"This Series May Soon do For Travel Guides What Hitchcock did for Film." —Chicago Tribune

"An Insider With Attitude."—Newsday

"This Book Understands All That." —Chicago Tribune

"A New Series From Itinerant Genius Dan Levine." —Elle Magazine

"Ultra Hip Travel Tomes."—Atlanta Journal-Constitution

"At Once Witty and Irreverent." —Toronto Sun

"Sharp Writing and a Thrilling Layout." —San Francisco Examiner

"If it's Cutting Edge You Want in a City That Teeters Between Conservative and Revolutionary, This is the Book to Buy."—Toronto Sun

"It's Hip to be There." —Chicago Sun-Times

"Slangy and Wired, Yet so Explicit and Well-Written."—Prague Post

"No Other Guide Captures so Completely and Viscerally What it Feels Like to be Inside the City."—San Francisco Bay Guardian

"Brutally Honest Insiders Give You the Straight Scoop on Where to be Seen so You Don't Feel or Look Like a Tourist."—Fitness Magazine

"Biting." —Library Journal

"Refreshingly Frank."—MSNBC

"A Dynamite Guide Packed with Attitude and the Opinions to Back it Up."—Amazon.com

"Razzle-Dazzle Design." —USA Today

"Refreshingly Sharp." —Consumer Reports

"One Guide That Doesn't Shrink From Expressing Opinions."—Boston Globe

"Opinionated, Mildly Caustic and Very Stylish."—Baltimore Sun

MGM
RICK SPRINGFIELD
EFX
THE CITY OF
ENTERTAINMENT

Also From Avant-Guide

Avant-Guide Chicago
Avant-Guide Disney World & Orlando
Avant-Guide London
Avant-Guide Miami
Avant-Guide New Orleans
Avant-Guide New York City
Avant-Guide Paris
Avant-Guide Prague
Avant-Guide San Francisco
Avant-Guide Toronto

Coming Soon...

Avant-Guide Amsterdam
Avant-Guide Barcelona
Avant-Guide Boston
Avant-Guide Cuba
Avant-Guide Los Angeles
Avant-Guide Shanghai
Avant-Guide Washington, DC

About Series Director Daniel Levine

Daniel Levine is a leading international trend hunter with a sharp eye for discovering pioneers in the world's ever-changing cultural landscape. He has written 10 best-selling guidebooks, produced travel television for HBO and NBC, and appeared as a travel trend expert on every major TV network in the US. Described as an "itinerant genius" by Elle magazine, Daniel has also been called the 21st-century Arthur Frommer for his stylish writing and contemporary approach to the world of travel. Daniel began his career researching and writing significant portions of the legendary guidebook *Europe on $50-a-Day*. During eight years with publishing giant Simon & Schuster he also wrote nine other best-selling travel books, from California and Florida to London and Italy. Daniel splits his time between Avant-Guide offices in the US and Europe.

Avant-Guide Online

avantguide.com is the place to go for up-to-the moment reports on the latest travel trends and current cultural events worldwide. Sign up for free membership and you'll also have access to daily updates on the newest hotels, restaurants, shops and sights. You can also make real-time reservations for almost every hip hotel in the world. As a service to the Avant-Guide community, we negotiate low rates directly with many hotels and have tapped directly into the reservations systems of many more. Our goal is to offer preferred service for every hotel recommended by Avant-Guide, but our reviewers are fiercely independent and have no relationship whatsoever with any of them.

Avant-Guide Lifestyle Network (AGLN)—A Private Members Club

Do you share our passion for avant urban adventures? Apply for VIP Status in the Avant-Guide Lifestyle Network and receive exclusive benefits including international concierge services that provide access to the inaccessible. Members also benefit from early travel alerts, hotel upgrades, preferred restaurant reservations, priority line passes and invites to special Avant-Guide events, showroom sales and more. See avantguide.com for details.

Our Select Network Of Destinations And Venues

Avant-Guide is a global-lifestyle media company offering a robust range of stylish, information-based products and services related to travel and entertainment. By identifying and creating new, unique and fashionable experiences in the world's most exciting places, Avant-Guide is focused on being the foremost authority on progressive destinations, goods and services worldwide. In the process we are assembling an influential community of progressive travelers and a select network of destinations, merchants and service providers who cater to them. Members of the Avant-Guide community are welcome to nominate avant destinations, but should be aware that being recommended by Avant-Guide is at our sole discretion, and we never accept discounts or payment in return for positive coverage.

Write To Us

Keeping our ears close to the ground includes listening closely to what our readers have to say. People often send us great stories about their avant experiences and we love to hear your comments. See what others have to say on our website and write to us at VIP@avantguide.com. Our hard-working interns respond personally to every email!

Our Future

Avant-Guide is growing rapidly, covering an increasing number of locations worldwide. Our goal is to be the world's leading source of stylish destination information across all media, including printed guidebooks, digitally, and on the Web. Let us know what you think.

THE AVANT-GUIDE MANIFESTO

Life is a Sensory Pilgrimage to be Enjoyed and Savored

Avant-Guide continuously wanders the contemporary cultural landscape in search of hip hotels, extraordinary restaurants, unique shops and the best nightlife. We are particularly attracted to unique places and one-of-a-kind experiences that we haven't encountered before, especially when they are innovative and have distinctive personalities. We work hard to make each Avant-Guide culturally courageous in exactly the same way, with informed listings, stylish prose, and a sexy package that doesn't make you stick out like a tourist.

Life is Too Short to Wade Through Exhaustive Lists

We go to great lengths to accurately research and edit the information you need. And we deliver it in a way that's both easy and pleasurable to use. Each listing is heavily cross-referenced, painstakingly mapped and intensively indexed. And Avant-Guide understands the importance of drawing a bright line between what you have to experience and what is not worth getting out of bed for.

Truth & Independence

Avant-Guide never accepts discounts or payments in exchange for positive coverage. Our worldwide network of informational omnivores are passionate about spotting emerging experiences long before they devolve into popular trends. But our visits to restaurants, clubs and other establishments are anonymous, and expenses are paid by Avant-Guide. Few other guides can make this claim.

Listings Key

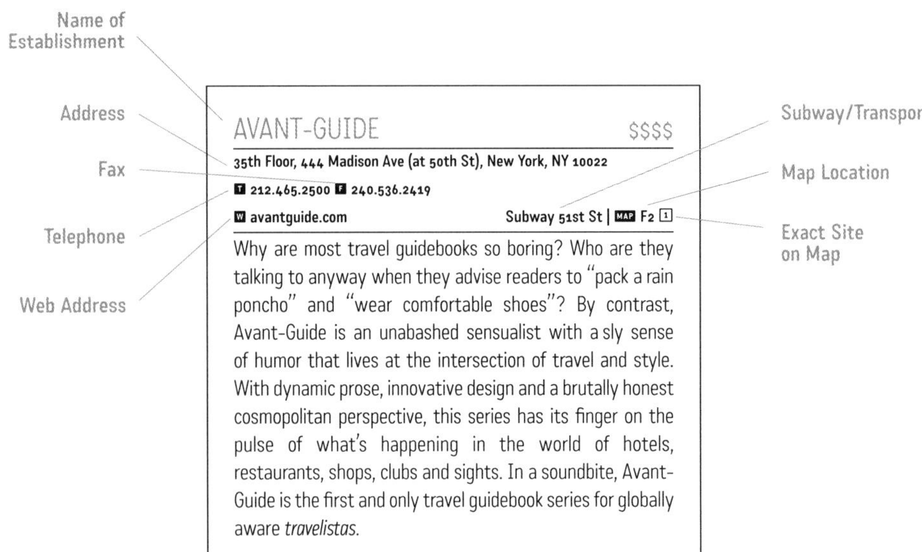
Name of Establishment
Address
Fax
Telephone
Web Address
AVANT-GUIDE $$$$
35th Floor, 444 Madison Ave (at 50th St), New York, NY 10022
T 212.465.2500 F 240.536.2419
W avantguide.com Subway 51st St | MAP F2 1
Why are most travel guidebooks so boring? Who are they talking to anyway when they advise readers to "pack a rain poncho" and "wear comfortable shoes"? By contrast, Avant-Guide is an unabashed sensualist with a sly sense of humor that lives at the intersection of travel and style. With dynamic prose, innovative design and a brutally honest cosmopolitan perspective, this series has its finger on the pulse of what's happening in the world of hotels, restaurants, shops, clubs and sights. In a soundbite, Avant-Guide is the first and only travel guidebook series for globally aware *travelistas*.
Subway/Transport
Map Location
Exact Site on Map

What The $$$$ Mean

HOTELS
Per-night prices of a standard room.

$	under $100
$$	$100–$200
$$$	$201–$300
$$$$	$301–$400
$$$$$	over $400

RESTAURANTS
Average price of one meal.

$	under $20
$$	$20–$35
$$$	$36–$50
$$$$	$51–$75
$$$$$	over $75

Empire Press Media, Inc., New York www.avantguide.com | vip@avantguide.com **Series Director** Daniel Levine **Photo Editor** Narita Penelope Johnson **Design** >o< Mowshe Studio | ka+li6+mig+push+ya5 | www.mowshe.cz **Writers** Peter J. Schaffer, Melania Viccone-Smith, Gary Lippman, Hillary Verona, J. P. Hills, David Schuman **Associate Editor** Andy Markowitz **Fact Checking** Prescott Mills, Amy Thompson **Chief Copy Editor** Peter Metzenbaum **Photography** Cornelis van Voorthuizen, LVCVB **Digital Cartography Copyright** © Empire Press Media, Inc. **Font** Katarine by Tomáš Brousil **Strategy & Partnerships** Gabor George Burt **Communications Director** Westley Overcash **Interns** Rachel Prescott, Sarah Lisey **Very Special Thanks** Fran & Alan Levine, Veronique Keys, Jonathan Pontell/Generation Jones, Da Jamb, Declan King, Pinky, James Kinsella, PB8, Lisa-Kim Ling Kuan, Jim Kwiatkowski.

ISBN 1-891603-29-9 Second Edition

Printed in the Czech Republic | Distributed in North America by Publishers Group West

CONTENTS

1	SLEEP	9
	reservations	11
	the $20 upgrade	11
	best hotels to...	11
	hotels a—z	12
	directory: hotels	27
	maps: hotels	29
2	EAT	35
	reservations	37
	buffets	37
	who's who: celebrity restaurateurs	37
	restaurants a—z	38
	directory: restaurants	59
	maps: restaurants	63
3	SHOP	69
	malls	71
	markets	74
	the best day spas	74
	10 things to buy	76
	shops a—z	77
	directory: shops	89
	maps: shops	95
4	PLAY	101
	best bars to...	103
	sex scenes	104
	bars & clubs a—z	105
	directory: bars & clubs	117
	maps: bars & clubs	119
5	EXPLORE	125
	the best of las vegas	127
	the best tours	128
	sights a—z	129
	directory: sights	143
	maps: sights	145
6	GAME	151
	comps & players clubs	153
	gambling lessons	153
	laws & taxes	154
	casino ten commandments	154
	where to play	154
	the games	155
7	KNOW	161
	know your neighborhoods	163
	leaving the airport	164
	local transport	165
	history in a hurry	166
	INDEXES	169

You can win a battle
but not a war..

SLEEP 1

1 | SLEEP

Most of the city's major resort hotels are bunched together along a 4-mile stretch of the Strip. With few exceptions—most notably the new Wynn Las Vegas—newer resorts on the south and center part of the Strip (like Mandalay Bay and the Bellagio) are nicer and more expensive than the older ones on the north end (like Stardust and the Sahara). Downtown's Fremont Street is home to some famous-but-stodgy old school hotels that retain sincere Rat Pack appeal. You can often find great deals here along with plenty of retro charm. The latest trend in Vegas hotelling is the hotel within the hotel. Started by the Four Seasons atop Mandalay Bay, it now includes The Mansions adjacent to the MGM Grand, SkyLofts atop MGM Grand, and THEhotel next to Mandalay Bay. The hotels in this book represent the very best in each price category that Las Vegas has to offer. All present something special in the way of local color and character. And we have gone to great lengths to uncover the very best of the city's budget hotels. Every establishment listed here meets our strict criteria for service, facilities and value. Hotels get extra points for shower power, room service reaction time, a sound system when you want it, and silence when you don't. Then, of course, there's the cool factor...

Reservations

Getting the best deal is definitely avant. Before booking a hotel, check out avantguide.com where you can make real-time reservations for many of the establishments we recommend. As a service to the Avant-Guide community, we negotiate low rates directly with a large number of hotels and have tapped directly into the reservations systems of many more. Our goal is to offer preferred service for as many of the hotels listed in every Avant-Guide book as we can. However, our reviewers are fiercely independent and have no relationship whatsoever with any of the establishments we recommend. Members of the Avant-Guide Lifestyle Network (AGLN) can also score many extras, including preferred rooms, automatic late checkouts, and special services and amenities appropriate to making our members feel like the VIPs they are. See our website for details.

The $20 Upgrade

Almost anywhere you stay, you should always ask for a view of the Strip. At the same time, it can't hurt to ask for an upgrade to a suite as well. You could simply tell the clerk it's your (choose one) honeymoon/anniversary/first time to Vegas. But some people swear that, upon checking in, you can get an instant upgrade by discreetly greasing the desk clerk. When sliding your reservation info or credit card over the counter, include a semi-hidden $20 bill and ask if an upgrade to a suite is available. The clerk will understand exactly what's happening, but of course that doesn't guarantee he'll cooperate. There simply may be no suites available. Be prepared to lose your $20... but, hey, you're in Vegas to gamble.

Best Hotels To...

Spot Celebrities
The Bellagio
Hard Rock Hotel
Mandalay Bay
THEhotel
The Palms
Wynn Las Vegas

Dance All Night in the Bars
Hard Rock Hotel
Mandalay Bay
New York-New York
The Palms
The Venetian

Have a Secret Affair
Four Seasons
Main Street Station
Monte Carlo
The Orleans
SkyLofts at MGM

Flaunt Your PhD in Kitsch
Caesars Palace
Luxor
New York-New York
Paris Las Vegas
Treasure Island
The Venetian

Kick Back With Kids
Circus Circus
Excalibur
MGM Grand
Rio
Stratosphere
Westin Casuarina

Play in the Pool
The Bellagio
Caesars Palace
Flamingo Las Vegas
Hard Rock Hotel
Mandalay Bay

Have a Rat Pack Experience
Algiers Hotel
El Cortez
Four Queens
Fremont Hotel & Casino
Sahara

What The $$$$ Mean

Our $ estimates are based on the per-night prices of a standard room. These can swing dramatically, depending on season, so use this as a guide.

$	= under $100
$$	= $100–$200
$$$	= $201–$300
$$$$	= $301–$400
$$$$$	= over $401

Aladdin/Planet Hollywood Hotel $$$$

3667 Las Vegas Blvd S (at Harmon), Strip

T 702.785.5555 or 877.333.9474

W aladdincasino.com MAP E2 33

This 39-story resort and casino is a suitably over-the-top Vegas-style spectacle. Opened in 2000 with an expensive and kitschy Arabian Nights theme, the hotel became mired in red ink and was soon acquired by Planet Hollywood and Starwood Hotels who are renovating and renaming the property. First and foremost, the best thing about this hotel is its stellar location, in the exact center of the Strip, next to Paris and across from the Bellagio. The second best thing is the mammoth **Desert Passage** shopping mall, which is also being rebranded. In addition to suites, there are two room types: standard guest rooms, which are on the small side for Vegas, and executive rooms, which are a bit larger. Each accommodation has excellent marble bathrooms with lots of counter space and separate showers and tubs. The best have Strip views. Multi-line phones and high-speed Internet access (for a fee) are also standard. The bottom line here is that this is a great place to stay if you can score a room for far less than you'd pay at any of its neighbors.

2567 Rooms: a/c | tv | tel | web | minibar | rm svc | gym

Algiers Hotel $

2845 Las Vegas Blvd S (at Riviera), Strip

T 702.735.3311 or 800.732.3361

W algiershotel.com MAP G1 1

Situated in the hinterlands of the Strip directly opposite Circus Circus, the Algiers is the motor lodge that time forgot: a pink twin-story motel that's a kitschy throwback to yesterdecade. In a city where ten years is ancient history, the Algiers, which was built in 1953, is positively prehistoric. The appeal of the hotel is not retro, it's the real old thing, complete with particle-board ceilings, naugahyde couches and a kidney-shaped swimming pool right in the middle of the parking lot. There's even a small, dimly-lit bar that's been favored by locals since Rat Pack days. While rooms here are too basic for the caviar set, they are large, clean, neat and thoroughly serviceable.

106 Rooms: a/c | tv | tel

Arizona Charlie's East $$

4575 Boulder Hwy (at Indios), East Side

T 702.951.5800 or 877.951.0002

W azcharlies.com MAP L2 2

This "locals" casino with a vaguely Wild West theme is a very well maintained property with comfortable motel-style guest rooms and a remarkably friendly staff. Some light sleepers have remarked about thin walls, bathrooms can be cramped and we don't like the wall-mounted soap dispensers in the showers. But we've received no complaints about this hotel's low prices. Suites are roughly double the size of basic rooms and include a separate sitting area. Facilities include an intimate casino and low-priced buffet. And the hotel's "no smoking" rooms are some of the few budget rooms we know of that actually smell like they've never been smoked in. AC-East's slightly out-of-the-way location is not walkable to anywhere, but it's only about 15-minutes' drive to the Strip.

303 Rooms: a/c | tv | tel | web | rm svc | gym

Bally's $$$

3645 Las Vegas Blvd S (at Flamingo), Strip

T 702.739.4111 or 888.742.9248

W ballyslv.com MAP E2 3

Bally's positions itself as a sophisticated antidote to the pop-art antics of its neighbors. The hotel's plaza entrance, in which moving walkways glide you past tall palm trees, colorful neon columns and cascading fountains, feels quite restrained compared to Paris, next door. Beyond the requisite bustling casino, are two 26-story towers filled with top-class guest rooms. Renowned for being some of the largest accommodations in the city, each is decorated with contemporary furnishings and filled with all the trimmings you'd expect from a very good hotel, including marble floors in the john. Although some people think North Tower rooms are slightly nicer, we like those in the South Tower facing the Strip and the Bellagio across the street. There's also a terrific, large outdoor pool area and one of the best gyms in town. In no way is Bally's a "hip" hotel, but services and facilities are great and the location is tops.

2814 Rooms: a/c | tv | tel | web | minibar | rm svc | gym

Barbary Coast $$$$

3595 Las Vegas Blvd S (at Flamingo), Strip

T 702.737.7111 or 888.227.2279

W barbarycoastcasino.com MAP E2 4

Barbary Coast is an older hotel, as small as it is schmaltzy, that looks and feels like it belongs Downtown instead of on a sizzlingly spectacular intersection across from behemoths Caesars, Bally's and the Bellagio. Guest rooms are average-sized and likeable, decorated in the hotel's trademark turn-of-the-century San Francisco motif with neo-Victorian wall coverings, heavy furnishings and busy floral carpeting. The best have four-

poster beds and Whirlpool tubs. You can often get good deals here which, in our opinion, is the best reason to stay.

200 Rooms: a/c | tv | tel | web

Bellagio $$$$$

3600 Las Vegas Blvd S (at Flamingo), Strip

T 702.693.7444 or 888.987.6667

W bellagioresort.com MAP E2 5

The theme of the 36-story Bellagio is opulence on the shores of Italy's Lake Como, complete with choreographed prancing waters outside and a Tuscan quarry's worth of marble within. The resort's magnificent lobby stuns with a ceiling blooming with thousands of sculptor Dale Chihuly's whimsical colored-glass flowers, a drama that's mimicked by a spectacular indoor conservatory of fresh flowers and trees just around the corner. The hotel's luxe extends to handsomely appointed guestrooms with acres of marble, data ports, hair dryers and multiple telephone lines. The best rooms face the Strip and overlook the resort's huge lake. Newer Spa Tower rooms feature marble entries, flat-panel televisions, high-tech minibars and automatic drapes. The Bellagio is no longer the most expensive hotel on the Strip, but it still scores top marks in many categories, from swimming area (with 2 lap pools) and production show (Cirque du Soliel's "O") to a tasteful lineup of four-star restaurants. The resort even boasts the city's top-rated valet and garage parking. The hotel's best PR gimmick? Children under 18 are supposedly not allowed in unless they're staying there, which, of course, is a great perk for gamblers who hate kids.

4205 Rooms: a/c | tv | tel | web | minibar | rm svc | gym

Boulder Station $$

4111 Boulder Hwy (at Desert Inn), East Side

T 702.432.7777 or 800.683.7777

W boulderstation.com MAP G2 6

Station resorts—including Sunset, Palace and Texas Stations—are the largest family of "locals" casino-hotels in Vegas. All are united by big gaming rooms, an enormous array of dining options and low-cost nightly entertainment. This member of the clan, situated a few minutes by car from the Strip, is vaguely inspired by a turn-of-the-century train station. Guestrooms continue the Victorian theme with dark woods and heavy furnishings. Standard rooms are average sized, unspectacularly decorated and contain lots of extras including iron, hairdryer and coffeemakers. There are only a dozen suites, but each is particularly attractive and includes a large dining table, canopy bed, etched glass partitions and

The Bellagio Lobby

a huge Jacuzzi bathtub. Rooms on high floors have good views of the Valley. The hotel's extensive Kids Quest activity center, which offers complete supervision for children six weeks to 12 years, makes Boulder Station a good choice for families.

300 Rooms: a/c | tv | tel | web | rm svc

Caesars Palace $$$$$

3570 Las Vegas Blvd S (at Flamingo), Strip

T 702.731.7110 or 800.634.6661

W caesars.com MAP E2 7

Opened in 1966, Vegas' first major themed resort remains one of the best. The theme, of course, is Ancient Rome, complete with copious marble statuary and toga-clad cocktail waitresses. And every guest is supposed to feel like an emperor: It's "Caesars," plural, no apostrophe, a fantastic, sprawling resort that continues to burnish its image as high-roller heaven. Its ornate casino, decorated with Olympian wall art, remains the gaming area of choice for the world's biggest whales. The location is perfect, restaurants are superb, entertainment is plentiful and

Caesars Palace

the spectacular Forum Shops are hysterically terrific. Happily, lavish bacchanalian luxury extends to the guestrooms, which are well-sized and well-stocked. Almost all contain separate dressing areas and snazzy marble-clad bathrooms with double sinks and shampoos in Roman-column bottles. Older rooms in the lower-rent Centurion Tower can be kitschy and fun, containing canopied beds (with mirrored ceilings) and Jacuzzi tubs right in the bedrooms. Many newer Palace Tower rooms have his and her baths and duel-head showers. Others have whirlpool tubs, massive beds, and floor-to-ceiling windows. All are generously appointed and larger than average. Of course, you've got to be a freakin' Rockefeller to get an enormous, two-story Fantasy Suite, but it's set with a circular bed, private sauna and quality home movie system. Surrounded by fountains, columns and sculptures, the Garden of the Gods swimming area is one of the most palatial poolscapes anywhere. And because Roman indulgence is the theme, topless sunbathing is encouraged at the Venus Pool. Even the gym raises camp to high art, equipped with a rock climbing wall, virtual reality cycle machines, Zen meditation garden, and a terrific view of the Strip.

3405 Rooms: a/c | tv | tel | web | minibar | rm svc | gym

Circus Circus $$

2880 Las Vegas Blvd S (at Circus Circus), Strip

T 702.734.0410 or 800.634.3450

W circuscircus-lasvegas.com MAP G1 9

Circus Circus is a Vegas classic. Opened in 1968, the city's second major theme resort (after Caesars) has always been oriented toward families with entertainment for all ages. And even though equating gambling with clowns is akin to promoting cigarettes with cartoon characters, this resort remains one of our top choices for couples with kids. The gaming and circus aspect of the resort are fully integrated, with the casino occupying the main floor while trapeze fliers and high-wire daredevils perform free-of-charge overhead (daily, every half-hour from 11am-midnight). There are games of skill and chance on the Midway Mezzanine, and the **Adventuredome**—America's largest indoor theme park—is just out back. "Circus Jerkus" is regularly disparaged by locals as a classless grind joint with low table minimums and small-denomination slot machines. Not to mention that pesky kids are running around everywhere. But the hotel is also loved for offering some of the lowest rates on the Strip and every brow of dining option from **The Steak House**

to McDonald's. Thankfully the circus theme is restrained in the guest rooms, most of which are comfortably non-descript. Rooms in the older towers are larger than those in the newer building, and south-facing rooms in the Skyrise Tower are best for views of the Strip.

3770 Rooms: a/c | tv | tel | web | minibar | rm svc | gym

El Cortez $

600 Fremont St (at 6th), Downtown

T 702.385.5200 or 800.634.6703

W elcortez.net MAP I2 10

El Cortez feels old, smells like moth balls and the average age of its guests is dead. And that's why we love it. In a town that places little value on history, this hotel—opened in 1941—is a welcome step backward. The El (or "The Hell", or "ElCo"), as it is affectionately known, is the perfect choice for tightwads with a well-developed sense of irony. Even the 24-hour coffee shop has a look and prices that are rooted in history. The laughably small registration desk is tucked into a corner of a gaming floor that still has an air of the Wild West about it. Accommodations are very clean, nicely furnished and well-sized, but predictably average, without niceties like in-room movies and dataports that even Motel 6 now offers. And the bathrooms are some of the smallest in town. The cheapest are queen-bedded rooms above the casino. For just a few bucks more you can get something on a high floor with good views over the **Fremont Street Experience**, which is just two blocks away. Check in, drop your bags, then go downstairs to win some nickles.

299 Rooms: a/c | tv | tel

Excalibur $$$

3850 Las Vegas Blvd S (at Tropicana), Strip

T 702.597.7700 or 800.937.7777

W excalibur-casino.com MAP D2 11

Totally kitschy, thoroughly ridiculous and eminently likeable, the enormous Excalibur is a mid-market, family-oriented theme hotel that takes its inspiration from England's medieval times. Sharing its spectacular intersection with New York-New York, the Tropicana and MGM Grand, the Excalibur is a whimsical faux-stone castle that's all turrets, spires and towers, complete with a moat and a drawbridge of sorts. A huge casino is, of course, the main attraction here (think of a dungeon with slots), sandwiched between the Disneyesque Medieval Village shopping arcade upstairs, and midway games with strolling minstrels in the Fantasy Faire below. Ranging from the Steakhouse at Camelot to the Round Table Buffet, even the restaurants never step out of character. Needless to say, Excalibur is very kid-oriented (the pool area is especially full of ankle biters) and those who come here without their own are duly warned. Boldly-colored guestrooms, set with heavy, dark wood furnishings and a smattering of wrought-iron fixtures are far warmer than most real castles we've been in, and comparable to good hotel rooms anywhere. And prices here are reasonable; low even, compared to real estate nearby.

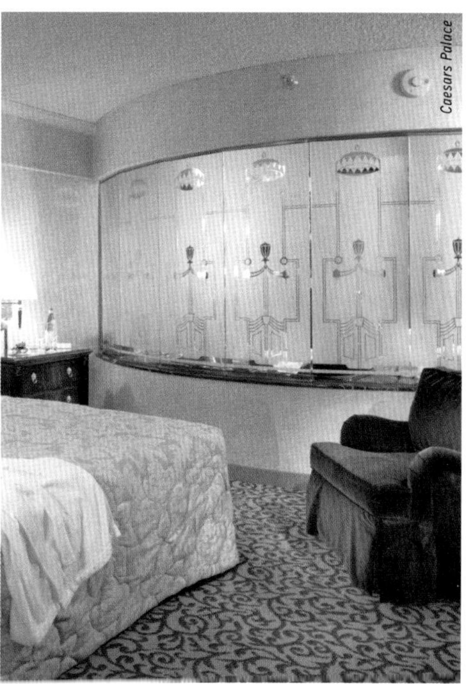
Caesars Palace

4008 Rooms: a/c | tv | tel | web | minibar | rm svc | gym

Fitzgerald's $

301 Fremont St (at 4th), Downtown

T 702.388.2400 or 800.274.5825

W fitzgeraldslasvegas.com MAP I2 12

Forget potatoes and famine because Irish fantasy, not Ireland, is the theme at this excellent Downtown hotel, directly under the **Fremont Street Experience** canopy. Guests are welcomed by Mr. O'Lucky—an enormous jolly leprechaun grinning beside a neon rainbow and pot of gold—into a buzzing casino full of gamblers hoping for the luck of the Irish. As you might imagine, green is the color of choice here, and motifs featuring four-leaf clovers are

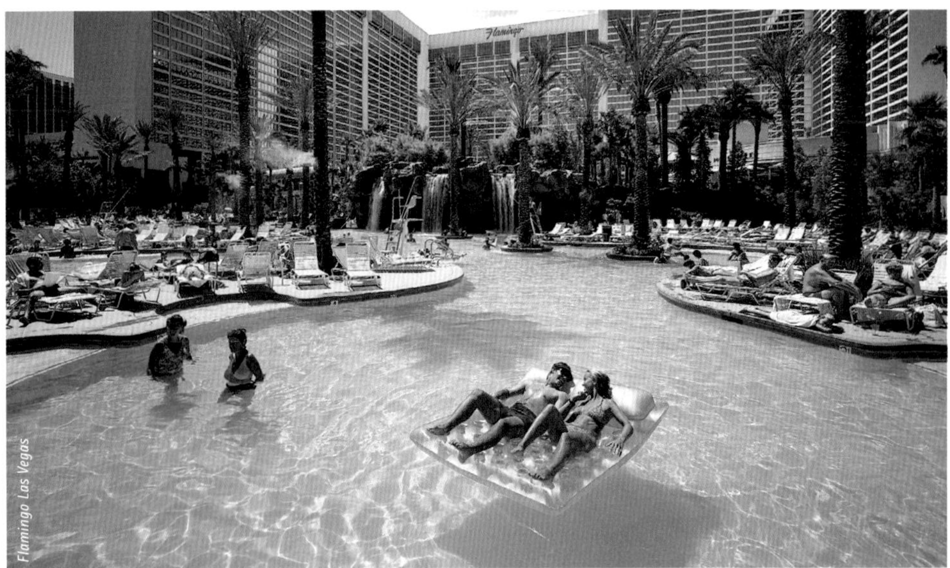
Flamingo Las Vegas

repeated ad nauseum. There are even Blarney Stones said to be sourced directly from Blarney Castle. Go on, kiss one. At 34-stories, the Fitz is the tallest Downtown hotel. That translates into high levels of hospitality and terrific views of either the Strip to the south or mountains to the north. Standard accommodations are fine and unexciting. "21 Club" rooms, on the 21st floor, are a bit nicer and come with evening turn-down service, coffeemakers and irons. And Jacuzzi suites, with their immense wrap-around windows are terrific. Fitzgerald's is a thoroughly acceptable place to stay, especially if you score a good rate.

652 Rooms: a/c | tv | tel | web | minibar | rm svc | gym

Flamingo Las Vegas $$$$

3555 Las Vegas Blvd S (at Flamingo), Strip

T 702.733.3111 or 800.732.2111

W flamingolasvegas.com MAP E2 13

Mobster Benjamin "Bugsy" Siegel's 107-room Flamingo was one of the first resort hotels on the dusty road that would soon become the Strip. Now completely rebuilt, the Flamingo is an extravagant tropical themed playground attracting the upper middle market with its unassailable location and solid quality. Guestrooms are conservative but efficient, filling six towers surrounding a tropical grotto. Many different building stages have produced a large number of room configurations, but most are spacious and perfectly appointed. Suites can be downright grand in both scale and character. More than most of its neighbors, the Flamingo feels like a full-blown resort mainly due to its extensive grounds that include swimming pools, tennis courts, and the **Flamingo Las Vegas Wildlife Habitat**—rambling gardens stocked with Mandarin ducks, African penguins, Chilean flamingos and three-story waterfalls cascading into Koi fish ponds. There's a terrific pool area too. And that fantastic pink and orange sign on the building's south side: A glowing goblet of flashing feathers waving in a neon breeze.

3642 Rooms: a/c | tv | tel | web | minibar | rm svc | gym

Four Seasons Las Vegas $$$$$

3960 Las Vegas Blvd S (at Four Seasons), Strip

T 702.632.5000 or 800.819.5053

W fourseasons.com MAP C2 14

The Four Seasons is an unusual and wonderful place to stay. The hotel markets itself as a non-gaming property and something of a "sanctuary" from all the madness you find elsewhere. Parking is civilized and there is a quiet lobby and check-in. But that's only part of the story. Because it's a hotel-within-a hotel, occupying the 35th to 39th floors of Mandalay Bay, the Four Seasons is just an elevator ride away from all the wonderful facilities of its host. Views are magnificent and conservatively plush guestrooms look the same as any Four

Seasons anywhere, which in our estimation is this hotel's only drawback. The Four Seasons has its own pool and spa, but these are trumped by those belonging to Mandalay Bay, both of which are open to you. Only the Four Seasons' service can't be topped.

424 Rooms: a/c | tv | tel | web | minibar | stereo | rm svc | gym

Four Queens $

202 Fremont St (at Casino Center), Downtown

T 702.385.4011 or 800.634.6045

W fourqueens.com MAP I2 15

Hard by the Fremont Street Experience, the time-honored Four Queens harks back to the Vegas of old, what with garish lighting, plenty of mirrors and a chandeliered casino that's home to the world's largest slot machine. Despite its provocative name and fetching New Orleans French Quarter motif (think 70's fern bar with hurricane-lamp chandeliers), the Four Queens was named in 1966 for the original owner's quartet of daughters. Bright rooms are set with solid furnishings, many of which include Victorian-style four-poster beds—queen-size, of course. And like other hotels in the immediate neighborhood, prices are well on this side of reasonable. South Tower rooms are a bit nicer and quieter. There's no pool, no spa and no business center because the 4Q's is made for meat-eating gamblers for whom such facilities are unnecessary frou-frou. In short: a classic

700 Rooms: a/c | tv | tel | web | minibar | rm svc | gym

Fremont Hotel & Casino $$

200 Fremont St (at 3rd), Downtown

T 702.385.3232 or 800.634.6182

W fremontcasino.com MAP I2 16

Another Downtown institution, The Fremont is a deconstructed gem that's lovable, warts and all. The theme of this hotel appears to be the very street upon which it makes its home, which is a novelty in a town that's famous for appropriating the culture of other places. Because it's one of the smallest properties fronting the **Fremont Street Experience**, the hotel usually offers better service and a friendlier reception than its larger neighbors. And finding your room, or retrieving your car, isn't fraught with aggravation. Bathrooms are miniature and rooms are smaller than average, but what they lack in size they make up for in content. Good furnishings are complimented by an in-room coffeemaker, refrigerator and safe, as well as a table, chairs and a sofa. And rates are typically half what they'd be at a comparable place on the Strip.

452 Rooms: a/c | tv | tel | web

Four Seasons Las Vegas

Golden Nugget $$$

129 Fremont St (at Casino Center), Downtown

T 702.385.7111 or 800.634.3454

W goldennugget.com MAP I2 17

The best Downtown hotel is not only the most famous one on Fremont Street, it is also the only one that wouldn't be out of place on the Strip. From its white marble and gold-leaf facade to the record-busting 61-pound Hand Of Faith gold nugget that's displayed just beside the gift shop, this is a richly swellegant place. Only the nickel slot machines and $2 Blackjack tables belie the clientele. Marble-clad public areas set with flamboyant bronze statuary lead to nicely appointed guestrooms dressed with half-canopied beds and club chairs atop cream-colored carpets. Rooms in the newer South Tower are a bit smaller than those in the older North Tower, but they're usually a bit cheaper too. Frou-frou bath packages include lots of flowery smelling things like French-milled soap (whatever that is). While rates usually offer good value for money, they feel particularly low for the hotel's 27 luxury apartments and six penthouse suites. Facilities and services are plentiful and include a top-of-the-line spa and an outdoor heated swimming pool—a rarity for a Downtown hotel.

1907 Rooms: a/c | tv | tel | web | minibar | rm svc | gym

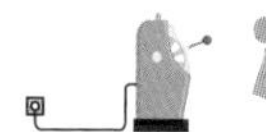

Hard Rock Hotel $$$$

4455 Paradise Rd (at Harmon), East Side

T 702.693.5000 or 800.473.7625

W hardrockhotel.com MAP K1 18

The Hard Rock is a theme palace of the highest order; magnetically attractive to hipsters who wouldn't be caught dead in the cafes of the same name or wearing the company's idiotic logo T-shirts. The theme, of course, is the music that will never die, played at medium-to-high sound levels, and musical memorabilia—usually signed guitars and MTV costumes—double as wall art. The hotel perpetually overflows with hormonal 20-somethings; not the heaviest gamblers to be sure, but they look good, like to drink and create a jubilant atmosphere in which every night is a party, often attended by genuine rock stars. Guestrooms are spacious and stylishly decorated with contempo furnishings, XL TVs, and quality marble baths. The best overlook the tropical pool area and the Strip beyond. Standard guestrooms contain no stereos or CD players, but the hotel gets it right with a terrific showroom (**The Joint**), a popular dance club (**Body English**), sexy leather-clad cocktail waitresses and several good restaurants. They also have cool purple felt-covered gaming tables, chips with the visages of rock royalty, and one of the very best pool areas in the city—known for swim-up Blackjack tables, sandy "beaches" and string bikinis (though the female/male ratio is probably greater at the equally fabulous Mandalay Bay pool where men are a decade older and several zeros richer). Despite the fact that it's a car ride from the Strip, the Hard Rock Hotel is a great place to stay.

668 Rooms: a/c | tv | tel | web | minibar | rm svc | gym

Harrah's $$$$

3475 Las Vegas Blvd S (at Flamingo), Strip

T 702.369.5000 or 800.427.7247

W harrahsvegas.com MAP F2 19

With an enviable location right in the heart of the hustle, Harrah's is a very good hotel with a street-party theme. The celebratory atmosphere starts outside, at the **Carnival Court**, one of the Strip's few open-air bars. Pass under the hotel's trademark neon globe into a busy casino built with confetti-pattern carpeting and fiber-optics embedded in the ceiling that burst like fireworks in patterns of light and color. In the "party pits," dealers wear wacky hats and are encouraged to jump around and scream with the patrons. Visually, this place can't compete with the Grand Canal down the block or the volcano across the street, but you will find fully-loaded deluxe guestrooms with small sitting areas, sound-proofed walls, blackout draperies, in-room coffeemakers, Web TV and excellent bedside reading lights. Some rooms have Whirlpool tubs and even the smallest suites have second televisions in the bathrooms. The swimming pool isn't spectacular, but it's wet and in the sun so it serves its purpose.

2700 Rooms: a/c | tv | tel | web | minibar | rm svc | gym

Imperial Palace $$

3535 Las Vegas Blvd S (at Flamingo), Strip

T 702.731.3311 or 800.634.6441

W imperialpalace.com MAP E2 20

Imperial Palace's faultless location, sandwiched between Harrah's and the Flamingo, has a lot to do with its appeal. Compared to its neighbors, this hotel's enormous blue-roofed pagoda facade seems downright restrained and almost, dare we say, classy. The interior, on the other hand, opts for a downmarket pan-Asian theme, with bamboo, jade and carved wood trimmings that feel vaguely like the entire continent without singling out any one country. Standard guestrooms riff on the Pacific Rim theme with rattan chairs and colorful soft goods—drapery, spreads and carpeting. Get one facing the Strip and you'll have a private balcony overlooking the action. If your thoughts are more toward Thailand, do like we do and opt for one of the fun and funky, excessively-mirrored Luv Tub rooms, which come with a giant sunken Whirlpool bath. At the end of the day, Imperial Palace suffers from bad feng shui. We also like the breathalyzers mounted in the hallway leading to the parking garage. But what it lacks in glamour and design it deducts from the final bill.

2700 Rooms: a/c | tv | tel | web | minibar | rm svc | gym

Las Vegas Hilton $$$

3000 Paradise Rd (at Riviera), East Side

T 702.732.5111 or 800.732.7117

W lv-hilton.com MAP G1 21

Hello, my name is the Las Vegas Hilton, the city's largest convention hotel. It's a huge place filled with somewhat starchy, cookie-cutter rooms that are within walking distance to one of the largest convention centers in the world. Despite a somewhat incongruous Star Trek theme, the Hilton is a high-quality business-oriented hotel, featuring well-appointed and spacious rooms with small TVs and average-sized bathrooms. Those with king beds also come with sofas. One benefit of staying in such a corporate place is that if the businesspeople are not around then rates go down and upgrades become plentiful.

3174 Rooms: a/c | tv | tel | web | minibar | rm svc | gym

Las Vegas Hilton

Luxor $$$$

3900 Las Vegas Blvd S (at Reno), Strip

T 702.262.4000 or 800.288.1000

W luxor.com MAP D2 22

Like the ancient wonder of the world it's based on, this awestriking black glass pyramid is a bona fide architectural marvel. Like a high kitsch neo-Egyptian wonderland, the resort is decked out with colossal Ramses statues, animatronic camels and a walking, talking King Tut that moves around the attractions level by remote control. The Luxor has had its problems. The black pyramid turned out to be almost invisible under the night sky, the powerful light that shoots out the top is a magnate for insects and bats, and, supposedly, many Chinese visitors won't gamble or sleep here because they think it's bad luck to play inside what is essentially a tomb. But we love this place. In the main building, guestrooms are accessed via "inclinators" that travel at a 39-degree angle along the pyramid's slope. Accommodations are spacious, each built with a sloping glass wall on one side and front doors that open onto a balcony overlooking the pyramid's atrium. It's a swanky place with upmarket furnishings and restrained Egyptianesque decor, and the suites are some of the nicest we've seen anywhere. Get a Jacuzzi Room and you can enjoy a soak directly under the sloped glass, so you can float on your back and look up at the stars. Most of the other rooms in the pyramid contain no tubs at all, only showers. Newer guest rooms, located in a pair of adjacent towers, are traditionally shaped, of top quality, and beautifully appointed with impressive details. The hotel has a terrific spa and an excellent pool area, not to mention one of the biggest casinos in town.

4408 Rooms: a/c | tv | tel | web | minibar | rm svc | gym

Main Street Station $$

200 N Main St (at Stewart), Downtown

T 702.387.1896 or 800.713.8933

W stationcasinos.com MAP J1 23

Situated two blocks from Fremont Street, this Station hotel doubles as a fascinating antique museum with a hodgepodge of oddities thrown in for good measure. That means lots of old-fashioned furnishings, stained glass, hardwood railroad benches, wrought-iron fences, century-old Belgian street lamps, carved mahogany cabinetry behind the registration desk, a chandelier from a Parisian opera house

Mandalay Bay and THEhotel

and several from the El Presidente Hotel in Buenos Aires, a rail car that was once owned by author Louisa May Alcott, and another one that belonged to US President Teddy Roosevelt. And, oh yeah, there's a heavily grafittied section of the Berlin Wall behind the urinals in the men's toilets by the Garden Court Buffet. Happily, guest rooms are far less cluttered, relatively spacious and well-appointed, with a decent-sized sitting area and homey wooden shutters. Odd-numbered rooms face north and have good far-away views of the Strip. Beware those facing north suffer from highway noise. There's no spa, no pool, and not even room service. But prices are usually terrific and the **Triple-7**, one of the city's best-loved brew pubs, is right downstairs.

452 Rooms: a/c | tv | tel | web | minibar | rm svc | gym

Mandalay Bay $$$$$

3950 Las Vegas Blvd S (at Mandalay Bay), Strip

T 702.632.7777 or 877.632.7000

W mandalaybay.com MAP C2 24

A cosmopolitan hotel in the best sense of the word, Mandalay Bay is aimed squarely at moneyed 30- and 40-somethings who are looking for a more sophisticated experience than the Hard Rock can deliver. Named for a mythical place in a Rudyard Kipling novel, Mandalay Bay is vaguely South Pacific in feel, with lots of lush foliage, carved stone and tropical gewgaws. Behind the gold-mirrored facade are richly-decorated rooms conceived by designer Anita Brooks, that are beautifully outfitted with floor-to-ceiling windows, lighted closets, and some of the finest bathrooms in Vegas—each with separate tubs and showers (so you can sit in the tub and watch someone shower) and handy toilet-side telephones (so you can chat while sitting on the can). Request one facing north if you want a great view of the Strip. Suites can be very sweet indeed; the best being two-story, house-sized affairs with amazing 180-degree vistas over Vegas. And rooms on the 34th floor have unique musical themes recalling the House of Blues, downstairs. Other lobby-level hotspots include the bar **Red Square**, **Rumjungle** dance club, and a half-dozen of the city's most desirable restaurants. Yet, perhaps the best reason to stay at this "party in a box" is to hang out at their huge backyard water park, a lush tropical extravaganza of sand beaches, waterfalls, a "lazy river" ride and a wave pool that can generate swells up to six feet high (you can rent boogie boards!). Open only to hotel guests, we think it's the best hotel pool in the world. The resort is home to one of Vegas's top spas too, as well as the swanky Four Seasons Hotel, which occupies the top five floors.

3309 Rooms: a/c | tv | tel | web | minibar | stereo | rm svc | gym

MGM Grand $$$$

3799 Las Vegas Blvd S (at Tropicana), Strip

T 702.891.1111 or 800.646.7787

W mgmgrand.com **MAP D2 25**

The emerald-green "City of Entertainment" is one of the largest resorts in the world and a litany of outsized statistics that includes Vegas's largest casino, a 17,000-seat arena for concerts and boxing matches, not one, but two showrooms, and even a **Lion Habitat** for Metro and his fellow MGM mascots. Yet, despite its hugeness, the hotel never feels overwhelming. Guestrooms, which occupy four 30-story towers, are average sized and decently furnished. Basic suites are about 50% larger than standard rooms, and split-level suites on the top floors are elaborate, sprawling affairs that are usually reserved for high rollers. From Moroccan "Casablanca" to Southern "Gone With the Wind," each room is decorated in a playful Hollywood film motif. The biggest and nicest rooms are in the Grand Tower. The adjacent Mansions, encompassing 29 huge Mediterranean-style villas, is one of the most exclusive places to stay in the entire city. Fitted with private indoor pools, outdoor gardens and exercise rooms, they are coveted even by high-rollers. There's an enormous video arcade, a childcare center, and a terrific swimming pool too. The MGM may not make your pulse race like you've just placed your entire life-savings on 15-Black, but it's astonishing just the same.

5034 Rooms: a/c | tv | tel | web | minibar | rm svc | gym

The Mirage $$$$

3400 Las Vegas Blvd S (at Spring Mountain), Strip

T 702.791.7111 or 800.374.9000

W themirage.com **MAP F2 26**

Local historians—to use the term loosely—often speak of The Mirage as the resort that presaged Vegas' swanky postmodern age. Put succinctly, the Mirage, which opened in late 1989, was the first "respectable" hotel on the Strip; a sophisticated place with an astute sense of style that replaced cheap schlock with high-priced glitz—epitomized by the fire-belching volcano in its front yard. Guestrooms in the hotel's 29-story Y-shaped tower (which was also copied all over town) are exceedingly comfortable, tastefully furnished and well-sized. Marble baths, overstuffed chairs, duel-line telephones and a dressing table with a make-up mirror are all standard. Executive rooms come with Jacuzzi tubs and stand-alone showers. The best rooms face the volcano and have excellent views of the Strip. The worst are those below the tenth story facing the parking garage.

The Mirage Check-In Area

Penthouse suites, which are actually on the top five floors, are coveted perks won by heavy betters. But even those pale next to the private villas out back, each with a putting green and its own swimming pool. The Mirage remains one of the best hotels in town. Its Polynesian theme is a terrific excuse to feature the lushest landscaping in Vegas as well as an extraordinary indoor tropical "rainforest" that almost makes the casino smell healthy and fresh. It's not cheap and most guests are too old to remember Gilligan's Island. But The Mirage comes with a spectacular coral reef aquarium behind the front desk, a Dolphin Habitat, a **Secret Garden** for white tigers and other exotic animals, and a lush pool area that makes you feel like swinging from vine to vine.

3044 Rooms: a/c | tv | tel | web | minibar | rm svc | gym

Monte Carlo $$$

3770 Las Vegas Blvd S (at Tropicana), Strip

T 702.730.7777 or 800.311.8999

W monte-carlo.com **MAP D2 27**

If you've ever been to Monaco then you've no doubt seen the *inferior* version of the Place du Casino, with its gas lit promenades, cascading fountains, ornate statuary and fanciful arches. Unlike Paris or The Venetian, both of which feel more Disneyesque, the Monte Carlo exudes the sophisticated James

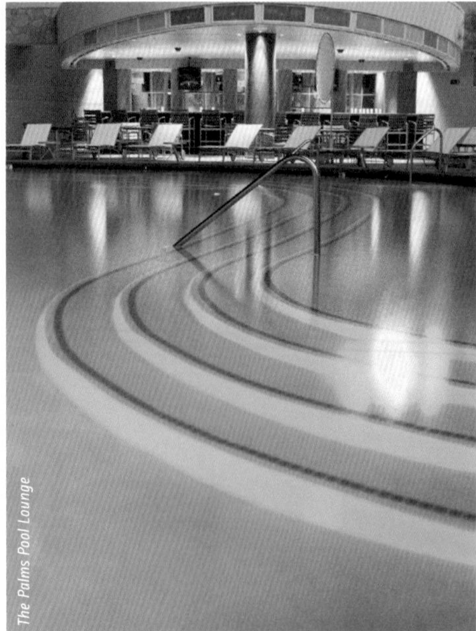

Bondian version of Europe that Europeans could only wish for. Guestrooms are attractive, and standard rooms are more than standard in size. Each has lots of marble and overstuffed chairs. And service is excellent. There's a good shopping arcade, a full-service health spa and salon, and six different swimming pools including a wave pool and a raft ride on Easy River. In the casino this Old World theme means high-limit baccarat and some of the few European-style single-o Roulette tables in town. On the whole, the Monte Carlo is a nice place that would be the most amazing resort in any other city. But situated between New York-New York and the Bellagio, it barely rates a yawn.

3002 Rooms: a/c | tv | tel | web | minibar | rm svc | gym

Motel 6 — $

195 E Tropicana Ave (at Koval), East Side

T 702.798.0728 or 800.466.8356

W motel6.com — MAP D2 [28]

Why is Motel 6 listed in a guide of this fine caliber? Because it's a good last-minute option to know about just in case you need a very cheap place to flop very close to the Strip. Hey, it's not like you're moving in permanently. Beneath one of the finest neon signs around is a sprawling double-deck motel with clean rectangle guestrooms surrounding a swimming pool we hope you'll never use. There's a nonstop grocery on the premises and, of course, local phone calls are free.

602 Rooms: a/c | tv | tel | web

New York-New York — $$$$

3790 Las Vegas Blvd S (at Tropicana), Strip

T 702.740.6969 or 800.675.3267

W nynyhotelcasino.com — MAP D2 [29]

Of all the outrageous "advertecture" in Vegas, this abridged re-creation of the New York City skyline is the most astounding. The wacky facade—a cluster of scaled-down knock-offs including the Statue of Liberty, the Empire State Building, the Brooklyn Bridge and the Chrysler Building—is fronted by a pint-sized New York Harbor and full-sized **Manhattan Express** roller-coaster that dives into and around the property. It's such a visual feast that we can stare at it for an hour and still not believe our eyes. Guestrooms, located in the hotel's "skyscrapers," are warmly decorated and of uniformly high standard. Although not particularly large, most are art deco in design and very comfortable. There are drawbacks, however. The health club is small, the pool area is poorly designed and those unlucky enough to get a room next to the roller coaster may be disturbed by screaming white-knucklers. There aren't any great restaurants here and, believe it or not, the hotel has no buffet. But the public areas are stunning interpretations of Greenwich Village, Park Avenue and Times Square (with a ball that drops each night at midnight). There's a large Coney Island themed arcade, graffiti covered mailboxes and steaming manhole covers embedded in cobblestones. The only thing missing is beggars slouched in the doorways. Just like living in the real New York, it's great to roll out of bed, walk downstairs, and find yourself in the center of the universe.

2035 Rooms: a/c | tv | tel | web | minibar | rm svc | gym

The Orleans — $$

4500 W Tropicana Ave (at Decatur), West Side

T 702.365.7111 or 800.675.3267

W orleanscasino.com — MAP D1 [30]

Situated about a mile west of the Strip, the Orleans' location is its only downer. But that's the tradeoff for keeping prices low. "Orleans," of course, refers not to France but to New Orleans, with nods to the Quarter, the Garden District and Mardi Gras. That translates into plantation shutters, faux cast-iron railings and other hackneyed references to the Big Easy. The hotel is light and bright and good Cajun bands actually perform in the lounge. Best of all, the Orleans vies with the Venetian for the largest standard guestrooms in the city; each is a mini-suite with a couch and a reading desk, representing one of the best

price-quality ratios in the city. On-site shopping is limited to a newsstand and a liquor store, which gives you an idea of the clientele; it's a very popular "locals" hotel, drawing natives with a 70-lane bowling alley (which is open nonstop!) and a 12-screen multiplex. There's also a better-than-average pool area, a large video arcade and a youth activity center for children under 12.

1460 Rooms: a/c | tv | tel | web | minibar | rm svc | gym

The Palms $$$

4321 W Flamingo Rd (at Arville), West Side

T 702.942.7777 or 866.942.7770

W thepalmslasvegas.com MAP E1 31

The Palms gets it right with its unique positioning as a hip "locals" hotel. Situated across from the Rio, the 42-story Palms is just far enough from the Strip to attract natives, yet it's so full of stylish spaces (**Little Buddha Café, N9ne, Ghostbar**) that it pulls in black-cladders visiting from the coasts. The resort's garden beach theme is reflected in wood floors, landscaped trellises and honey-colored lighting. Guest rooms are well sized and those on higher floors have good views of the Strip. All rooms feature jumbo televisions, coffeemakers, Web TV and Neutrogena bath products. Professional athletes often choose the Palms because the hotel's owners, the Maloof family, also own the Sacramento Kings basketball team. Some suites have seven-and-a-half-foot beds. There's an avant bamboo-studded "pool lounge" too, with a lavender-colored swimming pool, swim-up Blackjack, and several 30-seat "relaxation pools" filled just high enough to submerge your chaise lounge. The hotel also includes a 14-screen movie theater and an IMAX cinema.

447 Rooms: a/c | tv | tel | web | minibar | stereo | rm svc | gym

Paris Las Vegas $$$$$

3655 Las Vegas Blvd S (at Harmon), Strip

T 702.946.7000 or 888.266.5687

W paris-lv.com MAP E2 32

With clever, scaled-down replicas of Paris' greatest hits, this much-loved hotel has gotten the most superficial aspects of its namesake right. We love the beautiful casino in which gaming tables sit under fabulous faux Art Nouveau-style Metro arches. The cobblestoned **Le Boulevard** is one of the nicest shopping arcades in the city, and, predictably, the restaurants are terrific. But make no mistake, this *petite* City of Light still has more in common with Nevada's City of Lights: the staff greets everyone with a smile (sometimes in a Southern drawl), there are large bars of soap in the bathrooms (in cute little containers), and dogs are not allowed on the property (*quelle horreur!*). Accommodations in the mansard-roofed tower are well-sized, restrained in design and stuffed with all the extras you'd expect from a top hotel, including full-length and make-up mirrors. Get a corner room facing the Strip and you'll have a view of the Eiffel Tower out one window and the Arc de Triomphe out the other. In addition to its wonderful ground-zero location, the best thing about staying here is that Paris rarely feels too big or too crowded. The privileged atmosphere is safeguarded by intelligent interior design that puts things on a relatively human scale. The boutiques are small and even the buffet is divided into cozy dining rooms complete with fireplaces and mirrors angled off the walls. Of course, just like its namesake, this Paris isn't cheap. But it's in line with the other "cities" on the Strip and is better than most of them.

2916 Rooms: a/c | tv | tel | web | minibar | rm svc | gym

Rio $$$

3700 W Flamingo Rd (at Valley View), West Side

T 702.252.7777 or 800.752.9746

W playrio.com MAP E1 34

You probably wouldn't choose red and purple for your own neon sign, but that's the trademark of these 51-story towers just west of the Strip. If you believe the hype then every day here is a Brazilian Carnival. And because they're probably raking in millions of dollars each day, why shouldn't it be? Sarcasm aside, Rio is one of the most popular off-Strip hotels and its allure is multi-fold: First, this is an all-suite hotel—oversized rooms, actually—which means that even the cheapest ones are large. And they're well furnished with coffeemakers and refrigerators. There are floor-to-ceiling windows to the outside and windows in the shower through which you can watch TV. Furthermore, the Rio is one of the last remaining hotels offering "honeymoon suites" with Jacuzzi tubs. Yet, across the board, prices are lower than you'd pay for something similar on Las Vegas Boulevard. Rio is also fun, especially for families. Parents and kids come to witness the frequent Masquerade Show in the Sky, in which suspended parade floats sail through Masquerade Village, a flashy shopping, dining and entertainment complex. There is a very good swimming area with waterfalls, a sandy "beach" and a wave pool, terrific views from the hugely successful rooftop **VooDoo Lounge**, and the **Carnival World Buffet** is the most popular in Vegas. Oh, and their cocktail waitresses have got the sexiest girl-from-Ipanema uniforms in the city. Does all this mean you should stay here? If the price is light then, by all means, yes. Otherwise, choose something hipper and closer to the action.

2554 Rooms: a/c | tv | tel | web | minibar | rm svc | gym

Sahara $$

2535 Las Vegas Blvd S (at Sahara), Strip

T 702.737.2111 or 888.696.2121

W saharahotelandcasino.com MAP G1 35

Despite numerous expansions and renovations over the years, the Sahara delivers big doses of nostalgia and remains an old school spot that attracts people who are, well, old. Moroccan is the hotel's theme, one that extends into comfortably-remodeled guest rooms that will win no style awards, but are priced just as comfortably. That, of course, is the big attraction. Not all accommodations here are created equal and the worst rooms are very small. The best are in the Tangiers Tower, where the deluxe rooms are located. And Retro Suites are decked out with naugahyde and tiki touches. Some even have balconies overlooking the Strip. Back downstairs, amidst onion domes and colorful Arabian tiles, you'll find $1 Blackjack, the mammoth NASCAR Cafe, and several genuinely fun attractions related to speed (as in velocity, not the drug).

2100 Rooms: a/c | tv | tel | web | rm svc | gym

SkyLofts at MGM $$$$$

3799 Las Vegas Blvd S (at Tropicana), Strip

T 702.891.3832 or 800.646.5638

W skyloftsmgmgrand.com MAP D2 36

Skylofts are 51 lavish, two-story suites on the top floors of the MGM Grand hotel. Designed by architect Tony Chi with modern, luxurious furnishings, each condo-type accommodation contains one, two or three bedrooms with a large dining area, plus floor-to-ceiling windows (with great views and remote-control drapes) and lots of flat panel TVs, including one embedded in the bathroom mirror. The larger lofts also have Bang & Olufsen audio and video equipment, a steam room and infinity edge Jacuzzi spa tubs. And some even come with a pool table. Round-the-clock pampering includes butler service for unpacking your luggage and customizing your bar. Of course, all this luxury is not for the faint of wallet: Prices start at about $1000 per night.

51 Rooms: a/c | tv | tel | web | minibar | stereo | rm svc | gym

Stardust $$

3000 Las Vegas Blvd S (at Desert Inn), Strip

T 702.732.6111 or 800.824.6033

W stardustlv.com MAP F2 37

Stardust is old school and smells like it. Unlike its neighbors, this hotel is blissfully theme-less and appears to have no plans to get with the times. The hotel fills the niche for a solid mid-priced property on the Strip, offering very good rooms with few frills. Forget family attractions. In fact, forget attractions at all. With the exception of eight bars, an on-site liquor store and Wayne Newton, who performs here most evenings, the hotel is relatively unencumbered by diversions. Accommodations in the West Tower are a bit nicer, but those in the East Tower are a bit larger and many have full balconies with sliding glass doors. Those on high floors have very good views of the Strip or Downtown.

2431 Rooms: a/c | tv | tel | web | minibar | rm svc | gym

Stratosphere $$$

2000 Las Vegas Blvd S (at Main), Strip

T 702.380.7777 or 800.998.6937

W stratospherehotel.com MAP H1 38

It could take a lifetime of psychoanalysis to understand why the tallest observation tower in America suffers from such low self-esteem. But that's how it is: the Strat clearly has an outsized ego, yet remains one of the worst-loved buildings in the city. The resort's biggest problem is not height, but location, secluded on the northernmost edge of the Strip. Of course, bad location usually translates into good prices, and that's particularly true at this solid mid-range property with better-than-average rooms. Unfortunately, none of the accommodations are in the tower itself, but all are comfortable and contemporary and well-equipped with extras like hairdryers and clock radios. The hotel doubled in size in late 2001 and suites in the newer wing are particularly nice, with some offering excellent views over the city from the cozy confines of the Jacuzzi. There's also a beautiful eighth-floor pool deck with plenty of room for lounging and tanning.

2500 Rooms: a/c | tv | tel | web | minibar | rm svc | gym

Sunset Station $$

1301 W Sunset Rd (at I-95), Henderson

T 702.547.7777 or 888.319.4655

W stationcasinos.com MAP K2 39

One of the city's best-loved "locals" casinos, Sunset Station is a Spanish Mediterranean-style low-rise that attracts low-rollers in droves. The smart interior, which is festooned with iron balconies, faux-brick house fronts and a cool Gaudiesque bar, is intended to recall Barcelona. Yet scratch the surface and this place is pure Vegas. In addition to some 800 nickel slot machines and a large Bingo room, the hotel offers a ten-table Poker parlor, a micro-brewery specializing in German-style lagers, and a multiplex movie theater that regularly screens

independent and foreign films. The casino itself is large, but with fewer than 500 rooms, the hotel is downright intimate by Vegas standards. Guestrooms are bright and clean and thoroughly serviceable. You'll need a car, though: Sunset Station is situated about 20 minutes from the Strip, across from the **Galleria Mall**.

448 Rooms: a/c | tv | tel | web | minibar | rm svc | gym

Terrible's $$

4100 Paradise Rd (at Flamingo), East Side

T 702.733.7000 or 800.640.9777

W terribleherbst.com MAP L1 40

With a name like Terrible's it's got to be good. Owned by the Herbst brothers, who made their fortune with the locally legendary Terrible Herbst gas stations, this relatively new hotel is the family's first foray into the gaming world. And by all measures it's a success. Despite having a good location just down the block from the Hard Rock, Terrible's caters primarily to locals. It's bright and friendly with very nice mid-range motel-style rooms that grow in size from Standard to King to Deluxe to Suite. All are stuffed with amenities like coffeemakers, hairdryers and clock radios. Rooms facing the courtyard are quieter than those facing the street. In addition to low prices, there's a lot to like here, including an attractive pool area, a lobby-level convenience store which stocks discount liquor and cigarettes, and a bank of Video Poker machines in the casino that pays out in gasoline from an affiliated station.

374 Rooms: a/c | tv | tel | web | rm svc

THEhotel $$$$

3950 Las Vegas Blvd S (at Mandalay Bay), Strip

T 702.632.7777 or 877.632.7800

W thehotelatmandalaybay.com MAP C2 41

A 43-story tower adjacent to Mandalay Bay, THEhotel is an all-suite, style-driven hotel in which every accommodation comes with separate living and sleeping areas stocked with flat panel televisions, private bars and plush furnishings. From the stunning 3-story wood and granite lobby to the luxe rooms created by Dougall Design Associates, the look here is NYC chic: minimalist black and gray with top-of-the-line facilities and original art by the likes of Jasper Johns, Robert Raushenberg, Andy Warhol, Richard Serra and Donald Judd. Guestrooms are some of the largest in Vegas, and each comes with two bathrooms equipped with more flat panel televisions. Service can be hit-or-miss and the bathroom toiletries are not up to snuff, but somehow this feels like quibbling. Ask for a free upgrade to a corner suite for a tad more space and better views. Or shell out for one of two-dozen enormous premium suites on the tower's top floors which are some of the finest we've seen anywhere. There's a great bar/lounge with billiards in the lobby that plays to all manner of black-collar workers: artists, graphic designers, video producers. And, of course, all guests have access to the facilities and services of Mandalay Bay next door, including the fabulous pool areas. In short, this is one of our favorite hotels in Las Vegas.

THEhotel

1120 Rooms: a/c | tv | tel | web | minibar | stereo | rm svc | gym

Treasure Island $$$

3300 Las Vegas Blvd S (at Spring Mountain), Strip

T 702.894.7111 or 800.288.7206

W treasureislandlasvegas.com MAP F2 42

Originally themed after a Robert Louis Stevenson novel, TI recently modernized its pirate theme to be something more

akin to a sexy Caribbean getaway. Situated beside its sister hotel, the noble Mirage, Treasure Island is now one of the Strip's best midscale properties. Fronted by a replica of an Old World sea village and an artificial lagoon with a very real-looking, fully rigged frigate, the resort's wooden boardwalk entrance remains one of the most beguiling in Vegas—which, of course, is saying quite a lot. Guestrooms, which feature floor-to-ceiling windows, are upscale, oversized, and nicely decorated with quality furnishings, pleasant original artwork and marble baths. And most have high-speed Internet access. Amenities include a well-equipped spa and a generous pool area. And, although dining options cover all bases, none is worth going out of your way for. Still, we like this vaguely pirate-themed casino, if, for no other reason than, it strikes us as truth in advertising. The bottom line is that Treasure Island is a great place to visit if you can get a great deal.

2885 Rooms: a/c | tv | tel | web | rm svc | gym

The Venetian $$$$$

3355 Las Vegas Blvd S (at Sands), Strip

T 702.414.1000 or 888.283.6423

W thevenetian.com MAP F2 43

The Venetian's sanitized appropriation of Venice is a must see. Like New York-New York and Paris just down the road, this resort wows with replicas of famous urban landmarks, including the Doge's Palace, the Campanile, the Rialto Bridge (with a moving walkway!) and Piazza San Marco (complete with live pigeons). And upstairs (!) is the spectacular **Grand Canal Shoppes** mall featuring a lengthy "river" with real gondoliers. The hotel is a must-stay too, for its huge standard rooms (the largest in Vegas) and an all-around excellence that rates high on our Cool-O-Meter. Each accommodation has marble foyers and baths, a sunken living room with a convertible sofa and a couple of wing chairs, two big color TVs, a trio of phones, a mini bar and a fax/copier/printer (for an additional charge). And the newer Venezia Tower features bathrooms that are larger than most apartments. The resort's restaurant selection includes several of the biggest names in the city, the gyms are great (with rock climbing, spinning and therapeutic Watsu pools), and the amazing spa is an outpost of the venerable **Canyon Ranch**. But, back to the public areas which are simply jaw-droppingly amazing, with geometric black-and-beige marble floors like those in St. Mark's Cathedral, fantastic ceiling frescos, reproduction Renaissance-era paintings and even an outpost of the **Guggenheim Hermitage Museum**. And why not? The real Venice has a Guggenheim too. And this one's not sinking.

4049 Rooms: a/c | tv | tel | web | minibar | rm svc | gym

Westin Casuarina Hotel & Spa $$$

160 East Flamingo Rd (at Koval), East Side

T 702.836.9775 or 888.625.5144

W starwoodhotels.com MAP E2 44

This relatively new, 17-story chain hotel wins our praise for good quality at good prices, all in a great location just a few minutes' walk from the Strip. Westin is known for good beds and terry robes, plus dual-line cordless phones, in-room safes and coffeemakers. High speed Internet, 24/seven room service, a casino in the lobby and a small spa round out the offerings of this comparatively intimate hotel. There's a nice little swimming pool with teak chaise lounges, and even dogs are catered to with a "heavenly dog bed" and complimentary resort-baked biscuits. We recommend this one for both business people and families.

826 Rooms: a/c | tv | tel | web | minibar | rm svc | gym

Wynn Las Vegas $$$$$

3131 Las Vegas Blvd S (at Sands), Strip

T 702.770.7100 or 877.770.7077

W wynnlasvegas.com MAP F2 45

Legendary Las Vegas developer Steve Wynn, creator of the Bellagio, Treasure Island and the Mirage, is the man behind this new luxury resort for comfort-addicted alpha earners. Featuring an indoor, five-story "mountain" complete with a waterfall that cascades into a large artificial lake, the monolithic, bronze curvilinear hotel and casino is unusual in that it is meant to be experienced from the inside out, rather than the other way around like most of the other architectural showplaces on the Strip. Guestrooms are huge, as luxe as any on the Strip and fitted with floor-to-ceiling windows, high thread-count sheets, high-speed Internet and flat panel TVs. In addition to the requisite large casino (with radio frequency identification-embedded chips to deter casino cheats), the resort features a fine art museum stocked with Wynn's personal collection, an 18-hole championship golf course and an on-site Ferrari and Maserati dealership. And the location is great, next to the Venetian and across from the **Fashion Show Mall**. Despite comparatively high prices, reservations can be tough, as this is one of the city's hottest places to stay.

2700 Rooms: a/c | tv | tel | web | minibar | stereo | rm svc | gym

Map		Area	Hotel	Address	Phone	Website	Style Driven	Theme Driven	Club/Bar Scene	High Speed Internet	Spa	Pool	24/7 Room Service	Business Sense	Kid Friendly
			Very Expensive $$$$$												
E2	5	Strip	Bellagio	3600 Las Vegas Blvd S	702.693.7444	bellagioresort.com			★	★	★	★	★	★	
E2	7	Strip	Caesars Palace	3570 Las Vegas Blvd S	702.731.7110	caesars.com		★	★	★	★	★	★	★	★
C2	14	Strip	Four Seasons Las Vegas	3960 Las Vegas Blvd S	702.632.5000	fourseasons.com				★	★	★	★	★	★
C2	24	Strip	Mandalay Bay	3950 Las Vegas Blvd S	702.632.7777	mandalaybay.com			★	★	★	★	★	★	
E2	32	Strip	Paris Las Vegas	3655 Las Vegas Blvd S	702.946.7000	paris-lv.com		★	★	★	★	★	★	★	
D2	36	Strip	SkyLofts at MGM	3799 Las Vegas Blvd S	702.891.3832	skyloftsmgmgrand.com	★		★	★	★	★	★	★	★
F2	43	Strip	The Venetian	3355 Las Vegas Blvd S	702.414.1000	thevenetian.com		★	★	★	★	★	★	★	★
F2	45	Strip	Wynn Las Vegas	3131 Las Vegas Blvd S	702.770.7100	wynnlasvegas.com			★	★	★	★	★	★	
			Expensive $$$$												
K1	18	East Side	Hard Rock Hotel	4455 Paradise Rd	702.693.5000	hardrockhotel.com	★	★	★	★	★	★	★		
E2	33	Strip	Aladdin/Planet Hollywood	3667 Las Vegas Blvd S	702.736.0111	aladdincasino.com		★	★	★		★	★		★
E2	4	Strip	Barbary Coast	3595 Las Vegas Blvd S	702.737.7111	barbarycoastcasino.com				★			★		
E2	13	Strip	Flamingo Las Vegas	3555 Las Vegas Blvd S	702.733.3111	flamingolasvegas.com				★		★	★	★	★
F2	19	Strip	Harrah's	3475 Las Vegas Blvd S	702.369.5000	harrahsvegas.com			★	★		★	★	★	
D2	22	Strip	Luxor	3900 Las Vegas Blvd S	702.262.4000	luxor.com		★	★	★	★	★	★	★	★
D2	25	Strip	MGM Grand	3799 Las Vegas Blvd S	702.891.1111	mgmgrand.com			★	★	★	★	★	★	★
F2	26	Strip	The Mirage	3400 Las Vegas Blvd S	702.791.7111	themirage.com			★	★	★	★	★	★	
D2	29	Strip	New York-New York	3790 Las Vegas Blvd S	702.740.6969	nynyhotelcasino.com		★	★	★	★	★	★	★	★
C2	41	Strip	THEhotel	3950 Las Vegas Blvd S	702.632.7777	thehotelatmandalaybay.com	★			★	★	★	★	★	
			Moderate $$$												
I2	17	Downtown	Golden Nugget	129 Fremont St	702.385.7111	goldennugget.com				★		★	★	★	
G1	21	East Side	Las Vegas Hilton	3000 Paradise Rd	702.732.5111	lv-hilton.com				★	★	★	★	★	★
E2	44	East Side	Westin Casuarina Hotel & Spa	160 East Flamingo Rd	702.836.9775	starwoodhotels.com				★	★	★	★	★	★
E2	3	Strip	Bally's	3645 Las Vegas Blvd S	702.739.4111	ballyslv.com			★	★		★	★	★	
D2	11	Strip	Excalibur	3850 Las Vegas Blvd S	702.597.7700	excalibur-casino.com		★		★		★	★	★	★
D2	27	Strip	Monte Carlo	3770 Las Vegas Blvd S	702.730.7777	monte-carlo.com		★		★		★	★	★	
E1	31	West Side	The Palms	4321 W Flamingo Rd	702.942.7777	thepalmslasvegas.com	★		★	★	★	★	★	★	
E1	34	West Side	Rio	3700 W Flamingo Rd	702.252.7777	playrio.com		★	★	★		★	★	★	★
H1	38	Strip	Stratosphere	2000 Las Vegas Blvd S	702.380.7777	stratospherehotel.com				★		★	★	★	★
F2	42	Strip	Treasure Island	3300 Las Vegas Blvd S	702.894.7111	treasureislandlasvegas.com		★	★	★		★	★	★	

1 | DIRECTORY SLEEP

Map		Area	Hotel	Address	Phone	Website	Style Driven	Theme Driven	Club/Bar Scene	High Speed Internet	Spa	Pool	24/7 Room Service	Business Sense	Kid Friendly
			Inexpensive $$												
I2	16	Downtown	Fremont Hotel & Casino	200 Fremont St	702.385.3232	fremontcasino.com									
J1	23	Downtown	Main Street Station	200 N Main St	702.387.1896	stationcasinos.com								★	★
L2	2	East Side	Arizona Charlie's East	4575 Boulder Hwy	702.951.5800	azcharlies.com						★			★
G2	6	East Side	Boulder Station	4111 Boulder Hwy	702.432.7777	boulderstation.com						★		★	★
L1	40	East Side	Terrible's	4100 Paradise Rd	702.733.7000	terribleherbst.com						★		★	
K2	39	Henderson	Sunset Station	1301 W Sunset Rd	702.547.7777	stationcasinos.com						★		★	★
G1	9	Strip	Circus Circus	2880 Las Vegas Blvd S	702.734.0410	circuscircus-lasvegas.com		★		★		★	★		★
E2	20	Strip	Imperial Palace	3535 Las Vegas Blvd S	702.731.3311	imperialpalace.com		★		★		★	★	★	
D1	30	West Side	The Orleans	4500 W Tropicana Ave	702.365.7111	orleanscasino.com		★				★			
G1	35	Strip	Sahara	2535 Las Vegas Blvd S	702.737.2111	saharahotelandcasino.com		★				★			
F2	37	Strip	Stardust	3000 Las Vegas Blvd S	702.732.6111	stardustlv.com						★			
			Cheap $												
I2	10	Downtown	El Cortez	600 Fremont St	702.385.5200	elcortez.net									
I2	12	Downtown	Fitzgerald's	301 Fremont St	702.388.2400	fitzgeraldslasvegas.com									
I2	15	Downtown	Four Queens	202 Fremont St	702.385.4011	fourqueens.com									
D2	28	East Side	Motel 6	195 E Tropicana Ave	702.798.0728	motel6.com						★			
G1	1	Strip	Algiers Hotel	2845 Las Vegas Blvd S	702.735.3311	algiershotel.com									

Pack it				
aspirin	cd's	handcuffs	picnic blanket	sunglasses
backgammon set	clock	hat, scarf, gloves	playing cards	sunscreen
batteries	condoms	kite	power adapter	swim suit
beach towel	corkscrew	magazines	rolling paper	swiss army knife
binoculars	dvd's	massage oil	scented candles	umbrella
books	flip-flops	mp3 player	scrabble	video camera
camera	frisbee	phone charger	sexy underwear	warm sox

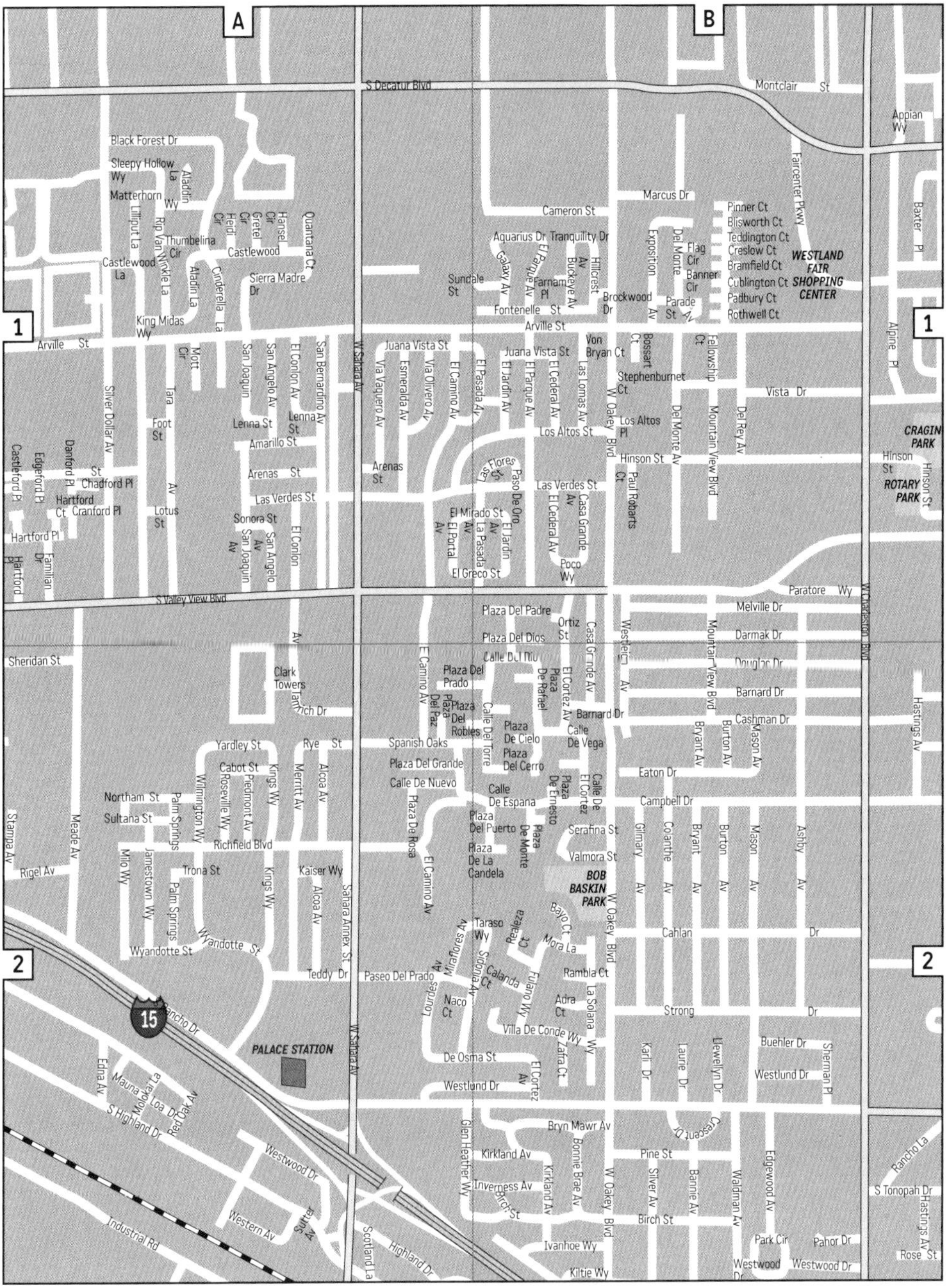

A
B
1
2

S Decatur Blvd
Montclair St
Appian Wy
Black Forest Dr
Sleepy Hollow La
Wy
Aladdin Wy
Matterhorn
Lilliput La
Rip Van Winkle La
Thumbelina Cir
Heidi Cir
Gretel Cir
Hansel Cir
Quantana Ct
Castlewood La
Castlewood
Aladdin La
Cinderella La
Sierra Madre Dr
King Midas Wy
Arville St
Mott Cir
Tara
Foot St
Silver Dollar Av
San Joaquin
San Angelo Av
El Conlon Av
San Bernardino Av
Lenna St
Lenna St
Amarillo St
Arenas St
Las Verdes St
Sonora St
San Joaquin Av
San Angelo Av
El Conlon
Lotus St
Av
Danford Pl
St
Chadford Pl
Castleford Pl
Edgeford Pl
Hartford Ct
Cranford Pl
Hartford Pl
Hartford Pl
Familian Dr
S Valley View Blvd
W Sahara Av
Juana Vista St
Via Vaquero Av
Esmeralda Av
Via Olivero Av
El Camino Av
El Pasada Av
El Jardin Av
El Parque Av
El Cederal Av
Las Lomas Av
Juana Vista St
Arenas St
Las Flores St
Paso De Oro
Los Altos St
Las Verdes St
Casa Grande Av
El Cederal Av
El Mirado St
Av
El Portal Av
La Pasada Av
El Jardin
Poco Wy
El Greco St
Cameron St
Aquarius Dr
Tranquility Dr
Galaxy Av
El Parque Av
Buckeye Av
Hillcrest
Farnam Pl
Sundale St
Fontenelle St
Brockwood Dr
Arville St
Von Bryan Ct
Bossart Ct
Stephenburnet Ct
W Oakey Blvd
Los Altos Pl
Hinson St
Paul Roberts Ct
Marcus Dr
Exposition Av
Del Monte
Flag Cir
Banner Cir
Parade St
Av
Ct
Fellowship
Del Monte Av
Mountain View Blvd
Del Rey Av
Vista Dr
Pinner Ct
Blisworth Ct
Teddington Ct
Creslow Ct
Bramfield Ct
Cublington Ct
Padbury Ct
Rothwell Ct
Faircenter Pkwy
WESTLAND FAIR SHOPPING CENTER
Baxter Pl
Alpine Pl
CRAGIN PARK
Hinson St
ROTARY PARK
Hinson St
Paratore Wy
W Charleston Blvd
Sheridan St
Clark Towers
Tamarich Dr
Av
Yardley St
Rye St
Cabot St
Roseville Wy
Wilmington Wy
Piedmont Av
Kings Wy
Merritt Av
Alcoa Av
Northam St
Sultana St
Palm Springs
Richfield Blvd
Stampa Av
Meade Av
Rigel Av
Milo Wy
Jamestown Wy
Trona St
Palm Springs
Kings Wy
Kaiser Wy
Alcoa Av
Sahara Annex St
Wyandotte St
Wyandotte St
Teddy Dr
Rancho Dr
15
PALACE STATION
Edna Av
Mauna Loa Dr
Mookai La
Red Oak Av
S Highland Dr
Westwood Dr
Western Av
Sutter Av
Industrial Rd
Scotland La
Highland Dr
W Sahara Av
Plaza Del Padre
Ortiz St
Plaza Del Dios
Casa Grande Av
Calle Del Rio
Plaza Del Prado
Plaza De Rafael
El Cortez Av
Plaza Del Paz
Plaza Del Robles
Calle Del Torre
Barnard Dr
Calle De Vega
Plaza De Cielo
Plaza Del Cerro
Spanish Oaks
Plaza Del Grande
Calle De Nuevo
Calle De Espana
Plaza De Ernesto
El Cortez
Calle De
Plaza De Rosa
Plaza Del Puerto
Plaza De Monte
Plaza De La Candela
Serafina St
Valmora St
El Camino Av
BOB BASKIN PARK
Taraso Wy
Realeza Ct
Bayo Ct
Mora La
Miraflores Av
Sidonia Ct
Calanda Av
Fulano Wy
Rambla Ct
Lourdes Av
Paseo Del Prado
Naco Ct
Adra Ct
La Solana Wy
Villa De Conde Wy
Zafra Ct
De Osma St
El Cortez Av
Westlund Dr
Melville Dr
Westlee Av
Darmak Dr
Douglas Dr
Mountain View Blvd
Barnard Dr
Cashman Dr
Bryant Av
Burton Av
Mason Av
Eaton Dr
Campbell Dr
Gilmary Av
Colanthe Av
Bryant Av
Burton Av
Mason Av
Ashby Av
Hastings Av
Cahlan Dr
Strong Dr
Karli Dr
Laurie Dr
Llewellyn Dr
Buehler Dr
Westlund Dr
Sherman Pl
Bryn Mawr Av
Crescent Dr
Glen Heather Wy
Kirkland Av
Pine St
Bonnie Brae Av
Inverness Av
Kirkland Av
Birch St
W Oakey Blvd
Silver Av
Bannie Av
Waldman Av
Edgewood Av
Birch St
Ivanhoe Wy
Kiltie Wy
Park Cir
Pahor Dr
Westwood Dr
Westwood Dr
Rancho La
S Tonopah Dr
Hastings Av
Rose St

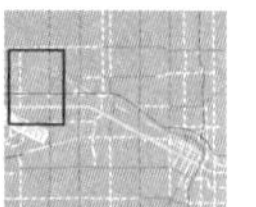

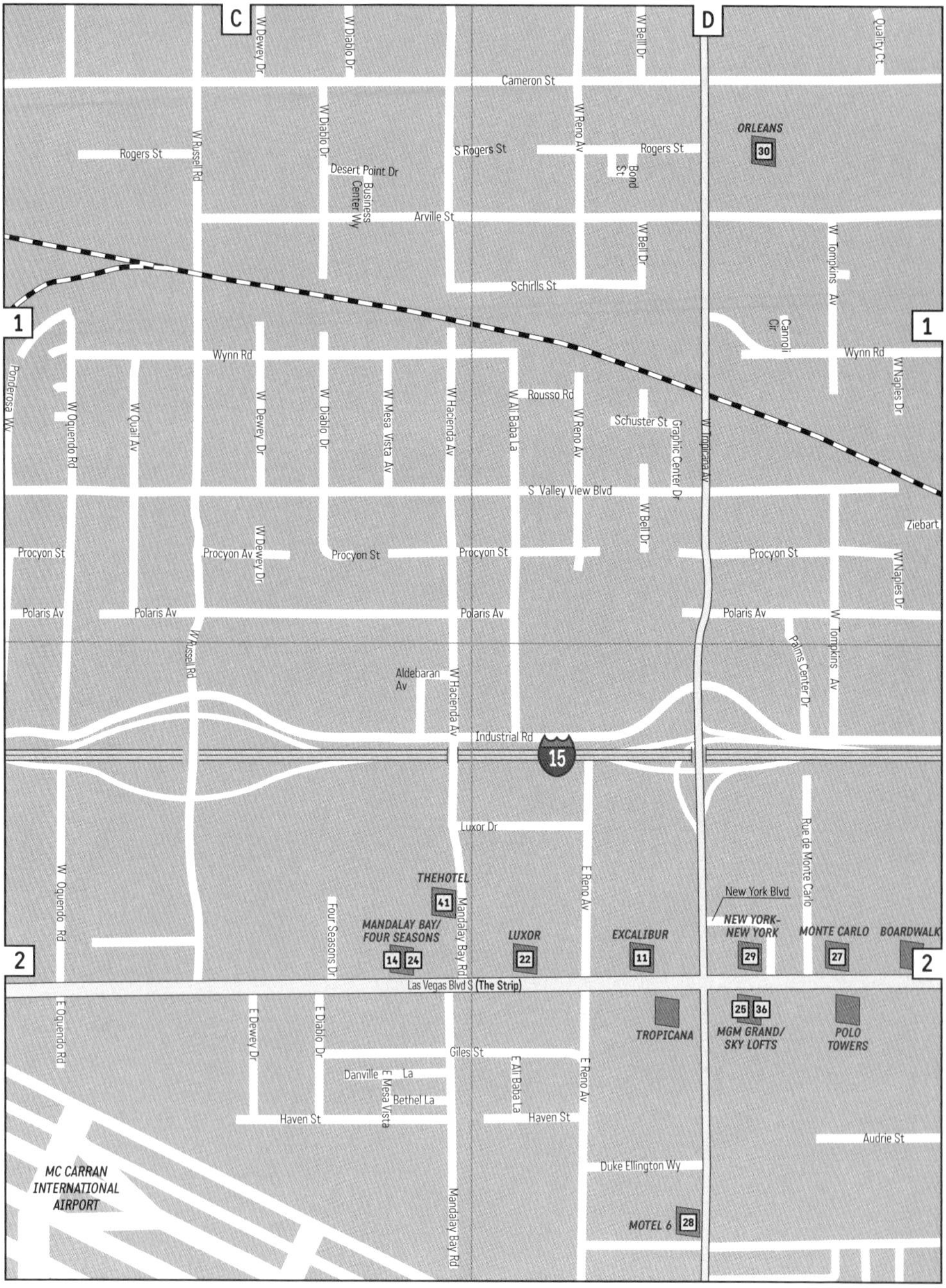

C
D
1
2

ORLEANS 30
THEHOTEL 41
MANDALAY BAY/ FOUR SEASONS 14 24
LUXOR 22
EXCALIBUR 11
NEW YORK-NEW YORK 29
MONTE CARLO 27
BOARDWALK
TROPICANA
MGM GRAND/ SKY LOFTS 25 36
POLO TOWERS
MOTEL 6 28
MC CARRAN INTERNATIONAL AIRPORT

W Dewey Dr
W Diablo Dr
W Bell Dr
Quality Ct
Cameron St
W Reno Av
Rogers St
W Russell Rd
S Rogers St
Desert Point Dr
Bond St
Business Center Wy
Arville St
W Tompkins Av
Schirlls St
Cannoli Cir
Wynn Rd
W Naples Dr
Ponderosa Wy
W Oquendo Rd
W Quail Av
W Mesa Vista Av
W Hacienda Av
W Ali Baba La
Rousso Rd
Schuster St
Graphic Center Dr
W Tropicana Av
S Valley View Blvd
Ziebart
Procyon St
Procyon Av
Polaris Av
W Russel Rd
Aldebaran Av
Palms Center Dr
Industrial Rd
15
Luxor Dr
Rue de Monte Carlo
E Reno Av
New York Blvd
W Oquendo Rd
Four Seasons Dr
Mandalay Bay Rd
Las Vegas Blvd S (The Strip)
E Oquendo Rd
E Dewey Dr
E Diablo Dr
Giles St
E Ali Baba La
Danville La
E Mesa Vista
Bethel La
Haven St
Audrie St
Duke Ellington Wy

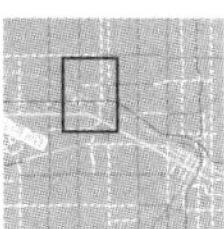

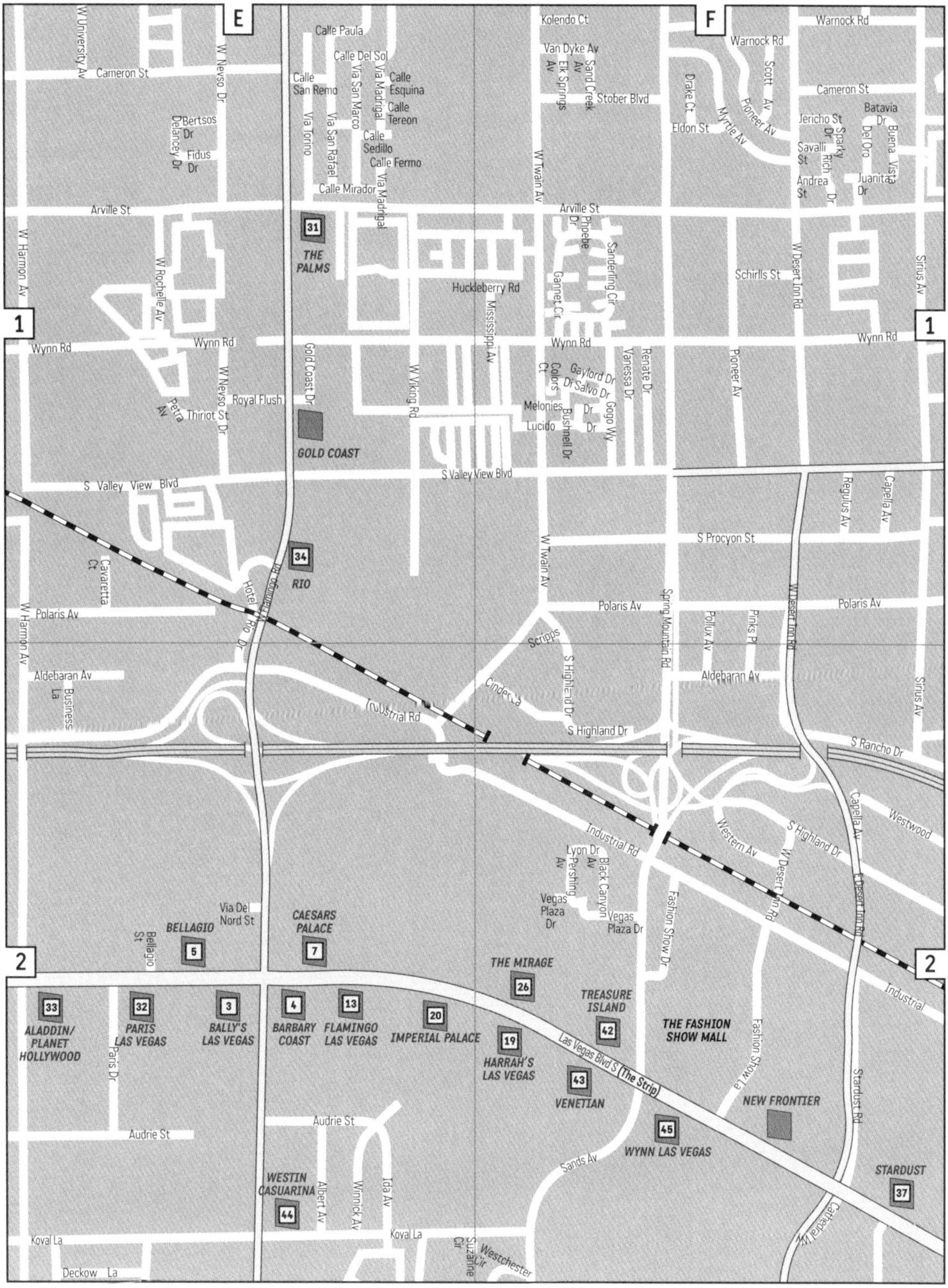

E F 1 2

31 THE PALMS
GOLD COAST
34 RIO
5 BELLAGIO
7 CAESARS PALACE
26 THE MIRAGE
42 TREASURE ISLAND
THE FASHION SHOW MALL
33 ALADDIN/ PLANET HOLLYWOOD
32 PARIS LAS VEGAS
3 BALLY'S LAS VEGAS
4 BARBARY COAST
13 FLAMINGO LAS VEGAS
20 IMPERIAL PALACE
19 HARRAH'S LAS VEGAS
43 VENETIAN
45 WYNN LAS VEGAS
NEW FRONTIER
37 STARDUST
44 WESTIN CASUARINA

W University Av
Cameron St
W Nevso Dr
Bertsos Dr
Delancey Dr
Fidus Dr
Calle Paula
Calle Del Sol
Calle San Remo
Via San Marco
Via Madrigal
Calle Esquina
Calle Tereon
Via Torino
Via San Rafael
Calle Sedillo
Calle Fermo
Calle Mirador
Kolendo Ct
Van Dyke Av
Elk Springs Av
Sand Creek Av
Stober Blvd
W Twain Av
Warnock Rd
Drake Ct
Scott Av
Pioneer Av
Eldon St
Myrtle Av
Jericho St
Batavia Dr
Sparky Dr
Del Oro
Buena Vista
Savalli St
Rich Dr
Andrea St
Juanita Dr
Arville St
W Harmon Av
W Rochelle Av
Phoebe Dr
Sanderling Cir
Huckleberry Rd
Garnet Cir
Mississippi Av
Schirlls St
W Desert Inn Rd
Sirius Av
Wynn Rd
Gold Coast Dr
W Viking Rd
Colors Ct
Gaylord Dr
Di Salvo Dr
Vanessa Dr
Renate Dr
Royal Flush
Petra Av
Thiriot St
Melonies Dr
Lucido Dr
Bushnell Dr
Gogo Wy
S Valley View Blvd
Regulus Av
Capella Av
S Procyon St
Cavaretta Ct
Hotel Rio Dr
Polaris Av
Spring Mountain Rd
Pollux Av
Pinks Pl
Scripps
S Highland Dr
Aldebaran Av
Business La
Cinderella
Industrial Rd
S Rancho Dr
Westwood
Western Av
Lyon Dr
Pershing Av
Black Canyon Av
Vegas Plaza Dr
Fashion Show Dr
E Desert Inn Rd
Via Del Nord St
Bellagio St
Industrial
Paris Dr
Las Vegas Blvd S (The Strip)
Fashion Show La
Stardust Rd
Audrie St
Sands Av
Albert Av
Winnick Av
Ida Av
Cathedral Wy
Koval La
Suzanne Cir
Westchester
Deckow La

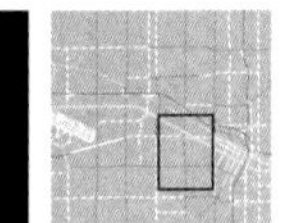

G
H
1
2
STARDUST 37
CIRCUS CIRCUS 9
RIVIERA
ALGIERS 1
SAHARA 35
STRATOSPHERE 38
LAS VEGAS HILTON 21
LAS VEGAS CONVENTION CENTER
LAS VEGAS COUNTRY CLUB
BAKER PARK
Las Vegas Blvd S (The Strip)
Circus Circus Dr
Kishner Dr
Convention Center Dr
Riviera Blvd
Paradise Rd
Av of the Hiltons
Joe W Brown Dr
Oakmont Pl
Oakmont Av
Oakmont Dr
Queens Courtyard Dr
Augusta Dr
Bel Air Cir
Bel Air Dr
Broadmoor Av
Vegas Valley Dr
Pinehurst Dr
Tam O'Shanter
Karen Av
Karen Ct
Lynnwood St
Van Patten St
Sherwood St
Kendale St
State St
S Maryland Pkwy
South Bridge La
Northbridge St
W Sahara Av
E Sahara Av
Tam Dr
W Cincinnati Av
W Cleveland Av
W Baltimore Av
W Boston Av
W St Louis Av
W Philadelphia Av
W Chicago Av
W New York Av
W Wyoming Ave
W Oakey Blvd
Industrial Rd
Highland Av
Western Av
Martin L King Blvd
Westwood Dr
Shadow La
Jaylar Cir
Ellis Av
Ormsby St
Mercedes Cir
Charmast La
Richard Ct
Ila St
Wall St
Fairfield Av
W Utah Av
W Imperial Av
W Colorado Av
S Commerce St
S Main St
E Imperial Av
E Colorado Av
E California St
E Utah Av
Casino Center Blvd
S 3rd St
S 4th St
Santa Clara Dr
Santa Paula Dr
Santa Rita Dr
Santa Rosa Dr
Santa Ynez Dr
Van Patten Pl
San Pablo Dr
Weldon Pl
Santa Paula Dr
El Centro Pl
Rexford Dr
Rexford Pl
E St. Louis Av
Bonita Av
Barbara Wy
Ellen Wy
E Oakey Blvd
Houssels Av
Griffith Av
Bracken Av
Sweeney Av
5th Pl
S 6th St
Park Paseo
S 7th St
Alhambra Cir
Alhambra Dr
Santiago St
Cordova St
Canosa Av
S 8th St
8th Pl
S 9th St
S 10th St
Franklin Av
Hasseth Av
Howard Av
Wengert Av
Norman Av
Jessica Av
Francis Av
Almond Tree La
S 11th St
Art and Mary Thomas La
S 13th St
San Pedro Av
Maroney St
Exley Av
Phillips Av
Canosa Cir
St. Joseph Cir
St. Jude Cir
S 14th St
Pardee Pl
S 15th St
Maria Elena Av
Chapman
Chapman Dr
Concordia Pl
S 16th St
Becke Cir
Hartke Pl
Curtis Dr
Hillside Pl
Cochran St
S 17th St
Spencer St
Talbot St
Pauline Wy
Kassabian Av
Lamplighter La
E St Louis Av
S Bruce St
Moore St
Casa Vegas St
Topanga St
Corona Av
Hermosa St
Laguna Av
Malibu St
La Canada St
La Jolla Av
El Segundo Av
Serenada Av
El Cajon St
Silver Mesa Wy
Raindance Wy
Golden Arrow Dr
Palora Av
Capistrano Av
Palma Vista Av
Izabella Av
Coronado Av
Iglesia St
Meteoro St
Del Mar Av
Playa Del Rey St
Sundown Dr
Talbot Cir
Seneca Dr
Medicine Man Wy
Caballero Wy
Berman St
Palma Vista Cir
La Varre Av
La Brisa Av
Balboa Av
Del Mar Pl
Del Mar Ct
El Toreador St
6

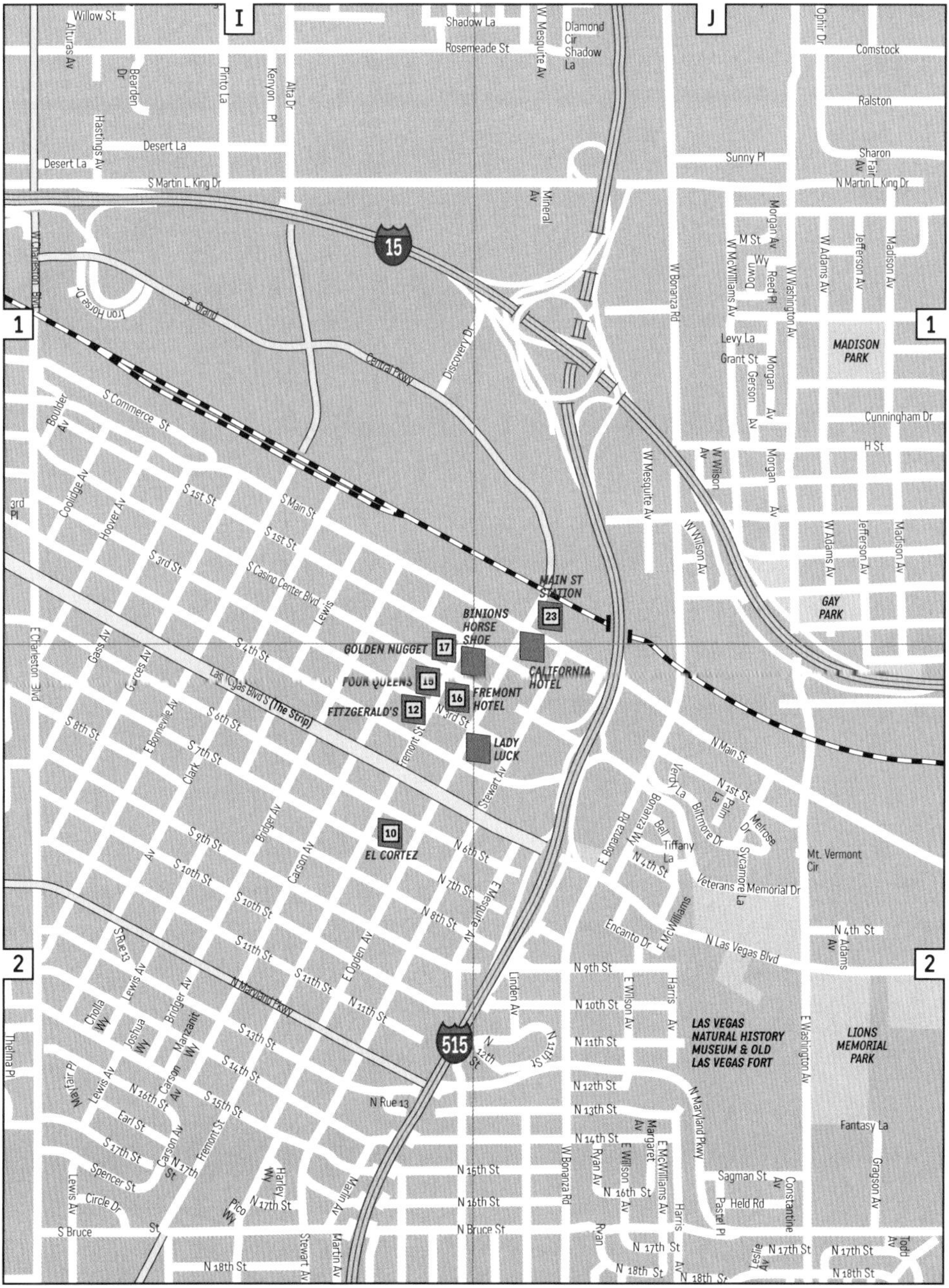

I
J
1
2

MAIN ST STATION 23
BINIONS HORSE SHOE
GOLDEN NUGGET 17
CALIFORNIA HOTEL
FOUR QUEENS 15
FREMONT HOTEL 16
FITZGERALD'S 12
LADY LUCK
EL CORTEZ 10
MADISON PARK
GAY PARK
LAS VEGAS NATURAL HISTORY MUSEUM & OLD LAS VEGAS FORT
LIONS MEMORIAL PARK
15
515

Willow St
Alturas Av
Bearden Dr
Hastings Av
Pinto La
Kenyon Pl
Alta Dr
Desert La
Shadow La
Rosemeade St
W Mesquite Av
Diamond Cir
Shadow La
Ophir Dr
Comstock
Ralston
Sunny Pl
Sharon Fair Av
S Martin L. King Dr
N Martin L. King Dr
Mineral Av
W Charleston Blvd
Iron Horse Dr
S Grand
Central Pkwy
Discovery Dr
W Bonanza Rd
M St
Down Wy
Morgan Av
Reed Pl
W McWilliams Av
W Washington Av
W Adams Av
Jefferson Av
Madison Av
Levy La
Grant St
Gerson Av
Cunningham Dr
H St
W Mesquite Av
W Wilson Av
S Commerce St
Boulder Av
Coolidge Av
Hoover Av
3rd Pl
S 1st St
S Main St
S 3rd St
S Casino Center Blvd
Lewis
Gass Av
Garces Av
S 4th St
Las Vegas Blvd S (The Strip)
E Charleston Blvd
S 8th St
E Bonneville Av
S 6th St
S 7th St
Clark
N 3rd St
Fremont St
Stewart Av
N Main St
Veri La
Bonanza Wy
N 1st St
Palm La
Biltmore Dr
Melrose Dr
Bell
Tiffany La
Sycamore La
Mt. Vermont Cir
E Bonanza Rd
N 4th St
Veterans Memorial Dr
E McWilliams
Encanto Dr
N 4th St
Adams Av
N Las Vegas Blvd
S 9th St
Bridger Av
Carson Av
S 10th St
N 6th St
N 7th St
E Mesquite Av
N 8th St
S Rue 13
Lewis Av
S 11th St
E Ogden Av
N 9th St
E Wilson Av
Harris Av
Cholla Wy
Joshua Wy
Bridger Av
Manzanita Wy
N Maryland Pkwy
N 11th St
Linden Av
N 10th St
E Washington Av
N 11th St
S 13th St
N 12th St
N 11th St
Thelma Pl
Mayfair Pl
Lewis Av
Carson Av
S 14th St
N 16th St
S 15th St
N 12th St
N Rue 13
N 13th St
N Maryland Pkwy
Fantasy La
Earl St
Carson Av
N 17th St
Fremont St
N 14th St
Margaret Av
E McWilliams Av
S 17th St
Spencer St
Harley Wy
Martin Av
N 15th St
W Bonanza Rd
Ryan Av
E Wilson Av
Sagman St
Constantine Av
Gragson Av
Lewis Av
Circle Dr
Pico Wy
N 17th St
N 16th St
N 16th St
Pastel Pl
Held Rd
S Bruce St
N Bruce St
Ryan
Harris Av
N 17th St
Leslie Av
N 17th St
N 17th St
Todd Av
N 18th St
Stewart Av
Martin Av
N 18th St
N 18th St
N 18th St

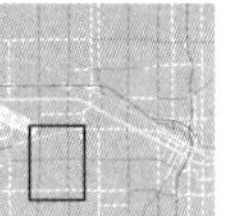

K
L
1
2

MC CARRAN INTERNATIONAL AIRPORT
HARD ROCK
18
TERRIBLE'S
40
UNIVERSITY OF NEVADA LAS VEGAS

Hensley St
Groff St
Finch
Elder
Davison
Charlton
Boone
Ashton
E Naples Dr
Hughes Center Dr
Corporate Dr
Sands Av
Paradise Rd
Swenson St
Albert Av
McKellar Cir
Calcaterra Cir
Kolson Cir
North Cir
Palos Verdes St
Voxna St
Visby La
Torsby Pl
Fredrika Dr
Royal Crest St
Hazelwood St
Daisy St
Mark Av
Gus Giuffre Dr
E Bell Dr
Palo Verde Rd
Thomas and Mack Dr
Palo Verde Cir
Sage Av
Swenson St
Colby
Durante St
E Harmon Av
E Twain Av
Laramore Dr
Bock St
Boyer St
Lulu Av
Radkovich Av
Toni Av
Shirley St
Wilbur St
Xanthippe La
Chatham Cir
Claymont St
Cottage Grove Av
Fairfax Cir
Grove Cir
Cottage Cir
Maryland Cir
Gym Dr
University Rd
Brussels St
Dorothy Av
Young St
Lulu Av
Turner St
E Katie Av
S Maryland Pkwy
Deirdre St
Ascot Dr
Del Mar
Escondido St
Elizabeth Av
Dorothy Av
Lorilyn Av
Santa Anita Dr
Living Desert
E Harmon Av
E University Av
E Nevso Dr
Heidi St
Hialeah Dr
Tamarus St
Algonquin Dr
E Flamingo Rd
Roberta St
Santa Anita Dr
Travis Cir
Caliente St
Gabriel Dr
Jupiter Ct
Newsom Cir
Puerto Verde La
Canterbury Ct
E Reno Av
E Viking Rd
E Katie Av
Colt Pl
Spencer St
Spencer St
Spencer St
Alto Verde
Camino Verde La
Arbol Verde Wy
Rockledge Wy
Kamden Wy
Avenida Del Sol
Silver Spur Cir
Avenida Del Luna
Newport Cove Dr
Carriage La
S Bruce St
Roxbury La
Roxford Dr
Ottawa Dr
Casey Ct
Corral Pl
Hallwood Dr
Rockledge Dr
Canterbury Dr
St
Heritageoaks La
Reno Ct
Surrey La
E Topicana Av
Coachman Cir
Irvin Cir
Sarah La
Stormy Cir
Ct
Whisper
Burnham Av
Waterford La
Osage Cir
Walteta Wy
Gabriel
Burnham Av
E Saddle Av
Shortleaf St
E Rochelle Av
E Nevso Dr
Tudur La
Omaha Cir
Celebrity Cir
Rancho Hills Dr
Renaissance Dr
Bridlewood Dr
Pine Breeze
Pinetop La
Portabello Rd
Amadeus Ct
Hoopa La
Jeffreys St
Woodpine Dr
Channel 10 Dr
Jeffreys St
Gaslight Cir
Mohigan Wy
Pima La
Delaware La
Saddle Pl
Latigo St
Dr
S Eastern Av
Paradise Village Wy
E Tompkins Av
Billman Av
Paradise Cove Dr
Astrotec Dr
Forever Dr
Sonrisa Wy
Domingo St
Sabado St
Evaline St
Los Reyes Ct
Resort Dr
Swan La
Whippoorwill Cir
Euclid St
Euclid St
Whippoorwill La
Blue Heron Ct
Madreperla St
Flagship Ct
Pacific Harbors Dr
Pacific St
E Reno Av
La Fortuna Av
La Cara Av
Malabar Av
Laconia Av
E Harmon Av
Albano Villa Ct
Batelli Ct
Flamingo Crest
Egret Cir
Saddlewood Ct
Topaz St
Kristen La
Paseo Del Ray
Garland Ct
E Saddle
Youngson Dr
Topaz St

39
2

EAT 2

The city's dining scene continues to grow and the massive influx of celebrity chefs continues unabated. There once was a time when foodies had to fly around the continent in order to sample the cooking of America's most celebrated chefs. Today, you can just take a cab. The new sophistication has even spilled over into the world of buffets, which has become more expansive and elaborate. Restaurants recommended by Avant-Guide represent the finest in each price category that the city has to offer. All present something new, unique or fashionable, or are very special in the way of local color and character. And we have gone to great lengths to uncover the very best of the city's lesser-known places. Regardless of budget—from burgers and sandwiches to steaks and seafood—with Avant-Guide in tow there's no excuse for a bad meal.

Our reviewers are fiercely independent and have no relationship whatsoever with any of the places we recommend.

Reservations

There are two ways to get reservations in Vegas. The first is to simply telephone and hope for the best. If this fails, phone your hotel's concierge, weeks before you check in if need be, and ask him or her to set you up. Even when reservations are "not accepted," you can often snag one simply by having your concierge phone for you. That's their job. Everything in Vegas works on the almighty tip, which means that nothing is impossible. For top restaurants, we advise you to reserve a table as far in advance as you can (The country code for the USA is 1; the city code for Las Vegas is 702. From Great Britain dial 00-1-702 plus the local number.).

Buffets

Las Vegas and buffets go together like Elvis and peanut butter. This AYCE embarrassment of riches began in the 1940s as loss leaders to woo gamblers into hotels. Today almost every major casino offers a buffet. You can still find a world-class-horrible one in which diners eat plates of congealed grease and get indigestion for as little as $8. But there are several excellent spreads too, many of which cost as much as an elegant restaurant. In addition to our favorites, listed below, you should know about the **Holiday Inn Boardwalk's Surf Buffet**, 3750 Las Vegas Blvd South (at Tropicana Ave–Strip; tel. 702.730.3100), which is the only buffet on the Strip open 24/seven. And there are few better values than **Main Street Station's Garden Court Buffet**, 200 North Main St (at Stewart Ave–Downtown; tel. 702.387.1896), where dorm food breakfasts, lunches and dinners are just about the cheapest you'll find.

Las Vegas' Celebrity Restaurateurs	
Chef/Owner	**Their Restaurants**
Brad Brennan	Commander's Palace
Tom Colicchio	Craftsteak
Alain Ducasse	Mix
Jean-Marie Josselin	808
Thomas Keller	Bouchon
Emeril Lagasse	Emeril's, Delmonico Steakhouse
Nobu Matsuhisa	Nobu
Maurizio Mazzon	Canaletto, Il Fornaio
Charlie Palmer	Aureole, Charlie Palmer Steak
Wolfgang Puck	Spago, Chinois, Postrio, Trattoria del Lupo
André Rochat	Alizé, André's
Guy Savoy	Guy Savoy
Julian Serrano	Picasso
Kerry Simon	Simon Kitchen
Joachim Splichal	Pinot Brasserie
Alessandro Stratta	Alex
Piero Selvaggio Valentino	Valentino
Jean-Georges Vongerichten	Prime Steakhouse

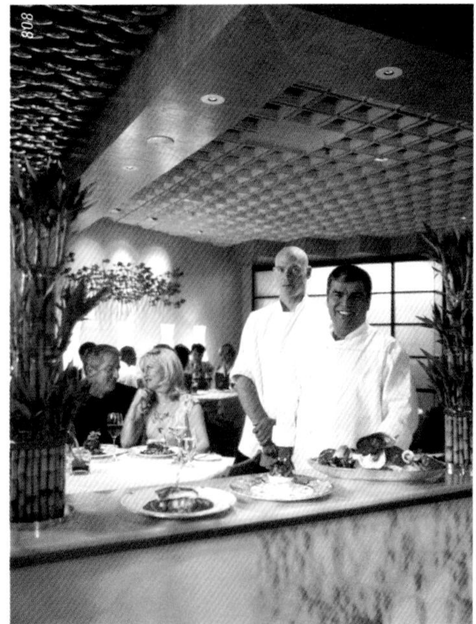

808 $$$$

Caesars Palace, 3570 Las Vegas Blvd S (at Flamingo), Strip

T 702.731.7110

ASIAN FUSION MAP E2 1

This great Asian-fusion restaurant gets its name from the Hawaiian area code and its inspiration from the Pacific Rim. In a word, food here is awesome. You could easily make a meal of sophisticated appetizers like seared scallops with white truffle mashed potatoes, and a "deconstructed ahi roll" with ahi tartar, avocado salsa and crab ceviche. The Hawaiian poke sampler is three tastes of fresh, marinated seafood presented in beautiful lacquer boxes. Mains are equally as inspired and served in a restrained, upscale room that includes chairs for singles facing a beautiful exhibition kitchen. Of course, all this goodness doesn't come cheaply, but portions are generous and quality is tops. This one's for foodies.

3950 $$$$

Mandalay Bay, 3950 Las Vegas Blvd S (at Mandalay Bay), Strip

T 702.632.7414

AMERICAN NEW MAP C2 2

3950 is that increasingly rare breed of Vegas restaurant: one without a branch in LA or New York and not connected with a celebrity chef. As a result, this serious food spot has remained mercifully under the radar of most visitors. But the restaurant's generously portioned meals rate as high as some others at twice the price. Steak takes pride of menu here, augmented by great starters that include plump shrimp cocktails, rich lobster bisque, and an enormous selection of wine (displayed in floor-to-ceiling acrylic vaults). Other winning mains include pan-seared sea bass with wild rice, and a stellar lobster and truffle macaroni and cheese. Reserve a soft suede and red leather booth and enjoy the lushly elegant dining room that is both good-looking and more-than-slightly wacky.

Ah Sin $$$

Paris Las Vegas, 3655 Las Vegas Blvd S (at Harmon), Strip

T 702.946.7000

ASIAN MAP E2 3

Offering Korean barbeque, Chinese noodles, Japanese sushi, Mongolian lamb chops and Malaysian lobster salad, you could be forgiven for imagining that this place would end up insulting numerous cuisines at once. Prepared at individual dining stations, food here is very good and far above the high-end food court it's nominally inspired by. Even desserts are special, including three different varieties of crème brûlé (Green Tea, Jasmine and Orange) and flavorful sorbets served in edible candy dishes. But great feng shui is the main draw. The dining room is a super-stylish place decked out with Buddha decor in which meals start with ritual hand washing. At night, **Risqué**, a sexy bar and club opens upstairs along with private outdoor terraces that are perfect for snogging.

Alex $$$$$

Wynn Las Vegas, 3131 Las Vegas Blvd S (at Sands), Strip

T 702.770.7100

FRENCH MAP F2 4

This sublime restaurant is headed by chef Alex Stratta, a disciple of the legendary Alaine Ducasse (**Mix**). It's also a swanky place to eat, drink and be very. The genuine art that adorns the walls of this intimate dining room is mimicked by original talent in a kitchen that turns out imaginative seasonal menus that might include cauliflower soup with caramelized endive and roasted chestnuts, warm pheasant salad with wild mushrooms, and John Dory with roasted fennel and white bean puree. And Stratta's trademark short ribs are available year-round. Wines, like everything else at Alex, are on the pricey side, starting at about $50.

Alizé $$$$

The Palms, 4321 W Flamingo Rd (at Arville), West Side

T 702.942.7777

FRENCH MAP E1 5

Small, loud and frenetic, Alizé is not for the faint of heart. But if you're looking for a sceney place to dine, this is your spot. Situated at the top of the Palms and filled with beautiful people, this is a place for views, both inside and out. Because the kitchen is headed by local hero André Rochat (André's), food here is very good. Winners on a menu that changes twice a year include black truffle-roasted guinea hen, and Black Angus steaks with green peppercorn and cognac cream sauce. Wines and cognacs are literally the centerpiece of this restaurant, as some 5,000 bottles are displayed in an ornate glass "cellar" in the middle of the dining room. Reserve by a window if you can.

Chef André Alizé

André's $$$$

401 S 6th St (at Bridger), Downtown

T 702.385.5016

FRENCH | **CLOSED** SUN | **OPEN** LATE MAP I2 6

Monte Carlo, 3770 Las Vegas Blvd S (at Tropicana), Strip

T 702.798.7151 MAP D2 106

Before celebrity chefs flooded in, André's was the best in town. In many ways it still is. This is a romantic, classic French institution that cooks up memorable meals in a one-of-a-kind location, a converted wood-frame house on a Downtown side street that's a favorite of C-level senior executives—CEO, CFO, CIO, CMO and the like. (The Monte Carlo dining room is more touristy.) Caviar, veal, foie gras, salmon... there's little here you've never tasted before, but these preparations are state of the art. The wine cellar is world class too.

Aureole $$$$

Mandalay Bay, 3950 Las Vegas Blvd S (at Mandalay Bay), Strip

T 702.632.7401

AMERICAN NEW MAP C2 7

A huge restaurant with a reputation to match, Charlie Palmer's New York transplant is a stunner, beloved for its New American cooking and for its Adam Tihany-designed four-story wine tower, where stewards strap on harnesses and are hoisted up like angels. Chef Palmer is known for complex concoctions and architectonic presentations. Indeed, Aureole serves some of the tallest food in town. Signature dishes include perfectly roasted caramelized chicken with chanterelles and herbs accompanied by gnocchi and red Swiss chard. Another hallmark dish is butter-braised lobster over lobster cannelloni with celery-root mousseline and wilted baby spinach. Several three-course menus are always on offer; the option to order à la carte is available at the bar only. And the wine list probably contains more fine bottles for under $50 than any other restaurant in Las Vegas.

Baja Fresh Mexican Grill $

1380 E Flamingo Rd (at Maryland), East Side

T 702.699.8920

MEXICAN MAP L1 8

4760 W Sahara Ave (at Decatur), West Side

T 702.878.7772 MAP A1 9

7501 W Lake Mead Blvd (at Buffalo), Northwest

T 702.838.4100 MAP B1 10

9310 S Eastern Ave (at Sunset), Henderson

T 702.563.2800 MAP K1 11

and other locations

Inauthentically healthful Mexican fast-food is the name of the game at these gourmet burrito joints. Fresh meats are roasted to order and topped with your choice of jack cheese, guacamole, or beans. There are good fish tacos too, plus a great selection of self-serve salsas.

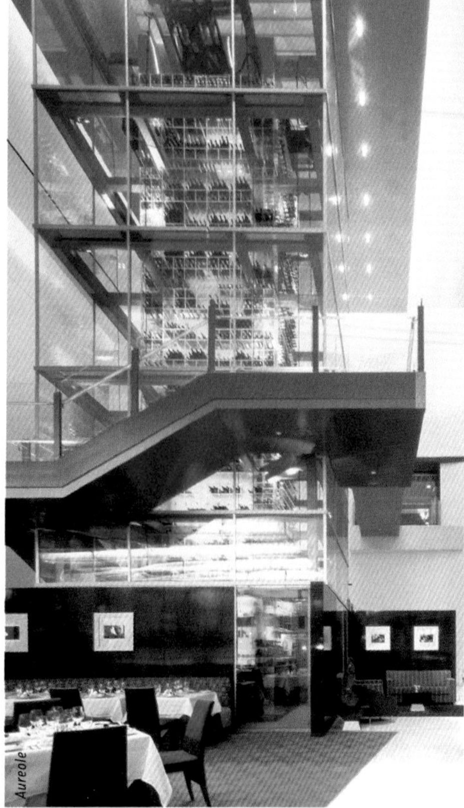

BANGKOK ORCHID $

4662 E Sunset Rd (at Mountain Vista), Henderson

T 702.458.4945

THAI MAP K2 12

A strip-mall exterior and bland cafe dining room belie the best Thai food in town. It's a mom-and-pop place with bad service to prove it, but if you're hankering for some spice, you won't be disappointed by the delicious tom kah kai, red curries, chili mint rice noodles, pork saté, and meaty pad Thai.

BELLAGIO BUFFET $$

The Bellagio, 3600 Las Vegas Blvd S (at Flamingo), Strip

T 702.693.7111

BUFFET | **OPEN** EARLY MAP E2 13

This king of Vegas buffets transcends the genre with an expansive smorgasbord of eclectic foods that run the gamut from high-quality salads and seafood to venison, roast duck and made-to-order pizzas. Even the salad bar wows with foie gras and eggplant. The weekend brunch selection is particularly excellent, and includes hand-carved meats, fruit salads, breads from LA's La Brea bakery and free-flowing champagne. Prices are about double that of other Strip buffets, but long lines suggest that it's worth it.

BIG AL'S OYSTER BAR $$

Orleans Hotel, 4500 W. Tropicana Ave. (Arville St.) , West Side

T 702.967.4930

CREOLE MAP D1 14

If you're looking for the best gumbo or jambalaya in Vegas go to **COMMANDER'S PALACE** or **EMERIL'S NEW ORLEANS FISH HOUSE**. But if you're looking for a top-of-the-line raw bar and shellfish house that won't break the bank, then Big Al's is your place. In addition to freshly shucked bivalves, the restaurant makes terrific oyster shooters, steamed clams and mussels, pan roasts and bouillabaisse, along with pasta dishes chunked out with seafood. And they've got lots of wines by the glass.

BIG MAMA'S RIB SHACK $$

2230 W Bonanza Rd (at Rancho), West Side

T 702.597.1616

AMERICAN REGIONAL MAP B2 15

Dargin McWhorter's mama is sadly gone, but her son still serves the same soulful recipes that are widely considered to be the best Southern in town. It's just a simple fast-food stand serving on disposable plates, but the food is excellent and includes delicately light fried shrimp, thick and meaty gumbo, Creole catfish, slow-cooked barbecued ribs, and fried chicken that's state of the art.

BINION'S COFFEE SHOP $

Binion's Casino, 128 Fremont St (at Ogden), Downtown

T 702.382.1600

DINER | **OPEN** NONSTOP MAP I2 16

If you can't leave Las Vegas without devouring a steak that's cheap enough to brag about, head straight for this Downtown casino diner where a slab of beef is sided with a baked potato, an Iceberg salad and a dinner roll for a measly $4.99. The best part is that this special is only available from 11pm to 7am. There are various other steak specials throughout the day, as well as a breakfast special (from 2am-2pm) that includes a slice of smoked ham that covers the entire plate. Note to coffee snobs: This is not the place to order a *doppio*.

Binion's Ranch Steakhouse $$$

Binion's Casino, 128 E Fremont St (at Ogden), Downtown

T 702.382.1600

STEAKHOUSE MAP J2 17

This timeless restaurant has been serving some of the city's top steaks since many of the Johnny-come-lately celebrity chefs were in diapers. Real men with pasta paunches still swear that Binion's serves the holy grail of steak: fist-sized portions of perfectly-grilled prime rib, lamb chops, New York steak, filet mignon and porterhouses. They've got fish and chicken dishes too, but why? Service is old school fantastic and the wood-paneled dining room is all swank, set with manly booths, aristocratic oils and masculine Wild West decor—not to mention a spectacular view over all of Las Vegas. In short, a Vegas classic.

Blue Agave Oyster & Chilé Bar $$$

The Palms, 4321 W Flamingo Rd (at Arville), West Side

T 702.942.7777

MEXICAN/SOUTHWESTERN | **OPEN** LATE MAP E1 18

Named for the plant from which tequila derives its flavor, Blue Agave is basically a lively Mexican/New Mexican with a huge selection of t'kill ya—over 150 at last count. In addition to traditional tortilla- and beans-based usuals, the kitchen turns out dependable steamed clams, oysters on the half shell, ceviche and roast lobster.

BOA Steakhouse $$$$

Caesars Forum Shops, 3500 Las Vegas Blvd S (at Flamingo), Strip

T 702.733.7373

STEAKHOUSE MAP E2 19

Straight from LA, this Vegas version of the celebrity-drenched Hollywood and Santa Monica hotspots is a worthy destination for a little surf-and-turf. There might be some famous faces in this very contemporary room, but with lighting so low it would be hard to see them anyway. Better yet, reserve a window table or one on the outdoor patios for prime Strip views, or fall into a leather booth and just enjoy the one you're with. Signature meals here are thick-cut, bone-in, dry-aged steaks blasted on a molten-hot grill. All come with a choice of rub and crust. Other offerings include black truffle nachos, halibut "T-bone," and fried free-range chicken with truffled macaroni and cheese. Caesar salads are prepared tableside, as are drinks, which are served from a fully loaded "martini cart."

Bouchon $$$$$

The Venetian, 3355 Las Vegas Blvd S (at Sands), Strip

T 702.414.6200

FRENCH MAP E2 20

Fresh off his four-star success with Per Se in New York's Time Warner Center, chef Thomas Keller is now being lauded as the best French chef in Las Vegas with this stellar bistro in the Venetian's Venezia Tower. Like top chefs everywhere, Keller serves simple food using the best ingredients. Lunch and dinner here are solid bistro offerings that could mean anything from onion soup, croque madame and a plate of French cheeses, to steak frites, roasted chicken and a grand plateau of fresh seafood. Created by Adam Tihany, the dining room's Belle Epoque decor consists of a pewter bar, an ornate floor mosaic and cathedral-height ceilings. Service is tops and reservations are so tough that even Jesus would have a hard time getting at table on Saturday night. Especially for those coveted patio tables. Bouchon also serves some of the best breakfasts in town, encompassing pastries and juices and other specialties, such as yogurt parfait. This one's for foodies.

The Buffet $

Golden Nugget, 129 Fremont St (at Casino Center), Downtown

T 702.385.7111

BUFFET | **OPEN** EARLY MAP I2 21

The best Downtown hotel also has the richest buffet in the neighborhood: a quality spread of traditional American fare that covers all the bases, from pasta salads and mountains of fresh fruit, to shrimp, turkey and prime rib. And regulars rave about the desserts.

Burger Bar $$

Mandalay Place, 3930 Las Vegas Blvd S (at Mandalay Bay), Strip

T 702.632.7777

AMERICAN MAP C2 22

Evidenced by the $60 Rossini burger made with Kobe beef, sautéed foie gras and shaved truffles, Hubert Keller's (**Fleur de Lys**) build-your-own-hamburger restaurant is far from the typical American drive-in. Less exotic offerings are no less special and include patties made with Black Angus beef, Colorado lamb and free-range turkey. Top yours with bacon, prosciutto, ham, pineapple, smoked salmon, grilled shrimp, marinated anchovies and a variety of cheeses, and you're in gourmet burger heaven. The surroundings are special too, built with cherrywood booths fitted with small-screen TVs.

Café Bellagio $$

The Bellagio, 3600 Las Vegas Blvd S (at Flamingo), Strip

T 702.693.7356

AMERICAN MAP E2 23

Situated in the bucolic Conservatory and open nonstop, this upscale coffee shop is the nicest place for a middle-of-the-night meal in Las Vegas. Food is good, not great, which means that you wouldn't necessarily choose this place during "normal" dining hours. But like the hotel it's located in, this is a swanky late night place for everything from eggs Benedict to steaks, with Keno at every table.

Café Lago $$

Caesars Palace, 3570 Las Vegas Blvd S (at Flamingo), Strip

T 702.731.7110

AMERICAN MAP E2 24

Las Vegas's top coffee shop goes way beyond java, offering a lengthy list of superior dishes from both the Old and New worlds. Breakfast, lunch and dinner buffets are served throughout the week, but you can choose to order à la carte or just come for a snack. They've got killer desserts too.

Canaletto $$$

The Venetian, 3355 Las Vegas Blvd S (at Sands), Strip

T 702.733.0070

ITALIAN MAP E2 25

A sister to the popular Californian Il Fornaio chain, this two-story restaurant offers a somewhat romantic setting for some good, fast-casual cuisine that includes good seafood risotto and squid ink pasta, very good wood-fired meats and fish, and some of the best pizza around. And regulars exclaim they've got one of the best bread baskets in Las Vegas. Its position overlooking the Venetian canal also puts Canaletto high on our Kitsch-O-Meter, a good thing considering where you are. The best seats are "al fresco," on St. Marks Square, beside passing gondolas and strolling musicians.

Capriotti's Sandwich Shop $

322 W Sahara Ave (at Industrial), West Side

T 702.474.0229

SANDWICHES | **CLOSED** SUN | **OPEN** EARLY | NO CARDS MAP G1 26

4983 W Flamingo Rd (at Decatur), West Side

T 702.222.3331 MAP E1 27

450 S Buffalo Dr (at Alta), Northwest

T 702.838.8659 MAP B1 28

3981 E Sunset Rd (at Sandhill), Henderson

T 702.898.4904 MAP K2 29

and other locations

If you like sub sandwiches you'll love this low-key Formica affair known for fresh ingredients that are over-stuffed into foot-long rolls. All the deli hits are here, but the shop is best known for permutations created with fresh-roasted turkey like Cole Turkey (turkey, cole slaw, cheese and Russian dressing), and a complete Thanksgiving dinner sandwich called The Bobby (turkey, stuffing, cranberry sauce and mayonnaise). There's not much to the décor; think about ordering to-go.

Carnival World Buffet $$

Rio, 3700 W Flamingo Rd (at Valley View), West Side

T 702.252.7757

BUFFET | **OPEN** EARLY MAP 30

Perhaps because it's one of the biggest in town, this buffet is the one most locals love most. With almost a dozen different cuisines to choose from—from Mongolian grills to milkshakes—this is one place where you can have the world on a plate; a "food court" world, that detractors say is low on quality and big on lines that can launch you into an eater's coma. Everyone, however, agrees that for the spectacle of sheer excess, this place is unrivaled. Weekend brunches are justifiably famous, but few dining experiences are worth an hour's wait. Sign up for Rio's slot club before heading to the buffet and you'll be shuttled to the express line.

Craftsteak

Charlie Palmer Steak $$$$

Four Seasons, 3960 Las Vegas Blvd S (at Four Seasons), Strip

702.632.5120

STEAK MAP 31

New York chef Charlie Palmer (**Aureole**) has two top restaurants in the high-rise that's home to both the Four Seasons and Mandalay Bay. Avant visionaries describe this subdued dining room as a luxurious oasis; a steakhouse where women feel as welcome as men. Aside from outstanding beef, the kitchen is known for white bean and arugula soup, applewood-smoked Atlantic salmon, and a bevy of wonderful side dishes. Don't forget the platinum.

The Cheesecake Factory $$

Caesars Forum Shops, 3500 Las Vegas Blvd S (at Flamingo), Strip

702.792.6888

AMERICAN | **OPEN** LATE MAP 33

750 S Rampart Blvd (at Alta), West Side

702.951.3800 MAP 34

Eat dessert first at this hyperactive industrial restaurant specializing in some three dozen varieties of its eponymous pastry. From chocolate to cherry, there is such an embarrassment of cheesecake riches that it verges on gastroporn. The dining room is a lively spot that's also known for moderate prices and good people-watching. Lots of people love this Factory for its main meals too, which encompass literally hundreds of entrees and read like a survey of middle-American cooking (pastas, pizzas, salads, seafood, steaks, sandwiches and more). Expect a wait on weekends.

Chinois $$$

Caesars Forum Shops, 3500 Las Vegas Blvd S (at Flamingo Rd), Strip

702.737.9700

CHINESE/FRENCH MAP E1 35

Just a mention of Chinois is enough to make most foodies swoon. Long regarded as Wolfgang Puck's best restaurant in L.A., this branch bustles nightly with diners who are wowed by the eatery's reputation, and rarely disappointed with the food. Groundbreaking when it first opened a generation ago, the restaurant still serves the same quirky East-meets-West cuisine that equals seriously good food. The menu is just about equally split between old-time signature dishes

and new creations. The most famous of the former are chicken salad with sweet mustard-ginger vinaigrette, sharply spiced Shanghai lobster, and whole fried catfish with ponzu sauce. Many of the best newer dishes come from a separate vegetarian menu featuring stir-fries and pancake-wraps, along with an excellent sushi bar.

Coachman's Inn $$

3240 S Eastern Ave (at Desert Inn), East Side

T 702.731.4202

AMERICAN | OPEN NONSTOP MAP G2 36

Coachman's Inn is a good-value grill where locals go to chow down on American comfort foods like prime rib, roast pork, chicken-fried steak and liver-and-onions. Built with dark woods, beamed ceilings, a fireplace—and no windows, the vibe is of a casual and cozy mountain chalet. Quality is high because everything is made right here. And the kitchen is open all night.

Coffee Pub $

The Plazas, 2800 W Sahara Ave (at Paseo Del Prado), West Side

T 702.367.1913

CAFÉ | OPEN EARLY MAP A2 37

Good coffee steamed by professional baristas is just the beginning at this "pub" that's also loved by local jitterati for its croissants, quiche, soufflés and pastries. It's a casual place with both indoor and patio seating with plenty of good people-watching.

Commander's Palace $$$$

Desert Passage, 3667 Las Vegas Blvd S (at Harmon), Strip

T 702.892.8272

CREOLE MAP E2 38

The original Commander's, in New Orleans' Garden District, is where many of that city's star chefs were nurtured, including Paul Prudhomme and Emeril Lagasse. This Vegas branch has quickly matured into one of this city's very best restaurants, wowing with Creole dishes that are as good as the original. Signature meals include thick and hearty turtle soup, seared jumbo crab cakes over fire-roasted corn, and pecan-crusted red snapper. Order a side of grits and goat cheese with everything and finish with Bananas Foster or their classic bread pudding soufflé. Commander's Sunday jazz brunch is special, but it lacks the same haute-Creole authenticity as the Big Easy original.

Craftsteak $$$$

MGM Grand, 3799 Las Vegas Blvd S (at Tropicana), Strip

T 702.891.7318

STEAK MAP D2 32

Tom Colicchio, who co-owns New York's Gramercy Tavern, has pulled off the unimaginable: creating one of the best steakhouses in a city full of steak places. The menu and decor are a homage to the Great American Steak House: straightforward and traditional. Top quality grain- or grass-fed aged steaks, along with many braised fish and poultry selections, are served à la carte, and meant to be paired with a starch and vegetable of your choice. The results are exemplary. Add an enormous list of excellent sides like roasted green beans, asparagus, Jerusalem artichokes, shiitake mushrooms and creamed spinach, and an extraordinary 500-strong wine list, and you have a restaurant worthy of your last meal. Open for dinner only.

Cravings $$

The Mirage, 3400 Las Vegas Blvd S (at Spring Mountain), Strip

T 702.791.7111

BUFFET | OPEN EARLY MAP F2 39

The Mirage buffet goes upscale in this Adam Tihany-designed space with a dozen cooking stations creating foods from around the world. Open for breakfast, lunch, dinner and weekend champagne brunch, this is one buffet in which quality matches quantity, and the rush to the salad bar is not impeded by so many human blobstacles.

Delmonico $$

The Venetian, 3355 Las Vegas Blvd S (at Sands), Strip

T 702.414.3737

STEAK MAP F2 40

Emeril Lagasse kicks it up a notch at this Venetian meatery. Like any classic steakhouse, porterhouse is the cut of choice, along with bone-in rib eye steak, double-cut pork chops, tender lamb shank on a bed of risotto, melt-in-your-mouth chateaubriand, baked jumbo Gulf shrimp, and chicken for two, which is carved tableside. Get garlic mashed potatoes with everything, and a bottle of wine from a list that's almost as long as *War and Peace*.

The Egg & I $

4533 W Sahara Ave (at Arville), West Side

T 702.364.9686

AMERICAN | OPEN EARLY MAP A1 41

Eggs (and you) are the name of the game at Brad Burdsall and Suzanne Altreche's beloved West Side breakfast spot. Think

Eiffel Tower

omelets, frittatas, huevos rancheros, and a worthy eggs Benedict smothered in hollandaise sauce. Most everything is sided with potatoes plus your choice of bread. The food is plentiful and the coffee is bottomless, ensuring you'll leave full and jittery.

Eiffel Tower $$$$

Paris Las Vegas, 3655 Las Vegas Blvd S (at Harmon), Strip

T 702.948.6937

FRENCH MAP E2 42

Kitschy surroundings notwithstanding—or because of them—the ET restaurant is considered one of the most romantic in town. Start with the view, in which you can gaze out the 12th-floor window of the Eiffel Tower at the fountains of Lake Como across the street. Then turn to the deluxe menu, which features superb, if conservative, renditions of enduring Parisian favorites. Add excellent service and you have a seriously good meal. The food is generally terrific, if you like gently browned foie gras, duck a l'orange, sautéed venison medallions and hazelnut soufflé. Wines are expensive and reservations are tough, especially if you want a table close to the window. Arrive by sunset and don't forget to bring a date.

Emeril's New Orleans Fish House $$$$

MGM Grand, 3799 Las Vegas Blvd S (at Tropicana), Strip

T 702.891.7374

CREOLE MAP D2 44

Now consisting of God-knows-how-many-restaurants, TV chef Emeril Lagasse's empire continues to grow, cashing in on one of America's best-known culinary brands. It's all served in an unfussy New Orleans atmosphere that's more casual up front and just slightly fancier in back. The most coveted seats for single diners are at the bar, where you can watch the masters in action. Neo-Cajun seafood is the soul of this kitchen where you can expect to find such inventive dishes as andouille-crusted redfish with Creole meuniere sauce, lump crab and sundried-tomato cheesecake. The turf menu is limited, but if you want meat, Emeril's other local restaurant, **Delmonico Steakhouse**, offers more "bam" for the buck.

Bobby Baldwin Burgers at Fix

Fleur de Lys

Fix $$$$

The Bellagio, 3600 Las Vegas Blvd S (at Flamingo), Strip

T 702.693.7111

AMERICAN MAP E2 45

Serving upscale wood-fired American comfort foods—with sides of hand-cut fries and macaroni and cheese—Fix is a suitably trendy place for good eating. It's a style-heavy, contemporary architectonic space with big tables, wooden floors and a dramatic curved ceiling. And service is top-notch. Meals visit no new ground, but consist of first-quality dry-aged steaks, fresh seafood and free-range poultry, the best of which are prepared on the grill. Surprises come in the form of Bobby Baldwin Burgers, a trio of Kobe beef sliders, freshly-fried potato chips served with blue cheese dressing, and bubble gum vanilla floats for dessert. Because it's owned by nightlife impresario Andrew Sasson (**Light**, **Caramel**, Mist), the atmosphere is buzzy and energetic, with the cocktail bar evolving into something of a singles scene.

Fleur de Lys $$$$

Mandalay Bay, 3950 Las Vegas Blvd S (at Mandalay Bay), Strip

T 702.632.7777

FRENCH MAP C2 46

Hubert Keller has bested his landmark San Francisco restaurant with this dramatic space featuring embossed wood ceilings, triple-height stone walls and a live floral sculpture consisting of thousands of fresh-cut roses. It's a swanky setting for a stellar meal that might start with marinated venison with a confit of shallots, move to Colorado lamb shanks and end with artisanal cheeses and sumptuous desserts. There is no carte as diners must choose from three-, four- and five-course fixed-price meals (about $70-$90) that encompass meat, seafood and vegetarian selections. Food is excellent but seating is tight. Think about forgoing a big meal in favor of a nosh from a separate appetizer menu that's available in the adjacent little DJ lounge—the back door to Keller's wonderful food without requiring the same commitment.

Garduños $$

The Palms, 4321 W Flamingo Rd (at Arville), West Side

T 702.942.7777

MEXICAN MAP E1 47

The Fiesta, 2400 N Rancho Dr (at Lake Mead), North Las Vegas

T 702.631.7000 MAP B2 48

Think Mexican TGI Fridays and you have a good idea of what this much-loved locals restaurant is all about. Brightly colored and friendly, you can count on tasty and ample portions of south-of-the-border specialties like blue enchiladas, crab posole (green chili stewed with crab), sautéed red snapper, and the best sopaipillas in the desert. Not to mention a 300-

strong margarita menu. Order guacamole (prepared tableside) with everything. And crucially, the salsas are tops. There's a popular margarita brunch too, served weekends.

Grand Lux Café $$

The Venetian, 3355 Las Vegas Blvd S (at Sands), Strip

T 702.414.3888

AMERICAN | **OPEN** NONSTOP MAP E2 49

Perhaps the best all-nighter on the Strip, Grand Lux is so good we actually go here even during daylight hours. This cafe is known for American comfort food including breakfasts, pizza, pot roast, Asian nachos, crabcakes, oven-roasted mussels, salads, burgers, sandwiches, pork tenderloin, grilled chicken, pastas and tons more. They've even got a separate bar. Portions are HUGE and because it's part of the Cheesecake Factory chain, you have to have dessert.

Guy Savoy $$$$$

Caesars Palace, 3570 Las Vegas Blvd S (at Flamingo), Strip

T 702.731.7110

FRENCH MAP E2 50

Michelin three-star chef Guy Savoy opened this, his first restaurant in the United States, in 2005. Rich, expensive and definitely one only for serious gastronauts, Savoy is known for state-of-the-art signature dishes like artichoke soup laced with fresh black truffles and perfect slim slices of Parmesan, and brilliant oysters *en nage glacée*, cooked in their own juices and turned into a soothing jelly. The 75-seat restaurant is located on the second floor of Caesars' new luxury tower.

Harrie's Bagelmania $

855 E Twain Ave (at Swenson), East Side

T 702.369.3322

BAGELS | **OPEN** EARLY MAP L1 51

When you need a bagel, Harrie's is a good place to know about. In addition to well-made bread rings, this simple New York-style shop offers a wide range of fillings, from orthodox to conservative and reform. It's also one of the few places between Chicago and LA that stocks all manner of smoked fish, from nova and sturgeon, to sable, chubs and whitefish.

Hush Puppy $$

7185 W Charleston Blvd (at Rainbow), West Side

T 702.363.5988

AMERICAN REGIONAL MAP A1 52

1820 N Nellis Blvd (at Lake Mead), Northeast

T 702.438.0005 MAP J2 53

Catfish is the specialty at this Southern seafooder; they've got two kinds and the "farm-raised" is better. Side it with well-seasoned cornmeal hush puppies, crisp coleslaw, and

Le Village Buffet

pickled green tomatoes from a big vat and you have an always-busy soul food spot that's worth leaving the casino for. There are other menu items too, but most are forgettable.

In-N-Out Burger $

4888 Industrial Rd (at Tropicana), West Side

T 800.786.1000

BURGERS | **OPEN** LATE | NO CARDS — MAP D2 54

2900 W Sahara Ave (at Teddy), West Side

T 800.786.1000 — MAP A2 108

51 N Nellis Blvd (at Charleston), East Side

T 800.786.1000 — MAP J2 55

4705 S Maryland Pkwy (at University), East Side

T 800.786.1000 — MAP K1 56

and other locations

In-N-Out is the holy grail of fast-food burgers. The menu is short and to the point: hamburgers, cheeseburgers, french fries and beverages. Period. Potatoes are sliced fresh in-house. And the beef patties are grilled to order and topped with fresh iceberg lettuce, tomato, pickles and Thousand Island dressing. Tell the counter monkey to add grilled onions and prepare to taste heaven.

Isla Mexican Kitchen & Tequila Bar $$

Treasure Island, 3300 Las Vegas Blvd S (at Spring Mountain), Strip

T 702.894.7111

MEXICAN — MAP F2 57

Mexican cuisine with a modern twist is the motto of this terrific, if inauthentic, South of the Border eatery. The best meals are those that you can't get anywhere else, like crispy rock shrimp tacos; crab, shrimp and snapper tostadas; chipotle meatballs; and lobster guacamole—which is made tableside from a roving cart. The tequila bar is impressive too, offering an enormous variety, along with excellent flavored margaritas made with fresh-squeezed juices. It's fun eating in a jazzy environment created by Jeffrey Beers (**Tabu**) with fanciful light fixtures and plenty of colorful original art.

Le Café Île St. Louis $$

Paris Las Vegas, 3655 Las Vegas Blvd S (at Harmon), Strip

T 702.739.4111

CAFÉ | **OPEN** NONSTOP — MAP E2 58

It's hard to find a better breakfast in Vegas than the one served at this refined Parisian cafe. The menu dashes from gourmet omelets and eggs Benedict, to French toast with

bananas and caramel-pecan sauce. And good European coffees are served in individual pots. The best tables are "outside," under a faux sky.

Le Village Buffet $$

Paris Las Vegas, 3655 Las Vegas Blvd S (at Harmon), Strip

T 702.946.4966

BUFFET | **OPEN** EARLY — MAP E2 59

Leave it to the French to raise the lowly buffet to a fine dining experience. Le Village is almost, dare we say, fancy, and is easily one of the best—and most expensive—buffets in town. The dining room is relatively charming and intimate (you can even eat outside) and numerous buffet stations offer foods inspired by the country's various regions. These include hand-made crêpes, pâtés, quiches and meats like veal and duck smothered in heavy sauces. It's not French food, *per se*, but it's far better than the ordinary offerings at most other buffets. Desserts are particularly special, and include that New Orleans favorite, Bananas Foster (sautéed bananas in a rich caramel sauce).

Little Buddha Café $$$

The Palms, 4321 W Flamingo Rd (at Arville), West Side

T 702.942.7778

CHINESE/FRENCH | **OPEN** LATE — MAP E1 60

From the creator of the Buddha Bar in Paris (the real one), this restaurant serves Chinese-French foods (plus an impressive sushi bar) along with world music and some stylish settings. Choose poolside dining during good weather for the best in eater-tainment.

Little Buddha Café

Luv-It Frozen Custard $

505 E Oakey Blvd (at Las Vegas), Strip

T 702.384.6452

DESSERT | NO CARDS — MAP H1 61

Like macaroni 'n cheese and monster trucks, creamy frozen custard is a true-blue American invention. The Western Special is the ultimate Luv-It experience, topped with caramel, hot fudge, pecans and a maraschino cherry. It's so good you'll need extra napkins to clean up your drool.

Mayflower Cuisinier $$$

4750 W Sahara Ave (at Decatur), West Side

T 702.870.8432

CHINESE — MAP A1 62

Mayflower Cuisinier is one of the best Nouveau Chinese restaurants between New York and California, dishing out great noodles, perfect fish and delicate sauces that ensure almost every dish hits its intended mark. Regulars swear by the duck salad with plum vinaigrette, ginger-chicken ravioli, chicken potstickers, basil garlic scampi, and grilled lamb chops with creamy cilantro-mint sauce. The decor is strictly casual, which keeps prices light. And desserts are worth sticking around for—a rarity in Asian restaurants.

Memphis Championship Barbecue $$

2250 E Warm Springs Rd (at Eastern), East Side

T 702.260.6909

AMERICAN REGIONAL — MAP K2 63

4379 Las Vegas Blvd N (at Craig), North Las Vegas

T 702.644.0000 — MAP J2 64

Barbeque fans should make a pilgrimage to this rustic restaurant for the holy grail of meats: tender baby back ribs, slow-cooked in a pit with a combination of woods for 6 hours; fiery smoked hot links; barbecue pork shoulder; and Memphis-style chicken wings smothered with barbecue sauce. Owner Mike Mills is a four-time world champion in barbecue serving up the best food of its kind in Vegas. Even the sides—deep-fried dill pickles, baked beans and coleslaw—are terrific.

Outdoor Patio at Mon Ami Gabi

Portions are ample, prices are decent, there's a full bar and the woody atmosphere, filled with Elvis clutter, is appealing.

Mesa Grill $$$$

Caesars Palace, 3570 Las Vegas Blvd S (at Flamingo), Strip

T 702.731.7731

AMERICAN REGIONAL MAP E2 65

New York-based chef and popular Food Network personality Bobby Flay fires up Vegas with his trademark Southwestern cuisine. All his Iron Chef hits are here, including 16-spice rotisserie chicken and blue corn pancakes with barbecued duck and habañero sauce. There's lots to like here, and you could easily make a whole meal of appetizers like grilled tuna tostadas filled with barbecued duck, cornmeal crusted oysters, and lamb tacos with red chili-peanut barbeque sauce. Open for dinner only.

Metro Pizza $

1395 E Tropicana Ave (at Maryland), East Side

T 702.736.1955

PIZZA MAP K2 66

4001 S Decatur Blvd (at Flamingo), West Side

T 702.362.7896 MAP E1 67

4178 E Koval Ln (at Flamingo), East Side

T 702.312.5888 MAP E2 68

Metro is the pizza to call when you need an in-room delivery. If you're from New York or Naples, or perhaps even Chicago, then you won't be floored by the pizzas served here. But by most accounts, these are the best pies in Vegas, usually ordered by locals in the deep-dish variety. There's a decent pasta menu too.

Mix $$$$$

THEhotel, 3950 Las Vegas Blvd S (at Mandalay Bay), Strip

T 702.632.7777

FRENCH NEW MAP C2 69

On the 64th floor of THEhotel at Mandalay Bay, Mix is a colorful restaurant/bar/club/lounge hybrid with floor-to-ceiling windows offering sweeping views of the Strip. The open kitchen comes from French über-chef Alain Ducasse (Plaza Athenee in Paris, Louis XV in Monaco, Alain Ducasse in New York), whose minions whip up things like black truffle, foie gras and artichoke salad, and striped bass with spinach in a champagne reduction. Presentations are youthful, which fits the very contemporary dining room to a T. Set with small tables and egg-shaped dining pods beneath an enormous Murano glass chandelier, it's a rich space, with prices to match. The atmosphere is buzzy and food is good, but the city's best meals are not in this mix. The adjoining dark leather lounge appeals to Arab oil millionaires and stays open until 3am.

Mon Ami Gabi $$$

Paris Las Vegas, 3655 Las Vegas Blvd S (at Harmon), Strip

T 702.944.4224

FRENCH MAP E2 71

Solid French food and delightful bistro surroundings are the hallmarks of our favorite restaurant in the Paris resort, which is to say one of our favorite places to dine in Vegas. Think great steak frites, classic croque monsieur sandwiches, roast chicken and garlicky escargot, matched with beautiful surroundings and terrific people-watching from some of the only outdoor seating directly on the Strip. Unfortunately, these tables are first come, first served so cross your fingers and arrive early. It's usually open to midnight on weekends.

Montesano's Italian Deli $

4835 W Craig Rd (at Decatur), North Las Vegas

T 702.656.3708

ITALIAN AMERICAN | **CLOSED** SUN | **OPEN** EARLY MAP B1 72

Sahara Village Center, 3441 W Sahara Ave (at Valley View), West Side

T 702.876.0348 MAP A2 73

It's all in the *famiglia* at this small, authentic New York-style Italian deli known for meat-and-cheese sandwiches on home-baked bread. There are good pastas, pizzas and sausages too, plus a wide selection of Southern Italian desserts.

Mr. Lucky's 24/7 $

Hard Rock Hotel, 4455 Paradise Rd (at Harmon), East Side

T 702.693.5592

AMERICAN | **OPEN** NONSTOP MAP K1 70

This wonderful American diner in the main room of the Hard Rock is often something of a post-club scene spot, offering a great selection of party foods that run the gamut from huge shrimp cocktails to a delicious off-menu $7.77 steak and seafood special (just ask for it). There's usually some other specials too, served most nights from 11pm to 6am.

N9ne $$$$

The Palms, 4321 W Flamingo Rd (at Arville), West Side

T 702.933.9900

STEAK MAP E1 74

Owned by Michael Morton, who is the son of the founder of Morton's of Chicago and the brother of Hard Rock Cafe creator Peter Morton, N9ne is a serious restaurant with a genuine pedigree. Heading up the list of restaurants with monosyllabic names, it's also a trendy place for foodies who like their meals with an energetic atmosphere, and a glance around the contemporary room usually reveals sports celebs chowing on lobster bisque and big aged steaks, generic rich people dining on tuna tartare and herb-roasted salmon, and plenty of models eating nothing. A champagne and caviar bar with a fiber-optically lit drink rail takes pride of place, offering good sightlines for seeing and being sceney. Open for dinner only.

Nobu $$$$

Hard Rock Hotel, 4455 Paradise Rd (at Harmon), East Side

T 702.693.5090

JAPANESE NEW MAP K1 75

Chef Nobu Matsuhisa, a Japanese-Peruvian-Los Angeleno (by way of NYC, London, Milan and Miami) creates perfectly *genki* combinations like raw yellowtail with jalapeño peppers, barely

N9ne

cooked sashimi drizzled with garlic- and ginger-flavored olive oil, and monkfish-liver pâté with soy dressing and a gleaming dollop of caviar. Squid pasta—delicate segments of squid and asparagus glazed with butter and garlic sauce—is an extraordinary taste treat you won't soon forget. And, you can do no wrong ordering the multi-course Omakase menu (about $50 lunch; $75 dinner). Regulars begin with shots of Masu sake, served tequila-style in small cedar cups with salted rims.

Olives $$$

The Bellagio, 3600 Las Vegas Blvd S (at Flamingo), Strip

T 702.693.7223

MEDITERRANEAN | **OPEN** LATE MAP E2 76

Boston's Todd English brings his stylishly casual Mediterranean restaurant to the Bellagio shopping arcade. It's a pleasant space with mosaic tiling, an open kitchen and a colorful mobile hanging from a sculpted wood ceiling. But the best tables are on the patio overlooking the hotel's famous fountains. Top meals include grilled and chilled lobster claw cocktail, beef carpaccio served on crispy Roquefort polenta, and the restaurant's trademark flat breads topped with everything from figs and prosciutto to shrimp and

tomatoes. Pastas, sandwiches and grilled meats round out the offerings, all of which are beautifully presented.

Osteria del Circo $$$$

The Bellagio, 3600 Las Vegas Blvd S (at Flamingo), Strip

T 702.693.8150

ITALIAN MAP E2 77

Circo carries on the Maccioni family's whimsical theme of elegant dining under a stylized red-and-yellow circus canopy. Fancier than its name implies, this Adam Tihany-designed restaurant is one of the best Italians in Vegas, serving up delicious meals with unparalleled views overlooking Bellagio's "Lake Como" fountains and the landmarks of Paris across the street. Pastas are the mainstay of a kitchen that also excels with *dolci* like panna cotta with black currant syrup, a show-stopping bomba di ciocciolata, and the city's best tiramisu.

PF Chang's China Bistro $$

Desert Passage, 3667 Las Vegas Blvd S (at Harmon), Strip

T 702.836.0955

CHINESE MAP E2 78

4165 Paradise Rd (at Flamingo), East Side

T 702.792.2207 MAP L1 107

The PF Chang's which have been popping up all around California have spread to Vegas. They're popular because they're good, serving nouvelle Chinese meals to the masses. The interior is stylish, spacious and soaring. The bar is two-deep and drinks are suitably strong. Signature dishes include chicken lettuce wraps, crab wontons, lemon pepper shrimp, Malaysian chicken, and sautéed spicy eggplant. And it doesn't hurt that portions are big and prices are small. These places buzz nightly so you usually have to wait for a table. Officially reservations are not accepted, but that's nothing your hotel concierge can't get around.

Picasso $$$$$

The Bellagio, 3600 Las Vegas Blvd S (at Flamingo), Strip

T 702.693.7223

FRENCH NEW | CLOSED WED MAP E2 79

Julian Serrano, formerly of San Francisco's Masa, is the genius behind this top rated restaurant. He's also one of the few celebrity cooks in Vegas who is a permanent fixture in his own kitchen. There are two menus, a five-course *degustation* and a four-course *prix fixe*, each an imaginative feast of Frenchish flavors (think warm lobster salad, sautéed black bass, slow-roasted short ribs, and lamb roti). The equally opulent interior includes several Picasso paintings from the 1940s with a few ceramics thrown in for good measure. With so much going for it, snagging a table here can be tough. If you have trouble, ask for maitre d' Ryland Worrell and tell him who you are.

Piero Selvaggio Valentino $$$$

The Venetian, 3355 Las Vegas Blvd S (at Sands), Strip

T 702.414.3000

ITALIAN MAP E2 80

Chef Valentino's restaurant in Santa Monica was once rated tops for wine by Wine Spectator and lauded for serving "the

best Italian food in the United States" by *New York Times* food critic Ruth Reichl. That's the reputation this Vegas outpost strives to live up to and, according to fans, succeeds. Dinners here are always lengthy multi-course affairs, often involving several bottles of wine (there are over 1600 labels to choose from). You might begin with a crisp Pinot Grigio paired with caviar-filled cannoli; or crespelle, thin little pancakes made with fresh porcini mushrooms and a rich melt of fontina cheese. Handmade pastas tossed with tender baby squid or sweet tiny clams are typical of first courses, though it really depends on what came to market the morning you visit. A rich Barolo is the perfect accompaniment to rosemary-infused roasted rabbit, but is probably too powerful for the fantastically fragrant risotto with white truffles. It's dinner only, but PS Italian Grill, in front, is open all day and is about half the price.

Pink Taco $$

Hard Rock Hotel, 4455 Paradise Rd (at Harmon), East Side

T 702.693.5525

MEXICAN MAP K1 B1

Forget the stupid name and head to this funky Mexican cantina for very good carnitas, fish tacos, sweet-corn tamales and fresh-from-the-fryer tortilla chips with smoked-pepper salsas. Of course, tequila and margaritas are the drinks of choice. It's usually open until midnight on weekends.

Pinot Brasserie $$$

The Venetian, 3355 Las Vegas Blvd S (at Sands), Strip

T 702.414.8888

FRENCH MAP F2 B2

Joachim Splichal's Vegas outpost of his LA hotspot offers authentic French bistro meals in a rich, traditional setting. The best meals emerge from the rotisserie, though regulars also swear by the foie gras and steak frites. There's a raw bar too.

Postrio $$$$

The Venetian, 3355 Las Vegas Blvd S (at Sands), Strip

T 702.796.1110

AMERICAN MAP E2 B3

Soon after Wolfgang Puck earned his toque at Spago in LA, he opened Postrio on San Francisco's Post Street and wowed local foodies who know chow. This Vegas outpost serves San Francisco food with Mediterranean influences, like Dungeness crab gratin, potato galette with house-smoked sturgeon, and seafood risotto with shrimp, crab, mussels and clams. Of course there are meat and fowl choices too. The restaurant is also known for serving one of the best shrimp cocktails in Vegas, which is no small feat in itself. It's food to sigh for as you sit on the plaza overlooking Piazza San Marco.

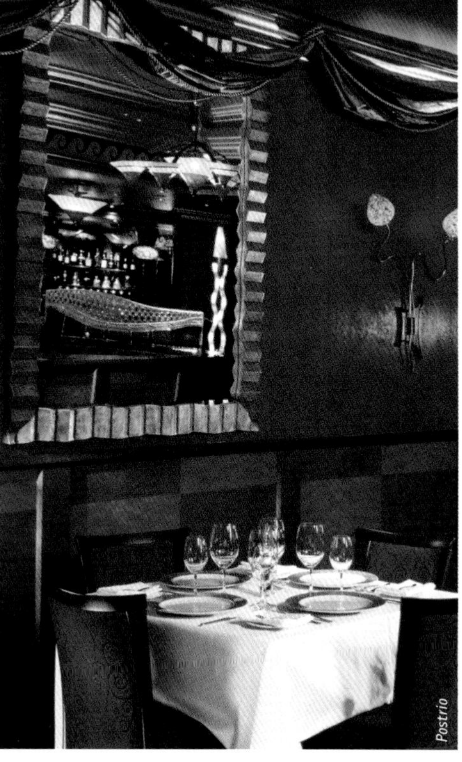
Postrio

Prime $$$$

The Bellagio, 3600 Las Vegas Blvd S (at Flamingo), Strip

T 702.693.7111

STEAK MAP E2 B4

New York superchef Jean-Georges Vongerichten's entry into the Vegas dining scene comes in the form of this magnificent Bellagio steakhouse overlooking the hotel's famous fountains. Sure they've got perfect steaks, but that's not tough to find in this part of the world. This is the one top beef place where we would forgo steak in favor of something more demonstrative of the chef's talents. Try the spiced rack of lamb, potato goat cheese terrine, fantastic chick-pea fries, or duck breast with shallots, ginger and rosemary.

Picasso

Prime

Roasted Bean $

The Mirage, 3400 Las Vegas Blvd S (at Spring Mountain), Strip

T 702.791.7111

CAFÉ | **OPEN** EARLY MAP F2 85

Everything in the Mirage is terrific, so why should this cafe be an exception? The inspiration is old Vienna, complete with marble-topped tables and homemade pastries—sticky buns, Danishes, muffins—that make mornings a pleasure. There's good coffee too, plus a full range of quiches and sandwiches that go perfectly with *The New York Times*.

Romano's Macaroni Grill $$

2400 W Sahara Ave (at Rancho), West Side

T 702.248.9500

ITALIAN MAP A2 86

2001 N Rainbow Blvd (at Lake Mead), Northwest

T 702.648.6688 MAP B1 87

573 N Stephanie St (at Sunset), Henderson

T 702.433.2788 MAP K2 88

This large chain is known for above-average Italian-American food and a celebratory atmosphere that makes every meal entertaining. Portions are ginormous, the bread is terrific, the house vino is decent and the price is light. And the menu has more subdivisions than a Dallas suburb. Favorites include grilled chicken Caesar salad, lasagna, sweet sausage with roasted peppers and onions, and linguine with clams. Reservations are not accepted, but you can phone before you head out and they'll put you on the list.

San Francisco Shrimp Bar $

Golden Gate Hotel, 1 Fremont St (at Main), Downtown

T 702.382.6300

AMERICAN | **OPEN** NONSTOP MAP I1 89

They've got sandwiches, hot dogs, ice cream and salads, but the only reason to come here is for the 99¢ shrimp cocktail ($1.06 with tax), widely acknowledged as the first ever served in Las Vegas and still one of the most cherished Downtown institutions. Situated in the rear of the ground-floor casino, the Shrimp Bar is a simple buffet-style spot with a dozen cafe tables and a baby-grand piano that's often rollicking under the fingers of talented ragtimers. The crunchy, previously-frozen bay shrimp are not the best you've tasted, but they're plentiful, served in classic tulip glasses with a dollop of cocktail sauce and a packet of crackers, and they're available any time of day or night. It's an institution, see, because where else but Vegas can you get something so wonderful for under a buck?

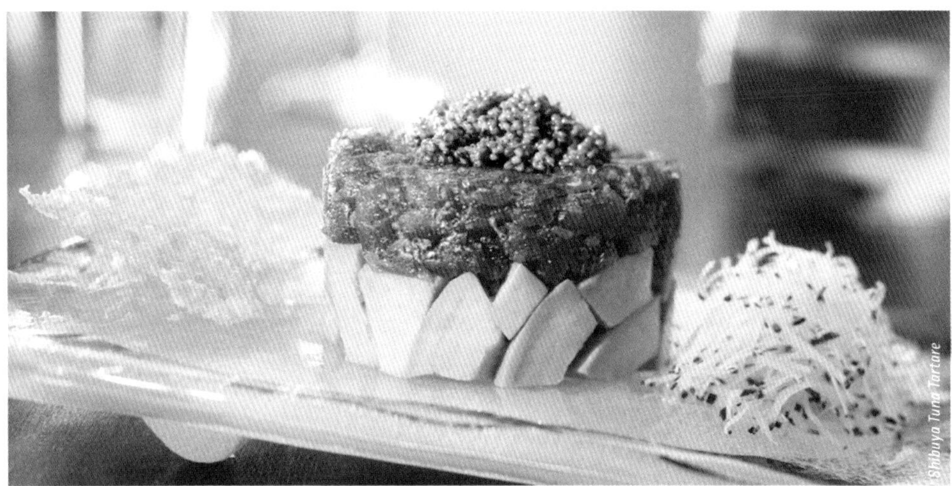
Shibuya Tuna Tartare

Shalimar $$

Citibank Park, 3900 Paradise Rd (at Flamingo), East Side

T 702.796.0302

INDIAN MAP L1 90

We include this fine Indian for the pleasure of animal-liberationists who will appreciate Shalimar's attention to well-spiced vegetarian curries and paneers, along with the usual biryanis, kormas and tandooris, plus skinless, fat free, charbroiled chicken, meat and seafood. It's not the best North India has to offer, but it's the best there is in this desert.

Shanghai Lilly $$$

Mandalay Bay, 3950 Las Vegas Blvd S (at Mandalay Bay), Strip

T 702.632.7409

CHINESE MAP C2 91

Mainly Cantonese in character, with a few Szechwan dishes thrown in for spice, Shanghai Lilly serves what many foodies consider to be the best Chinese in Vegas. There's a lot to like on the large and varied menu, and regular visitors to Hong Kong will recognize a lot here, including abalone and sea cucumber braised with oyster sauce, sautéed geo-duck clams with yellow chives, and pork chops marinated with fermented bean paste and chee hau sauce. Insiders swear by the crispy Hong Kong-style seafood noodles, which are pan-fried at high heat and served with shrimp, scallops, squid and lobster. Designed by Tony Chi & Associates with a water wall at the entrance, giant statues and diaphanous draperies hanging from triple-height ceilings, the room is so romantic that wives feel like mistresses and vice versa. Dinner only.

Shibuya $$$$

MGM Grand, 3799 Las Vegas Blvd S (at Tropicana), Strip

T 702.891.7777

JAPANESE MAP D2 92

Shibuya is a very good Japanese restaurant that gets marks here for its extensive sake list featuring some 60 brands. The kitchen is as comfortable preparing creative sushi like tuna tartar with caviar and spicy Tobiko, as it is cooking teppan dishes and modern meals like lobster with uni butter, and wild salmon in a sauce of lotus root, miso and ginger. And the sleek urban dining room is designed to wow.

Simon Kitchen & Bar $$$$

Hard Rock, 4455 Paradise Rd (at Harmon), East Side

T 702.693.5000

AMERICAN MAP K1 93

Hotshot hospitality consultant Elizabeth Blau teamed up with wannabe-celebrity chef Kerry Simon to create this energetic and playful dining spot for excellent meals without too much frou-frou. As evidenced by Chef Kerry's official bio, which boasts of his boyish good looks and that "starlets frequently appear on his arm," this restaurant unabashedly plays to young social strivers who like to have a good time. The food is souped-up American comfort food—tender meatloaf with garlic mashed potatoes, gooey macaroni and cheese gratin,

Spago

colossal crab cakes, and chicken curry that's delivered to the table in a Chinese take-out container. And the kitchen stays in character all the way to dessert that includes cotton candy and warm chocolate chunk cookies served with ice cold milk. Singles are catered to at the bar, where there is exceptional people-watching and a good grazing menu.

Sourdough Cafe $

Arizona Charlie's, 4575 Boulder Hwy (at Indios), East Side

T 702.951.5800

AMERICAN | **OPEN** NONSTOP — MAP H2 94

There's something about a 77-cent all-night breakfast that makes us giddy, and nowhere is that sensation more intense than at this champion of "locals" casinos where there are no less than seven different breakfast choices for under a buck, available Monday to Friday from midnight to 7am. Other great specials for breadlosers—like steak and eggs—cost about $2.50 and are served around the clock.

Spago $$$

Caesars Forum Shops, 3500 Las Vegas Blvd S (at Flamingo), Strip

T 702.369.0360

AMERICAN NEW — MAP E2 99

Wolfgang Puck is not just a great chef, he's a masterful businessman and publicist who has made his LA Spago one of the best known restaurants in America. Opened over a decade ago, this bright, clean, and colorful Vegas dining room is noisy and upbeat, and popular with celebrities, wannabes, tourists and even dedicated foodies. Chef Puck originally won fame serving imaginative "gourmet" pizzas. These thin-crust pies are about the size of your head, baked in a wood burning oven, and topped with things like duck sausage, shiitake mushrooms,

leeks and artichokes; combinations that were once considered to be on the culinary edge. The celebrated (and far from secret) off-menu meal at Spago is Jewish Pizza, a crispy ethnic pie topped with smoked salmon, crème fraiche, dill, red onion and dollops of caviar.

The Steak House $$$

Circus Circus, 2880 Las Vegas Blvd S (at Circus Circus), Strip

T 702.894.7111

STEAK MAP G1 96

Even people who hate kids brave this family-oriented hotel for its top rated steak room serving perfectly aged, mesquite-broiled meat. Huge portions and bargain prices conspire to make this place the best in its class. The oak-paneled dining room is more casual than most, but the food is strictly luxury. Lobster, lamb, fish and chicken also make appearances. They serve a good Sunday brunch too.

Sterling Brunch $$$$

Bally's, 3645 Las Vegas Blvd S (at Flamingo), Strip

T 702.739.4111

BUFFET | **CLOSED** MON-SAT | **OPEN** EARLY MAP E2 97

This Sunday-only affair is the world's ultimate brunch indulgence: an all-you-can eat buffet that includes everything from real caviar, smoked salmon and Maine lobster, to oysters, sushi, crêpes and sumptuous desserts. The meal usually devolves into a feeding frenzy that is as expensive as it is memorable, though all-you-can-drink Cordon Rouge champagne is sure to soften the blow of the bill. The Brunch is served in Bally's Steakhouse.

Sushi Roku $$$$

Caesars Forum Shops, 3500 Las Vegas Blvd S (at Flamingo), Strip

T 702.733.7373

JAPANESE MAP E2 98

Situated on the top floor of the Forum Shops, this Zen-like retreat is the antithesis of the opulent overabundance of everything that surrounds it. Like the eye of a storm, Sushi Roku is a tranquil sanctuary of dark wood and candlelight that strives hard to be as hip as its sister restaurants in LA. Flown in fresh daily, food here is good enough to please chopstick-wielding Japanophiles and includes all the requisite hits along with plenty of specialties like tuna tataki salad, seared yellowtail sashimi with ponzu and diced chilies, and crunchy shrimp tempura rolls. There's outdoor seating on a terrace too, offering good views of the Strip.

Terrazza $$$

Caesars Palace, 3570 Las Vegas Blvd S (at Flamingo), Strip

T 702.731.7731

ITALIAN MAP E2 99

Fronting the elaborate Garden of the Gods swimming pool area, Terrazza is an expansive and elegant Italian restaurant known for terrific al fresco dining and toothsome meals from an exhibition kitchen that turns cooking into a spectator sport. Northern specialties include risottos, veal chops, and a litany of wonderful pastas. Very good pizzas and focaccias emerge from their wood burning oven. The crowd is more upscale than most, as no shorts, T-shirts, sandals or tank tops are allowed. Jazz trios perform in the adjacent lounge Wednesday through Sunday evenings.

Top of the World $$$$

Stratosphere, 2000 Las Vegas Blvd S (at Main), Strip

T 702.380.7711

CONTINENTAL MAP H1 100

This restaurant gets "top" billing not for its cooking, but for its location, atop **Stratosphere Tower**. The schmancy revolving dining room is a great place to impress a date. The continental cuisine—steaks, chicken and seafood—is good, not great, but few star-crossed couples seem to care. And as long as you're here for love, be sure to order chocolate soufflé mousse, an impressive dessert that's whimsically shaped like the phallic tower in which you are sitting.

The Verandah $$$

Four Seasons, 3960 Las Vegas Blvd S (at Four Seasons), Strip

T 702.632.5000

AMERICAN | **OPEN** EARLY MAP C2 101

This American restaurant is one of the nicest coffee shops in Vegas. It's an elegant place with a comfortable dining room and one of the finest garden patios in town. Breakfasts are traditional Continental and egg affairs, and service is tops.

Village Seafood Buffet $$

Rio, 3700 W Flamingo Rd (at Valley View), West Side

T 702.252.7777

BUFFET MAP E1 102

There is not one, but two, buffets at Rio—the **Carnival World Buffet** and this exquisite seafooder brimming with swordfish, salmon, scallops, shrimp, calamari, king crab legs and more. If you're up to battling salad-dodging Jenny Craig rejects to get to mountains of shellfish, this is your place.

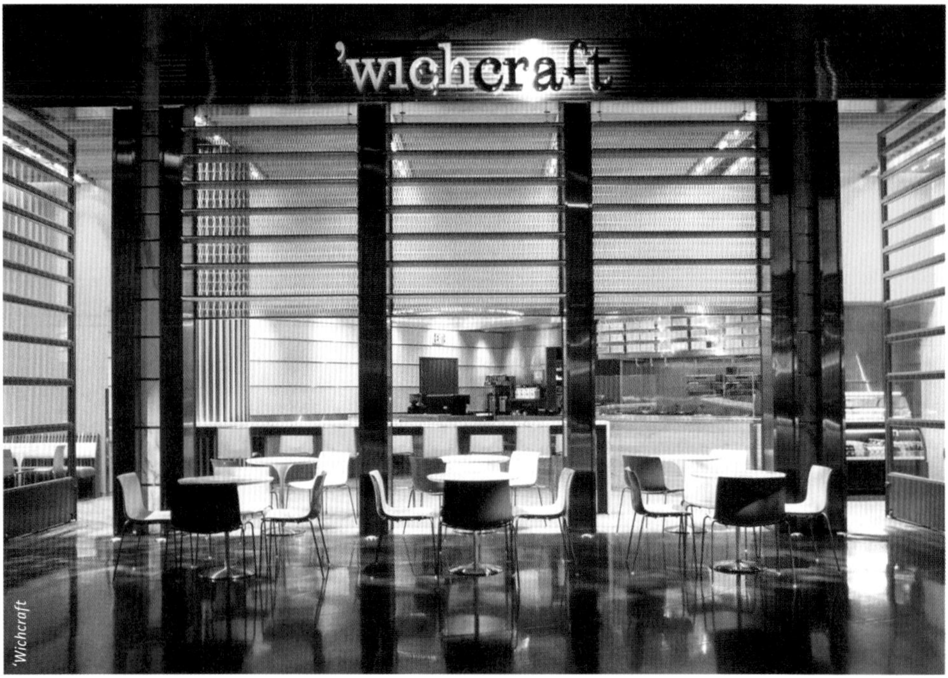

'wichcraft

'Wichcraft

Viva Mercado's $$

6182 W Flamingo Rd (at Jones), West Side

702.871.8826

MEXICAN MAP E1 103

Viva Mercado's is a family-owned restaurant serving up excellent Mexican-American "cuisine" that never quite escapes the confines of culinary cliché. We're talking big steak burritos, taquitos dorados, lobster and fish tacos, quesadillas and the like—cooked without animal fats. It's all set off by fiery habañera salsa and extinguished by raspberry margaritas.

'Wichcraft $

MGM Grand, 3799 Las Vegas Blvd S (at Tropicana), Strip

702.891.3166

SANDWICHES MAP D2 104

The brilliant chef Tom Colicchio (Craftsteak) is the mastermind behind this creative upscale sandwich bar. Forget peanut butter and jelly and think goat cheese, avocado, celery and watercress on multi-grain; roasted turkey, avocado, bacon and onion relish on ciabatta roll; and the best meatloaf sandwich you've ever tasted. And breakfasts bring the city's best sticky buns, rich scones and great coffee. Order from the counter person and bring your creation to a green plastic chair, the best of which face Studio Walk for good people-watching. The restaurant is open daily 8am-8pm.

Z'Tejas Grill $$

3824 S Paradise Rd (at Twain), East Side

702.732.1660

AMERICAN REGIONAL MAP L1 105

9560 W Sahara Ave (at Fort Apache), West Side

702.638.0610 MAP A1 108

Hot without being *haute*, Z'Tejas is a satisfying Southwestern/Cajun mini-chain with all its clichés in place. That means a large selection of Santa Fe and New Orleans-style favorites (shrimp and corn relleno, blackened tuna, jerk chicken, fish tacos, pork roast Veracruz) and cactus and coyote decor that leaves little to the imagination. Seating, either indoors or out, is comfortable, portions are huge, and prices are fine. They're known for a decent happy hour bar scene (Chambord margaritas), but Z'Tejas is popular with kids too. It's open weekends until midnight.

Map	Price	Cuisine	Restaurant	Location	Phone	Closed	Design Driven	Bar Scene	Top Food	Classic Vegas	Dining Alone	Romantic	Business Power	Kid Friendly	Outdoor Seating	Breakfast/Brunch	Dessert	After Midnight
The Strip																		
H1 61	$	Dessert	Luv-It Frozen Custard	505 E Oakey Blvd	702.384.6452					★	★			★	★		★	
F2 86	$	Café	Roasted Bean	The Mirage	702.791.7111						★			★		★		
D2 104	$	Sandwiches	'Wichcraft	MGM Grand	702.891.3166		★				★			★				
E2 13	$$	Buffet	Bellagio Buffet	The Bellagio	702.693.7111					★						★		
C2 22	$$	American	Burger Bar	Mandalay Place	702.632.7777		★				★			★				
E2 23	$$	American	Café Bellagio	The Bellagio	702.693.7356						★					★		
E2 24	$$	American	Café Lago	Caesars Palace	702.731.7110						★			★		★	★	
F2 39	$$	Buffet	Cravings	The Mirage	702.791.7111		★									★		
E2 49	$$	American	Grand Lux Café	The Venetian	702.414.3888											★	★	★
F2 57	$$	Mexican	Isla Mexican Kitchen	Treasure Island	702.894.7111			★			★							
E2 58	$$	Café	Le Café Île St. Louis	Paris Las Vegas	702.739.4111							★	★	★		★	★	★
E2 59	$$	Buffet	Le Village Buffet	Paris Las Vegas	702.946.4966		★			★				★		★		
E2 78	$$	Chinese	PF Chang's China Bistro	Desert Passage	702.836.0955						★			★				
E2 33	$$	American	The Cheesecake Factory	Caesars Forum Shops	702.792.6888									★			★	★
E2 3	$$$	Asian	Ah Sin	Paris Las Vegas	702.946.7000		★								★			
E2 25	$$$	Italian	Canaletto	The Venetian	702.733.0070							★						
E2 35	$$$	Chinese/French	Chinois	Caesars Forum Shops	702.737.9700				★		★		★					
E2 71	$$$	French	Mon Ami Gabi	Paris Las Vegas	702.944.4224						★	★		★	★	★		
E2 76	$$$	Mediterranean	Olives	The Bellagio	702.693.7223			★					★		★			★
F2 82	$$$	French	Pinot Brasserie	The Venetian	702.414.8888				★		★		★					
C2 91	$$$	Chinese	Shanghai Lilly	Mandalay Bay	702.632.7409		★					★		★				
E2 95	$$$	American New	Spago	Caesars Forum Shops	702.369.0360						★							
E2 99	$$$	Italian	Terrazza	Caesars Palace	702.731.7731								★		★			
G1 96	$$$	Steak	The Steak House	Circus Circus	702.894.7111					★			★			★		
C2 101	$$$	American	The Verandah	Four Seasons	702.632.5000							★			★	★	★	
E2 1	$$$$	Asian fusion	808	Caesars Palace	702.731.7110		★		★		★		★					
C2 2	$$$$	American New	3950	Mandalay Bay	702.632.7414		★				★		★					
D2 106	$$$$	French	André's	Monte Carlo	702.798.7151				★				★					
C2 7	$$$$	American New	Aureole	Mandalay Bay	702.632.7401		★	★	★		★	★	★					
E2 19	$$$$	Steakhouse	BOA Steakhouse	Caesars Forum Shops	702.733.7373		★						★	★				
C2 31	$$$$	Steak	Charlie Palmer Steak	Four Seasons	702.632.5120				★				★					

Map	Price	Cuisine	Restaurant	Location	Phone	Closed	Design Driven	Bar Scene	Top Food	Classic Vegas	Dining Alone	Romantic	Business Power	Kid Friendly	Outdoor Seating	Breakfast/Brunch	Dessert	After Midnight
E2 38	$$$$	Creole	Commander's Palace	Desert Passage	702.892.8272				★		★		★	★		★		
D2 32	$$$$	Steak	Craftsteak	MGM Grand	702.891.7318								★					
F2 40	$$$$	Steak	Delmonico	The Venetian	702.414.3737				★			★	★			★		
E2 42	$$$$	French	Eiffel Tower	Paris Las Vegas	702.948.6937					★		★						
D2 44	$$$$	Creole	Emeril's Fish House	MGM Grand	702.891.7374				★		★		★	★				
E2 45	$$$$	American	Fix	The Bellagio	702.693.7111		★		★				★					
C2 46	$$$$	French	Fleur de Lys	Mandalay Bay	702.632.7777				★			★	★					
E2 65	$$$$	US Regional	Mesa Grill	Caesars Palace	702.731.7731				★		★		★			★		
E2 77	$$$$	Italian	Osteria del Circo	The Bellagio	702.693.8150								★					
E2 80	$$$$	Italian	Piero Selvaggio Valentino	The Venetian	702.414.3000				★			★	★					
E2 83	$$$$	American	Postrio	The Venetian	702.796.1110						★		★					
E2 84	$$$$	Steak	Prime	The Bellagio	702.693.7111				★				★	★				
D2 92	$$$$	Japanese	Shibuya	MGM Grand	702.891.7777								★					
E2 97	$$$$	Buffet	Sterling Brunch	Bally's	702.739.4111	M–Sa				★						★		
E2 98	$$$$	Japanese	Sushi Roku	Caesars Forum Shops	702.733.7373						★							
H1 100	$$$$	Continental	Top of the World	Stratosphere	702.380.7711					★		★	★	★				
F2 4	$$$$$	French	Alex	Wynn Las Vegas	702.770.7100				★			★	★					
E2 20	$$$$$	French	Bouchon	The Venetian	702.414.6200				★			★	★					
E2 50	$$$$$	French	Guy Savoy	Caesars Palace	702.731.7110				★			★	★					
C2 69	$$$$$	French new	Mix	THEhotel	702.632.7777		★	★					★					
E2 79	$$$$$	French new	Picasso	The Bellagio	702.693.7223	W			★			★	★		★			
				Downtown														
I2 16	$	Diner	Binion's Coffee Shop	Binion's Casino	702.382.1600					★	★			★		★	★	★
I1 89	$	American	San Francisco Shrimp Bar	Golden Gate Hotel	702.382.6300					★	★							★
I2 21	$	Buffet	The Buffet	Golden Nugget	702.385.7111					★				★		★		
J2 17	$$$	Steakhouse	Binion's Steakhouse	Binion's Casino	702.382.1600					★			★	★				
I2 6	$$$$	French	André's	401 S 6th St	702.385.5016	Su			★	★		★			★			★
				East Side														
L1 107	$$	Chinese	PF Chang's China Bistro	4165 Paradise Rd	702.792.2207			★			★			★	★			
L1 8	$	Mexican	Baja Fresh Mexican Grill	1380 E Flamingo Rd	702.699.8920						★			★				
L1 51	$	Bagels	Harrie's Bagelmania	855 E Twain Ave	702.369.3322						★			★		★		
J2 55	$	Burgers	In-N-Out Burger	51 N Nellis Blvd	800.786.1000						★			★	★			

Map	Price	Cuisine	Restaurant	Location	Phone	Closed	Design Driven	Bar Scene	Top Food	Classic Vegas	Dining Alone	Romantic	Business Power	Kid Friendly	Outdoor Seating	Breakfast/Brunch	Dessert	After Midnight
K1 56	$	Burgers	In-N-Out Burger	4705 S Maryland Pkwy	800.786.1000						★			★	★			
K2 66	$	Pizza	Metro Pizza	1395 E Tropicana Ave	702.736.1955						★			★				
E2 68	$	Pizza	Metro Pizza	4178 E Koval Ln	702.312.5888						★			★				
K1 70	$	American	Mr. Lucky's 24/7	Hard Rock Hotel	702.693.5592						★			★		★	★	★
H2 94	$	American	Sourdough Cafe	Arizona Charlie's	702.951.5800						★			★		★		★
G2 36	$$	American	Coachman's Inn	3240 S Eastern Ave	702.731.4202					★				★				★
K2 63	$$	US Regional	Memphis Barbecue	2250 E Warm Springs Rd	702.260.6909						★			★	★			
K1 81	$$	Mexican	Pink Taco	Hard Rock Hotel	702.693.5525						★			★				
L1 90	$$	Indian	Shalimar	3900 Paradise Rd	702.796.0302									★				
L1 105	$$	US Regional	Z'Tejas Grill	3824 S Paradise Rd	702.732.1660									★	★			
K1 75	$$$$	Japanese new	Nobu	Hard Rock Hotel	702.693.5090		★		★		★		★		★			
K1 93	$$$$	American	Simon Kitchen & Bar	Hard Rock	702.693.5000		★	★			★		★		★	★	★	
				Henderson														
K2 11	$	Mexican	Baja Fresh Mexican Grill	9310 S Eastern Ave	702.563.2800						★			★				
K2 12	$	Thai	Bangkok Orchid	4662 E Sunset Rd	702.458.4945									★				
K2 29	$	Sandwiches	Capriotti's Sandwich	3981 E Sunset Rd	702.898.4904						★			★	★			
K2 88	$$	Italian	Romano's Macaroni Grill	573 N Stephanie St	702.433.2788									★				
				North Las Vegas														
B1 72	$	Ital–American	Montesano's Italian Deli	4835 W Craig Rd	702.656.3708	Su					★			★		★		
B2 48	$$	Mexican	Garduños	The Fiesta	702.631.7000									★	★			
J2 64	$$	US Regional	Memphis Barbecue	4379 Las Vegas Blvd N	702.644.0000						★			★	★			
				Northeast														
J2 53	$	US Regional	Hushy Puppy	1820 N Nellis Blvd	702.438.0005						★			★		★		
				Northwest														
B1 10	$	Mexican	Baja Fresh Mexican Grill	7501 W Lake Mead Blvd	702.838.4100						★			★				
B1 28	$	Sandwiches	Capriotti's Sandwich	450 S Buffalo Dr	702.838.8659						★			★	★			
B1 87	$$	Italian	Romano's Macaroni Grill	2001 N Rainbow Blvd	702.648.6688									★				
				West Side														
G1 26	$	Sandwiches	Capriotti's Sandwich	322 W Sahara Ave	702.474.0229	Su					★			★	★	★		
E1 27	$	Sandwiches	Capriotti's Sandwich	4983 W Flamingo Rd	702.222.3331						★			★	★			
A1 9	$	Mexican	Baja Fresh Mexican Grill	4760 W Sahara Ave	702.878.7772						★			★				
A2 37	$	Café	Coffee Pub	2800 W Sahara Ave	702.367.1913						★			★		★		

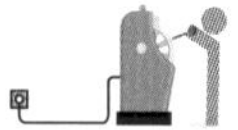

Map	Price	Cuisine	Restaurant	Location	Phone	Closed	Design Driven	Bar Scene	Top Food	Classic Vegas	Dining Alone	Romantic	Business Power	Kid Friendly	Outdoor Seating	Breakfast/Brunch	Dessert	After Midnight
D2 54	$	Burgers	In-N-Out Burger	4888 Industrial Rd	800.786.1000						★			★	★			★
A2 108	$	Burgers	In-N-Out Burger	2900 W Sahara Ave	800.786.1000						★			★	★			
E1 67	$	Pizza	Metro Pizza	4001 S Decatur Blvd	702.362.7896						★			★				
A2 73	$	Ital–American	Montesano's Italian Deli	3441 W Sahara Ave	702.876.0348						★			★				
A1 41	$	American	The Egg & I	4533 W Sahara Ave	702.364.9686						★			★		★		
D1 14	$$	Creole	Big Al's Oyster Bar	Orleans Hotel	702.967.4930						★			★				
B2 15	$$	US Regional	Big Mama's Rib Shack	2230 W Bonanza Rd	702.597.1616						★			★				
E1 30	$$	Buffet	Carnival World Buffet	Rio	702.252.7757					★				★		★		
E1 47	$$	Mexican	Garduños	The Palms	702.942.7777									★	★			
A1 52	$$	US Regional	Hush Puppy	7185 W Charleston Blvd	702.363.5988									★				
A2 86	$$	Italian	Romano's Macaroni Grill	2400 W Sahara Ave	702.248.9500									★				
A1 34	$$	American	The Cheesecake Factory	750 S Rampart Blvd	702.951.3800									★			★	
E1 102	$$	Buffet	Village Seafood Buffet	Rio	702.252.7777					★								
E1 103	$$	Mexican	Viva Mercado's	6182 W Flamingo Rd	702.871.8826									★		★		
A1 108	$$	US Regional	Z'Tejas Grill	9560 W Sahara Ave	702.638.0610									★	★			
E1 18	$$$	Southwestern	Blue Agave	The Palms	702.942.7777		★	★			★							★
E1 60	$$$	Chinese/French	Little Buddha Café	The Palms	702.942.7778						★							★
A1 62	$$$	Chinese	Mayflower Cuisinier	4750 W Sahara Ave	702.870.8432								★	★	★			
E1 5	$$$$	French	Alizé	The Palms	702.942.7777		★					★	★					
E1 74	$$$$	Steak	N9ne	The Palms	702.933.9900		★	★					★					

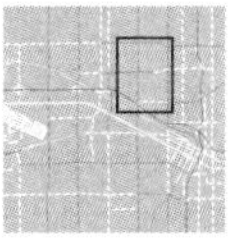

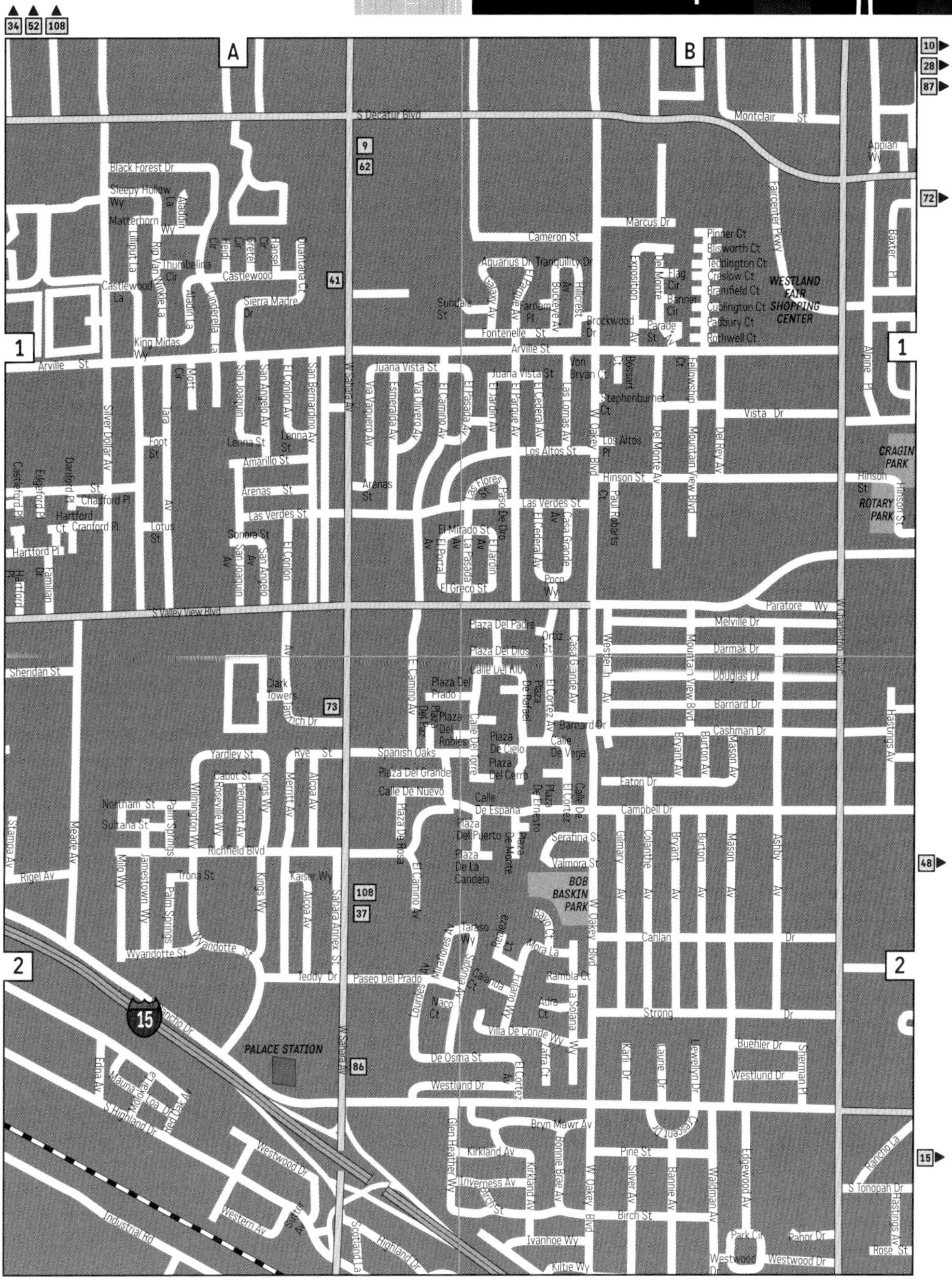

34 52 108
A
B
10
28
87
72
48
15
1
2

S Decatur Blvd
Montclair St
Appian Wy
Black Forest Dr
Sleepy Hollow Wy
Aladdin La
Matterhorn Wy
Lilliput La
Rip Van Winkle La
Thumbelina Cir
Heidi Cir
Gretel Cir
Hansel Cir
Quantana Ct
Castlewood
Castlewood La
Aladdin La
Cinderella La
Sierra Madre Dr
King Midas Wy
Arville St
Mott Cir
Faircenter Pkwy
Marcus Dr
Cameron St
Pinner Ct
Blisworth Ct
Teddington Ct
Creslow Ct
Bramfield Ct
Cuddington Ct
Padbury Ct
Rothwell Ct
WESTLAND FAIR SHOPPING CENTER
Baxter Pl
Aquarius Dr
Tranquility Dr
Galaxy Av
El Parque Av
Buckeye Av
Hillcrest
Exposition
Del Monte
Hag Cir
Banner Cir
Sundale St
Farnam Pl
Brockwood Dr
Parade St
Fontenelle St
Von Bryan Ct
Bossart Ct
Fellowship Ct
Alpine Pl
Juana Vista St
Via Vaquero Av
Esmeralda Av
Via Olivero Av
El Camino Av
El Pasada Av
El Jardin Av
El Parque Av
El Cederal Av
Las Lomas Av
W Oakey Blvd
Stephenburnet Ct
Vista Dr
Mountain View Blvd
Del Rey Av
Del Monte Av
Los Altos Pl
Los Altos St
Hinson St
CRAGIN PARK
ROTARY PARK
Hinson St
Silver Dollar Av
Tara Av
Foot St
San Joaquin
San Angelo Av
El Conlon Av
San Bernardino Av
W Sahara Av
Lenna St
Lenna St
Amarillo St
Arenas St
Arenas St
Las Verdes St
Sonora St
Castleford Pl
Edgeford Dr
Danford Dr
Chalford Pl
Hartford Ct
Cranford Pl
Lotus St
Hartford Pl
Hartford
Familian
Las Flores St
Paso De Oro
Las Verdes St
Casa Grande
Paul Roberts
El Mirado St
El Portal Av
La Pasada Av
El Jardin
El Cederal Av
Poco Wy
El Greco St
S Valley View Blvd
Paratore Wy
Melville Dr
Darmak Dr
Douglas Dr
Barnard Dr
Cashman Dr
W Charleston Blvd
Hastings Av
Plaza Del Padre
Ortiz St
Plaza Del Dios
Casa Grande Av
Calle Del Rio
Wester Ln
Sheridan St
Clark Towers
Lanoch Dr
Plaza Del Prado
Plaza De Rafael
El Cortez Av
Plaza Del Paz
Plaza Del Robles
Calle Del Torre
Plaza De Cielo
Calle De Vega
Barnard Dr
Bryant Av
Burton Av
Mason Av
Yardley St
Rye St
Spanish Oaks
Plaza Del Cerro
Plaza Del Grande
Eaton Dr
Cabot St
Roseville Wy
Piedmont Av
Kings Wy
Merritt Av
Alcoa Av
Calle De Nuevo
Calle De Espana
Plaza De Ernesto
El Cortez
Calle De
Campbell Dr
Northam St
Palm Springs
Wilmington Wy
Sultana St
Plaza De Rosa
Plaza Del Puerto
Plaza De Monte
Serafina St
Gilmary Av
Colanthe Av
Bryant Av
Burton Av
Mason Av
Ashby Av
Richfield Blvd
Stampa Av
Meade Av
Plaza De La Candela
Valmora St
Milo Wy
Jamestown Wy
Trona St
Kaiser Wy
El Camino Av
Rigel Av
Palm Springs
Kings Wy
Alcoa Av
Sahara Annex St
BOB BASKIN PARK
Taraso Wy
Realeza Ct
Bayo Ct
Mora La
Cahlan Dr
Wyandotte St
Wyandotte St
Miraflores Av
Eugenia Ct
Teddy Dr
Paseo Del Prado
Lourdes Av
Calandra Ct
Furano Wy
Rambla Ct
La Solana
Rancho Dr
Naco Ct
Adra Ct
Strong Dr
Villa De Conde Wy
Karli Dr
Laurie Dr
Lewellyn Dr
Buehler Dr
Sherman Pl
Zafra Ct
PALACE STATION
De Osma St
Edna Av
Mauna Loa Dr
Molokai Dr
Red Oak Av
S Highland Dr
Westlund Dr
El Cortez Av
Westlund Dr
Bryn Mawr Av
Crescent Dr
Glen Heather Wy
Kirkland Av
Bonnie Brae Av
Pine St
Westwood Dr
Kirkland Av
Inverness Av
W Oakey Blvd
Silver Av
Bannie Av
Waldman Av
Edgewood Av
Rancho La
S Tonopah Dr
Birch St
Birch St
Western Av
Industrial Rd
Sutter
Scotland La
Highland Dr
Ivanhoe Wy
Park Cir
Pahor Dr
Hastings Av
Rose St
Westwood Dr
Westwood Dr
Kiltie Wy
9
62
41
73
108
37
86
15

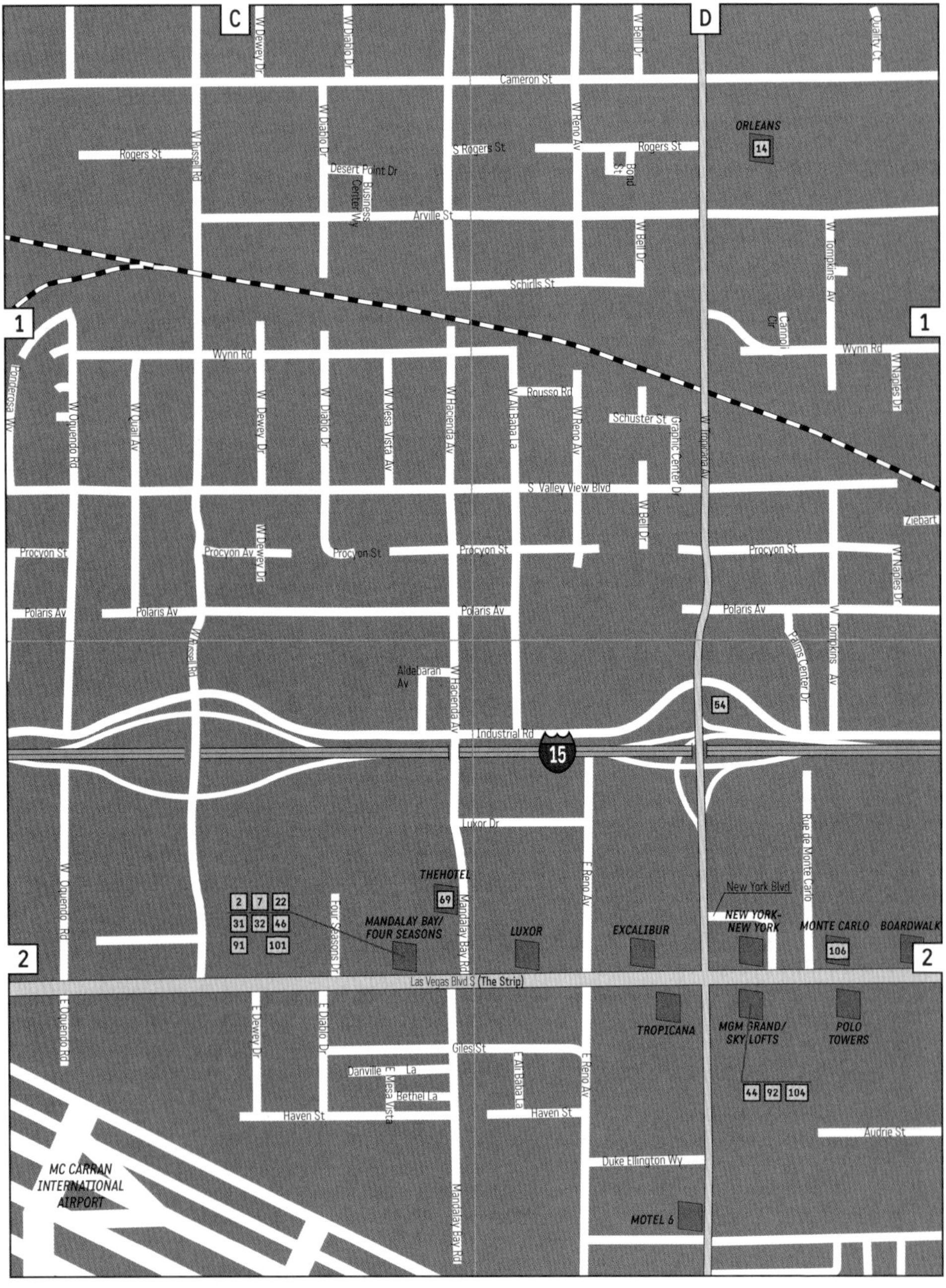

C
D
1
2

Cameron St
Rogers St
S Rogers St
W Russel Rd
W Dewey Dr
W Diablo Dr
Desert Point Dr
Business Center Wy
Arville St
W Reno Av
Bond St
W Bell Dr
Quality Ct
ORLEANS
14
W Tompkins Av
Schirlls St
Cannoli Cir
Wynn Rd
W Naples Dr
Ponderosa Wy
W Oquendo Rd
W Quail Av
W Mesa Vista Av
W Hacienda Av
W Ali Baba La
Rousso Rd
Schuster St
Graphic Center Dr
W Tropicana Av
S Valley View Blvd
Ziebart
Procyon St
Procyon Av
W Dewey Dr
Polaris Av
Palms Center Dr
Aldebaran Av
54
Industrial Rd
15
Luxor Dr
E Reno Av
Rue de Monte Carlo
New York Blvd
THEHOTEL
69
2 7 22
31 32 46
91 101
Four Seasons Dr
Mandalay Bay Rd
MANDALAY BAY/ FOUR SEASONS
LUXOR
EXCALIBUR
NEW YORK-NEW YORK
MONTE CARLO
106
BOARDWALK
Las Vegas Blvd S (The Strip)
E Oquendo Rd
E Dewey Dr
E Diablo Dr
TROPICANA
MGM GRAND/ SKY LOFTS
POLO TOWERS
Giles St
Danville La
E Mesa Vista
Bethel La
E Ali Baba La
Haven St
44 92 104
Audrie St
Duke Ellington Wy
MC CARRAN INTERNATIONAL AIRPORT
MOTEL 6

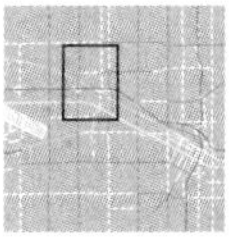

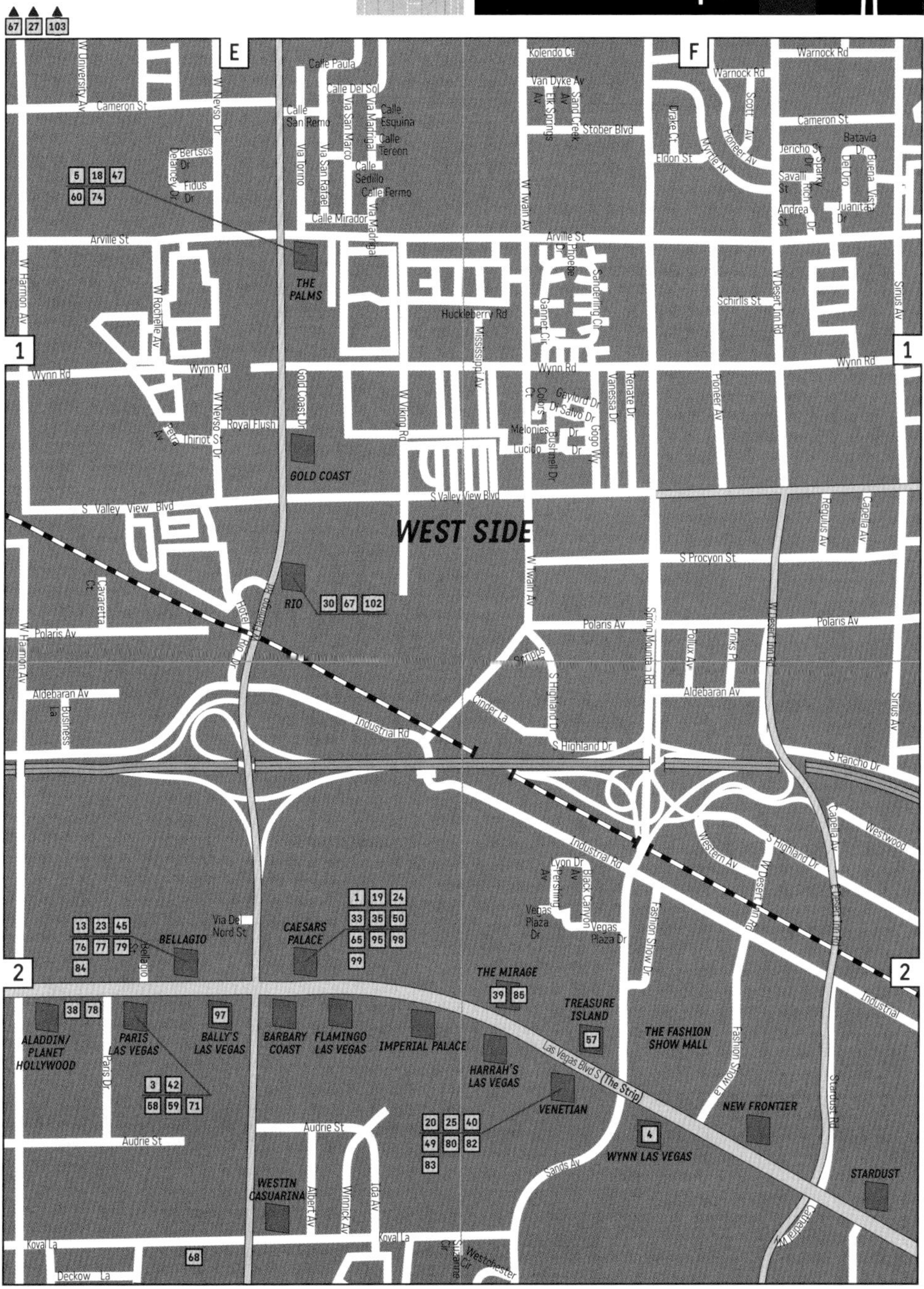

67 27 103

E
F
1
2

WEST SIDE

THE PALMS
5 18 47
60 74

GOLD COAST

RIO
30 67 102

BELLAGIO
13 23 45
76 77 79
84

CAESARS PALACE
1 19 24
33 35 50
65 95 98
99

THE MIRAGE
39 85

TREASURE ISLAND
57

THE FASHION SHOW MALL

ALADDIN/ PLANET HOLLYWOOD
38 78

PARIS LAS VEGAS
3 42
58 59 71

BALLY'S LAS VEGAS
97

BARBARY COAST

FLAMINGO LAS VEGAS

IMPERIAL PALACE

HARRAH'S LAS VEGAS

VENETIAN
20 25 40
49 80 82
83

NEW FRONTIER

WYNN LAS VEGAS
4

STARDUST

WESTIN CASUARINA

68

Cameron St
Arville St
Wynn Rd
S Valley View Blvd
Polaris Av
Aldebaran Av
Industrial Rd
S Highland Dr
S Rancho Dr
W Desert Inn Rd
Spring Mountain Rd
Fashion Show Dr
Las Vegas Blvd S (The Strip)
Sands Av
Audrie St
Koval La
Deckow La
Stardust Rd
W Harmon Av
W Nevso Dr
W Viking Rd
W Twain Av
Hotel Rio Dr
Paris Dr
Warnock Rd
Western Av

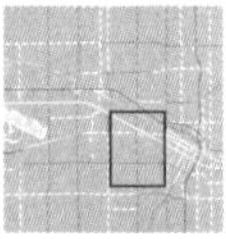

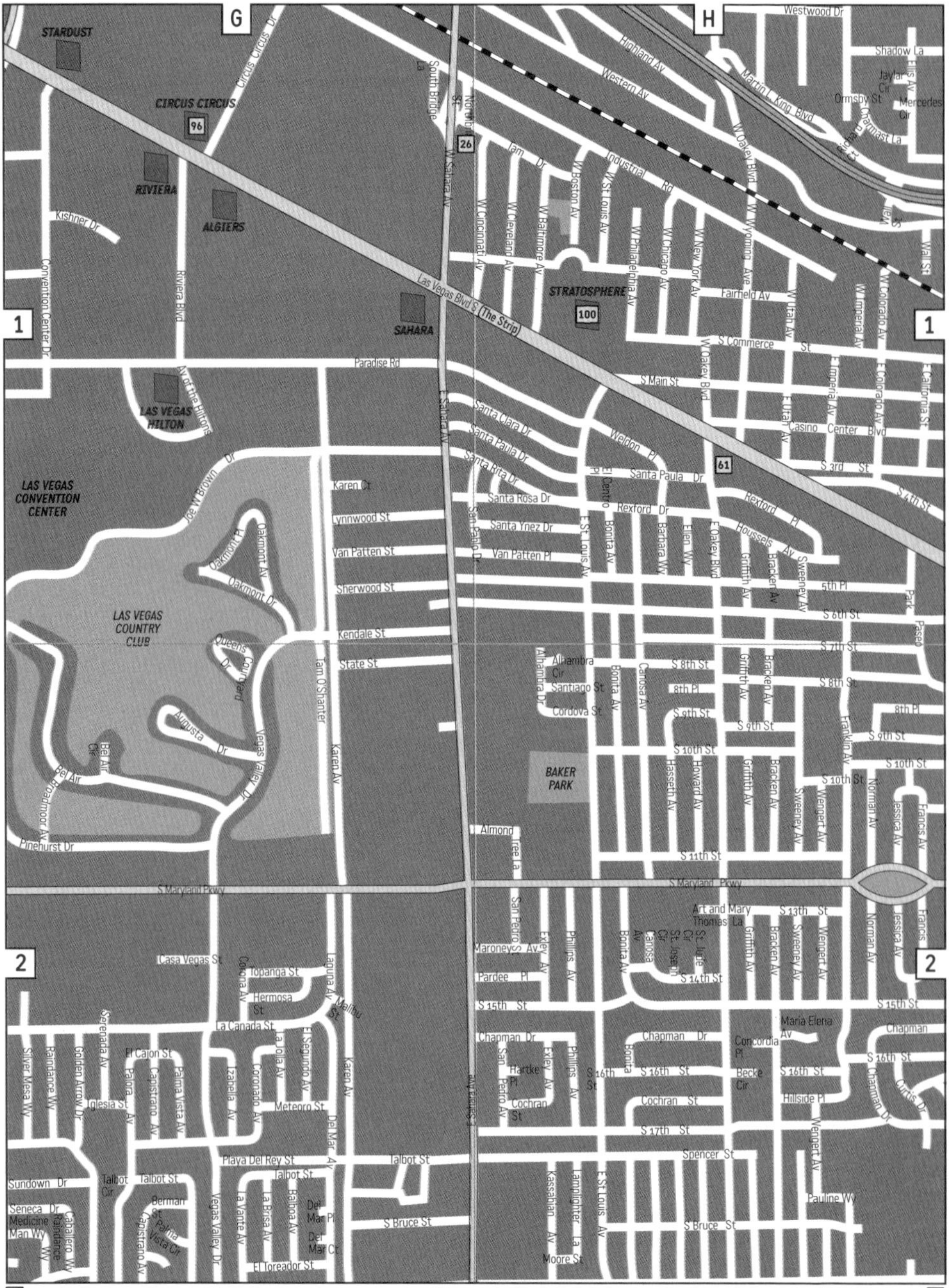
G
H
1
2
36
94
STARDUST
CIRCUS CIRCUS
96
RIVIERA
ALGIERS
SAHARA
STRATOSPHERE
100
26
61
LAS VEGAS HILTON
LAS VEGAS CONVENTION CENTER
LAS VEGAS COUNTRY CLUB
BAKER PARK
Las Vegas Blvd S (The Strip)
Circus Circus Dr
Kishner Dr
Convention Center Dr
Riviera Blvd
Paradise Rd
Av of the Hilton
Joe W Brown Dr
Oakmont Pl
Oakmont Av
Oakmont Dr
Queens Dr
Courtyard
Augusta Dr
Vegas Valley Dr
Bel Air Cir
Bel Air
Broadmoor Av
Pinehurst Dr
Karen Ct
Lynnwood St
Van Patten St
Sherwood St
Kendale St
State St
Tam O'Shanter
Karen Av
S Maryland Pkwy
South Bridge La
North Bridge St
W Sahara Av
E Sahara Av
Highland Av
Western Av
Industrial Rd
Iam Dr
W Cincinnati Av
W Cleveland Av
W Baltimore Av
W Boston Av
W St Louis Av
W Philadelphia Av
W Chicago Av
W New York Av
W Oakey Blvd
W Wyoming Ave
W Utah Av
W Imperial Av
W Colorado Av
Fairfield Av
Martin L King Blvd
Westwood Dr
Shadow La
Jaylar Cir
Ellis Av
Ormsby St
Mercedes Cir
Charmast La
Richfield Blvd
Main St
Wall St
S Commerce St
S Main St
E Imperial Av
E Colorado Av
E California St
E Utah Av
Casino Center Blvd
S 3rd St
S 4th St
Santa Clara Dr
Santa Paula Dr
Santa Rita Dr
Santa Rosa Dr
Santa Ynez Dr
Van Patten Pl
San Pablo Dr
Weldon Pl
El Centro Pl
Santa Paula Dr
Rexford Dr
Rexford Pl
E St Louis Av
Bonita Av
Barbara Wy
Ellen Wy
E Oakey Blvd
Houssels Av
Griffith Av
Bracken Av
Sweeney Av
5th Pl
S 6th St
S 7th St
Park Paseo
Alhambra Cir
Alhambra Dr
Santiago St
Cordova St
Canosa Av
S 8th St
8th Pl
S 9th St
S 10th St
Hassett Av
Howard Av
Wengert Av
Franklin Av
Norman Av
Jessica Av
Francis Av
S 11th St
Almond Tree La
San Pedro Av
Exley Av
Phillips Av
Art and Mary Thomas La
St. Jude Cir
St. Joseph Cir
S 13th St
Maroney Av
Pardee Pl
S 14th St
S 15th St
Chapman Dr
Maria Elena Av
Concordia Pl
Hartke Pl
Cochran St
S 16th St
Becke Cir
Hillside Pl
Curtis Dr
S 17th St
Spencer St
Pauline Wy
Kassabian Av
Lamplighter La
Moore St
S Bruce St
Casa Vegas St
Colonia Av
Topanga St
Hermosa St
Laguna Av
Malibu St
La Canada St
Serenada Av
El Cajon St
Silver Mesa Wy
Raindance Wy
Golden Arrow Dr
Palora Av
Capistrano Av
Palma Vista Av
Izabella Av
Coronado Av
La Jolla Av
El Segundo Av
Iglesia St
Meteoro St
Del Mar Av
Playa Del Rey St
Talbot St
Talbot Cir
Sundown Dr
Seneca Dr
Medicine Man Wy
Caballero Wy
Berman St
Palma Vista Cir
La Vante Av
La Brisa Av
Balboa Av
Del Mar Pl
Del Mar Ct
El Toreador St

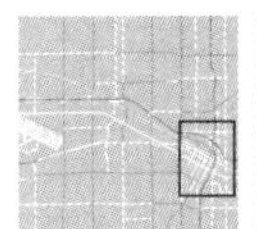

I
J
1
2
DOWNTOWN
MAIN ST STATION
89 BINIONS HORSE SHOE
GOLDEN NUGGET 21
16 17
CALIFORNIA HOTEL
FOUR QUEENS
FREMONT HOTEL
FITZGERALD'S
6
LADY LUCK
EL CORTEZ
MADISON PARK
GAY PARK
LAS VEGAS NATURAL HISTORY MUSEUM & OLD LAS VEGAS FORT
LIONS MEMORIAL PARK
15
515
64
53
55

Willow St
Alturas Av
Bearden Dr
Pinto La
Kenyon Pl
Alta Dr
Shadow La
Rosemeade St
W Mesquite Av
Diamond Cir
Shadow La
Comstock
Ralston
Sharon
Sunny Pl
Ophir Dr
Hastings Av
Desert La
Desert La
S Martin L King Dr
N Martin L King Dr
Mineral Av
M St
Morgan Av
W Adams Av
Jefferson Av
Madison Av
W McWilliams Av
Downy Wy
Reed Pl
W Washington Av
W Bonanza Rd
Levy La
Grant St
Gerson Av
Cunningham Dr
H St
W Wilson Av
W Mesquite Av
Morgan Av
W Adams Av
Jefferson Av
Madison Av
W Charleston Blvd
Iron Horse Dr
S Grand Central Pkwy
Discovery Dr
S Commerce St
Boulder Av
Coolidge Av
Hoover Av
S 1st St
S Main St
S 1st St
S 3rd St
S Casino Center Blvd
Lewis
Gass Av
Garces Av
S 4th St
Las Vegas Blvd S (The Strip)
E Charleston Blvd
S 8th St
E Bonneville Av
S 6th St
S 7th St
Clark
Fremont St
N 3rd St
Stewart Av
N Main St
N 1st St
Palm La
Biltmore Dr
Melrose Dr
Mt. Vermont Cir
Sycamore La
Veterans Memorial Dr
Tiffany La
N 4th St
Bonanza Wy
Bell
E Bonanza Rd
S 9th St
Bridger Av
Carson Av
S 10th St
S 10th St
N 6th St
N 7th St
N 8th St
E Mesquite Av
Encanto Dr
E McWilliams
N Las Vegas Blvd
N 4th St
Adams Av
S 11th St
S 11th St
E Ogden Av
N 11th St
N Maryland Pkwy
S Rue 13
Lewis Av
Chula Wy
Joshua Wy
Bridger Av
Manzanita Wy
S 13th St
S 14th St
S 15th St
Linden Av
N 9th St
N 10th St
E Wilson Av
Harris Av
N 11th St
N 12th St
N 11th St
E Washington Av
Thelma Pl
Mcnair Pl
Lewis Av
N 16th St
Carson Av
Earl St
S 17th St
Carson Av
Fremont St
N 17th St
N Rue 13
N 12th St
N 13th St
N 14th St
Margaret Av
N Maryland Pkwy
Fantasy La
Spencer St
Lewis Av
Circle Dr
S Bruce St
Harley Wy
N 17th St
Paco Wy
Martin Av
Stewart Av
Martin Av
N 15th St
N 16th St
N Bruce St
W Bonanza Rd
Ryan Av
E Wilson Av
E McWilliams Av
N 16th St
Harris Av
Sagman St
Constantine Av
Held Rd
Pastel Pl
Grayson Av
Ryan
N 17th St
N 18th St
N 18th St
N 18th St
Leslie Av
N 17th St
N 17th St
N 18th St
Todd Av

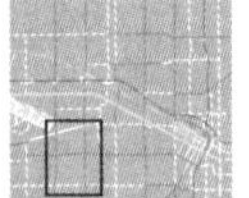

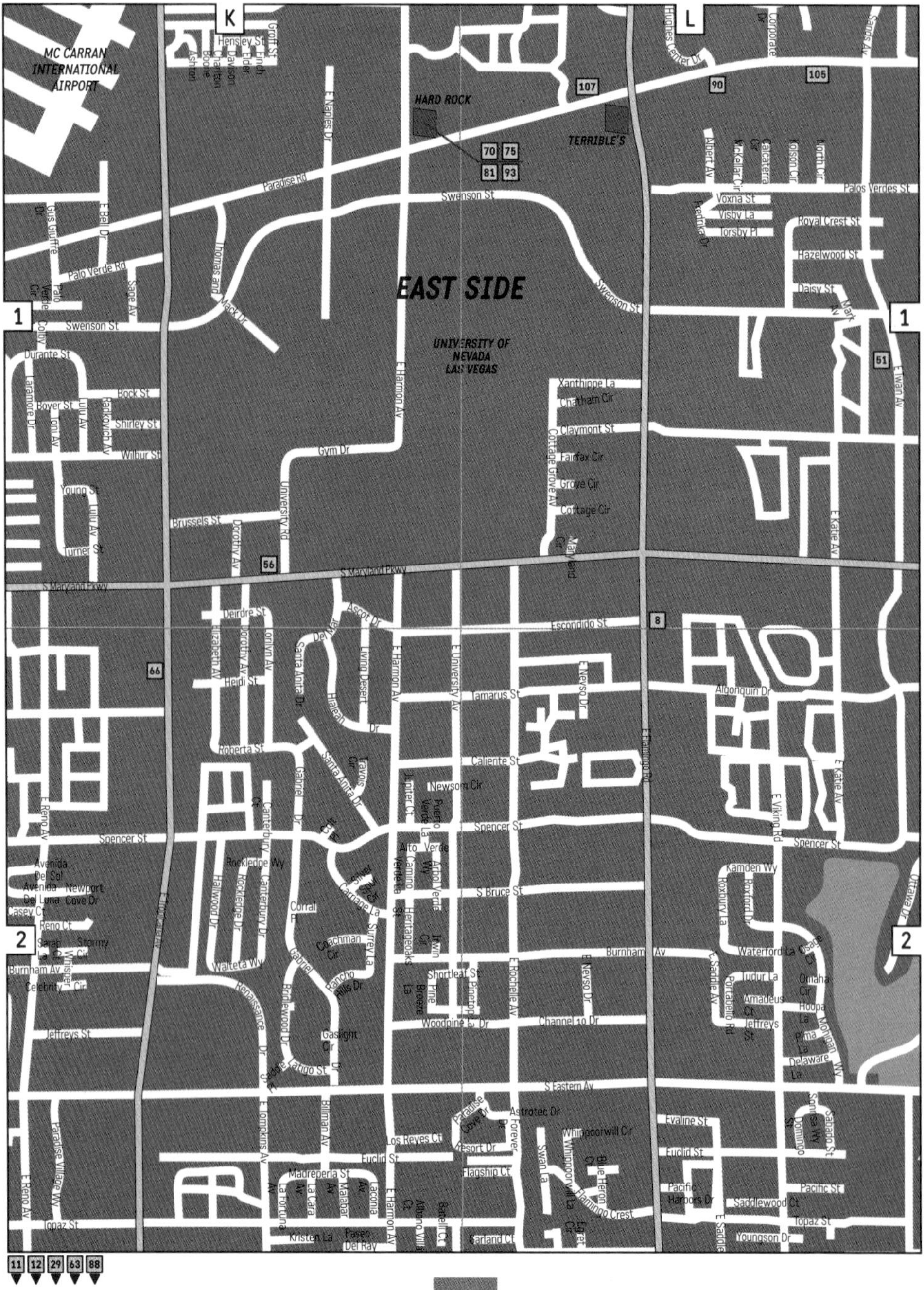

K
L
1
2

MC CARRAN INTERNATIONAL AIRPORT
HARD ROCK
TERRIBLE'S
EAST SIDE
UNIVERSITY OF NEVADA LAS VEGAS

107
90
105
70
75
81
93
51
56
66
8

Paradise Rd
Swenson St
Palo Verde Rd
S Maryland Pkwy
Spencer St
Burnham Av
S Eastern Av
Topaz St
E Harmon Av
E University Av
E Flamingo Rd
E Tropicana Av
E Katie Av
E Viking Rd
Hughes Center Dr
Palos Verdes St
Royal Crest St
Hazelwood St
Escondido St
Tamarus St
Algonquin Dr
Caliente St
S Bruce St
Woodpine Dr
Channel 10 Dr
Euclid St
E Reno Av
Gym Dr
University Rd
Brussels St
Cottage Grove Av
Maryland Cir
E Naples Dr
Thomas and Mack Dr

SHOP 3

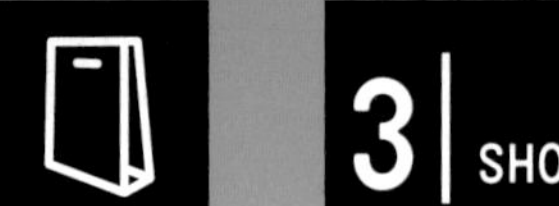

3 | SHOP

Vegas has become something of a couture shopper's mecca, with Gucci, Louis Vuitton and Versace outposts all over town. The city is also a great place to go binge-shopping just for the fun of it. Nowhere is trolling for clothes and gifts more entertaining than in these million-dollar malls with indoor rainstorms, animatronic gods, extravagant light shows and even a Grand Canal. Over the last few years, Las Vegas has also become an excellent shopping city for middle-of-the-road basics, and several off-price outlet malls have made the city a paradise for upscale bargainistas. And if you want something sparkly, or with sequins, or thoroughly infused with post-ironic kitsch, Vegas is your town, baby. In this guide, we focus on locally-owned stores and unusual shopping places, and highlight products that are not readily available everywhere else. Of course, there is no better souvenir you could bring home from Vegas than a fat wad of cash.

MALLS

BOULEVARD MALL | 3528 S Maryland Pkwy (at Desert Inn), East Side, T 702.732.8949, MAP **L1** [1] For many locals, the oldest shopping mall in Las Vegas remains one of its best. For ease-of-use and effortless location about five minutes east of the Strip, the Boulevard can't be beat. Most of the stores aim toward the mid to lower end of the market. But when it comes to staples, you can find just about anything you need here, at lower prices than you'd pay at the place with the talking Roman-god statues or the indoor thunderstorm.

150 Stores Include: B Dalton Booksellers, Bombay Company, The Body Shop, Brookstone, Dillard's, Express, Foot Locker, Frederick's of Hollywood, Gap, JC Penney, KB Toys, Lenscrafters, Macy's, Marshall's, Radio Shack, Sears, Victoria's Secret

DESERT PASSAGE | Aladdin/Planet Hollywood, 3663 Las Vegas Blvd S (at Harmon), Strip, T 888.800.8284, MAP **E2** [2] Like its nearest retailtainment competitors—the Forum Shops at Caesars and the Grand Canal Shops at the Venetian—this mall is a brilliantly themed space. As bicycle rickshaws pass, the occasional clang of a bell or cry of a seagull gives way to a genuine fake "thunderstorm" which darkens the "sky" with a rainy drizzle, reaches a thunderous crescendo, then blows away just as effortlessly. The faint background sounds of hustlers and hawkers are dead-on, some of the architecture is fantabulous, and the shop selection is very good. There's a particularly good collection of fine art galleries too, including Bernard K. Passman (black coral sculptures and jewelry), Thomas Kinkade (original prints), and Tresor (art glass and jewelry).

130 Stores Include: Aveda, BCBG Max Azria, bebe, Betsey Johnson, Clinique, Discovery Channel Store, Eddie Bauer, French Connection, GAP, Herve Leger, Hookah Gallery, Houdini's Magic Shop, Hugo/Hugo Boss, L'Occitane, Lucky Brand Dungarees, Metropolitan Museum of Art Store, Neighborhoodies, Origins, Sephora, Sharper Image, Stash Clothing, Steve Madden, Sur la Table, Swarovski, Tommy Bahama, Tumi, United Colors of Benetton, Urban Leather, Victoria's Secret

FASHION OUTLETS LAS VEGAS | 32100 Las Vegas Blvd S (at Primm), Primm, T 702.874.1400, MAP **C2** [3] Situated about 45-minutes south of the Strip on the California/Nevada border, Fashion Outlet is a great place to find low prices on high fashions, including designer labels from top brands. While things are not exactly cheap, there are some great deals (up to half-off) amongst a selection of goods that will keep you on the brandwagon. Discounted house- and kitchenware are also sold. Of course, there's the requisite food court too (including Hot Dog On-A-Stick!).

100 Stores Include: Bally, Banana Republic, Bath & Body Works, BCBG Max Azria, Burberry, Coach, Cole Haan, DC Shoes, Escada, GAP, Guess?, Izod, Jones New York, KB Toys, Kenneth Cole, Polo Ralph Lauren, Quiksilver, Reebok, Versace, Williams-Sonoma

FASHION SHOW MALL | 3200 Las Vegas Blvd S (at Spring Mountain), Strip, T 702.369.0704, MAP **F2** [4] The first mall on the Strip began the 21st Century with a $350 million upgrade that doubled the retail space and erected an enormous cloudlike canopy which "floats" above the mall's front plaza. Situated in the center of the Strip, the Fashion Show is a convenient place to Aberzombie away some time. And because the mall's major tenants are Lord & Taylor, Bloomingdale's Home, Nordstrom, Nieman Marcus, Saks Fifth Avenue, and Macy's, it's the perfect one-stop-shop for an important accessory you mistakenly left behind. Of course, there are lots of smaller stores too, plus the requisite food court. And we love that for $20 we can toss the keys to the parking valet and say "wash it."

200 Stores Include: Abercrombie & Fitch, Adrienne Vittadini, Apple, Bally, Banana Republic, Bang & Olufsen, Bath & Body Works, bebe, Betsey Johnson, Bloomingdale's Home, Coach, Cole Haan, Diesel, Dillard's, Eddie Rodriguez, Frederick's of Hollywood, GAP, Guess, LensCrafters, L'Occitane, Louis Vuitton, Lucky Brand, Lunettes, Macy's, Magic Zone, Neiman Marcus, Nordstrom, Optica, Paul Frank, Puma, Quiksilver, Robinsons-May, Saks Fifth Avenue, Sanrio, Steve Madden, Swarovski, Swatch, Talulah G, Tumi, Waldenbooks, Williams-Sonoma, Zara

THE FORUM SHOPS | Caesars Palace, 3500 Las Vegas Blvd S (at Flamingo), Strip, T 702.893.4800, MAP **E2** [5] The Forum Shops is one part mall, two parts entertainment event. We have been there tons of times and had enjoyable experiences without purchasing a thing. Yet, we are told that this whacked-out Roman theme mall with a Trevi Fountain look-alike at its core leads the nation in annual sales-per-square-foot. In any event, we stand by our assertion that the best reason to go—and you should go—is to witness one of the strangest interior environments anywhere. The Shops' *trompe l'oeil* sky has been

copied all over town, but few others continually transform from day to night, along with associated temperature changes. And no others have stores fronting "ancient" Roman streets, complete with classical statuary, ornate fountains, a laser light show, dancing waters, and moving, "talking" animatronic Roman gods. The tenants in this exhaustingly-large mall of Gap-to-Gucci boutiques are all over the retail map. In short, there's something for everyone here, from a Mickey Mouse key chain to a crisp Armani suit. The unforgettably silly **Fall of Atlantis** fountain show, located between the **Cheesecake Factory** and **Race for Atlantis**, usually happens on the hour.

160 Stores Include: Agent Provocateur, Anthropologie, Baccarat, Bally, bebe, Hugo Boss, Burberry, Bvlgari, Celine, Carolina Herrera, Christian Dior, Coach, David Yurman, Diesel, DKNY, Dolce & Gabbana, Emporio Armani, Ermenegildo Zegna, Escada, Estee Lauder, FAO Schwarz, Gianni Versace, Gucci, Guess, Houdini's Magic Shop, Juicy Couture, Kate Spade, Kenneth Cole, La Perla, Longchamp, Louis Vuitton, Lucky Brand Jeans, MaxMara, Nanette Lepore, Roberto Cavalli, Salvatore Ferragamo, Scoop NYC

THE GALLERIA AT SUNSET | 1300 W Sunset Rd (at Stephanie), Henderson, T 702.434.0202, MAP **K2** 6 This newish two-story gem is full with mallrats and anchored by several department stores—Dillard's, JC Penney and Robinsons-May, the last being the best reason to visit (those accessories! those sales! those prices!). Most of the stores are typical suburban fare, but for Vegas it all seems a bit upscale. Or maybe that's just because they have valet parking. The mall is located about 20 minutes from the Strip near I-95.

140 Stores Include: Abercrombie & Fitch, B. Dalton Bookseller, Dillard's, ExpressMen, Foot Locker, Gap, JCPenney, LensCrafters, No Fear, Robinsons-May, Sanrio, Sharper Image, Spencer Gifts, Victoria's Secret

THE GRAND CANAL SHOPPES | The Venetian, 3355 Las Vegas Blvd S (at Sands), Strip, T 702.414.4500, MAP **F2** 7 It's hard not to be shocked by the sheer audacity of recreating Venice's Grand Canal on the *upper* level of a desert casino resort. But this place, like the rest of the property, raises the bar on irony to become one of the top sights in the city. The Grand Canal Shoppes are a hoot. They're probably too fantastic, actually, because the scene is so breathtaking that shopping here seems an afterthought. Perhaps retailers think so too, because nothing really pops here. Sure, there's a few good names, but few people we know think of heading to these "shoppes" when setting out on a spree. The bottom line, frankly, is that you've just got to see this place. And as long as you're at it, why not get a gondola ride as well?

75 Stores Include: Burberry, Ca' d' Oro, Dolcé Due, Houdini's Magic Shop, Jimmy Choo, Kenneth Cole, Lido Beach Shop, Lladró, Mikimoto, Movado, Regis Galerie, Ripa de Monti, Sephora, Tolstoys

LAS VEGAS OUTLET CENTER | 7400 Las Vegas Blvd S (at Warm Springs), Strip, T 702.896.5599, MAP **C2** 8 Situated a few miles from the Strip, this enormous discount mall covers all the bases: clothing, jewelry, toys, shoes, housewares and the like. Prices seem to be about 25 to 65 percent below retail. It's located on the far southern end of the Strip.

130 Stores Include: Billabong, Black & Decker, Bose, Casio, Danskin, Etienne Aigner, Fossil, Izod, Jockey, Jones New York, Levi's/Dockers, London Fog, Mikasa, Motherhood Maternity, Nike, Reebok, Samsonite

LAS VEGAS PREMIUM OUTLETS | 875 S Grand Central Pkwy (at Charleston), West Side, T 702.474.7500, MAP **I1** 9 Of the several discount-outlet shopping centers in the Las Vegas brandscape, this is one of the newest and best. Reaching high and low, stores are all over the retail map. If you're not looking for this season's latest then bargains can be found, but good deals here are not always a given.

120 Stores Include: Adidas, Adrienne Vittadini, Armani Exchange, Bally, Banana Republic, Barneys New York, Bebe, Benetton, Betsey Johnson, Bottega Veneta, Brooks Brothers, Burberry, Calvin Klein, Camper, Carolina Herrera, Chanel, Christian Dior, Coach, Cole Haan, Diesel, DKNY, Dockers, Dolce & Gabbana, Eddie Bauer, Escada, Fendi, Furla, GF Ferre, Giorgio Armani, Gucci, Guess, Hugo Boss, Izod, Joan & David, Jockey, Kenneth Cole, L.L. Bean, La Perla, Lacoste, Lands' End, Levi's, L'Occitane, London Fog, Lucky Brand, MaxMara, Michael Kors, Nike, Pratesi, Puma, Quiksilver, Reebok, Rip Curl, Roberto Cavalli, Saks Fifth Avenue, Salvatore Ferragamo, Sanrio, Timberland, Tumi, Versace, Yves Saint Laurent

LE BOULEVARD | Paris Las Vegas, 3655 Las Vegas Blvd S (at Harmon), Strip, T 702.739.4111, MAP **E2** 10 What makes Le Boulevard special is the fact that it's a small mall built on a comparatively human scale. The theme, of course, is old Paris and the interior is built to look like a Parisian pedestrian thoroughfare, with brass lamps and cobblestone "streets." The shops that line the lanes are

The Grand Canal Shoppes

relatively intimate boutiques. We like this place because it doesn't even attempt to compete with the mainstream malls. Rather it offers a big selection of unique shops and goods you can't get anywhere else. Interspersed amongst the retail shops are a good French bakery (JJ's Boulangerie), an excellent patisserie (Lenotre), and even a bar where you can pause for a Pastis (Napoleon's).

20 Stores Include: Cigars du Monde, Judith Jack, L'Art de Paris, L'Oasis, La Cave, La Vogue, Lenôtre, Les Enfants, Les Mémoires, Lunettes, Presse News

MANDALAY PLACE | Mandalay Bay, 3950 Las Vegas Blvd S (at Mandalay Bay), Strip, T 702.632.9333, MAP **C2** 11 This newish shopping complex is located on a bridge connecting Mandalay Bay with the Luxor. It's something of an air-conditioned Ponte Vecchio containing lots of shops you won't find anywhere else in Vegas. Access it via Mandalay Bay, the Luxor or from a valet parking area beneath a grand circular skylight.

41 Stores Include: 55 Degrees Wine + Design, Art of Shaving, Chocolate Swan, Davidoff, GF Ferre, Lunettes, Max & Co., Mulholland, Musette, Nike Golf, Oilily, Portico, Reading Room, Samantha Chang, Sauvage, Skinklinic, Urban Outfitters

NEONOPOLIS | 400 Fremont St (at 4th), Downtown, T 702.477.0470, MAP **I2** 12 Anchored by a multi-screen cinema, this small, multi-hued mall across from the Fremont Street Experience has a clutch of rather standard shops, a large bowling center and even larger food court. It's worth a look around, if only to check out the numerous refurbished, vintage neon signs from around Vegas and the rest of the America.

10 Stores Include: Viva Vegas Gifts, Z&Z Apparel

VIA BELLAGIO | Bellagio, 3600 Las Vegas Blvd S (at Flamingo), Strip, T 702.693.7111, MAP E2 13 Via Bellagio, like the hotel in which it is located, is an overstated stroll through the world's luxury brands. Many of earth's most upscale retail establishments are represented here, playing to brandroids who have hit the big one. It might as well be Madison Avenue or the Faubourg Saint Honoré, except here the window shoppers are wearing T-shirts and holding Big Gulps.

10 Stores Include: Chanel, Dior, Fred Leighton, Giorgio Armani, Gucci, Hermès, Prada, Tiffany & Co., Yves Saint Laurent

WYNN LAS VEGAS SHOPS | Wynn Las Vegas, 3131 Las Vegas Blvd S (at Sands), Strip, T 702.770.7100, MAP F2 14 Shopping is as good a reason as any to check out this spectacular resort hotel. The brandwidth is small, but the selection is as upscale as Vegas gets.

20 Stores Include: Brioni, Cartier, Chanel, Dior, Gaultier, Gizmos, Graff, Jo Malone, Judith Leiber, La Flirt, Manolo Blahnik, Oscar de la Renta, Penske-Wynn Ferrari Maserati, w.ink, Wynn & Co. Watches

MARKETS

BROADACRES SWAP MEET | 2930 N Las Vegas Blvd (at Pecos), North, T 702.642.3777 | **CLOSED** SUN, MAP J2 15 For a quarter-century, Broadacres has been Nevada's favorite outdoor flea market. And with over 1000 sellers, it's the state's largest too. Goods here are split almost equally between old and new, and you can never tell what's going to turn up. Most of it, of course, is sub-brand trash, but there are some diamonds in this rough.

FANTASTIC INDOOR SWAP MEET | 1717 S Decatur Blvd (at Oakey), West Side, T 702.877.0087 | **CLOSED** MON-THURS, MAP B1 16 Hundreds of merchants selling mostly new merchandise make this an interesting place to explore each weekend. Most of the things here are cheap clothes, household items, perfumes and the like. But there are some good deals on dust-collectors you might actually want too.

THE BEST DAY SPAS

THE BATHHOUSE | THEhotel, 3950 Las Vegas Blvd S (at Mandalay Bay), Strip, T 877.632.9636, MAP C2 17 A showcase for avant design and luxurious treatments, the Bathhouse is positioning itself as the most stylish spa on the Strip. The decor, by the New York firm Richardson Sadeki, is stark and elegant, built with dark slate and a watery theme that runs throughout. Signature treatments are the crème brulée body wrap, a wasabi bath, and a mist spray-tanning unit that gives users a lasting tan in about 30 seconds. Of course they also offer massages, facials, and manicures and pedicures, along with scented steam rooms and numerous water pools.

CANYON RANCH SPACLUB | The Venetian, 3355 Las Vegas Blvd S (at Sands), Strip, T 702.414.3600, MAP F2 18 One of the largest and most awesome spas we've ever seen, Canyon Ranch is a respected place to work off last night's debauchery. Situated on the resort's fourth floor, signature services include the Mango Sugar Glo (conditioning body scrub, hydrotherapy tub immersion, full-body moisturizing), and Euphoria (candles, music, heated sage-infused face towels, aromatherapy scalp massage, warm botanical body mask, herbal bath and herb-infused oil massage). There are also gyms and weight rooms, therapeutic pools and a three-story rock-climbing wall.

ELEMIS SPA | Desert Passage, Aladdin/Planet Hollywood, 3667 Las Vegas Blvd S (at Harmon), Strip, T 866.935.3647, MAP E2 19 A large Moroccan-inspired spa, salon and fitness center, Elemis has the vague atmosphere of a Moorish retreat, with the aroma of mint tea and the whiff of exotic ritual. It's a very beautiful place, encompassing 35 private therapy rooms, six of which are designed for couples. Highlights of an extensive menu of pamperings are a Hawaiian four-hand massage, a coconut body rub and milk wrap, and a jasmine flower bath for two. They also have the only sensory-deprivation tank in Las Vegas.

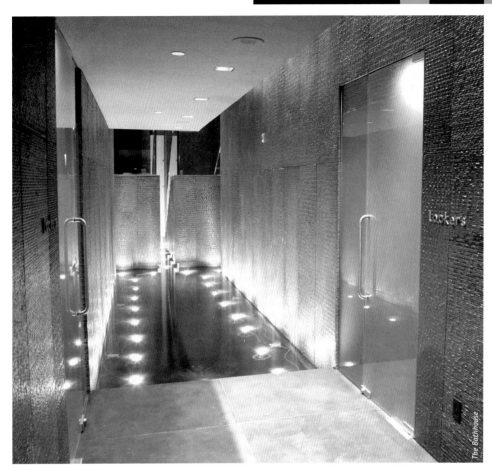

The Bathhouse

MGM Grand Spa | MGM Grand, 3799 Las Vegas Blvd S (at Tropicana), Strip, T 702.891.3077, MAP **D2** 20 Comfortable, soothing and very well decorated, the Spa is a wonderfully calm contrast to the craziness just outside the door. It's a large place with 30 treatment rooms, twin saunas, steam rooms and whirlpools, and an excellent fitness center. Pamperings for both men and women include the 55-minute Biodroga Triple C Treatment Special Facial, comprised of a papaya/pineapple exfoliant, extraction, steam, face massage, mask, and hot towel scented with rosemary and peppermint; and the Dreaming Ritual, a head-to-toe experience inspired by Australia's Aboriginals. involving an incense smudging ceremony, a warm foot soak, body exfoliation, mud mask, scalp treatment and massage.

Paris Spa by Mandara | Paris Las Vegas, 3655 Las Vegas Blvd S (at Harmon), Strip, T 702.946.4366, MAP **E2** 21 Although you can find Mandara spas all over the world, it's one luxury that you can't even get in the real Paris. In Vegas, it's one of the city's most luxurious places, with thirty treatment rooms and six grande suites featuring oversized whirlpool baths, double-headed showers and private lounges. Secreted on the hotel's second floor, the vibe is suitably tranquil and vaguely French Polynesian with copious fragrant flowers. Signature treatments include the Caviar Facial and Paris Pour Les Amoureux, a romantic package for *deux*.

10 Things to Buy

What: Dice Clock — Next to fuzzy dice, these timers are the quintessential lowbrow Las Vegas souvenir gift. Plus, your friends will never be late again.
Where: Bonanza Gift Shop

What: Siegfried & Roy Calendar — These corny calendars never made our list until Roy had an unfortunate run-in with a white tiger and was literally dragged offstage for the last time. Call it post-modern ironic kitsch.
Where: Siegfried & Roy Boutique

What: Las Vegas T-Shirt — Just walk down the Strip and you'll see signs offering 3 for $10; a deal that's hard to pass up when looking for some commemorabilia to bring home to the wife.
Where: On the Strip

What: Head-To-Toe Dealer's Uniform — Arrive to your weekly poker night in style, wearing a full-on Vegas dealer's outfit. And all your friends came back from Vegas with is a pack of used casino playing cards.
Where: Dealers Room Casino Clothiers

What: Elvis Glasses With Fake Sideburns Attached — Put these beauties on, perfect the Elvis sneer and you're ready for your Vegas close up. Even better with a gold lamé jumpsuit and a pair of blue suede shoes.
Where: Elvis-A-Rama Museum Shop

What: How to Beat the Slots Book — Strange but true: there is a system to playing slots, and every other game in Vegas for that matter. And as you know, you should bet with your head, not over it.
Where: Gamblers Book Club

What: Your Own Slot Machine — When you're ready to set up your own home casino this is the place to go. Tweak the wheels, show your friends, and soon you'll be able to tell your boss to you-know-what.
Where: Gamblers General Store

What: Liberace Refrigerator Magnets — What else can prove to your visitors and friends what good taste you have than a handful of these hard-to-find style markers?
Where: Liberace Museum Gift Shop

What: Showgirl Feather Headdress — Now you can prance around your living room just like a real starlet. Don one of these outlandish headdresses made of the finest genuine feathers and become the showgirl of your dreams.
Where: Rainbow Feather Company

What: Stripper-Type Breakaway Panties — We love stripping. But it's always difficult to step out of our panties without stumbling a bit. A little Velcro does the trick just like all the pros. Now all you need is a pole in your living room.
Where: Strings by Judith

55 Degrees Wine + Design

55 Degrees Wine + Design

Mandalay Place, 3950 Las Vegas Blvd S (at Mandalay Bay), Strip

T 702.632.9355 MAP C2 22

Constructed from steel, zebrawood, glass and resin, and more postmodern chic than any wine store we've ever seen, 55 Degrees stocks some 2,000 labels, ranging from $10 Spanish discoveries to more than $4,000 for a 1961 Chateau Latour. And flat screen PC tablets enable customers to access the store's inventory. There's an avant little tasting bar too. And we love those cool air-cushioned wine carriers.

Adult Superstore

3850 W Tropicana Ave (at Valley View), West Side

T 702.798.0144 MAP D1 23

This bi-level store is fully-stocked with high quality "literature," plus toys, gear and even novelty items all related to that thing you wanted to know about but were afraid to ask. And five-knuckle-shufflers are catered to with a substantial video arcade where you can try before you buy.

Agent Provocateur

Caesars Forum Shops, 3500 Las Vegas Blvd S (at Flamingo), Strip

T 702.696.7174 MAP E2 24

This London-based shop for sexy underthings would make Victoria blush. Classic ranges include bras and knickers, augmented by stockings, leather goods and footwear. Bellybutton chains, ankle bracelets, candles, soaps and perfumes too.

Albion Book Company

2466 E Desert Inn Rd (at Eastern), East Side

T 702.792.9554 MAP G2 25

There's not a whole hell of a lot of competition for used books in the vacuous wasteland of Vegas but, with more than 100,000 pre-read titles, Albion would be considered a damn good book shop just about anywhere. Prices are excellent and there's even some deals to be had in the rare-book room. It's in the Von's shopping center.

Big B's CDs & Records

Antique Mall

1495 E Flamingo Rd (at Algonquin), East Side

T 702.270.9910 MAP L2 [26]

Dealer Cheleen Morgan opened this 80-vendor mall a few years ago. There's lots of variety here, encompassing antiques and collectibles from cheap to chic. We especially like the specialty furniture that's hard to find elsewhere.

Antiques at the Market

6663 S Eastern Ave (at Sunset), East Side

T 702.307.3960 MAP K2 [27]

Nearly 70 dealers show their wares in this brick warehouse set back from the road behind a flower market. Look for everything from jewelry, clothing and furniture to books, toys and collectibles... all low- to no-brow.

The Art of Shaving

Mandalay Place, 3950 Las Vegas Blvd S (at Mandalay Bay), Strip

T 702.632.9355 MAP C2 [28]

The Art Of Shaving has an extensive collection of shaving creams, balms, oils, hair care and skincare products. What gets it mention here is the fact that it also offers the best hot towel shaves in town—perhaps anywhere; a traditional straightedge shave that includes a face and neck massage and hot aromatherapy towels. It's a genuine treat that every hedonist should be lucky enough to enjoy, and will make women wish they had facial hair.

The Attic

1018 S Main St (at Charleston), Downtown

T 702.388.4088 MAP I1 [29]

When you're trolling around town for cool retro duds, there is no better place to look than this two-story used clothing emporium. Nothing here is a steal, but you pay for good quality that ranges from 1950s dresses and stylish shoes to authentic Western wear, accessories and oddities that find there way into many local fashion shoots. There's some cool furniture too. Strangely, it costs a buck to get in, but they'll deduct it off any purchase.

Bare Essentials

4029 W Sahara Ave (at Valley View), West Side

T 702.247.4711 MAP A1 [30]

Local strippers gravitate to this clean and well-lighted strip mall shop selling all manner of slutwear, including belted lycra

booty shorts, sheer neon micro-dresses, break-away panties and the world's smallest G-string. Men are catered to with swimwear and thongs that include the custom-designed Whopper (and the Super Whopper).

Barnes & Noble

3860 Maryland Pkwy (at Twain), East Side

T 702.734.2900 MAP L1 31

2191 N Rainbow Blvd (at Lake Mead), Northwest

T 702.631.1775 MAP B1 32

567 N Stephanie St (at Sunset), Henderson

T 702.434.1533 MAP K2 33

America's largest bookstore chain has three outposts in Vegas offering America's greatest hits and trademark bright comfort. There's a good selection of discount books, an enormous magazine rack, a cozy cafe and a large area for music CDs and computer software.

Bass Pro Shops

Silverton Hotel, 8200 Industrial Rd (at Blue Diamond), Southwest

T 702.730.5200 MAP C1 34

Anglers, hunters and other animal lovers are catered to at this shop for the great outdoorsman (and woman). It's a huge space selling everything from clothing and lures to boats and golf gear. There's even an on-site rock climbing wall, archery and pistol ranges, and a huge fish-filled aquarium in which you can practice your cast.

Big B's CDs & Records

4761 S Maryland Pkwy (at Tropicana), East Side

T 702.732.4433 MAP K1 35

Big B's is a great place for used CDs because it stocks thousands of discs sold by starving university students from nearby UNLV. There's a strong electronica section and plenty of vinyl too, including tuff-to-find stuff you can try before you buy. This is also a fine place to look for new and used DVDs.

Blockbuster Video

4065 S Maryland Pkwy (at Flamingo), East Side

T 702.369.8105 MAP K1 36

3862 W Sahara Ave (at Valley View), West Side

T 702.364.1242 MAP A1 37

and other locations

America's mainstream rental chain can always be counted on to carry plenty of copies of the latest releases. Surprisingly, their foreign film selection is extensive as well. There are over 30 locations in Vegas, and this first one is closest to the Strip.

Bonanza Gift Shop

2460 Las Vegas Blvd S (at Sahara), Strip

T 702.385.7359 MAP G1 38

You've probably never seen more tacky crap in your life than the touristy schlock that fills the "World's Largest Souvenir Shop." But that's what makes this place great. Nothing about Bonanza is ironic; this place is real, man. Most of its customers really like fuzzy dice, blacklight art, snow globes and Vegas-emblazoned cup holders. Dice clocks are available in a variety of colors, shapes and sizes and make great gifts, as do the Roulette-wheel ashtrays, showgirl dolls, gold-colored Elvis glasses with fake sideburns attached, and liquor miniatures in ceramic bowling pins.

Borders Books, Music & Cafe

2323 S Decatur Blvd (at Sahara), West Side

T 702.258.0999 MAP A1 39

2190 N Rainbow Blvd (at Lake Mead), Northwest

T 702.638.7866 MAP B1 40

1445 W Sunset Rd (at Stephanie), Henderson

T 702.433.6222 MAP K2 41

Borders has a lot going for it, including an excellent selection of general books, a comfortable atmosphere to hang out in, and one of the best travel sections in the city.

British Foods, Inc.

Pioneer Shopping Sq., 3375 S Decatur Blvd (at Desert Inn), West Side

T 702.579.7777 MAP E1 42

You don't have to be a limey to enjoy the offerings in this food store for homesick Brits. Specialties include marmalade, sweets and teas, as well as frozen sausage rolls, black pudding and steak-and-kidney pies—all served up with the latest *Sunday Times.*

Buffalo Exchange

Pioneer Center, 4110 S Maryland Pkwy (at Flamingo), East Side

T 702.791.3960 MAP L1 43

From bowling shirts and prom dresses to stylish slippers and funky ties, there's always something cool at Buffalo Exchange. The mood here is quite retro, which means it's a great place to find a Rat Pack wardrobe for waltzing into the Sahara in style.

Ca'd'Oro

Venetian Grand Canal Shoppes, 3355 Las Vegas Blvd S (at Sands), Strip

T 702.696.0080 MAP F2 44

There are lots of great jewelry shops in Vegas, but this palace of gold is particularly fetching for it's authentic

imports that include pieces from Damiani and Charriol, as well as fine watches, hand-blown Murano glass chandeliers, beautiful custom tiles, Katherine Baumann clutches and lots more.

Carolina Herrera

Caesars Forum Shops, 3500 Las Vegas Blvd S (at Flamingo), Strip

T 702.893.4800 MAP E2 45

Herrera's third American store is home to the designer's secondary label, CH Carolina Herrera, a collection for men and women that includes everything from cotton shirts and hand-tailored suits to glam evening wear. Snazzy accessories include handbags and other leather goods, neckties, scarves and shoes.

Casey's Cameras

Liberace Plaza, 1550 E Tropicana Ave (at Spencer), East Side

T 702.736.0890 | CLOSED SUN MAP K2 46

This is where the city's professional photographers purchase their equipment. It's a vast store which sells almost every brand of digital and 35mm camera, plus a full range of video and other filmmaking equipment, from lighting to color processors. Casey's is also a good place to buy film in bulk at very low prices.

Chanel

Via Bellagio, 3600 Las Vegas Blvd S (at Flamingo), Strip

T 702.765.5505 MAP E2 47

You know this brand, and all the usual Chanel accessories are here. But what earns this boutique special mention from us are the one-of-a-kind items sold here that you can't get in Paris or New York: like Priscilla Presley's diamond-and-sapphire necklace for just $270,000.

Circuit City

4860 S Eastern Ave (at Tropicana), East Side

T 702.898.0500 MAP K2 48

5055 W Sahara Ave (at Decatur), West Side

T 702.367.9700 MAP A1 49

and other locations

One of the largest electronics chain stores in the West, this all-purpose megastore is a great place for name-brand audio and video. They've got a great selection of blank tapes and CDs too.

Cuba Libre

Hard Rock Hotel, 4455 Paradise Rd (at Harmon), East Side

T 702.693.5000 MAP K1 50

There are several stinky cigar bars in town, but this tiny shop/lounge is tops for its handsome leather club chairs, youth-infected atmosphere and huge selection of stogies. Portraits of Fidel and Che hang on the walls, but unfortunately, that's as close to Cuba as Cuba Libre gets.

Davante

Caesars Forum Shops, 3500 Las Vegas Blvd S (at Flamingo), Strip

T 702.737.8585 MAP E2 51

7866 W Sahara Ave (at Naples), West Side

T 702.798.8638 MAP A1 52

Davante is one of the coolest places in the city for Oliver Peoples, Matsuda, Kisura and other dandy frames. The store is beautiful (as are the assistants), and there's often an optometrist on hand to match your lenses.

Dead Poet Books

3858 W Sahara Ave (at Valley View), West Side

T 702.227.4070 MAP A1 53

From Adams to Zola, this fine shop stocks a full range of used books in most every genre imaginable. We especially like their small selection on Western Americana (including Vegas, of course), plus books-on-tape for the drive back to LA.

Dealers Room Casino Clothiers

4465 W Flamingo Rd (at Arville), West Side

T 702.362.7980 MAP E1 [54]

3507 S Maryland Pkwy (at Dumont), East Side

T 702.732.3932 MAP L1 [55]

Your friends think they're so cool, coming home from Vegas with authentic casino playing cards or professional-quality chips. You take it one step further and return with a full dealer's outfit: white shirt, black pants and an oversized orange bow tie. It works for wedding rentals too.

Don Pablo Cigar Co.

3025 Las Vegas Blvd S (at Stardust), Strip

T 702.369.1818 MAP F2 [56]

Located in the Gold Key Shops across from the Stardust, Don Pablo hand rolls cigars using top tobaccos and Cuban methods. And they'll prove it by offering you a free tour of the factory. Lots of smoking accessories are sold here too, including pipes and humidors.

Eddie Rodriguez

Fashion Show Mall, 3200 Las Vegas Blvd S (at Spring Mountain), Strip

T 702.369.0704 MAP F2 [57]

Think Men's Wearhouse with a Latin flair and you'll have a good idea of the offerings here. Expanded to a complete lifestyle collection, the brand now offers men's and women's clothing, shoes and home furnishings.

Elvis-A-Rama Museum Shop

3401 Industrial Rd (at Fashion Show), West Side

T 702.309.7200 MAP F2 [58]

This "king" of museum gift shops is cluttered with Elvis-related gifts that include everything from the silly to the ridiculous, like a swatch of pillowcase on which Elvis is said to have laid his head ($9), one of his credit cards ($3500), Elvis refrigerator magnets ($1-$4), Elvis fake-tattoos ($5) or Elvis mouse pads ($7). While you're at it, you may even wish to visit the museum's $3-million collection of cars and clothes.

FAO Schwarz

Caesars Forum Shops, 3500 Las Vegas Blvd S (at Flamingo), Strip

T 702.893.4800 MAP E2 [59]

Fronted by a giant Trojan horse (into which you can actually climb), this play palace is so awesome that most trophy children believe it when their parents tell them they're actually in a toy museum. It's a huge place, full of frivolity, that includes

Via Bellagio

house-sized stuffed animals, mini-Porsche automobiles that actually work, a wall of M&M chocolate candies sorted by color, and all manner of toys and games. Request entry into the private Best of FAO room where you can ogle ridiculously high-end toys, like a life-sized stuffed woolly mammoth ($6500) and a complete, kid-sized outdoor theater ($15,000).

Frederick's of Hollywood

Fashion Show Mall, 3200 Las Vegas Blvd S (at Spring Mountain), Strip

T 702.893.9001 MAP F2 [60]

The underwear maker to some of the best-undressed mistresses in Vegas, Frederick's has been well known to high-powered Hollywood executives for over half a century. Silk panties, string bikinis, naughty Marabou baby dolls... it's what our au pair will be wearing this summer.

Fry's Electronics

6845 Las Vegas Blvd S (at US 215), South

T 702.932.1400 MAP C2 [61]

You probably didn't come to Vegas to buy a new washing machine, but if you find yourself in need of a quick camera, laptop, phone accessory or blank CDs, Fry's is your store. Great prices and extensive stock make this place one of the only sure bets in Vegas.

Gamblers Book Club

620 S 11th St (at Charleston), Downtown

T 702.382.7555 | CLOSED SUN MAP I2 62

The largest and best bookshop of its kind in the world, Gamblers is a specialized paradise in which you can learn how to beat the slots and find those elusive copies of *Robbing the One-Armed Bandits* by Charles Lund and *Caro's Book of Tells* by Mike Caro. They've got poker software too, including our favorite, "Turbo Texas Hold'em."

Gamblers General Store

800 S Main St (at Hoover), Downtown

T 702.382.9903 MAP I1 63

When you're ready to set up your own home casino, this is your one-stop-shop for gaming hardware: slot and poker machines, roulette and blackjack tables, and dice and cards. The General Store is probably the largest gambling supply store in the world. A craps table goes for a cool $4000, but there are plenty of cheaper souvenirs too, like dice earrings, Vegas ties, a massive book selection, classic photos and an enormous variety of poker chips. Some states don't allow private ownership of slot machines, but we won't tell them if you won't.

Gypsy Caravan Antique Mall

1302 S Third St (at Colorado), West Side

T 702.868.3302 MAP H1 64

The caravan is eight railroad cottages, each painted red, white and blue and following a theme. One is filled with shabby chic antiques and furniture, another contains vintage clothing.

Ice Accessories

Caesars Forum Shops, 3500 Las Vegas Blvd S (at Flamingo), Strip

T 702.696.9700 MAP E2 65

Accessories are women's best friends. And Ice is full of friends. We love their dazzling hair clips and bands, stylish totes, statement-making costume jewelry, and cocktail rings from the likes of Konstantin, David Yurman, Isabelle Fiore and Lulu Guinness.

Il Prato

Venetian Grand Canal Shoppes, 3355 Las Vegas Blvd S (at Sands), Strip

T 702.733.1235 MAP F2 66

A pint-size shop for hand-crafted Venetian carnival masks and other little gifts from Veneto, like glass-tip quills, tooled-leather journals and wax-seal kits. Masks range from small ceramic ones to luxury papier-mâché headdresses. And they've got matching, hand-sewn costumes that include copper bustiers encrusted with Swarovski crystals, by designer Alfredo Lagia.

International Marketplace

5000 S Decatur Blvd (at Tropicana), West Side

T 702.889.2888 MAP D1 67

International Marketplace is a good place to know about when you need some cooking ingredients that are not strictly middle-American. We're talking Chinese, Japanese, Indonesian, Mexican, Italian and Mediterranean, to name but a few world cuisines that require ingrediants stocked here.

Jacqueline Jarrot

Desert Passage, 3663 Las Vegas Blvd S (at Harmon), Strip

T 702.731.3200 MAP E2 68

Women flock to this shop for up-market jewelry and handbags from some 300 designers, both known and not. Look for great

rings, necklaces and broaches from the likes of Francesco Biasia, Isabella Fiore, Miguel Ases, Vass Ludacer and Petro Zilla.

Judith Leiber Boutique

Caesars Forum Shops, 3500 Las Vegas Blvd S (at Flamingo), Strip

T 702.893.4800 MAP E2 69

No high-end accessory is more distinctively Las Vegas than a JL bag. They're not cheap, of course, but nowhere else has a rhinestone-studded purse shaped like the king of spades seemed more tasteful. We like this store for its unusual selection of high-end goods that you really can't get anywhere else.

Juicy Couture

Caesars Forum Shops, 3500 Las Vegas Blvd S (at Flamingo), Strip

T 702.893.4800 MAP E2 70

J-Lo wannabes pile into Juicy's first American store for the label's trademark terry apparel that includes best-selling sweat suits, bikini bottoms and zip jackets customized by embroidering your own name. Ribbed tanks, hot pink drawstring pants and velour hoodies are also hits with angels on-the-go.

Lee's Discount Liquor

3480 Flamingo Rd (at Pecos), East Side

T 702.458.5700 MAP L2 71

1780 S Rainbow Blvd (at Oakey), West Side

T 702.870.6300 MAP A1 72

and other locations

The name doesn't lie, because Lee's offers some of the best prices around, matched by a truly unbeatable number of bottles. Beer? One of the state's largest selections of microbrews is here, along with a full roster of imports. "T'kill-ya" you say? They've got over 100 brands for stocking the limo bar. There's even a good selection of wine, plus porno mags by the register.

Leonard's Wide Shoes

3999 Las Vegas Blvd S (at Four Seasons), Strip

T 702.895.9993 MAP C2 73

Las Vegas is full of big people. And people with wide feet. And that's just about all you need to know about this bigfoot mecca, home of the world's widest shoes. Needless to say, this is a destination store for freaks wearing wide or double-wide kickers. And they have a huge selection. According to owner Leonard Lipkin, lots of customers plan their Vegas vacations around their need for new shoes.

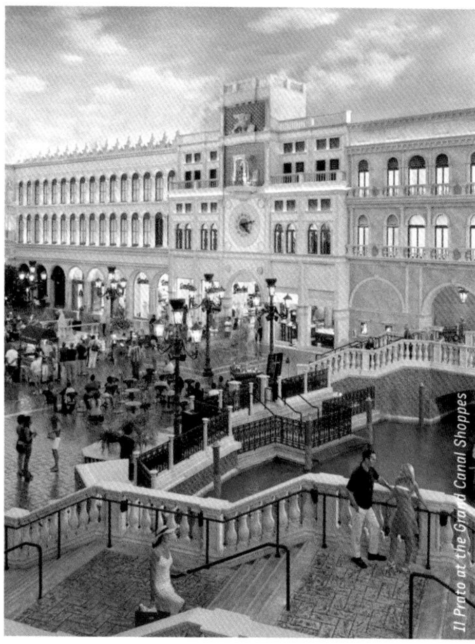

Il Prato at the Grand Canal Shoppes

Liberace Museum Gift Shop

1775 E Tropicana Ave (at Spencer), East Side

T 702.798.5595 MAP K2 74

Vegas glitz (read: kitsch) is the theme running through many of our gift store picks, but nowhere is this aesthetic more stark than in the gift shop of Mr. Showmanship. Skip the CDs and head straight for the seediest, like miniature pianos, crystal candelabra, chandeliers, refrigerator magnets, and clothing with little keyboard logos.

M&Ms World & Ethel M. Chocolates

Showcase Mall, 3785 Las Vegas Blvd S (at Tropicana), Strip

T 702.736.7611 MAP D2 75

If there was ever a job assignment to make travel writers consider changing professions, it's this four-story candy store that dares to call itself a museum. Picture us, adults with college degrees, wandering around diligently taking notes about M&M-themed coffee mugs, beanbags, crayons, keychains, lunchboxes and calculators, while sweating, wild-eyed shoppers race from display to display. There's even a silly 3D short film (in which Red loses his "M" at the poker table) to assail your by-now itchy eyes. **Avant-Guide Fun Fact**: The last American citizen named "Ethel" died in 1981.

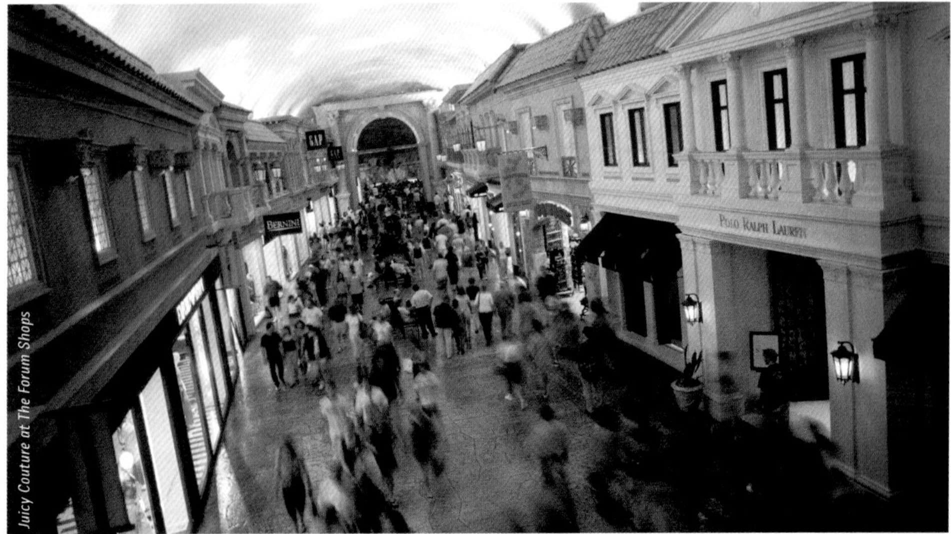

Juicy Couture at The Forum Shops

Merlin's Mystic Shop

Excalibur, 3850 Las Vegas Blvd S (at Tropicana), Strip

T 702.597.7251 — MAP D2 76

You forgot your rabbit's foot at home and are in dire need of a replacement amulet before you hit the tables. Merlin's comes to the rescue with a diverse collection of crystals and lucky charms. On your return visit, you can blow your winnings on strange things as diverse as glow-in-the-dark stickers and a toilet-brush holder in the shape of a skull.

Mr. Bill's Pipe & Tobacco

4441 W Flamingo Rd (at Arville), West Side

T 702.221.9771 — MAP E1 77

4510 E Charleston Blvd (at Lamb), Northeast

T 702.459.3400 — MAP I2 78

And other locations

If you're on the pipe, then Mr. Bill is your man, stocking lots of varieties of loose tobacco, as well as one of the city's best cigar selections, stored in walk-in humidors. Accessories include cool lighters and smokers' jewelry too. Smokers' jewelry?!

Musette

Mandalay Place, 3950 Las Vegas Blvd S (at Mandalay Bay), Strip

T 702.632.9333 — MAP C2 79

A chic boutique for women with fashion sense that's more Los Angeles than Las Vegas, Musette offers a well-edited selection of clothes and accessories from labels like Dolce & Gabbana, Earl Jean, Juicy Couture and Three Dots.

Nanette Lepore

Caesars Forum Shops, 3500 Las Vegas Blvd S (at Flamingo), Strip

T 702.893.9704 — MAP E2 80

Ultra feminine and totally chic, Nanette Lepore creates fabulous clothes for sophisticated urbanites. Look for flirty dresses, perfectly-cut jackets and lots of other clothes for women that were inspired by combing through vintage shops around the world.

Neiman Marcus

Fashion Show Mall, 3200 Las Vegas Blvd S (at Spring Mountain), Strip

T 702.731.3636 — MAP F2 81

One of the anchors of the Fashion Show Mall, this multi-level department store is well stocked with moderate to luxury fashions for men, women and children. The stock is broad, ranging from classics by Ermenegildo Zegna, Hugo Boss and Brioni, to contemporaries by Roberto Cavalli, Gucci and Paul Smith. And the women's shoe department is one of the best in town.

Nicolas & Osvaldo Antiques

2020 E Charleston Blvd (at Eastern), East Side

T 702.386.0238 | CLOSED SUN-MON — MAP I2 82

When you're looking for upmarket Vegas style, you can do no better than this small antiques shop specializing in

Neiman Marcus at Fashion Show Mall

estate pieces. Think bronze sculptures, 18th and 19th century furniture, art glass and American pottery. And amazingly, N&O has been around for over three decades.

Oculus

Caesars Appian Way Shops, 3500 Las Vegas Blvd S (at Flamingo), Strip

702.731.4850 MAP E2 83

Probably the coolest place in the city for Oliver Peoples, Matsuda, Kisura and other dandy frames. The shop will sell you glasses to go, or they will fit yours with replacement lenses on the premises.

Opportunity Village

921 S Main St (at Charlston), Downtown

702.383.1082 MAP I1 84

A decent selection of everything anyone might give away—clothing, toys, housewares, books—all at rock-bottom prices. The "opportunity" here is not just lucking out on a terrific find, it's providing jobs and money to people with disabilities.

Paiute Tribal Smoke Shop

1225 N Main St (at Paiute), Northeast

702.387.6433 MAP J2 85

Not only does Paiute have some of the lowest prices in Vegas, but they also have an awesome selection of smokes that includes plenty of obscure brands. There's cigars (Partagas, Macanudo, Hoyo de Monterey) and pipe tobacco too. And because it's a tribal smoke shop, taxes go to the Paiute Nation rather than the state of Nevada. Best of all, there's drive-thru service!

Paradise Electro Stimulations

1509 W Oakey Blvd (at Western), West Side

702.474.2991 MAP H1 86

Secreted behind a very plain facade lies the retail showroom of Paradise Electro Stimulations, a specialist sex-machine maker creating some of the most unusual toys anywhere. If you think you've seen it all, visit this turbo-charged vibrator store that's known for a unique type of stimulation device that uses electrical impulses rather than simple vibrations to make you quiver. They come in all shapes and sizes and our friend Patricia swears they really work a charm.

Rainbow Feather Company

1036 S Main St (at Boulder), Downtown

702.598.0988 MAP I1 87

File this one under Wacky Las Vegas: an entire retail store devoted to every commercially available feather in the world. Sure, showgirls shop here, but so does anyone looking for genuine boas, jewelry and fans fashioned from some of the most colorful feathers anywhere. You can even stuff a pillow: Turkey, chicken, goose, duck, pheasant, ostrich and peacock plumage is sold by the pound.

Unica Home

Ray's Beaver Bag

727 Las Vegas Blvd S (at Charleston), Downtown

T 702.386.8746 MAP I2 88

Daniel Boone and the Unabomber would both love this totally wacky one-of-a-kind trading post for foxtail caps, beeswax candles, buffalo jerky and moose milk. Outfitting hard-core mountain men and survivalists, the shop looks like a film set with front loading guns, Hudson Bay blankets, cast iron belt buckles, animal pelts and beaded elk-skin pipe bags made by Native American injuns.

The Reading Room

Mandalay Place, 3950 Las Vegas Blvd S (at Mandalay Bay), Strip

T 702.632.9333 MAP C2 89

First the Strip gets a fine art gallery. And now a high-end bookstore? What is happening to lowbrow Las Vegas? This tiny, independently owned bookshop—in which three is truly a crowd—has quickly become an unlikely, and somewhat ironic, cultural center stocking art books, fiction and nonfiction, and hosting regular readings.

Record City

4555 E Charleston Blvd (at Lamb), East Side

T 702.457.8626 MAP I2 90

300 E Sahara Ave (at Santa Clara), East Side

T 702.452.7719 MAP G1 91

and other locations

You wouldn't know it from the outside, but this excellent shop carries a huge selection of the best-priced used CDs in the city. They've got everything, including LPs and cassettes, and few titles ever top $8.

Red Rooster Antique Mall

307 W Charleston Blvd (at Martin Luther King), Northwest

T 702.382.0067 MAP I1 92

We love this place for its enormous selection of well-chosen antiques, furniture, collectibles and one-of-a-kind items. It's an appropriately dusty spot with some 50 stalls offering lots of treasures hidden amongst the junk. Red Rooster is housed in a former bottling plant near I-15.

Ripa di Monti

Venetian Grand Canal Shoppes, 3355 Las Vegas Blvd S (at Sands), Strip

T 702.733.1004 MAP F2 93

Ripa di Monti is known for really nice Venetian art-glass creations ranging from glass-bead necklaces and earrings to stunning vases. Nothing is cheap.

Roberto Cavalli

Caesars Forum Shops, 3500 Las Vegas Blvd S (at Flamingo), Strip

T 702.893.0369 MAP E2 94

1960s Italian pimp sensibility informs the exotic prints and bold colors of Cavalli's collections. It's perfect for Las Vegas. Look for sex-reeking designs for men and women made with leather and fur. Think snake aviator sunglasses, chiffon baby-doll dresses, tiger-print jeans and billowy pirate-style shirts.

Saks Fifth Avenue

Fashion Show Mall, 3200 Las Vegas Blvd S (at Spring Mountain), Strip

T 702.733.8300 MAP F2 95

Saks is a great store. They have terrific selections of women's designer wear (Armani, Gucci, Prada, Yves Saint Laurent) and excellent, if conservative, men's offerings. The shoe department is legendary, and prices are not too far out of this world.

Savers Thrift Shop

3145 E Tropicana Ave (at McLeod), East Side

T 702.433.1402 MAP K2 96

5130 W Spring Mountain Rd (at Decatur), West Side

T 702.220.7350 MAP E1 97

and other locations

Thrifting is not great in Vegas, primarily because most of the people donating stuff have closets full of crap. That said, this mini-chain is the very best shop of its kind in town. There is always something good to be found here and because the

inventory is extremely well organized, shopping is a breeze. The shops are strongest in clothing, but housewares, jewelry and furniture are also on offer.

Scoop NYC

Caesars Forum Shops, 3500 Las Vegas Blvd S (at Flamingo), Strip

T 702.734.0026 — MAP E2 98

This New York fashion sensation brings its "ultimate closet" concept to Vegas with this trendy store selling must-have staples: low-rise cords, luxe velvet fitted jackets, pencil skirts, Fair Isle sweaters, embroidered velvet scarves and the latest Jimmy Choos.

Serges Showgirl Wigs

953 E Sahara Ave (at Maryland), East Side

T 702.732.1015 | CLOSED SUN — MAP G1 99

Showgirl or not, Serges is the place to get big hair for stage or street. They claim to be the world's largest rug retailer and it may be true. There are thousands of synthetic and natural pieces to choose from.

Sheplers Western Store

4700 W Sahara Ave (at Decatur), West Side

T 702.258.2000 — MAP A1 100

3025 E Tropicana Ave (at McLeod), East Side

T 702.898.3000 — MAP K2 101

When you're achy-breaking for real cowgirl clothes, Sheplers is the authentic spot in Vegas to find everything from scarves and hats to boots and chaps. The aesthetic here is not city slicker, it's the real McCoy.

Showcase Slots & Antiquities

4305 S Industrial Rd (at Flamingo), West Side

T 702.740.5722 — MAP E2 102

Antique slot machines can be beautiful works of art, and some of the best masterpieces are sold here, along with some original Wurlitzer jukeboxes, Coca-Cola dispensers and other utilitarian Americana. Even if you're not buying, this place doubles as the finest museum of its kind in Vegas. The store is located directly behind the Bellagio.

Siegfried & Roy Boutique

The Mirage, 3400 Las Vegas Blvd S (at Spring Mountain), Strip

T 702.791.7111 — MAP F2 103

There are lots of magic shops in Vegas selling floating this and disappearing that. But the gift store attached to Siegfried & Roy's former theater trumps them all with magical merchandise like white tiger plush toys, S&R pajamas, and even the same boxer shorts the boys wear.

Slightly Sinful

1232 Las Vegas Blvd S (at Park Paseo), Strip

702.387.1006 — MAP H1 104

Couples who like to play games are the mainstay of this bedroom fantasy shop selling ersatz outfits for schoolgirls, nurses, maids and the like. Other popular items are corsets in satin and leather, crotchless underwear, and bras with holes cut into the cups. Go get 'em tiger.

Strings by Judith

4970 Arville St (at Tropicana), West Side

T 702.873.7820 — MAP D1 105

Ever wonder where strippers buy their clothes? In the world of pole dancing, this place is legendary for its huge lines of string bikinis, sheer nylon dresses, micro shorts, glittery leggings and other sexy stagewear, some designed by Judith herself. Appropriately, it's located in a little strip mall.

Superpawn

1611 Las Vegas Blvd S (at 3rd), Downtown

T 702.642.1133 — MAP H1 106

2300 E Charleston Blvd (at Fremont), East Side

T 702.477.3040 — MAP I2 107

3270 S Valley View Blvd (at Desert Inn) West Side

T 702.364.1103 — MAP F1 108

and other locations

Before paying top prices at some electronics superstore, pop into this pawn shop where you just might find what you're looking for at cents on the dollar. Even if you don't, it's a fascinating, über-Vegas cultural experience. Super cheap CDs too.

Talulah G

Fashion Show Mall, 3200 Las Vegas Blvd S (at Spring Mountain), Strip

T 702.737.6000 — MAP F2 109

Talulah G is a burgeoning boutique offering designer clothing and accessories from designers such as Michael Stars, Seven for All Mankind, Paper Denim and Cloth, and Chloe. Owner Meital Grantz's aesthetic rides the line between edgy and classic, featuring styles that are trendy but seem to also have longevity.

Thriller Clothing Company

855 E Twain Ave (at Swenson), East Side

T 702.732.2780 MAP L1 110

Custom made or off-the-rack, Thriller creates and sells some of the most provocative stage- and streetwear in Vegas. And that's saying a lot. They also carry some of the trendiest labels from LA and NYC, including shoes and accessories. And prices are surprisingly light.

Tiffany & Co.

Via Bellagio, 3600 Las Vegas Blvd S (at Flamingo), Strip

T 702.693.7111 MAP E2 111

It's good to know about Tiffany when you need to celebrate or say "I'm sorry." There's a great selection of baubles here, and everything looks that much better when presented in the store's trademark sea-blue packaging. This is the store to visit after hitting it big on Megabucks.

Toe Rings and Foot Things

Holiday Inn Boardwalk, 3750 Las Vegas Blvd S (at Harmon), Strip

T 702.735.2400 MAP D2 112

Local strippers flock to this Tacky 'R Us shop for the largest selection of toe bands in sterling silver and 14-karat gold. Other body jewelry includes foot beads and ankle bracelets in all sizes. Honestly, we've never seen anything like this place anywhere.

Tower Records

4580 W Sahara Ave (at Decatur), West Side

T 702.364.2500 MAP A1 113

The best of the music chain stores stocks plenty of indie stuff along with major labels. It's a huge space, with a separate area for classical, plus some good deals on new releases, listening stations and a bargain bin.

Unica Home

7540 S Industrial Rd (at Eldorado), East Side

T 702.616.9280 MAP C1 114

The most avant homeware store in Vegas, Unica is a great place to browse for everything from barware and furniture to games, pet accessories, soap, watches and artwork. We've seen Boroullec lounge chairs, hand-blown glass perfume bottles, Philippe Starck beds, Tonsil toothbrush holders, Mensa card games for kids, Alessi Mami pots, and ice bat the uglydoll. It's situated across I-15 from the Premium Outlet Mall.

Village Meat & Wine

Village East Plaza, 5025 S Eastern Ave (at Tropicana), East Side

T 702.736.7575 | CLOSED SUN-MON MAP K2 115

Whether you're throwing a party in your suite or just planning a romantic snuggle, Village Meat and Wine comes to the gourmet's rescue with caviar, pâté, fine cheeses and wines from around the world.

Virgin Megastore

Caesars Forum Shops, 3500 Las Vegas Blvd S (at Flamingo), Strip

T 702.696.7100 MAP E2 116

You could easily spend hours combing through CDs, videos and CD-ROMs in this expansive complex. There's a decent indies section and lots of listening booths to hear new music. But beware the greasy headphones.

Vosges Haut Chocolat

Caesars Forum Shops, 3500 Las Vegas Blvd S (at Flamingo), Strip

T 702.893.4800 MAP E2 117

Vosges scours the world for ingredients for their exotic truffles, each of which come with a story and instructions on how to eat them correctly. The Vincent Gallo, for example, is draped in bittersweet chocolate and contains Italian taleggio cheese, organic walnuts, and Tahitian vanilla beans.

Wild Oats Community Market

7250 W Lake Mead Blvd (at Tenaya), Northwest

T 702.942.1500 MAP B1 118

Vegas' best and biggest healthist supermarket stocks a terrific selection of organic produce, natural foods, plus a salad bar, noodle bar, sandwiches and pizza-by-the-slice. Body care products and homeopathic medicines too.

The Wine Cellar & Tasting Room

Rio, 3700 W Flamingo Rd (at Valley View), West Side

T 702.247.7962 MAP E1 119

This retail arm of the Rio hotel's famous Tasting Room easily stocks the best selection of wine in the city (50,000 bottles!). There's always a resident sommelier on hand to assist you, even if you're only buying a $7 bottle of plunk. Best of all, many of the bottles are available by the glass, so you can try before you buy.

Map	Area	Shop	Address	Phone	Closed	Design Driven	Celebrity Clientele	Only in Las Vegas
		FASHION & BEAUTY						
		Accessories						
I1 29	Downtown	The Attic	1018 S Main St	702.388.4088				★
I1 87	Downtown	Rainbow Feather Company	1036 South Main St	702.598.0988			★	★
K2 101	East Side	Sheplers Western Store	3025 E Tropicana Ave	702.898.3000				
L1 110	East Side	Thriller Clothing Company	855 E Twain Ave	702.732.2780				
F2 44	Strip	Ca d'Oro	Venetian Grand Canal Shoppes	702.696.0080				★
E2 45	Strip	Carolina Herrera	Caesars Forum Shops	702.893.4800		★		
E2 47	Strip	Chanel	Via Bellagio	702.765.5505		★		
E2 65	Strip	Ice Accessories	Caesars Forum Shops	702.696.9700			★	
E2 68	Strip	Jacqueline Jarrot	Desert Passage	702.731.3200				
E2 69	Strip	Judith Leiber Boutique	Caesars Forum Shops	702.893.4800				
C2 79	Strip	Musette	Mandalay Place	702.632.9333		★	★	
E2 80	Strip	Nanette Lepore	Caesars Forum Shops	702.893.9704		★		
E2 98	Strip	Scoop NYC	Caesars Forum Shops	702.734.0026		★		
100	West Side	Sheplers Western Store	4700 W Sahara Ave	702.258.2000				
		Clothing—Basics						
L1 55	East Side	Dealers Room Casino Clothiers	3507 S Maryland Pkwy	702.732.3932				★
K2 101	East Side	Sheplers Western Store	3025 E Tropicana Ave	702.898.3000				
L1 110	East Side	Thriller Clothing Company	855 E Twain Ave	702.732.2780				
E2 70	Strip	Juicy Couture	Caesars Forum Shops	702.893.4800		★		
E1 54	West Side	Dealers Room Casino Clothiers	4465 W Flamingo Rd	702.362.7980				★
A1 100	West Side	Sheplers Western Store	4700 W Sahara Ave	702.258.2000				
		Clothing—Designer						
E2 45	Strip	Carolina Herrera	Caesars Forum Shops	702.893.4800		★		
F2 57	Strip	Eddie Rodriguez	Fashion Show Mall	702.369.0704				
E2 70	Strip	Juicy Couture	Caesars Forum Shops	702.893.4800		★		
E2 80	Strip	Nanette Lepore	Caesars Forum Shops	702.893.9704		★	★	
E2 94	Strip	Roberto Cavalli	Caesars Forum Shops	702.893.0369		★	★	
		Clothing—Multilabel Stores						
C2 79	Strip	Musette	Mandalay Place	702.632.9333		★	★	
E2 98	Strip	Scoop NYC	Caesars Forum Shops	702.734.0026		★		
F2 109	Strip	Talulah G	Fashion Show Mall	702.737.6000		★	★	

Map		Area	Shop	Address	Phone	Closed	Design Driven	Celebrity Clientele	Only in Las Vegas
			Clothing—Vintage & Thrift						
I1	29	Downtown	The Attic	1018 S Main St	702.388.4088				★
I1	84	Downtown	Opportunity Village	921 S Main St	702.383.1082				
L1	43	East Side	Buffalo Exchange	4110 S Maryland Pkwy	702.791.3960				
K2	96	East Side	Savers Thrift Shop	3145 E Tropicana Ave	702.433.1402				
H1	64	West Side	Gypsy Caravan Antique Mall	1302 S Third St	702.868.3302				★
E1	97	West Side	Savers Thrift Shop	5130 W Spring Mountain Rd	702.220.7350				
			Cosmetics, Fragrance & Grooming						
G1	99	East Side	Serges Showgirl Wigs	953 E Sahara Ave	702.732.1015	SU		★	★
C2	28	Strip	The Art of Shaving	Mandalay Place	702.632.9355		★		
E2	47	Strip	Chanel	Via Bellagio	702.765.5505		★	★	
			Department Stores						
F2	81	Strip	Neiman Marcus	Fashion Show Mall	702.731.3636				
F2	95	Strip	Saks Fifth Avenue	Fashion Show Mall	702.733.8300				
			Eyewear						
E2	51	Strip	Davante	Caesars Forum Shops	702.737.8585		★	★	
E2	83	Strip	Oculus	Caesars Appian Way Shops	702.731.4850		★	★	
A1	52	West Side	Davante	7866 W Sahara Ave	702.798.8638		★		
			Handbags						
F2	44	Strip	Ca d'Oro	Venetian Grand Canal Shoppes	702.696.0080		★		★
E2	68	Strip	Jacqueline Jarrot	Desert Passage	702.731.3200		★		
E2	69	Strip	Judith Leiber Boutique	Caesars Forum Shops	702.893.4800		★		
			Jewelry						
I1	87	Downtown	Rainbow Feather Company	1036 S Main St	702.598.0988			★	★
F2	44	Strip	Ca d'Oro	Venetian Grand Canal Shoppes	702.696.0080				★
E2	47	Strip	Chanel	Via Bellagio	702.765.5505		★	★	
E2	65	Strip	Ice Accessories	Caesars Forum Shops	702.696.9700		★		
E2	68	Strip	Jacqueline Jarrot	Desert Passage	702.731.3200		★		
F2	93	Strip	Ripa di Monti	Venetian Grand Canal Shoppes	702.733.1004		★		★
E2	111	Strip	Tiffany & Co.	Via Bellagio	702.693.7111		★		
D2	112	Strip	Toe Rings and Foot Things	Holiday Inn Boardwalk	702.735.2400				
			Lingerie						
E2	24	Strip	Agent Provocateur	Caesars Forum Shops	702.696.7174		★	★	

Map		Area	Shop	Address	Phone	Closed	Design Driven	Celebrity Clientele	Only in Las Vegas
F2	60	Strip	Frederick's of Hollywood	Fashion Show Mall	702.893.9001				
H1	104	Strip	Slightly Sinful	1232 Las Vegas Blvd S	702.387.1006				★
A1	30	West Side	Bare Essentials	4029 W Sahara Ave	702.247.4711				
D1	105	West Side	Strings by Judith	4970 Arville St	702.873.7820			★	★
			Shoes						
K2	101	East Side	Sheplers Western Store	3025 E Tropicana Ave	702.898.3000				
L1	110	East Side	Thriller Clothing Company	855 E Twain Ave	702.732.2780				
E2	45	Strip	Carolina Herrera	Caesars Forum Shops	702.893.4800				
C2	73	Strip	Leonard's Wide Shoes	3999 Las Vegas Blvd S	702.895.9993				★
A1	100	West Side	Sheplers Western Store	4700 W Sahara Ave	702.258.2000				
			HOME						
			Antiques & Auction Houses						
I2	88	Downtown	Ray's Beaver Bag	727 Las Vegas Blvd S	702.386.8746				★
L2	26	East Side	Antique Mall	1495 E Flamingo Rd	702.270.9910				★
K2	27	East Side	Antiques at the Market	6663 S Eastern Ave	702.307.3960				★
I2	[illegible]	East Side	Nicolás & Osvaldo Antiques	2020 E Charleston Blvd	702.386.0238	SU-MO			★
I1	92	Northwest	Red Rooster Antique Mall	307 W Charleston Blvd	702.382.0067				★
H1	64	West Side	Gypsy Caravan Antique Mall	1302 S Third St	702.868.3302				★
E2	102	West Side	Showcase Slots & Antiquities	4305 S Industrial Rd	702.740.5722			★	★
			Home Furnishings						
I1	63	Downtown	Gamblers General Store	800 S Main St	702.382.9903				★
C1	114	East Side	Unica Home	7540 S Industrial Rd	702.616.9280				
F2	93	Strip	Ripa di Monti	Venetian Grand Canal Shoppes	702.733.1004		★		★
			Lighting & Tableware						
C1	114	East Side	Unica Home	7540 S Industrial Rd	702.616.9280		★		
F2	44	Strip	Ca d'Oro	Venetian Grand Canal Shoppes	702.696.0080				★
			LIFESTYLE						
			Books & Magazines						
I2	62	Downtown	Gamblers Book Club	620 S 11th St	702.382.7555	SU			★
G2	25	East Side	Albion Book Company	2466 E Desert Inn Rd	702.792.9554				★
L1	31	East Side	Barnes & Noble	3860 Maryland Pkwy	702.734.2900				
K2	33	Henderson	Barnes & Noble	567 N Stephanie St	702.434.1533				
K2	41	Henderson	Borders Books & Music	1445 W Sunset Rd	702.433.6222				

Map	Area	Shop	Address	Phone	Closed	Design Driven	Celebrity Clientele	Only in Las Vegas
B1 32	Northwest	Barnes & Noble	2191 N Rainbow Blvd	702.631.1775				
B1 40	Northwest	Borders Books & Music	2190 N Rainbow Blvd	702.638.7866				
C2 89	Strip	The Reading Room	Mandalay Place	702.632.9333		★		★
A1 39	West Side	Borders Books & Music	2323 S Decatur Blvd	702.258.0999				
A1 53	West Side	Dead Poet Books	3858 W Sahara Ave	702.227.4070				★
		Cameras & Electronics						
H1 106	Downtown	Superpawn	1611 Las Vegas Blvd S	702.642.1133				★
K2 46	East Side	Casey's Cameras	1550 E Tropicana Ave	702.736.0890	SU			
K2 48	East Side	Circuit City	4860 S Eastern Ave	702.898.0500				
I2 107	East Side	Superpawn	2300 E Charleston Blvd	702.477.3040				★
C2 61	South	Fry's Electronics	6845 Las Vegas Blvd S	702.932.1400				
A1 49	West Side	Circuit City	5055 W Sahara Ave	702.367.9700				
F1 108	West Side	Superpawn	3270 S Valley View Blvd	702.364.1103				★
		Discount Outlets						
C2 3	Primm	Fashion Outlets Las Vegas	32100 Las Vegas Blvd S	702.874.1400				
C2 8	Strip	Las Vegas Outlet Center	7400 Las Vegas Blvd S	702.896.5599				
I1 9	West Side	Las Vegas Premium Outlets	875 S Grand Central Pkwy	702.474.7500				
		Food & Drink						
L2 71	East Side	Lee's Discount Liquor	3480 Flamingo Rd	702.458.5700				
K2 115	East Side	Village Meat & Wine	5025 S Eastern Ave	702.736.7575	SU			★
B1 118	Northwest	Wild Oats Community Market	7250 W Lake Mead Blvd	702.942.1500				
C2 22	Strip	55 Degrees Wine + Design	Mandalay Place	702.632.9355		★	★	★
D2 75	Strip	M&Ms World & Ethel M. Chocolates	3785 Las Vegas Blvd S	702.736.7611				★
E2 117	Strip	Vosges Haut Chocolat	Caesars Forum Shops	702.893.4800		★	★	
E1 42	West Side	British Foods, Inc.	3375 S Decatur Blvd	702.579.7777				★
D1 67	West Side	International Marketplace	5000 S Decatur Blvd	702.889.2888				
A1 72	West Side	Lee's Discount Liquor	1780 S Rainbow Blvd	702.870.6300				★
E1 119	West Side	The Wine Cellar & Tasting Room	Rio	702.247.7962			★	★
		Gifts, Novelties & Museum Stores						
I1 63	Downtown	Gamblers General Store	800 S Main St	702.382.9903				★
I2 88	Downtown	Ray's Beaver Bag	727 Las Vegas Blvd S	702.386.8746				★
K2 74	East Side	Liberace Museum Gift Shop	1775 E Tropicana Ave	702.798.5595				★
G1 99	East Side	Serges Showgirl Wigs	953 E Sahara Ave	702.732.1015	SU		★	★

Map	Area	Shop	Address	Phone	Closed	Design Driven	Celebrity Clientele	Only in Las Vegas
G1 [38]	Strip	Bonanza Gift Shop	2460 Las Vegas Blvd S	702.385.7359				★
F2 [44]	Strip	Ca d'Oro	Venetian Grand Canal Shoppes	702.696.0080				★
E2 [59]	Strip	FAO Schwarz	Caesars Forum Shops	702.893.4800			★	
F2 [66]	Strip	Il Prato	Venetian Grand Canal Shoppes	702.733.1235		★		★
D2 [75]	Strip	M&Ms World & Ethel M. Chocolates	3785 Las Vegas Blvd S	702.736.7611				★
D2 [76]	Strip	Merlin's Mystic Shop	Excalibur	702.597.7251				★
F2 [103]	Strip	Siegfried & Roy Boutique	The Mirage	702.791.7111				★
F2 [58]	West Side	Elvis-A-Rama Museum Shop	3401 Industrial Rd	702.309.7200				★
		Music & Video						
K1 [35]	East Side	Big B's CDs & Records	4761 S Maryland Pkwy	702.732.4433				★
L1 [36]	East Side	Blockbuster Video	4065 S Maryland Pkwy	702.369.8105				
I2 [90]	East Side	Record City	4555 E Charleston Blvd	702.457.8626				
G1 [91]	East Side	Record City	300 E Sahara Ave	702.452.7719				
E2 [116]	Strip	Virgin Megastore	Caesars Forum Shops	702.696.7100				
A1 [37]	West Side	Blockbuster Video	3862 W Sahara Ave	702.364.1242				
A1 [113]	West Side	Tower Records	4580 W Sahara Ave	702.364.2500				
		Malls						
I2 [12]	Downtown	Neonopolis	400 Fremont St	702.477.0470				
L1 [1]	East Side	Boulevard Mall	3528 S Maryland Pkwy	702.732.8949				
K2 [6]	Henderson	The Galleria at Sunset	1300 W Sunset Rd	702.434.0202				
C2 [3]	Primm	Fashion Outlets Las Vegas	32100 Las Vegas Blvd S	702.874.1400				
E2 [2]	Strip	Desert Passage	3663 Las Vegas Blvd S	888.800.8284				★
F2 [4]	Strip	Fashion Show Mall	3200 Las Vegas Blvd S	702.369.0704				
E2 [5]	Strip	The Forum Shops	Caesars Palace	702.893.4800		★		★
F2 [7]	Strip	The Grand Canal Shoppes	The Venetian	702.414.4500		★		★
C2 [8]	Strip	Las Vegas Outlet Center	7400 Las Vegas Blvd S	702.896.5599				
E2 [10]	Strip	Le Boulevard	Paris Las Vegas	702.739.4111				
C2 [11]	Strip	Mandalay Place	Mandalay Bay	702.632.9333				
E2 [13]	Strip	Via Bellagio	Bellagio	702.693.7111			★	
F2 [14]	Strip	Wynn Las Vegas Shops	Wynn Las Vegas	702.770.7100			★	
I1 [9]	West Side	Las Vegas Premium Outlets	875 S Grand Central Pkwy	702.474.7500				

Map	Area	Shop	Address	Phone	Closed	Design Driven	Celebrity Clientele	Only in Las Vegas
		Musical Instruments						
H1 106	Downtown	Superpawn	1611 Las Vegas Blvd S	702.642.1133				★
I2 107	East Side	Superpawn	2300 E Charleston Blvd	702.477.3040				★
F1 108	West Side	Superpawn	3270 S Valley View Blvd	702.364.1103				★
		Outdoor Markets						
J2 15	North	Broadacres Swap Meet	2930 N Las Vegas Blvd	702.642.3777	SU			
B1 16	West Side	Fantastic Indoor Swap Meet	1717 S Decatur Blvd	702.877.0087	MO–TH			
		Sex Shops						
H1 104	Strip	Slightly Sinful	1232 Las Vegas Blvd S	702.387.1006				★
D1 23	West Side	Adult Superstore	3850 W Tropicana Ave	702.798.0144				
H1 86	West Side	Paradise Electro Stimulations	1509 W Oakey Blvd	702.474.2991				★
		Spas						
C2 28	Strip	The Art of Shaving	Mandalay Place	702.632.9355		★		
F2 18	Strip	Canyon Ranch SpaClub	The Venetian	702.414.3600			★	
E2 19	Strip	Elemis Spa	Desert Passage	866.935.3647				
D2 20	Strip	MGM-Grand Spa	MGM Grand	702.891.3077				★
E2 21	Strip	Paris Spa by Mandara	Paris Las Vegas	702.946.4366				
C2 17	Strip	The Bathhouse	THEhotel	877.632.9636		★	★	★
		Sporting Goods						
I1 63	Downtown	Gamblers General Store	800 S Main St	702.382.9903				★
I2 88	Downtown	Ray's Beaver Bag	727 Las Vegas Blvd S	702.386.8746				★
C1 34	Southwest	Bass Pro Shops	8200 Industrial Rd	702.730.5200				
		Tobacco						
K1 50	East Side	Cuba Libre	Hard Rock Hotel	702.693.5000		★		
I2 78	Northeast	Mr. Bill's Pipe & Tobacco	4510 E Charleston Blvd	702.459.3400				
J2 85	Northeast	Paiute Tribal Smoke Shop	1225 N Main St	702.387.6433				★
F2 56	Strip	Don Pablo Cigar Co.	3025 Las Vegas Blvd S	702.369.1818				★
E1 77	West Side	Mr. Bill's Pipe & Tobacco	4441 W Flamingo Rd	702.221.9771				
		Toys						
E2 59	Strip	FAO Schwarz	Caesars Forum Shops	702.893.4800			★	
D2 76	Strip	Merlin's Mystic Shop	Excalibur	702.597.7251				
F2 103	Strip	Siegfried & Roy Boutique	The Mirage	702.791.7111				★

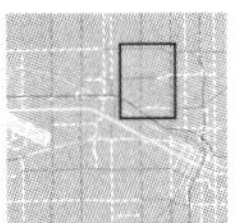

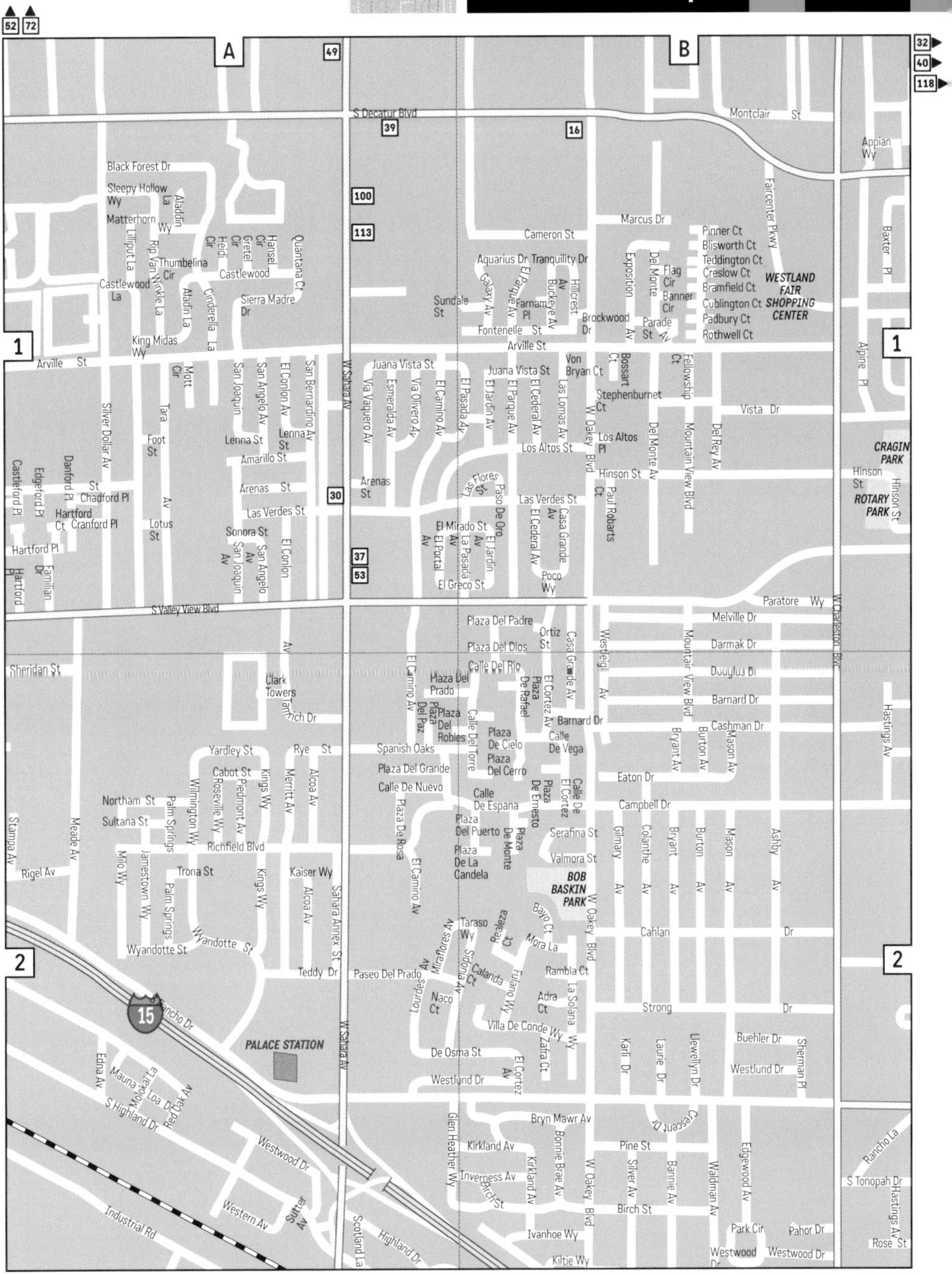

52 72

A
B
1
2

32 40 118

49 39 16 100 113 30 37 53

S Decatur Blvd
Montclair St
Appian Wy
Black Forest Dr
Sleepy Hollow Wy
Aladdin La
Matterhorn Wy
Lilliput La
Rip Van Winkle La
Thumbelina Cir
Heidi Cir
Gretel Cir
Hansel Cir
Quantana Ct
Castlewood
Castlewood La
Sierra Madre Dr
Aladin La
Cinderella La
King Midas Wy
Cameron St
Marcus Dr
Farcenter Pkwy
Baxter Pl
Pinner Ct
Blisworth Ct
Teddington Ct
Creslow Ct
Bramfield Ct
Cublington Ct
Padbury Ct
Rothwell Ct
WESTLAND FAIR SHOPPING CENTER
Aquarius Dr
Tranquility Dr
Galaxy Av
El Parque Av
Buckeye Av
Hillcrest
Exposition Av
Del Monte
Flag Cir
Banner Cir
Parade St
Sundale St
Farnam Pl
Fontenelle St
Brockwood Dr
Arville St
Alpine Pl
Juana Vista St
Von Bryan Ct
Bossart Ct
Fellowship Ct
Mott Cir
San Joaquin
San Angelo Av
El Conlon Av
San Bernardino Av
W Sahara Av
Via Vaquero Av
Esmeralda Av
Via Olivero Av
El Camino Av
El Pasada Av
El Jardin Av
El Parque Av
El Cederal Av
Las Lomas Av
Stephenburnet Ct
Vista Dr
Silver Dollar Av
Tara Av
Foot St
Lenna St
Amarillo St
W Oakey Blvd
Los Altos Pl
Los Altos St
Del Monte Av
Mountain View Blvd
Del Rey Av
CRAGIN PARK
Hinson St
ROTARY PARK
Arenas St
Las Flores St
Paso De Oro
Las Verdes St
Casa Grande Av
Paul Robarts
Castleford Pl
Edgeford Pl
Danford St
Chadford Pl
Hartford Ct
Cranford Pl
Lotus St
Sonora St
El Conlon
Hartford Pl
Hartford Pl
Familian Dr
El Mirado St
El Portal Av
La Pasada Av
El Jardin
El Greco St
Poco Wy
S Valley View Blvd
Paratore Wy
Melville Dr
W Charleston Blvd
Plaza Del Padre
Ortiz St
Plaza Del Dios
Westleigh Av
Darmak Dr
Sheridan St
Calle Del Rio
Douglas Dr
Clark Towers
Tamarich Dr
Plaza Del Prado
Plaza De Rafael
El Cortez Av
Barnard Dr
Hastings Av
Plaza Del Paz
Plaza Del Robles
Calle Del Torre
Plaza De Cielo
Calle De Vega
Cashman Dr
Bryant Av
Burton Av
Mason Av
Yardley St
Rye St
Spanish Oaks
Plaza Del Cerro
Cabot St
Roseville Wy
Piedmont Av
Kings Wy
Merritt Av
Alcoa Av
Plaza Del Grande
Calle De Nuevo
Eaton Dr
Northam St
Wilmington Wy
Palm Springs
Calle De Espana
Plaza De Ernesto
Calle De El Cortez
Campbell Dr
Sultana St
Plaza De Rosa
Plaza Del Puerto
De Monte
Serafina St
Gilmary Av
Colanthe Av
Ashby Av
Stampa Av
Meade Av
Richfield Blvd
Milo Wy
Valmora St
Rigel Av
Trona St
Kaiser Wy
Plaza De La Candela
BOB BASKIN PARK
Jamestown Wy
Sahara Annex St
Taraso Wy
Realeza Ct
Bayo Ct
Wyandotte St
Mora La
Cahlan Dr
Teddy Dr
Paseo Del Prado
Miraflores Av
Lourdes Av
Sidonia Av
Calanda Ct
Fulano Wy
Rambla Ct
15
S Rancho Dr
Naco Ct
Adra Ct
La Solana Wy
Strong Dr
Villa De Conde Wy
PALACE STATION
Zafra Ct
Karli Dr
Laurie Dr
Lewellyn Dr
Buehler Dr
Sherman Pl
De Osma St
Westlund Dr
Edna Av
Mauna Loa Dr
Molokai La
Red Oak Av
S Highland Dr
Bryn Mawr Av
Crescent Dr
Rancho La
Glen Heather Wy
Kirkland Av
Bonnie Brae Av
Pine St
Silver Av
Bannie Av
Waldman Av
Edgewood Av
Westwood Dr
S Tonopah Dr
Inverness Av
Birch St
Western Av
Sutter Av
Industrial Rd
Scotland La
Highland Dr
Ivanhoe Wy
Park Cir
Pahor Dr
Rose St
Westwood Dr
Kiltie Wy

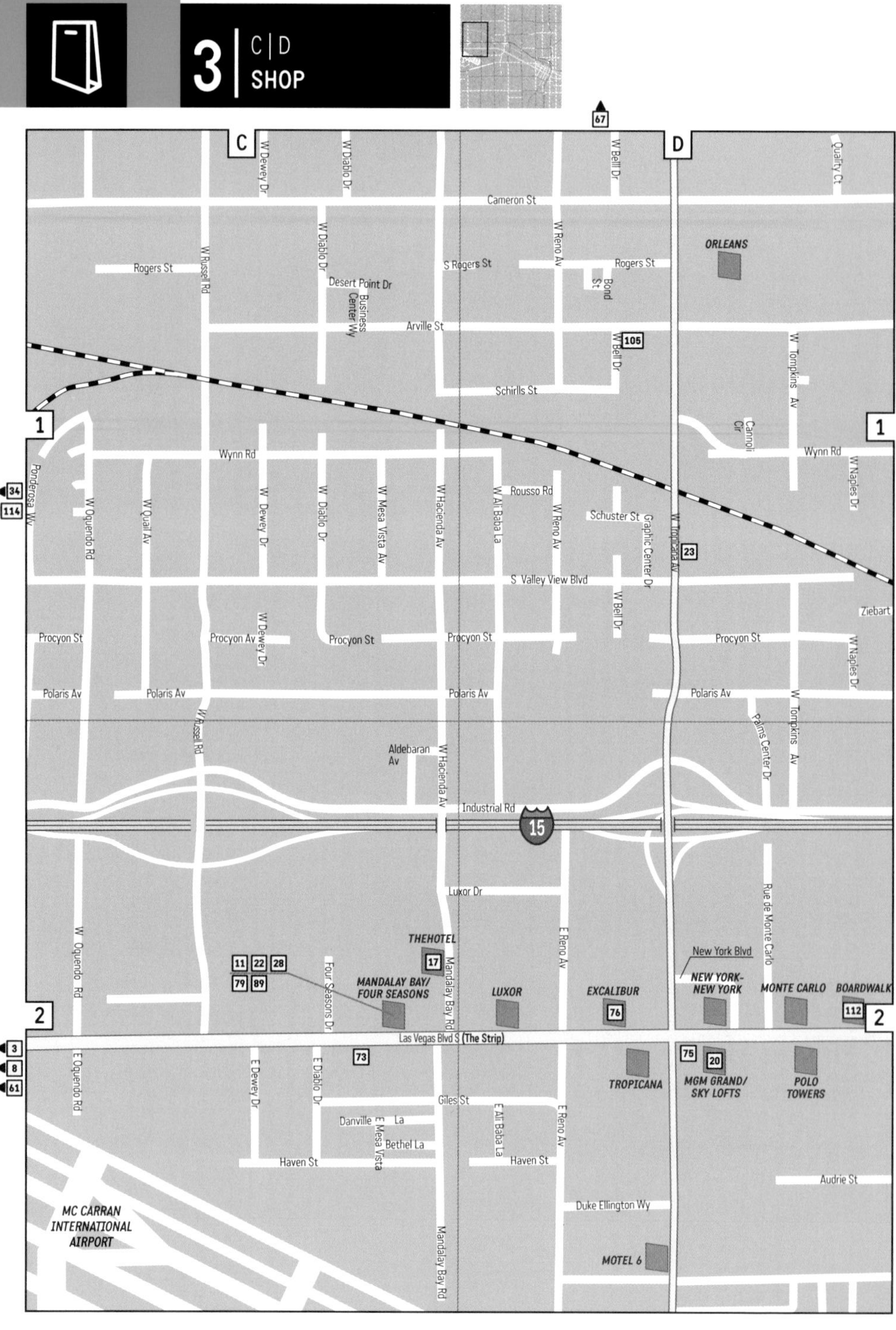

ORLEANS
THEHOTEL
MANDALAY BAY/ FOUR SEASONS
LUXOR
EXCALIBUR
NEW YORK-NEW YORK
MONTE CARLO
BOARDWALK
TROPICANA
MGM GRAND/ SKY LOFTS
POLO TOWERS
MOTEL 6
MC CARRAN INTERNATIONAL AIRPORT
Cameron St
Rogers St
S Rogers St
Desert Point Dr
Business Center Wy
Arville St
Schirlls St
Wynn Rd
Rousso Rd
Schuster St
Graphic Center Dr
S Valley View Blvd
Procyon St
Procyon Av
Polaris Av
Aldebaran Av
Industrial Rd
Luxor Dr
New York Blvd
Las Vegas Blvd S (The Strip)
Giles St
Danville La
Bethel La
Haven St
Duke Ellington Wy
Audrie St
Ziebart
Cannoli Cir
Bond St
Quality Ct
Ponderosa Wy
W Dewey Dr
W Diablo Dr
W Bell Dr
W Reno Av
W Russell Rd
W Tompkins Av
W Naples Dr
W Oquendo Rd
W Quail Av
W Mesa Vista Av
W Hacienda Av
W Ali Baba La
W Tropicana Av
Palms Center Dr
Rue de Monte Carlo
Four Seasons Dr
Mandalay Bay Rd
E Reno Av
E Oquendo Rd
E Dewey Dr
E Diablo Dr
E Mesa Vista
E Ali Baba La
15

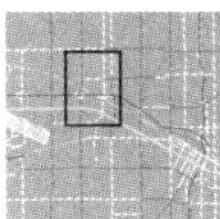

42 97

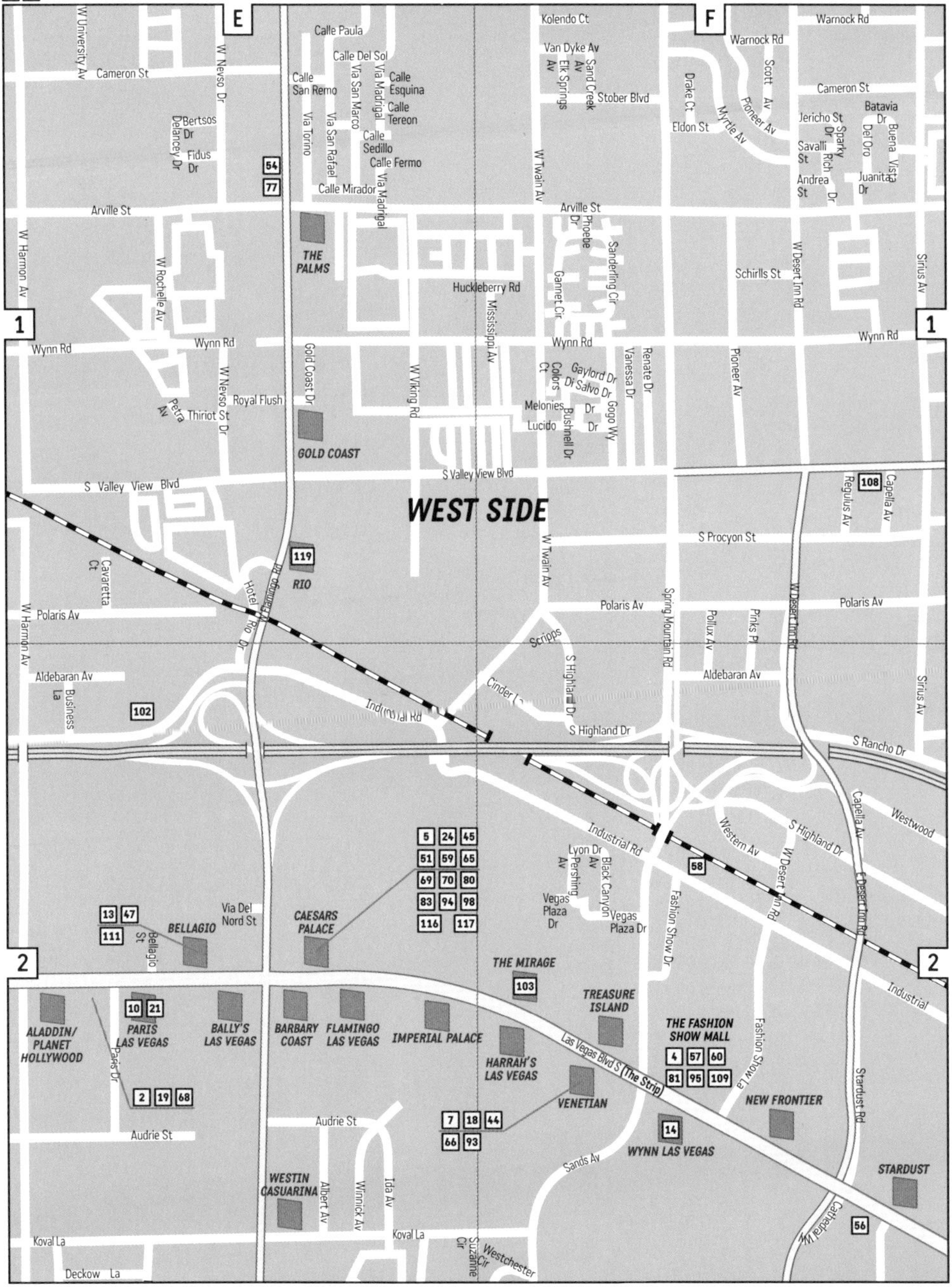

E
F
1
2

WEST SIDE

THE PALMS
54 77
GOLD COAST
RIO 119
102
108
BELLAGIO 13 47 111
CAESARS PALACE
5 24 45
51 59 65
69 70 80
83 94 98
116 117
THE MIRAGE 103
58
TREASURE ISLAND
THE FASHION SHOW MALL
4 57 60
81 95 109
ALADDIN/ PLANET HOLLYWOOD
PARIS LAS VEGAS 10 21
2 19 68
BALLY'S LAS VEGAS
BARBARY COAST
FLAMINGO LAS VEGAS
IMPERIAL PALACE
HARRAH'S LAS VEGAS
VENETIAN
7 18 44
66 93
WYNN LAS VEGAS 14
NEW FRONTIER
STARDUST
56
WESTIN CASUARINA

W University Av
Cameron St
W Nevso Dr
Bertsos Dr
Delancey Dr
Fidus Dr
Calle Paula
Calle Del Sol
Calle San Remo
Via Torino
Via San Marco
Via Madrigal
Calle Esquina
Calle Tereon
Via San Rafael
Calle Sedillo
Calle Fermo
Calle Mirador
Kolendo Ct
Van Dyke Av
Av
Elk Springs
Sand Creek Av
Stober Blvd
W Twain Av
Drake Ct
Eldon St
Myrtle Av
Warnock Rd
Scott Av
Pioneer Av
Jericho St
Sparky Dr
Batavia Dr
Del Oro
Buena Vista
Savalli St
Rich Dr
Andrea St
Juanita Dr
Arville St
W Harmon Av
W Rochelle Av
Phoebe Dr
Sanderling Cir
Garnet Cir
Huckleberry Rd
Mississippi Av
W Desert Inn Rd
Schirlls St
Sirius Av
Wynn Rd
Gold Coast Dr
W Viking Rd
Colors Ct
Gaylord Dr
Di Salvo Dr
Vanessa Dr
Renate Dr
Melonies Dr
Lucido Dr
Bushnell Dr
Gogo Wy
Royal Flush
Petra Av
Thiriot St
S Valley View Blvd
Regulus Av
Capella Av
S Procyon St
Cavaretta Ct
Hotel Rio Dr
Flamingo Rd
Polaris Av
Spring Mountain Rd
Pollux Av
Pinks Pl
Scripps
S Highland Dr
Aldebaran Av
Business La
Cinder La
Industrial Rd
S Rancho Dr
Westwood
Western Av
Lyon Dr
Pershing Av
Black Canyon Av
Vegas Plaza Dr
Fashion Show Dr
Via Del Nord St
Bellagio St
Paris Dr
Industrial
Las Vegas Blvd S (The Strip)
Fashion Show La
Stardust Rd
Audrie St
Sands Av
Albert Av
Winnick Av
Ida Av
Cathedral Wy
Koval La
Deckow La
Suzanne Cir
Westchester

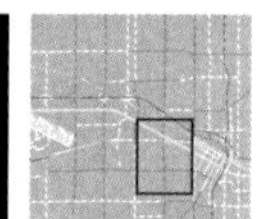

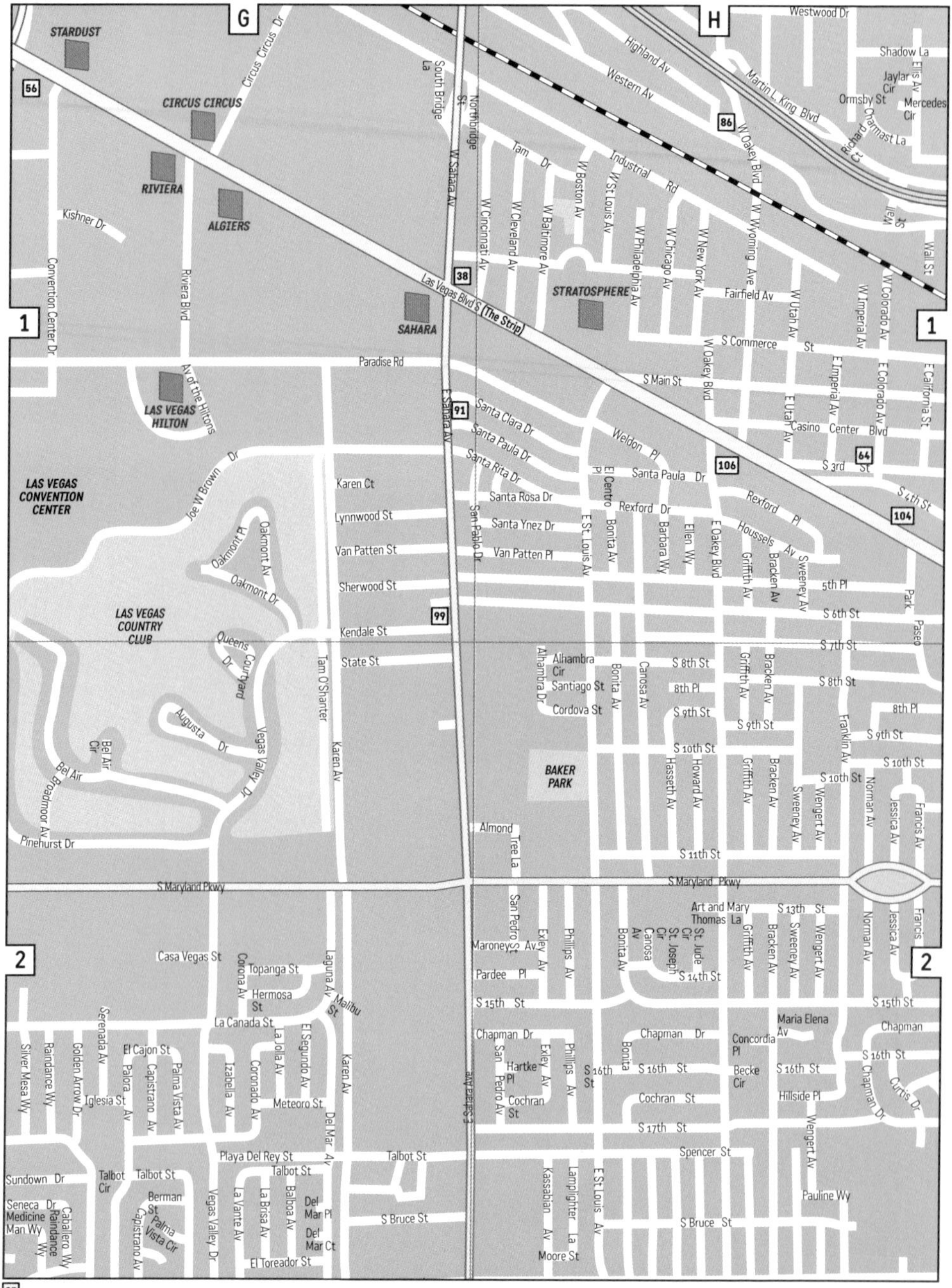

G
H
1
2

STARDUST
CIRCUS CIRCUS
RIVIERA
ALGIERS
SAHARA
STRATOSPHERE
LAS VEGAS HILTON
LAS VEGAS CONVENTION CENTER
LAS VEGAS COUNTRY CLUB
BAKER PARK

Las Vegas Blvd S (The Strip)
Paradise Rd
S Maryland Pkwy
W Sahara Av
E Sahara Av
Convention Center Dr
Riviera Blvd
Circus Circus Dr
Av of the Hilitons
Joe W Brown Dr
Kishner Dr
Karen Av
Karen Ct
Tam O'Shanter
Santa Clara Dr
Santa Paula Dr
Santa Rita Dr
Santa Rosa Dr
Santa Ynez Dr
San Pablo Dr
Van Patten St
Van Patten Pl
Sherwood St
Kendale St
State St
Lynnwood St
Oakmont Av
Oakmont Dr
Oakmont Pl
Queens Courtyard Dr
Augusta Dr
Vegas Valley Dr
Bel Air Cir
Bel Air
Broadmoor Av
Pinehurst Dr
Highland Av
Western Av
Martin L. King Blvd
Industrial Rd
W Oakey Blvd
E Oakey Blvd
Fairfield Av
S Commerce St
S Main St
Casino Center Blvd
S 3rd St
S 4th St
S 6th St
S 7th St
S 8th St
S 9th St
S 10th St
S 11th St
S 13th St
S 14th St
S 15th St
S 16th St
S 17th St
Weldon Pl
Rexford Dr
Rexford Pl
Houssels Av
E St. Louis Av
Bonita Av
Franklin Av
Norman Av
Jessica Av
Francis Av
Park Paseo
Almond Tree La
San Pedro Av
Exley Av
Phillips Av
Chapman Dr
Cochran St
Spencer St
Talbot St
S Bruce St
Playa Del Rey St
El Toreador St
Sundown Dr
Pauline Wy
Westwood Dr
Shadow La
Wall St

56
86
38
91
106
64
104
99
25

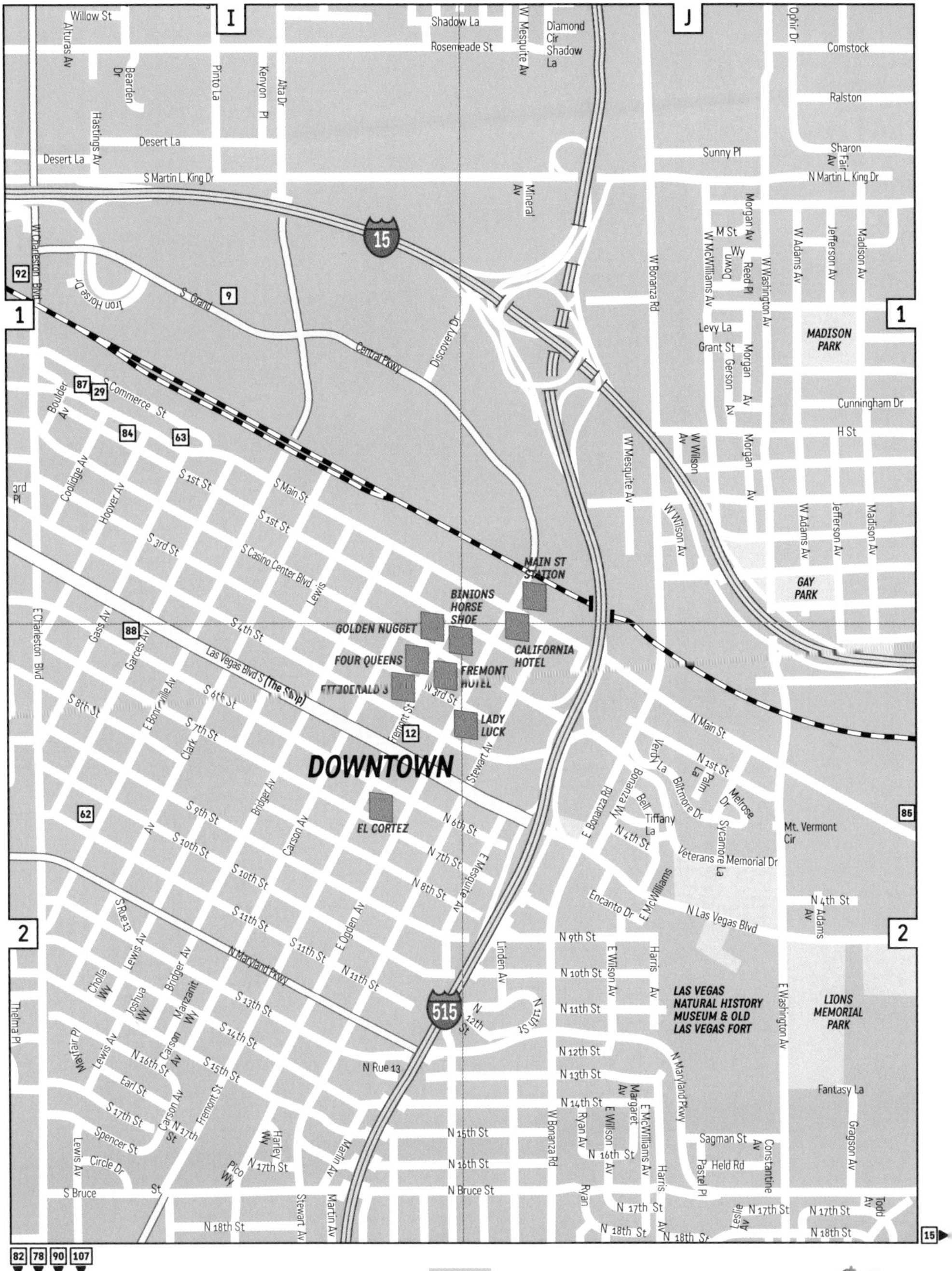

I
J
1
2

Willow St
Alturas Av
Bearden Dr
Hastings Av
Pinto La
Kenyon Pl
Alta Dr
Desert La
Desert La
S Martin L. King Dr
Shadow La
Rosemeade St
W Mesquite Av
Diamond Cir
Shadow La
Mineral Av
Ophir Dr
Comstock
Ralston
Sharon Fair Av
Sunny Pl
N Martin L. King Dr
15
W Charleston Blvd
Iron Horse Dr
S Grand
Central Pkwy
Discovery Dr
M St
Morgan Av
Dowd Wy
Reed Pl
W McWilliams Av
W Washington Av
W Adams Av
Jefferson Av
Madison Av
W Bonanza Rd
Levy La
Grant St
Gerson Av
Morgan Av
MADISON PARK
Cunningham Dr
H St
W Wilson Av
Morgan Av
W Mesquite Av
W Wilson Av
W Adams Av
Jefferson Av
Madison Av
GAY PARK
92
9
87
29
84
63
88
62
12
86
15

Boulder Av
S Commerce St
Coolidge Av
3rd Pl
Hoover Av
S 1st St
S Main St
S 1st St
S 3rd St
S Casino Center Blvd
Lewis
MAIN ST STATION
BINIONS HORSE SHOE
GOLDEN NUGGET
CALIFORNIA HOTEL
FOUR QUEENS
FREMONT HOTEL
FITZGERALD'S
LADY LUCK
EL CORTEZ
DOWNTOWN
E Charleston Blvd
Gass Av
Garces Av
S 4th St
Las Vegas Blvd S (The Strip)
S 6th St
S 8th St
E Bonneville Av
S 7th St
Clark
Fremont St
N 3rd St
Stewart Av
N Main St
Verdy La
N 1st St
Palm La
Bonanza Wy
Biltmore Dr
Melrose Dr
Bell
Tiffany La
Sycamore La
Mt. Vermont Cir
E Bonanza Rd
N 4th St
Veterans Memorial Dr
S 9th St
Bridger Av
Carson Av
N 6th St
Av
S 10th St
N 7th St
E Mesquite Av
S 10th St
N 8th St
Encanto Dr
E McWilliams
N Las Vegas Blvd
N 4th St
Adams Av
S Rue 13
S 11th St
S 11th St
E Ogden Av
Lewis Av
Bridger Av
N Maryland Pkwy
N 11th St
Linden Av
N 9th St
E Wilson Av
Harris Av
Cholla Wy
Joshua Wy
Marzanit Wy
S 13th St
515
N 12th St
N 11th St
N 10th St
N 11th St
LAS VEGAS NATURAL HISTORY MUSEUM & OLD LAS VEGAS FORT
E Washington Av
LIONS MEMORIAL PARK
Thelma Pl
Mayfair Pl
Lewis Av
N 16th St
Carson Av
S 14th St
S 15th St
N 12th St
N Rue 13
N 13th St
N Maryland Pkwy
Fantasy La
Earl St
S 17th St
Carson Av
N 17th St
Fremont St
N 14th St
W Bonanza Rd
Ryan Av
Margaret Av
E Wilson Av
E McWilliams Av
Gragson Av
Spencer St
Harley Wy
N 17th St
N 15th St
Sagman St
Constantine Av
Lewis Av
Circle Dr
Pico Wy
Martin Av
N 16th St
N 16th St
Harris Av
Pastel Pl
Held Rd
S Bruce
St
N Bruce St
Ryan
N 17th St
Leslie Av
N 17th St
N 17th St
Todd Av
N 18th St
Stewart Av
Martin Av
N 18th St
N 18th St
N 18th St
82
78
90
107

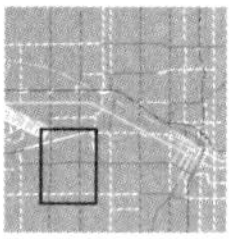

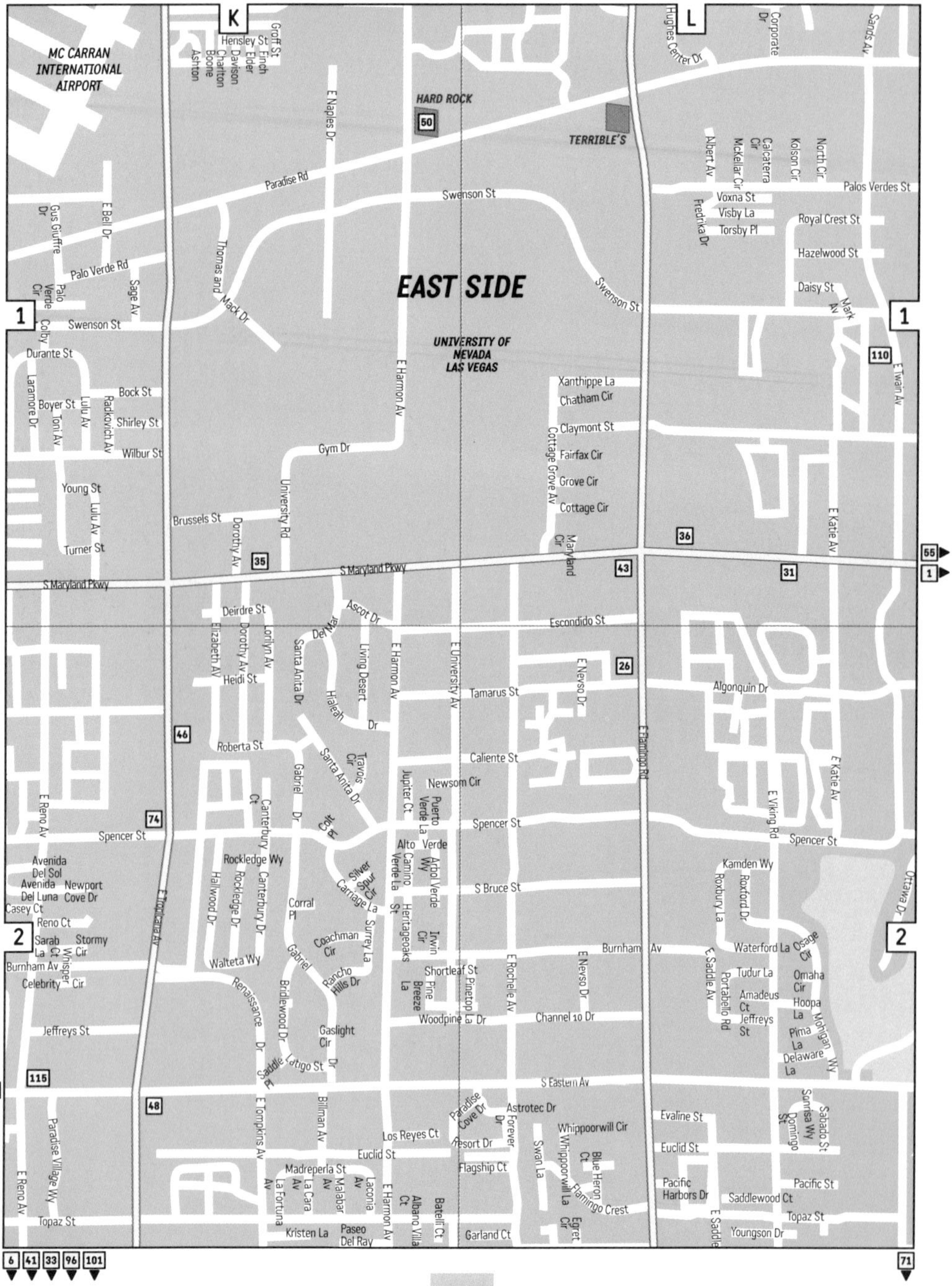

K L

MC CARRAN INTERNATIONAL AIRPORT

HARD ROCK

50

TERRIBLE'S

EAST SIDE

UNIVERSITY OF NEVADA LAS VEGAS

Hensley St
Groff St
Finch
Elder
Davison
Chalton
Boone
Ashton
E Naples Dr
Hughes Center Dr
Corporate Dr
Sands Av
Paradise Rd
Albert Av
McKellar Cir
Calcaterra Cir
Kolson Cir
North Cir
Palos Verdes St
Voxna St
Visby La
Torsby Pl
Fredrika Dr
Royal Crest St
Hazelwood St
Daisy St
Mark Av
Swenson St
Gus Giuffre Dr
E Bell Dr
Thomas and Mack Dr
Palo Verde Rd
Palo Verde Cir
Sage Av
Colby
Durante St
Laramore Dr
Boyer St
Toni Av
Lulu Av
Radkovich Av
Bock St
Shirley St
Wilbur St
Young St
Turner St
E Harmon Av
Gym Dr
University Rd
Brussels St
Dorothy Av
Xanthippe La
Chatham Cir
Claymont St
Cottage Grove Av
Fairfax Cir
Grove Cir
Cottage Cir
Maryland Cir
E Twain Av
E Katie Av
110
36
35
43
31
55
1
S Maryland Pkwy
Deirdre St
Ascot Dr
Escondido St
Elizabeth Av
Lorilyn Av
Del Mar
Santa Anita Dr
Living Desert
E University Av
E Nevso Dr
26
Heidi St
Hialeah Dr
Tamarus St
Algonquin Dr
E Flamingo Rd
46
Roberta St
Santa Anita Dr
Travis Cir
Caliente St
Gabriel Dr
Jupiter Ct
Newsom Cir
Canterbury Ct
Puerto Verde La
E Viking Rd
E Reno Av
74
Spencer St
Colt Pl
Alto Camino Verde La
Verde Wy
Arbol Verde
Avenida Del Sol
Avenida Del Luna
Newport Cove Dr
Rockledge Wy
Hallwood Dr
Rockledge Dr
Canterbury Dr
Corral Pl
Silver Spur Cir
Carriage La
Surrey La
S Bruce St
Heritageoaks St
Kamden Wy
Roxbury La
Roxford Dr
Ottawa Dr
Casey Ct
Reno Ct
Sarah La
Stormy Ct
Whisper Cir
Burnham Av
Celebrity Cir
Walteta Wy
Coachman Cir
Irvin Cir
Waterford La
Osage Cir
E Saddle Av
Tudur La
Omaha Cir
Amadeus Ct
Hoopa La
Jeffreys St
Pima La
Mohigan Wy
Delaware La
Portabello Rd
Gabriel
Rancho Hills Dr
Shortleaf St
Pine Breeze La
Pinetop La
E Rochelle Av
Renaissance Dr
Bridlewood Dr
Gaslight Cir
Woodpine Dr
Channel 10 Dr
Jeffreys St
E Tropicana Av
115
Saddle Pl
Latigo St
S Eastern Av
27
48
E Tompkins Av
Billman Av
Paradise Cove Dr
Astrotec Dr
Forever Dr
Evaline St
Sonrisa Wy
Domingo St
Sabado St
Paradise Village Wy
Los Reyes Ct
Resort Dr
Swan La
Whippoorwill Cir
Whippoorwill La
Euclid St
Madreperla St
Flagship Ct
Blue Heron Ct
Pacific Harbors Dr
Saddlewood Ct
Pacific St
E Reno Av
La Fortuna Av
La Cara Av
Malabar Av
Laconia Av
Albano Villa Ct
Batelli Ct
Flamingo Crest
Egret Cir
Topaz St
Kristen La
Paseo Del Ray
Garland Ct
E Saddle
Youngson Dr
2

6 41 33 96 101 71

PLAY 4

Vegas is brimming with voguish scene spots straining for the hipster audience with votive candles and avant flavored martinis. Many of these design-heavy places are called "ultralounges," swanky cocktail lounge/danceclub hybrids that are distinguished not by clientele, but by their extravagant decor and high cover charges. Another development is the transformation of hotel pool areas into outdoor nightclubs in which you can relax on lounges while DJs spin under the stars. And the city's danceclubs are some of the most exciting in the country. Lots of major spaces, backed by top promoters and insanely rich landlords, keeps the quality very high. Wherever you choose to go, phone ahead, use the VIP entrance and know that a discreet "tip" to the door goon can usually get you past the velvet ropes in a hurry.

Best Bars To...

Spot Celebrities
Caramel
Light
Mix
Pure

Have a Secret Affair
Cellar Lounge
Drai's
Polo Lounge

Luck Into a Threesome
The Center Bar
Club Rio
Free Zone
OPM
Rumjungle
Tabu

Bring Your Own Date
Double Down Saloon
Fontana Bar
Ivan Kane's Forty Deuce
Paymon's Hookah Lounge
Peppermill's Fireside Lounge
Pink E's Lounge

Go Slumming
Cue Club
Double Down Saloon
Ellis Island Lounge
Tommy Rocker's

Be Impressed With The City
Foundation Room
Ghostbar
Moorea Beach Ultra Lounge
Risqué
Teatro
VooDoo Lounge

Dance All Night
Backstreet Saloon & Dancehall
Body English
Gipsy
Ra
Rain
Studio 54

Cheetah's Girls

SEX SCENES

Prostitution is illegal in Las Vegas and all of Clark County. Of course, the fact that hookers abound is the city's worst kept secret. And we'd be surprised if this city's most powerful financiers (read: casinos) don't tacitly protect their most important customers (read: you). Theoretically, however, you could end up being charged with a crime.

STRIP CLUBS | There are almost as many strip clubs in Vegas as there are pawn shops and check-cashing stores. Quality varies, however, and can be as gristly as a $1.99 steak. Some places are even clip joints, promising one thing then providing another, while taking lots of your cash in the process. The places listed here are all 100% pure beef. When taking a taxi, be certain to tell the driver which club you want to visit and be firm; cabbies are often paid kickbacks to drop unsuspecting tourists at clip joints.

CHEETAH'S TOPLESS LOUNGE | 2112 Western Ave (at Wyoming), West Side, T 702.384.0074, MAP **H1** [1] Überbunny women, an almost equal ratio of customers and employees, and more silicone than an Intel factory makes this place the top choice for perverts everywhere. It's a topless joint with a half-dozen stages, a free (bad) food buffet Monday through Friday from 7am to 2pm, and reduced-price lap dances daily from 5am to 8pm.

CLUB PARADISE | 4416 Paradise Rd (at Harmon), East Side, T 702.734.7990, MAP **L1** [2] Another top spot for nature enthusiasts, this upscale "club" offers several dance floors, good sightlines, an appetizer menu and tons of beautiful women with ankle-bracelets and gravity-defying pneumatic breasts. It's located across from the Hard Rock Hotel.

CRAZY HORSE TOO | 2476 Industrial Rd (at Sahara), West Side, T 702.382.8003, MAP **H1** [3] The favorite of locals (who get in free through the back door), CH2 is a topless joint with lots of women, a laid-back atmosphere, and... well, that's about it. There's a pool table and a lingerie shop next door where you can pick up something nice for the wife.

OLYMPIC GARDENS CABARET | 1531 Las Vegas Blvd S (at Wyoming), Strip, T 702.385.8987, MAP **H1** [4] Olympic Gardens is famous around these parts for serving up some of the finest fake parts anywhere, on eight stages. Barbie-shaped women who, mathematically, shouldn't even be able to stand up straight, are wriggling and jiggling all over the club. OG also has male dancers upstairs, most nights between 9pm and 2am.

Backstreet Saloon & Dancehall

5012 S Arville Rd (at Tropicana), West Side

T 702.876.1844 **MAP D1 5**

It's just a neighborhood country and western bar, but one that's so friendly it could convince you to cut the mullet and move out of Arkansas. This is a good place to know for casual camaraderie, especially on Sunday afternoons beginning at 4pm, when they host one of the most popular weekly beer parties in Vegas.

The Beach

365 Convention Center Dr (at Paradise), East Side

T 702.731.1925 **MAP G1 6**

The Beach is the place where you're certain to meet the drunken frat boy of your dreams. It's the kind of pop-dance spot where local radio stations promote parties, ladies nights are many, waitresses wear bikinis (and let you do body shots), and half the crowd looks like they got in with fake IDs. Go with a mission and dressed to the 69's.

Body English

Hard Rock Hotel, 4455 Paradise Rd (at Harmon), East Side

T 702.693.4000 | Closed MON-THURS **MAP K1 7**

Secreted down a grand staircase, Body English is a medium-sized, bi-level nightclub spinning hip-hop, house and rock to a good looking crowd of adultescents. The space takes its design cues from the fantasy of a rock star's mansion with crystal chandeliers, black mirrored walls, and bars on the mezzanine offering a perch from which to take in the dance floor below. And there's a one-way mirror in the VIP.

Boston Grill & Bar

Mountain View Center, 3411 S Jones Blvd (at Spring Mountain), West Side

T 702.368.0750 **MAP E1 8**

The Boston is a solid backer of local rockers, giving them a stage most every night of the week. If you're a talent scout looking for the feral Vegas sound, this is the first stop on your tour. It's a cavernous space in the middle of nowhere with cheap drinks and late hours.

The Buffalo

4640 Paradise Rd (at Naples), East Side

T 702.733.8355 **MAP K1 9**

This gay Levis and leather bar is the Real McCoy. Home to the phallocentric Satyricons Motorcycle Club, it sometimes degenerates into a parody of heteroflexible bipsters (blue-collar hipsters, often accessorized with pit bulls), which, of course, is the best time to see it. It's best when they're putting on a beer bust, usually Sundays at 4pm and Fridays at 9pm, but it's safest to phone first.

Caramel

Bellagio, 3600 Las Vegas Blvd S (at Flamingo), Strip

T 702.693.8300 MAP E2 [10]

Low-slung leather sofas, wheat-grass planters, and one-way mirrors looking out onto the casino floor are the hallmarks of this upscale Bellagio lounge. The club is co-owned by nightlife impresarios Chris Barish and Andrew Sasson (**Light, Mist**), who have worked hard to recreate a refined New York atmosphere. That translates into an easygoing mix of business types and black-clad "alcoholiques" who drink from the top shelf. There's occasional dancing, but conversation is the main thing. Order one of the specialty drinks served in chocolate and caramel-coated martini glasses. No cover.

Carnival Court

Harrah's, 3475 Las Vegas Blvd S (at Sands), Strip

T 702.369.5000 MAP F2 [11]

One of the Strip's only outdoor bars, this always-colorful sidewalk party shifts into high gear most weekends at midnight when Cook E. Jarr rules the roost for late-nite sets of traditional party anthems backed by canned musical accompaniment and a huge tip jar on center stage. He's so schmaltzy you can get coronary thrombosis just looking at the guy. Throw in some bottle-juggling bartenders and a frat party atmosphere, and you have a wonderfully horrible Vegas experience that shouldn't be missed.

Cellar Lounge

3601 W Sahara Ave (at Valley View), West Side

T 702.362.6268 MAP A1 [12]

If you're serious about jazz, seek out the Cellar, where Strip musicians drop by after their last shows to play for fun, not money. Jam sessions can be hit-or-miss, but when they're on a roll it's often 'til sunrise.

The Center Bar

Hard Rock Hotel, 4455 Paradise Rd (at Harmon), East Side

T 702.693.5000 MAP K1 [13]

True to its name, the Center Bar is the axis around which the Hard Rock Casino revolves. From its elevated position, drinkers can gun around the entire room, ogling a flaxen-haired dealer there, looking at a biker-chick cocktail waitress there, all while chatting up a spandexed and siliconed waif or three right here. Each night, like clockwork, the volume is cranked up a few notches as locals in middle-youth with buns of steel pour in to hit on and ignore each other in turn. Often when you go—and you should go—getting anywhere close to a bartender is all but impossible. A quick escape to the Sports Deluxe or Pink Taco in the rear solves your problems so you can make a B-line straight back to the action-in-the-round.

Club Rio

Rio, 3700 W Flamingo Rd (at Valley View), West Side

T 702.252.7777 | Closed SUN-TUES MAP E1 [14]

This big, popular club books dance bands like the Boogie Knights as well as local DJs who spin popular 80s music, Latin beat, Top 40, hip-hop and house. It's a big space, attracting a thirtysomething suburban crowd, and has a reputation as a place for people looking to hit a speed hump. Their dress code (collar shirts/cocktail dresses) is strict.

Crown & Anchor

1350 E Tropicana Ave (at Maryland), East Side

T 702.739.8676 MAP K2 [15]

Everything at the C&A—except the crowd—is authentically English, right down to the ploughman's lunches, ciders on tap and dart boards on the wall. You can even shoot pool on the balcony. It's a downmarket dive catering to a mixed crowd of UNLV students, casino workers and even a few local media types thrown in for good measure. And it's busy most every night of the week, especially Tuesdays. There's a decent jukebox and better-than-average live rock and blues on the weekends.

Cue Club

953 E Sahara Ave (at Paradise), East Side

T 702.735.2884 MAP G2 [16]

No yuppies allowed at this true-blue, dim and dank pool hall for local waitstaff and service types. Set with 46 regulation tables, the club hosts frequent tournaments and offers a beer-and-burgers menu. Monday night is ladies' night. Open nonstop.

Double Down Saloon

4640 Paradise Rd (at Harmon), East Side

T 702.791.5775 MAP K1 [17]

This quintessential, smoke-filled, seedy Vegas hipster dive is a youth-infected embodiment of Sin City, complete with Goth chicks, post-work suits, pre-work strippers, belle boys, trannies and casino stiffs—all lubricated with cheap drinks and good tunes from the city's most eclectic jukebox. Go against your better reasoning, order "ass juice," the house drink, then order it again.

Ivan Kane's Forty Deuce

Drai's

Barbary Coast, 3595 Las Vegas Blvd S (at Flamingo), Strip

T 702.737.7801 | Closed MON-TUES MAP E2 18

For those who like to wake up at the crack of noon, there's this fabulous late-nighter. Hollywood producer-turned-restaurateur Victor Drai's place is a swanky restaurant-cum-lounge, offering several different intimately-sized rooms, all of which are nicely decorated and refreshingly unflashy. The music is fashionable: deep house and trance, and things heat up around 3am.

Dylan's Dance Hall & Saloon

4660 Boulder Hwy (at Indios), East Side

T 702.451.4006 | Closed SUN-TUES MAP L2 19

In early December, when the National Finals Rodeo is in town, Dylan's transforms into its unofficial headquarters. The rest of the year this is the achy-breakyest country club in town, featuring a full schedule of local DJs and occasional bands. There's a huge dance floor, kountry karaoke on Wednesdays, free line-dance lessons Wednesdays-Saturdays from 7.30-9pm, and food and drink specials throughout the week.

The Eagle

3430 E Tropicana Ave (at Pecos), East Side

T 702.458.8662 MAP K2 20

Yet another jeans and rawhide bar, the Eagle gets ink here for its underwear nights on Wednesdays and Fridays, when barely-dressed customers are treated to free wells and drafts from 10pm-3am. But come to think of it, scantily-dressed boys can get free drinks at gay bars most anytime.

Ellis Island Lounge

Ellis Island, 4178 Koval Ln (at Flamingo), East Side

T 702.733.8901 MAP E2 21

Just off the Strip, beyond the glitter, is an Old Skool hotel that's unknown to most visitors—hip ones anyhow. But hidden in the corner of the lobby restaurant is a swanky red lounge with cushioned booths, friendly ancient bartenders, strong drinks made with top-shelf brands, and homemade beers for about $2 a pint. You might want to avoid the place at midnight on Tuesdays when it packs out with karaoke singers. Then again, this is Vegas and some of the impersonators are so good you'll swear they're channeling the dead.

Fontana Bar

Bellagio, 3600 Las Vegas Blvd S (at Flamingo), Strip

T 702.693.7989 MAP E2 22

Even when there's no crooner hamming it up on stage, the Fontana is a great choice for a swoony drink. The room is plush, the drinks are perfectly mixed by bartenders who, in another city, might have become pharmacologists, and the amazing Bellagio fountains are in full view from the comfort of your sofa. Unfortunately, the canned music sometimes wanders into elevator territory, but you can't have everything.

Foundation Room

Mandalay Bay, 3950 Las Vegas Blvd S (at Mandalay Bay), Strip

T 702.632.7631 MAP C2 23

On the top floor of Mandalay Bay, the Foundation Room is a wonderful Moroccan theme lounge run by the House of Blues downstairs. Inside is sexy and indulgent; a comfortable space for corporate geldings and beautiful people imbibing very good cocktails. And the view of the Strip from the balcony is extraordinary. Most of the week this is a members-only club, though if you gamble steadily enough you may be able to score some comps from the floor manager. Otherwise it's open to the public only on Monday and Wednesday nights, and reservations for Wednesdays must be made in advance.

Free Zone

610 E Naples Rd (at Paradise), East Side

T 702.794.2300 MAP K1 24

If you're looking for the pinkest party in town, it's at Free Zone, a fun and festive bar with a United Colors of Benetton crowd that's almost always staging some special event or another. Sometimes it's karaoke, sometimes it's drag. And when nothing's happening, a quick visit here will dial you in to where the party is. It's located directly across from the Buffalo.

Ghostbar

The Palms, 4321 Flamingo Rd (at Arville), West Side

T 702.938.2666 MAP E1 25

Great lighting is what makes a place, and this quintessential ultra-lounge illuminated in shrouds of grays and greens gets the luminosity just right. Along with highly stylized Jetsons-esque design, intimate seating on metallic Eero Saarinen Tulip chairs, and wonderful views from floor-to-ceiling windows, Ghostbar, on the 55th floor, has a cool skytop patio too. Arrive early or late to avoid the lines to get in.

Gilley's Dancehall Saloon

New Frontier, 3120 Las Vegas Blvd S (at Stardust), Strip

T 702.794.8200 MAP F2 26

Gilley's and the New Frontier go together like tornados and trailer parks. If you're serious about chew, this CW spot is the first place you should visit when they let you out of jail. All the stereotypes are in place here, from boots and belt buckles and a mechanical bull, to the barbecue menu and live bands most every night.

Gipsy

4605 Paradise Rd (at Harmon), East Side

T 702.731.1919 MAP K1 27

A single, large space with a sunken dance floor, Gipsy is Vegas's oldest and most popular gay nightclub, attracting a youthful, ambisexterous crowd with Top 40, hip-hop and deep house. The club has long been a sweaty mainstay of the city's gay scene, popular for its no-frills atmosphere and anything-goes attitude. Things get going 'round midnight, and Monday is Latin Night.

Gordon Biersch Brewery

Hughes Center, 3987 Paradise Rd (at Flamingo), East Side

T 702.312.5247 MAP L1 28

Founded in Northern California, Gordon Biersch brings its excellent beer and good World Cuisine to this popular off-Strip gathering place. By day, it's a fashionable place for tie-wearing power-lunchers. By night, it's an even more popular local hotspot with a well-deserved reputation as a place to find Mr. Right Now. Friday Happy Hour is a particularly good time to booze-bond with the receptionist of your dreams.

House of Blues

Mandalay Bay, 3950 Las Vegas Blvd S (at Mandalay Bay), Strip

T 702.632.7600 MAP C2 29

Top bands, a diverse national booking policy, and a great venue all converge to make HoB the top room in the city for live music. When a household name is not in the House, local bands take the stage so that there's something happening in this 1900-seat theater most every night of the week. Their members-only **Foundation** is on the 43rd floor.

Ice Las Vegas

200 E Harmon Ave (at Koval), East Side

T 702.699.9888 MAP E2 30

The city's largest freestanding dancespace has an enormous sound-system and calls itself a "meta-club," as in metamorphosis, because of it's ever-changing interior. In short, this is a playground for baggier-than-thou twentynothings with novelty facial hair, and those who want to get to know them. There are excellent dance floors for grooving and an embarrassment of niches for snogging. And the party usually lasts until dawn.

Ivan Kane's Forty Deuce

Mandalay Place, 3930 Las Vegas Blvd S (at Mandalay Bay), Strip

T 702.632.9442 MAP C2 31

Because local laws forbid nude dancing on casinos' premises, we're seeing lots of lounges pushing limits without ever crossing them. Ivan Kane's is the best of this genre, recalling days that probably never were, when burlesque meant striptease done in feathers and fedoras with a small jazz combo setting the beat. The interior is dimly lit, plush and sultry, and the dancers are really pretty good. Is it worth a 20-spot to get in? With tongue firmly in cheek, it is.

The Joint

Hard Rock Hotel, 4455 Paradise Rd (at Harmon), East Side

T 702.226.4650 MAP L1 32

The Joint is a decent place to catch a show. It's a cavernous 1600-seat theater with excellent sound and fine sightlines augmented by closed-circuit video screens. The national acts which parade through here are a remarkable smorgasbord of A-list, aging and one-hit talent. Don't get stuck with General Admission tickets on the balcony or you'll end up standing with a mob far away from the action.

Light

Bellagio, 3600 Las Vegas Blvd S (at Flamingo), Strip

T 702.693.8300 | Closed MON-WED MAP E2 33

Trendy, crowded and good for dancing, Light is the second link in a posh New York-based mini-chain. It's also one of the few places in Vegas in which you can see real art dealers canoodling with good actors, along with an A-list of hipsters from the coasts. Past the velvet ropes you'll find minimalist chic with lots of private, candle-lit tables and a huge sunken dance floor, beyond which go-go dancers gyrate to Ashanti and Ja Rule. High cover charges and exorbitant bottle service fees translate into lots of pretty candy on rich guys' arms.

Mix

THEhotel, 3950 Las Vegas Blvd S (at Mandalay Bay), Strip

T 702.632.9500 MAP C2 34

Adjacent to the Alain Ducasse restaurant of the same name, Mix is an expensive Euro style lounge for aristobrats on the top floor of the TheHotel at Mandalay Bay. The design is swank and sultry, with wall to wall leatherette décor and an expansive patio set with oversized lounge beds offering glorious views of the Strip. It's a beautiful place that often books good electronica DJs, but high prices and large doses of attitude seem to attract people with more dollars than sense.

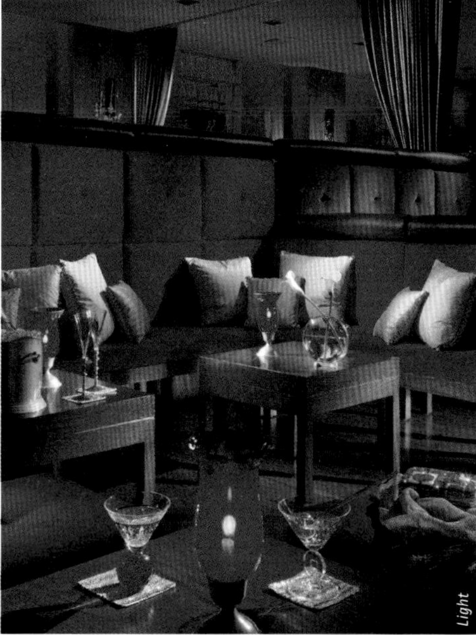
Light

Monte Carlo Pub & Brewery

Monte Carlo, 3770 Las Vegas Blvd S (at Harmon), Strip

T 702.730.7777 MAP D2 35

If you're serious about beer, you've got to visit this excellent brewpub which serves a half-dozen varieties of expertly made barley pop along with huge helpings of atmosphere. The location is great and the food is pretty good. Live dance bands play most weekend nights, and they're never so bad you'll want to cry in your High Roller Red.

Moorea Beach Ultra Lounge

Mandalay Bay, 3950 Las Vegas Blvd S (at Mandalay Bay), Strip

T 702.632.7777 MAP C2 36

During warm months, after 10pm, the VIP area of the Mandalay Bay pool area transforms into an upscale South

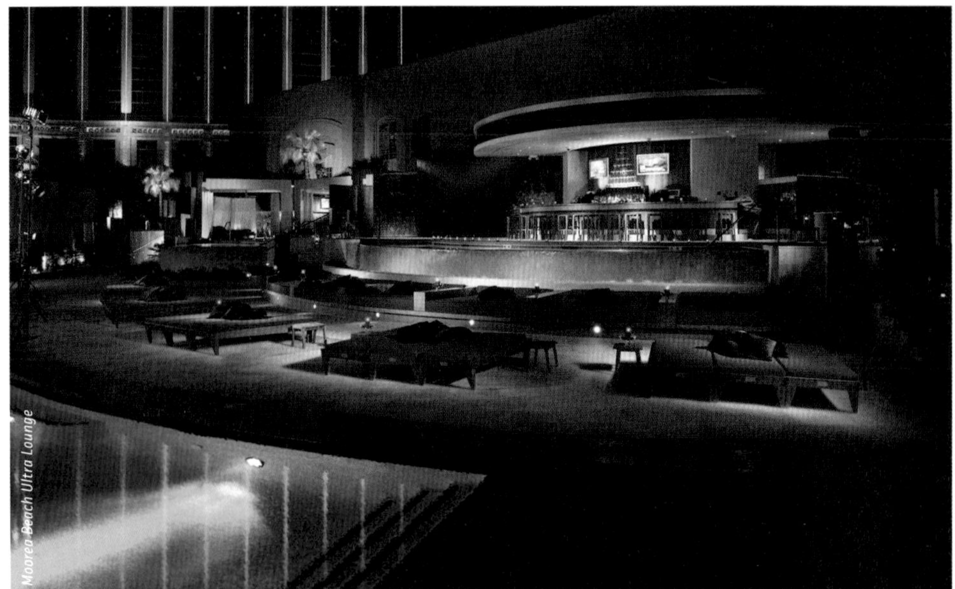

Beach-inspired nightclub. With good electronica DJs, beautiful people, tropical drinks and lounges on the sandy shoreline of Mandalay's beach, the vibe can be sublime.

OPM

Caesars Forum Shops, 3500 Las Vegas Blvd S (at Flamingo), Strip

T 702.387.3840 MAP E2 37

East meets West at this contemporary Asianesque danceclub and lounge with state-of-the art lighting and sound. Situated on a curtained balcony above **Chinois**, Wolfgang Puck's Asian/French restaurant, OPM is a good place to either get your groove-on on the large dance floor, or rock the kasbah in the hookah lounge with low slung seating. And Puck's sushi, dim sum and desserts are served until 3am. You can sometimes find free passes on the club's website (www.o-pm.com).

Paymon's Hookah Lounge

Tiffany Square Plaza, 4147 S Maryland Pkwy (at Flamingo), East Side

T 702.731.6030 | Closed SUN-MON MAP L1 38

8380 W Sahara Ave (at Durango), West Side

T 702.731.6030 MAP A1 39

Even before everything Islamic was in vogue, Hookah Lounge knew that smoking from Turkish water pipes was cool. Dark and loungy, with lots of Oriental rugs and throw pillows, these heady spots are welcome surprises in the middle of strip malls a few blocks from the Strip. Their house specialty is apple martinis, but the hook is the hookah, a tall waterpipe filled with your choice of over a dozen scented tobaccos (try jasmine). Don't forget to bring a date.

Peppermill's Fireside Lounge

2985 Las Vegas Blvd S (at Stardust), Strip

T 702.735.7635 MAP G1 40

Enter through the front door, slink past the nondescript diner—it's a rouse to keep the unknowing away—and make your way to the wonderfully clichéd old-school lounge in back. Wrapped with mirrors, set with cozy sunken sofas, and anchored by a fire pit with flames that erupt from a pool of bubbling water, this retro hip spot is perfect for snogging. Share your lust over a "Scorpion," the Lounge's specialty cocktail that's served in a glass as big as your head. It's located across from the Stardust.

Pink E's Lounge

3695 W Flamingo Rd (at Valley View), West Side

T 702.252.4666 MAP E1 41

This pink pool hall-cum-nightclub across from the Rio has become a hugely popular place for local rockers to play some stick. High-decibel music, chicks on the make and a party

atmosphere rage all week long. It's worst on weekends when they post goons at the door and scam $12 from amateurs who don't know better. Stick to the beginning of the week, when it's free and full of strippers, Harley guys, casino workers and sharks like you.

Polo Lounge

Polo Towers, 3745 Las Vegas Blvd S (at Harmon), Strip

T 702.261.1000 **MAP D2 42**

It's surprising that almost nobody knows about the lounge atop Polo Towers, because this hideaway piano bar in a timeshare condominium complex has it all: great drinks, conversational noise levels, eclectic local crowd and killer Strip views from the comfort of your booth. Keep this one to yourself.

Pure

Caesars Palace, 3570 Las Vegas Blvd S (at Flamingo), Strip

T 702.731.7873 **MAP E2 43**

White-on-white decor is as pure as the pedigree of this posh bi-level nightclub whose investors include Celine Dion, Shaquille O'Neal and Andre Agassi. The main room features oversized beds, three bars and a VIP area overlooking the dance floor, where house, R&B and hip-hop are served. And a spiral staircase leads up to a swanky dance terrace with a fire pit, a water wall, and panoramic views of the Strip. The **Pussycat Dolls Lounge** is next door.

Pussycat Dolls Lounge

Caesars Palace, 3570 Las Vegas Blvd S (at Flamingo), Strip

T 702.369.4998 **MAP E2 44**

The Pussycat Dolls, an ad-hoc dance troupe that originated in LA's Viper Room, made a name for themselves with a burlesque-style cabaret that incorporated a revolving cast of Hollywood starlets, including Christina Aguilera, Carmen Electra, Gwen Stefani and Brittany Murphy. Dressed in pinup-style with fishnets and stilettos, this nightly song and dance burlesque is meant to hark back to the 1930s with shticks that include swings from the ceiling and torch singers lounging in giant champagne glasses.

Ra

Luxor, 3900 Las Vegas Blvd S (at Reno), Strip

T 702.262.4949 | Closed SUN-TUES **MAP D2 45**

Named for the Egyptian sun god, Ra is a great space, featuring a seriously good sound system, duel bars, plenty of seating and a dynamite lighting package. When the music is good, this place is unbeatable. Wednesdays are usually winners,

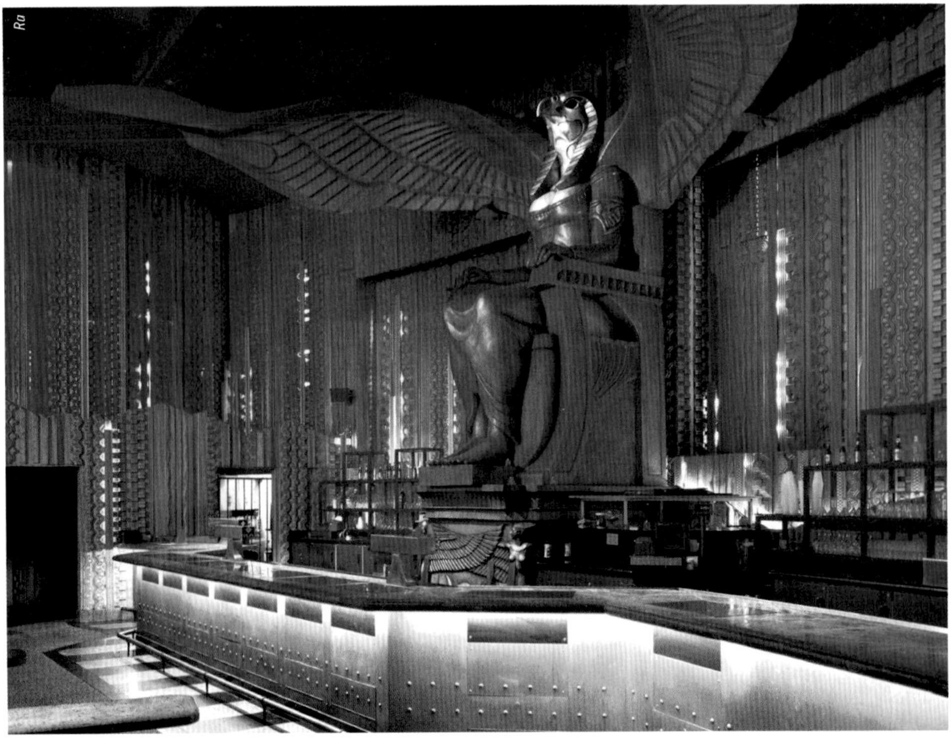

Ra

featuring deep house and a groovy crowd. Other nights can be a grab-bag, sometimes reaching mighty low with bikini contests and silly promotions.

Rain

The Palms, 4321 W Flamingo Rd (at Arville), West Side

T 702.942.6832 MAP E1 46

A large, stereotypical danceclub with all the required accoutrements (fake fog, cool pyrotechnics, elaborate lighting), Rain is a good choice for anyone looking to drop a mint to shimmy on the same floor with any number of small-town lawyers and liposucked women with pneumatic breasts. The decor is suitably wonderful, set with midcentury-modern sofas, glass and bamboo cocktail tables, and an elevated dance floor surrounded by a moat of dry ice. Plus, there's grown women dancing in cages. Don't want to wait up to an hour to pay a $30 cover charge? There is always the option of booking a Skybox for cool $1,500.

Red Square

Mandalay Bay, 3950 Las Vegas Blvd S (at Mandalay Bay), Strip

T 702.632.7407 MAP C2 47

A posh, commie-Russian themed boite, Red Square is a single beautiful room with terrific lighting, comfortable seating, retro agit-prop art, a good blini-and-caviar menu and an ice-topped bar with a peerless selection of vodkas, from South African "Savannah Royal" to Norwegian "Gabouegset." Comrades-in-the-know order the house martini, made with Moskovskaya vodka, sweet vermouth and a trio of blue-cheese-stuffed olives. Forget "Better Dead Than Red"—the line on this place is it's hip to be Square. Ask to see Lenin's head inside the walk-in freezer. Really.

Risqué

Paris Las Vegas, 3655 Las Vegas Blvd S (at Harmon), Strip

T 702.946.4589 MAP E2 48

Situated above **Ah Sin** restaurant, this chic ultra lounge is a suitably luxe place to sit back with a drink or take to the small

Rain

dance floor. Seating is on plush couches, expansive ottomans and large daybeds hidden on balconies that are so great they need to be reserved a week in advance. Plus there's an outdoor balcony overlooking the Strip. Otherwise, this place feels so aspirational that it leaves us flat. Witness male and female restrooms separated by a translucent wall creating silhouetted views of the opposite gender. Needless to say, it's a design element that backfires. Phone in the afternoon and request a free front-of-the-line upgrade.

Rumjungle

Mandalay Bay, 3950 Las Vegas Blvd S (at Mandalay Bay), Strip

T 702.636.7404 MAP C2 49

Rambunctious techno, Top 40 and Latin beats are the mainstays of this ridiculously ultra-high-tech drinkery. The highlights here are the amazing collection of rums, the full-stop gorgeous postmodernist bar and a multi-tiered dance floor that features more African percussionists and slutty go-go dancers than a rich kid's Bar Mitzvah. The burbanite crowd is pretty standard and, because rave is not the rave here, they're often less edgy then other nightspots. But drinks are decently priced, the food is better than it needs to be, and good flow makes finding a sleep-over date relatively easy to come by. The long line to get in can be avoided with dinner reservations.

Sand Dollar Blues Lounge

3355 Spring Mountain Rd (at Polaris), West Side

T 702.871.6651 MAP F1 50

The best true-blues bar in town, the Sand Dollar is an unsanitized original that attracts aficionados who are somewhat older and much less pretty than the people who are paying $30 at that blues "House" on the Strip. That's not to say there aren't plenty of perky youngsters grooving here too, but the vibe here is real and regulars are passionate about supporting an excellent, accessible music scene that offers something good and live most every night of the week. Bands usually take the stage at 10pm.

Risqué

Shadow

Caesars Palace, 3570 Las Vegas Blvd S (at Flamingo), Strip
T 702.731.7110 MAP E2 51

It was just a matter of time before casinos muscled in on pervy strip club territory; there's just too much money to be made from flesh. At Shadow, nude looking lasses writhe behind backlit scrims while dancing "hosts" mingle with the crowd and expensive drinks are poured by the bar. If this works, can casino lap dances be far behind? Either way, we'll stick with **Cheetah's** down the street, thank you very much.

Studio 54

MGM Grand, 3799 Las Vegas Blvd S (at Tropicana), Strip
T 702.891.7254 | Closed SUN-MON MAP D2 52

There may not be mountains of coke on the tables, and the door policy is far more relaxed than the original, but this massive, four-level disco is one of the best-loved danceterias in town. Lots of different rooms assure there's something for everyone, except, perhaps for truly hip people. Make your way to the top where you'll find some of the best chillout spaces in town. It's claimed that the original Studio 54 moon hangs over the dance floor. Tuesdays attract serious local clubbers (strippers get VIP cards) and weekends are the preserve of amateurs.

Tabu

MGM Grand, 3799 Las Vegas Blvd S (at Tropicana), Strip
T 702.891.7183 MAP D2 53

We hate the hyped-up name of this ultra lounge, because we know, of course, that there is nothing prohibitive inside—except the price of the drinks. But that's the price we pay to marinate in this very avant space with posh living room decor, a model waitstaff and cool interactive projections on the tabletops that move with the swish of your hand. We also like Tabu because you can actually meet new friends here, many of whom seem to be MBAs (Married But Availables). There is a small dance floor too, but that's not what this place is about.

Teatro

MGM Grand, 3799 Las Vegas Blvd S (at Tropicana), Strip
T 702.891.1111 MAP D2 54

We love this super-stylish bar at the entrance to Studio Walk. Designed by Adam Tihany, it's a futuristic and theatrical pod-shaped space with plush, Ferrari-red leather upholstery and pretty servers clad in black and white uniforms by Tadashi Shojiare. And behind the bar, serious mixologists create some of the finest cocktails in the city.

Tommy Rocker's

4275 S Industrial Rd (at Flamingo), West Side
T 702.261.6688 MAP E2 55

Located around the corner from the Rio, TR is a divey beer bar that can usually be counted on for something indigenous, cheap and fun. Local musicians play here in droves, often in impromptu jams. The bar can be good anytime, but really hits its stride on weekends after 11pm.

Triple 7 Brewpub

Main Street Station, 200 N Main St (at Ogden), Downtown
T 702.387.1896 MAP J1 56

One of the best places to imbibe Downtown, 777 serves five well-crafted home brews along with a wide selection of snacks,

Tabu

from gourmet pizzas to oysters and sushi. And their garlic fries are some of the best on the planet. The warm and woody 1930s warehouse atmosphere is fitted with antique fixtures and big-screen sports TVs, and offers live music most nights.

V Bar

The Venetian, 3355 Las Vegas Blvd S (at Sands), Strip

T 702.414.3200 MAP F2 57

From the gorgeous staff to the chic minimalist décor by Manhattan-based Meyer Davis Studio, everything is beautiful at this trend-heavy lounge in which crème de la crème out of towners rub body parts with on-the-posh-side locals. V Bar also pulls in the best-looking off-duty strippers and, on weekends, can be packed tighter than Jordan in an A-cup. Brad Johnson of Hollywood's Sunset Room and Will Regan and David Rabin of New York's Lotus joined forces to create this soulful space without attitude. Get tanked on their trademark apple martinis, and dance to soulful R&B and jazzy house or just shimmy in your seat by the bar.

Vivid

The Venetian, 3355 Las Vegas Blvd S (at Sands), Strip

T 702.992.7970 MAP F2 58

The world's leading porn production company is leveraging its good name to create this crimson colored nightclub and lounge with expensive drinks, a booming sound system and hordes of horny visitors from small town America. The visual hooks here are three-dimensional holographic images of dancing girls projected onto "trans-screens," large panels of glass hung high above the dance floor. But there's a lingering stench of testosterone and desperation. For a real danceclub experience this is not the place to go. For blondes in short black dresses, your appetite may be satisfied.

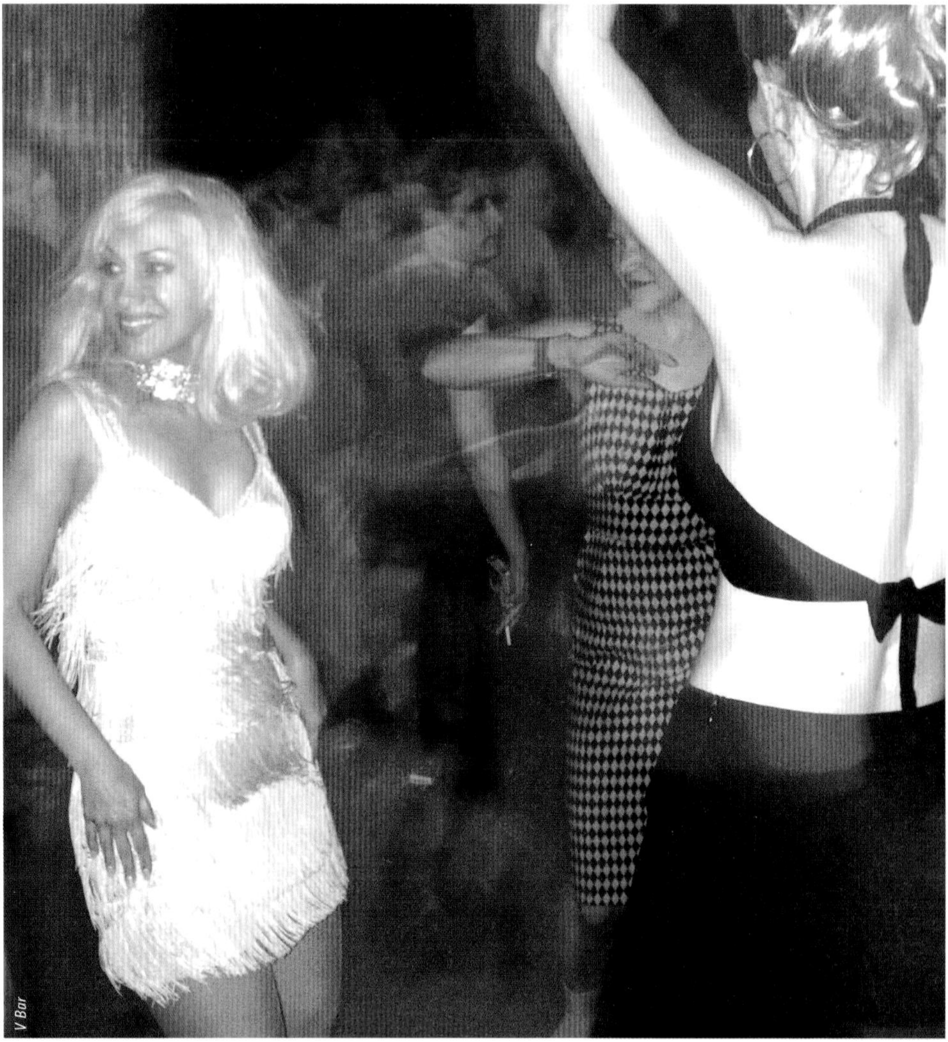

V Bar

VooDoo Lounge

Rio, 3700 W Flamingo Rd (at Valley View), West Side

T 702.247.7800 MAP E1 59

Secreted on the top floor of the Rio, and commanding a spectacular view of the Strip resorts, VooDoo Lounge is a great place for a drink—provided you can get past the huge line of middle-aged tourists and the stupid bouncer at the foot of the elevators who's there to weed out jeans-wearers and god-knows-who else. It's a popular place because there's something for everybody: bartenders who toss bottles, waitresses in sexy slit skirts, bands playing everything jazzy from swing to bop, and an outdoor patio that affords unobstructed vistas from the Stratosphere to Mandalay Bay. Beware the fishbowl-sized red voodoo drink and the mediocre Cajun-Creole "cuisine."

Map	Venue	Address	Phone	Closed	ApresWork	Lounge	Good Food	Dance Club	Brewpub/Beer Bar	Quiet Conversation	Gay/Lesbian	Live Entertainment	Outdoors
		The Strip											
E2 [10]	Caramel	Bellagio	702.693.8300			★							
F2 [11]	Carnival Court	Harrah's	702.369.5000									★	★
E2 [18]	Drai's	Barbary Coast	702.737.7801	M-Tu		★	★			★			
E2 [22]	Fontana Bar	Bellagio	702.693.7989			★						★	
C2 [23]	Foundation Room	Mandalay Bay	702.632.7631			★							★
F2 [26]	Gilley's Dancehall Saloon	New Frontier	702.794.8200					★	★			★	
C2 [29]	House of Blues	Mandalay Bay	702.632.7600									★	
C2 [31]	Ivan Kane's Forty Deuce	Mandalay Place	702.632.9442									★	
E2 [33]	Light	Bellagio	702.693.8300	M-W				★					
C2 [34]	Mix	THEhotel	702.632.9500			★	★			★			
D2 [35]	Monte Carlo Pub & Brewery	Monte Carlo	702.730.7777		★		★		★	★			
C2 [36]	Moorea Beach Ultra Lounge	Mandalay Bay	702.632.7777			★		★					★
H1 [4]	Olympic Gardens Cabaret	1531 Las Vegas Blvd S	702.385.8987		★							★	
E2 [37]	OPM	Caesars Forum Shops	702.387.3840				★	★					
G1 [40]	Peppermill's Fireside Lounge	2985 Las Vegas Blvd S	702.735.7636		★	★				★			
D2 [42]	Polo Lounge	3745 Las Vegas Blvd S	702.261.1000			★				★			
E2 [43]	Pure	Caesars Palace	702.731.7873					★					★
E2 [44]	Pussycat Dolls Lounge	Caesars Palace	702.369.4998									★	
D2 [45]	Ra	Luxor	702.262.4949	Su-Tu				★					
C2 [47]	Red Square	Mandalay Bay	702.632.7407		★		★						
E2 [48]	Risqué	Paris Las Vegas	702.946.4589			★		★					★
C2 [49]	Rumjungle	Mandalay Bay	702.636.7404				★	★					
E2 [51]	Shadow	Caesars Palace	702.731.7110			★						★	
D2 [52]	Studio 54	MGM Grand	702.891.7254	Su-M				★					
D2 [53]	Tabu	MGM Grand	702.891.7183			★		★					
D2 [54]	Teatro	MGM Grand	702.891.1111		★	★				★			
F2 [57]	V Bar	The Venetian	702.414.3200			★		★					
F2 [58]	Vivid	The Venetian	702.992.7970			★		★					
		Downtown											
J1 [56]	Triple 7 Brewpub	Main Street Station	702.387.1896		★		★		★	★		★	

Map		Venue	Address	Phone	Closed	ApresWork	Lounge	Good Food	Dance Club	Brewpub/Beer Bar	Quiet Conversation	Gay/Lesbian	Live Entertainment	Outdoors
East Side														
K1	7	Body English	Hard Rock Hotel	702.693.4000	M–Tr				★					
L1	2	Club Paradise	4416 Paradise Rd	702.734.7990									★	
K2	15	Crown & Anchor	1350 E Tropicana Ave	702.739.8676		★		★		★	★			★
G2	16	Cue Club	953 E Sahara Ave	702.735.2884						★				
K1	17	Double Down Saloon	4640 Paradise Rd	702.791.5775						★				
L2	19	Dylan's Dance Hall & Saloon	4660 Boulder Hwy	702.451.4006	Su–Tu				★	★			★	
E2	21	Ellis Island Lounge	4178 Koval Ln	702.733.8901		★	★	★		★	★			
K1	24	Free Zone	610 E Naples Rd	702.794.2300							★	★		
K1	27	Gipsy	4605 Paradise Rd	702.731.1919					★			★		
L1	28	Gordon Biersch Brewery	3987 Paradise Rd	702.312.5247		★		★		★	★			
E2	30	Ice Las Vegas	200 E Harmon Ave	702.699.9888					★					
L1	38	Paymon's Hookah Lounge	4147 S Maryland Pkwy	702.731.6030	Su–M		★	★			★			
G1	6	The Beach	365 Convention Center Dr	702.731.1925					★					
K1	9	The Buffalo	4640 Paradise Rd	702.733.8355						★		★		
K1	13	The Center Bar	Hard Rock Hotel	702.693.5000		★								
C2	20	The Eagle	3430 E Tropicana Ave	702.458.8662						★		★		
L1	32	The Joint	Hard Rock Hotel	702.226.4650							★		★	
West Side														
D1	5	Backstreet Saloon & Dancehall	5012 S Arville Rd	702.876.1844					★	★			★	
E1	8	Boston Grill & Bar	3411 S Jones Blvd	702.368.0750				★		★			★	
A1	12	Cellar Lounge	3601 W Sahara Ave	702.362.6268			★				★		★	
H1	1	Cheetah's Topless Lounge	2112 Western Ave	702.384.0074		★	★						★	
E1	14	Club Rio	Rio	702.252.7777	Su–Tu				★					
H1	3	Crazy Horse Too	2476 Industrial Rd	702.382.8003		★	★						★	
E1	25	Ghostbar	The Palms	702.938.2666			★							★
A1	39	Paymon's Hookah Lounge	8380 W Sahara Ave	702.731.6030			★	★						
E1	41	Pink E's Lounge	3695 W Flamingo Rd	702.252.4666			★			★				
E1	46	Rain	The Palms	702.942.6832					★					
F1	50	Sand Dollar Blues Lounge	3355 Spring Mountain Rd	702.871.6651							★		★	
E2	55	Tommy Rocker's	4275 S Industrial Rd	702.261.6688						★			★	
E1	59	VooDoo Lounge	Rio	702.247.7800			★						★	★

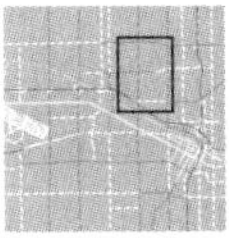

39

A

B

S Decatur Blvd
Montclair St
Appian Wy
Black Forest Dr
Sleepy Hollow Wy
Aladdin La
Matterhorn Wy
Lilliput La
Rip Van Winkle La
Thumbelina Cir
Heidi Cir
Gretel Cir
Hansel Cir
Quantana Ct
Castlewood
Castlewood La
Aladdin La
Cinderella La
Sierra Madre Dr
King Midas Wy
Faircenter Pkwy
Baxter Pl
Marcus Dr
Cameron St
Pinner Ct
Blisworth Ct
Teddington Ct
Creslow Ct
Bramfield Ct
Cublington Ct
Padbury Ct
Rothwell Ct
WESTLAND FAIR SHOPPING CENTER
Aquarius Dr
Tranquility Dr
Galaxy Av
El Paraiso Av
Buckeye Av
Hillcrest
Farnam Pl
Exposition
Del Monte
Flag Cir
Banner Cir
Brockwood Dr
Parade St
Sundale St
Fontenelle St
1
Arville St
Arville St
Mott Cir
San Joaquin
San Angelo Av
El Conlon Av
San Bernardino Av
W Sahara Av
Juana Vista St
Juana Vista St
Von Bryan Ct
Bossart Ct
Fellowship Ct
Alpine Pl
Via Vaquero Av
Esmeralda Av
Via Olivero Av
El Camino Av
El Pasada Av
El Jardin Av
El Parque Av
El Cederal Av
Las Lomas Av
W Oakey Blvd
Stephenburnet Ct
Vista Dr
Silver Dollar Av
Tara
Foot St
Lenna St
Lenna St
Amarillo St
Del Monte Av
Mountain View Blvd
Del Rey Av
Los Altos Pl
Los Altos St
CRAGIN PARK
Castleford Pl
Edgeford Pl
Danford Pl
St
Chadford Pl
Arenas St
Arenas St
Las Flores St
Paso De Oro
Hinson St
Hinson St
Hinson St
Ct
Paul Robarts
Las Verdes St
Las Verdes St
ROTARY PARK
Hartford Ct
Cranford Pl
Lotus St
Av
Sonora St
El Mirado St
Av
Av
El Jardin
Casa Grande
Hartford Pl
Hartford
Familian Dr
San Joaquin Av
San Angelo Av
El Conlon
El Portal Av
La Pasada
El Cederal Av
Poco Wy
El Greco St
Paratore Wy
S Valley View Blvd
Plaza Del Padre
Ortiz St
Melville Dr
12
Av
Plaza Del Dios
Casa Grande Av
Westleigh Av
Darmak Dr
Sheridan St
Calle Del Rio
Douglas Dr
Clark Towers
El Camino Av
Plaza Del Prado
Plaza De Rafael
El Cortez Av
Mountain View Blvd
W Charleston Blvd
Barnard Dr
Tamarack Dr
Plaza Del Paz
Plaza Del Robles
Calle Del Torre
Barnard Dr
Hastings Av
Cashman Dr
Plaza De Cielo
Calle De Vega
Bryant Av
Burton Av
Mason Av
Yardley St
Rye St
Spanish Oaks
Plaza Del Cerro
Cabot St
Plaza Del Grande
Eaton Dr
Kings Wy
Merritt Av
Alcoa Av
Calle De Nuevo
Northam St
Palm Springs
Wilmington Wy
Roseville Wy
Piedmont Av
Calle De Espana
Plaza De Ernesto
Calle De El Cortez
Campbell Dr
Sultana St
Plaza Da Rosa
Plaza Del Puerto
De Monte
Plaza
Serafina St
Stamba Av
Meade Av
Richfield Blvd
Gilmary Av
Colanthe Av
Bryant Av
Burton Av
Mason Av
Ashby Av
Milo Wy
Jamestown Wy
Plaza De La Candela
Valmora St
Rigel Av
Trona St
Kaiser Wy
Kings Wy
Alcoa Av
Sahara Annex St
El Camino Av
BOB BASKIN PARK
Palm Springs
Taraso Wy
Realeza Ct
Bayo Ct
W Oakey Blvd
Wyandotte St
Wyandotte St
Miraflores Av
Cahlan Dr
Mora La
2
Teddy Dr
Paseo Del Prado
Sidonia Av
Calanda Ct
Fulano Wy
Rambla Ct
2
Lourdes Av
Naco Ct
Adra Ct
La Solana Wy
Rancho Dr
15
Strong Dr
Villa De Conde Wy
Zafra Ct
Karli Dr
Laurie Dr
Lewellyn Dr
Buehler Dr
Sherman Pl
PALACE STATION
W Sahara Av
De Osma St
Edna Av
Mauna Loa La
Mona Loa Dr
Red Oak Av
Westlund Dr
El Cortez Av
Westlund Dr
S Highland Dr
Bryn Mawr Av
Crescent Dr
Glen Heather Wy
Bonnie Brae Av
Westwood Dr
Kirkland Av
Pine St
Edgewood Av
Rancho La
Kirkland Av
Inverness Av
W Oakey Blvd
Silver Av
Bannie Av
Waldman Av
S Tonopah Dr
Birch St
Birch St
Hastings Av
Industrial Rd
Western Av
Sutter Av
Scotland La
Highland Dr
Ivanhoe Wy
Park Cir
Pahor Dr
Rose St
Kiltie Wy
Westwood Dr
Westwood Dr

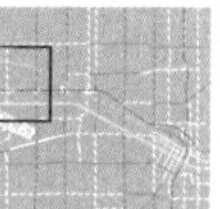

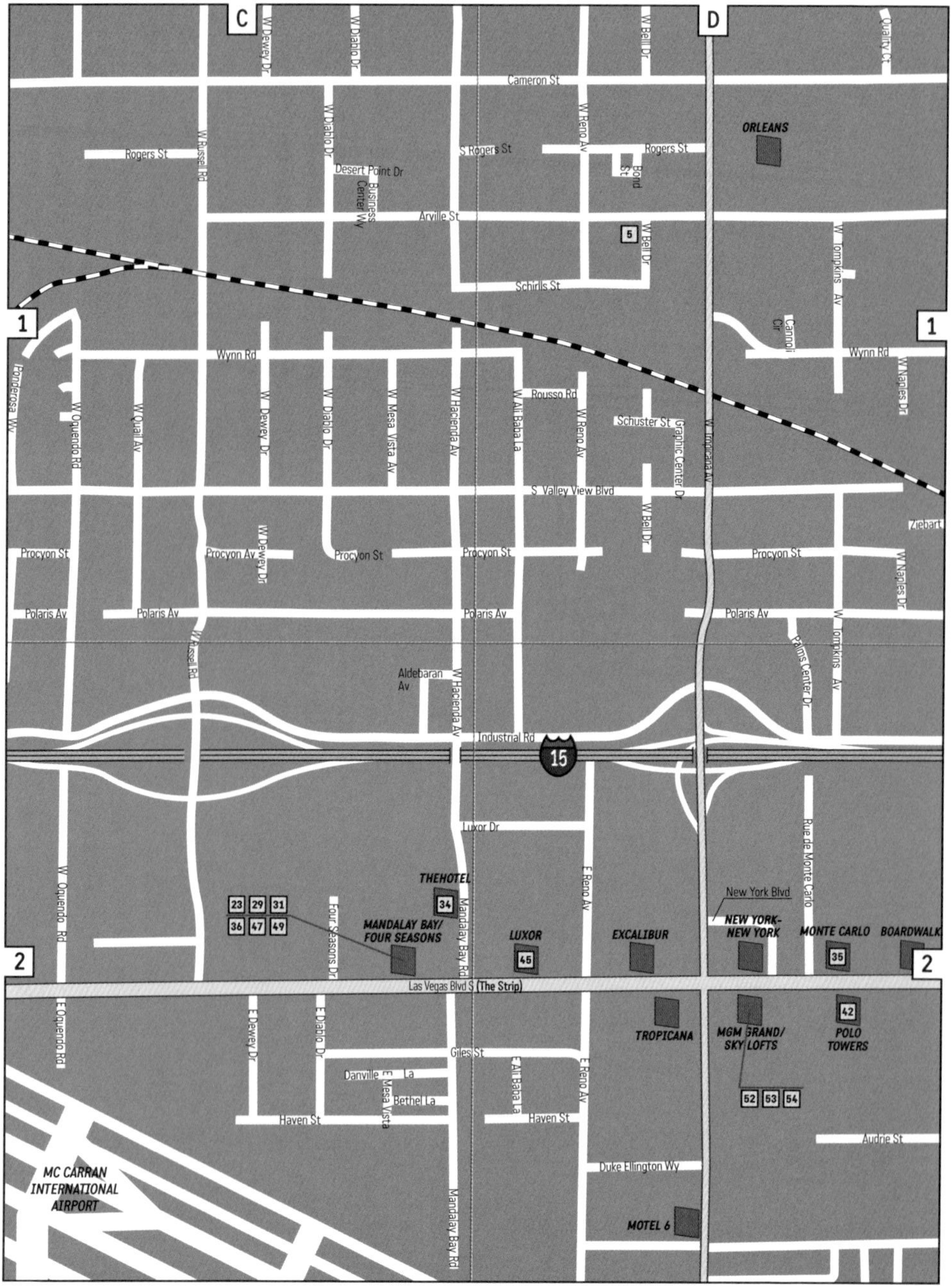

C
D
1
2

W Dewey Dr
W Diablo Dr
W Bell Dr
Quality Ct
Cameron St
ORLEANS
Rogers St
W Russell Rd
W Diablo Dr
W Reno Av
S Rogers St
Rogers St
Desert Point Dr
Business Center Wy
Bond St
Arville St
W Bell Dr
W Tompkins Av
Schirlls St
Cannoli Cir
Wynn Rd
Wynn Rd
Ponderosa Wy
W Oquendo Rd
W Quail Av
W Dewey Dr
W Diablo Dr
W Mesa Vista Av
W Hacienda Av
W Ali Baba La
Rousso Rd
W Reno Av
Schuster St
Graphic Center Dr
W Tropicana Av
W Naples Dr
S Valley View Blvd
W Bell Dr
Ziebart
Procyon St
Procyon Av
W Dewey Dr
Procyon St
Procyon St
Procyon St
W Naples Dr
Polaris Av
Polaris Av
Polaris Av
Polaris Av
W Tompkins Av
Palms Center Dr
W Russel Rd
Aldebaran Av
W Hacienda Av
Industrial Rd
15
Luxor Dr
W Oquendo Rd
THEHOTEL
E Reno Av
Rue de Monte Carlo
New York Blvd
23 29 31
36 47 49
34
Four Seasons Dr
MANDALAY BAY/ FOUR SEASONS
Mandalay Bay Rd
LUXOR
45
EXCALIBUR
NEW YORK-NEW YORK
MONTE CARLO
35
BOARDWALK
Las Vegas Blvd S (The Strip)
E Oquendo Rd
E Dewey Dr
E Diablo Dr
TROPICANA
MGM GRAND/ SKY LOFTS
42
POLO TOWERS
Giles St
Danville La
E Mesa Vista
Bethel La
E Ali Baba La
E Reno Av
52 53 54
Haven St
Haven St
Audrie St
MC CARRAN INTERNATIONAL AIRPORT
Duke Ellington Wy
Mandalay Bay Rd
MOTEL 6

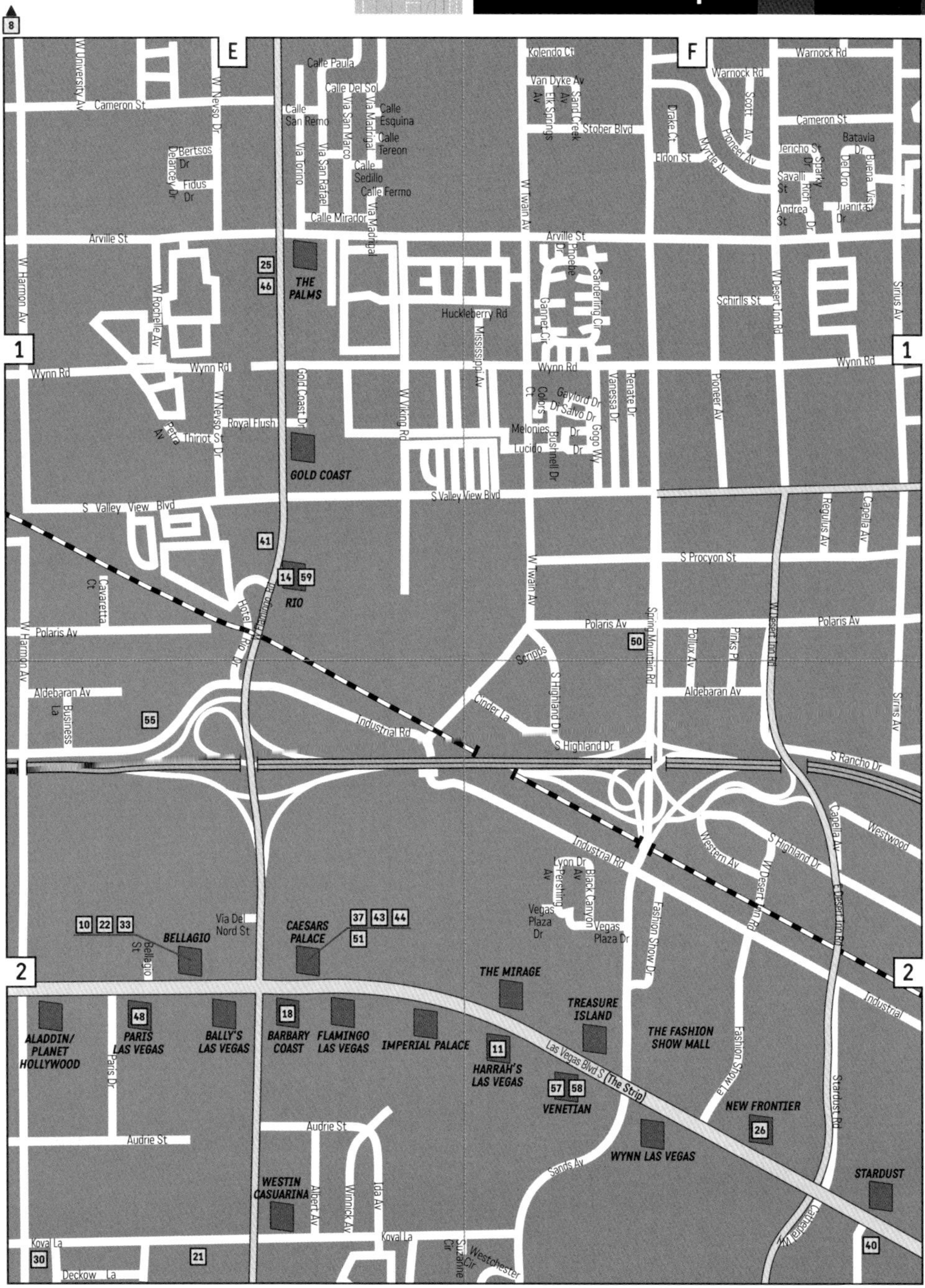

8

E
F
1
1
2
2

25
46
THE PALMS
GOLD COAST
41
14
59
RIO
50
55
10
22
33
BELLAGIO
CAESARS PALACE
37
43
44
51
THE MIRAGE
TREASURE ISLAND
THE FASHION SHOW MALL
ALADDIN/ PLANET HOLLYWOOD
48
PARIS LAS VEGAS
BALLY'S LAS VEGAS
18
BARBARY COAST
FLAMINGO LAS VEGAS
IMPERIAL PALACE
11
HARRAH'S LAS VEGAS
57
58
VENETIAN
NEW FRONTIER
26
WYNN LAS VEGAS
STARDUST
40
WESTIN CASUARINA
30
21

W University Av
Cameron St
W Nevso Dr
Bertsos Dr
Delancey Dr
Fidus Dr
Calle Paula
Calle Del Sol
Calle San Remo
Via San Marco
Via Madrigal
Calle Esquina
Calle Tereon
Via Torino
Via San Rafael
Calle Sedillo
Calle Fermo
Calle Mirador
Kolendo Ct
Van Dyke Av
Elk Springs Av
Sand Creek Av
Stober Blvd
Warnock Rd
Drake Ct
Scott Av
Pioneer Av
Eldon St
Myrtle Av
Cameron St
Jericho St
Batavia Dr
Savalli St
Sparky Dr
Del Oro
Buena Vista
Rich Dr
Andrea St
Juanita Dr
Arville St
W Twain Av
W Harmon Av
W Rochelle Av
Phoebe Dr
Sanderling Cir
Huckleberry Rd
Garnet Cir
Schirlls St
W Desert Inn Rd
Sirius Av
Wynn Rd
Mississippi Av
Gold Coast Dr
W Viking Rd
Colors Ct
Gaylord Dr
Di Salvo Dr
Vanessa Dr
Renate Dr
Pioneer Av
Royal Flush
Petra Av
Thiriot St
Melonies Dr
Lucido Dr
Bushnell Dr
Gogo Wy
S Valley View Blvd
Regulus Av
Capella Av
S Procyon St
Cavaretta Ct
Hotel Rio Dr
Flamingo Rd
Polaris Av
Spring Mountain Rd
Pollux Av
Pinks Pl
Scripps
S Highland Dr
Aldebaran Av
Business La
Cinder La
Industrial Rd
S Rancho Dr
Westwood
Western Av
Lyon Dr
Pershing Av
Black Canyon Av
Vegas Plaza Dr
Fashion Show Dr
Via Del Nord St
Bellagio St
Industrial
Las Vegas Blvd S (The Strip)
Paris Dr
Fashion Show La
Stardust Rd
Audrie St
Sands Av
Albert Av
Winnick Av
Ida Av
Koval La
Suzanne Cir
Westchester
W Cathedral
Deckow La

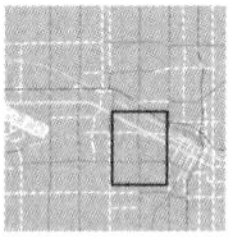

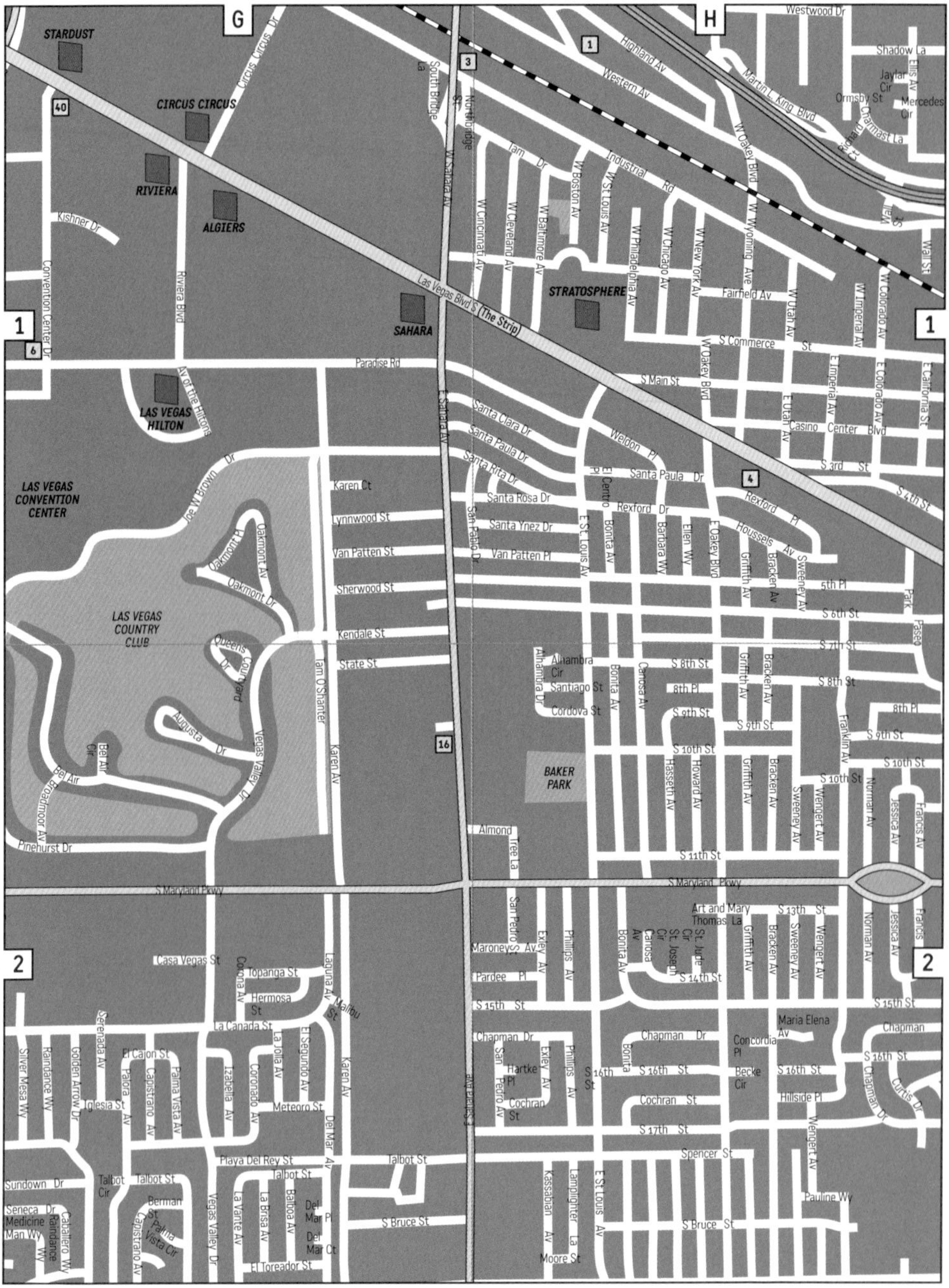
G
H
1
2
STARDUST
CIRCUS CIRCUS
RIVIERA
ALGIERS
STRATOSPHERE
SAHARA
LAS VEGAS HILTON
LAS VEGAS CONVENTION CENTER
LAS VEGAS COUNTRY CLUB
BAKER PARK
Las Vegas Blvd S (The Strip)
Westwood Dr
Shadow La
Jaylar Cir
Ormsby St
Mercedes Cir
Ellis Av
Highland Av
Western Av
Martin L. King Blvd
Richard Ct
Charmast La
W Oakey Blvd
W Wyoming Ave
Industrial Rd
Wall St
Circus Circus Dr
South Bridge La
Northbridge St
W Sahara Av
Tam Dr
W Boston Av
W St Louis Av
W Cincinnati Av
W Cleveland Av
W Baltimore Av
W Philadelphia Av
W Chicago Av
W New York Av
Fairfield Av
W Utah Av
W Imperial Av
W Colorado Av
Kishner Dr
Convention Center Dr
Riviera Blvd
Paradise Rd
Av of the Hilton
S Commerce St
S Main St
E Imperial Av
E Colorado Av
E California St
Casino Center Blvd
E Utah Av
S 3rd St
S 4th St
E Sahara Av
Santa Clara Dr
Santa Paula Dr
Santa Rita Dr
Santa Rosa Dr
Santa Ynez Dr
San Pablo Dr
Van Patten Pl
Weldon Pl
El Centro Pl
Rexford Dr
Rexford Pl
Bonita Av
Barbara Wy
Ellen Wy
E Oakey Blvd
E St Louis Av
Houssels Av
Griffith Av
Bracken Av
Sweeney Av
5th Pl
S 6th St
Park Paseo
Joe W Brown Dr
Karen Ct
Lynnwood St
Van Patten St
Sherwood St
Kendale St
State St
Oakmont Pl
Oakmont Av
Oakmont Dr
Queens Courtyard Dr
Augusta Dr
Vegas Valley Dr
Bel Air Cir
Bel Air
Broadmoor Av
Pinehurst Dr
Tam O'Shanter
Karen Av
S 7th St
Alhambra Cir
Alhambra Dr
Santiago St
Cordova St
Canosa Av
S 8th St
8th Pl
S 9th St
S 10th St
Hasseth Av
Howard Av
Wengert Av
Franklin Av
Norman Av
Jessica Av
Francis Av
Almond Tree La
S 11th St
S Maryland Pkwy
Casa Vegas St
Corona Av
Topanga St
Hermosa St
Laguna Av
Malibu St
La Canada St
La Jolla Av
El Segundo Av
Karen Av
Silver Mesa Wy
Raindance Wy
Golden Arrow Dr
Serenada Av
El Cajon St
Palora Av
Capistrano Av
Palma Vista Av
Izabella Av
Coronado Av
Meteoro St
Iglesia St
Del Mar Av
Playa Del Rey St
Talbot St
Sundown Dr
Talbot Cir
Berman St
Palma Vista Cir
Seneca Dr
Medicine Man Wy
Raindance Wy
Caballero Wy
Vegas Valley Dr
La Vante Av
La Brisa Av
Balboa Av
Del Mar Pl
Del Mar Ct
El Toreador St
S Bruce St
San Pedro Av
Maroney Av
Pardee Pl
S 15th St
Chapman Dr
Exley Av
Phillips Av
Hartke Pl
Cochran St
S 16th St
Art and Mary Thomas La
St. Jude Cir
St. Joseph Cir
S 13th St
S 14th St
Maria Elena Av
Concordia Pl
Becke Cir
Hillside Pl
Curtis Dr
S 17th St
Spencer St
Kassabian Av
Lamplighter La
E St Louis Av
Pauline Wy
Moore St
1
3
4
6
16
40

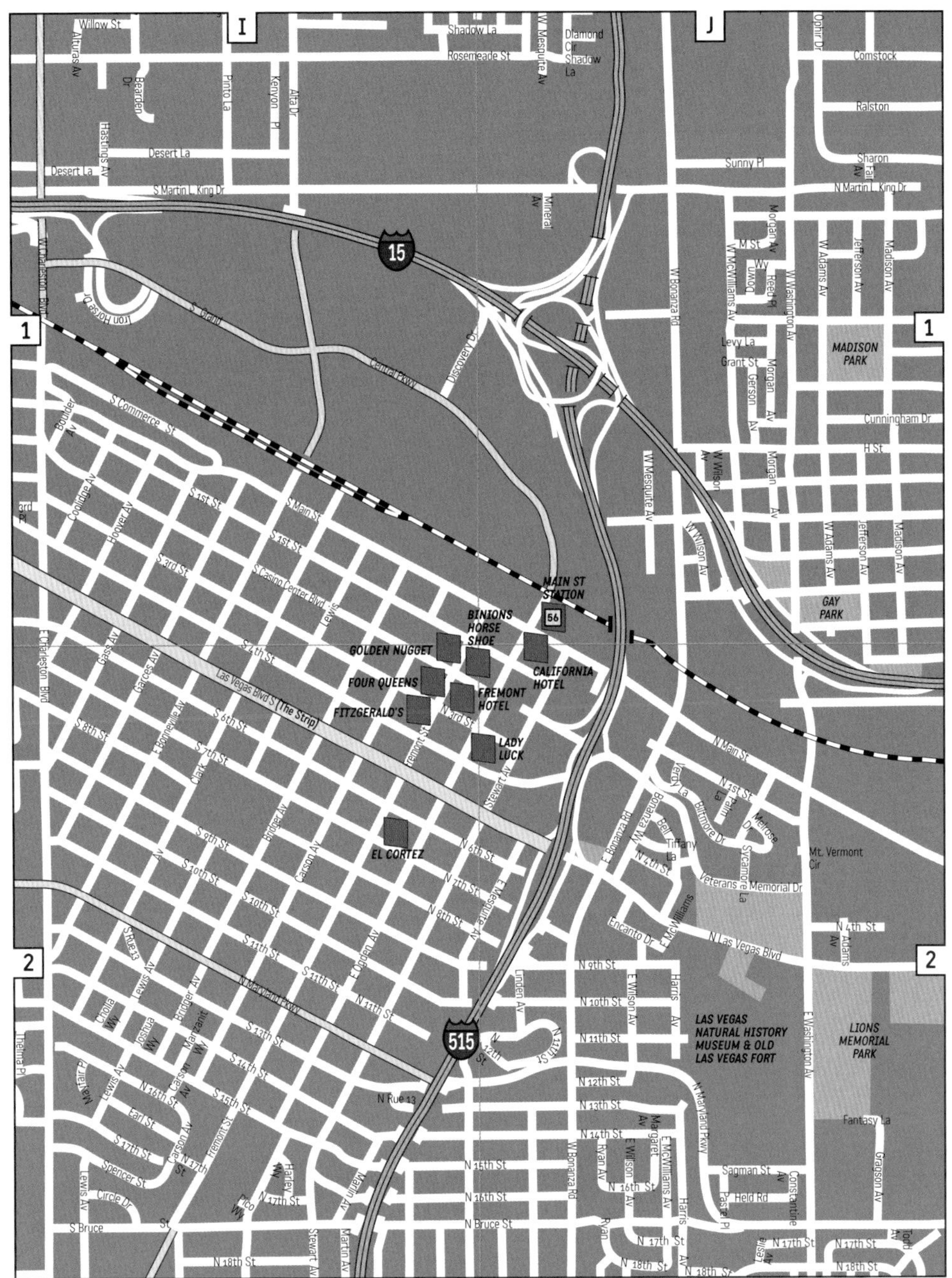
I
J
1
2
MAIN ST STATION
BINIONS HORSE SHOE
GOLDEN NUGGET
CALIFORNIA HOTEL
FOUR QUEENS
FREMONT HOTEL
FITZGERALD'S
LADY LUCK
EL CORTEZ
MADISON PARK
GAY PARK
LAS VEGAS NATURAL HISTORY MUSEUM & OLD LAS VEGAS FORT
LIONS MEMORIAL PARK
15
515
56
Willow St
Shadow La
Rosemeade St
Diamond Cir
W Mesquite Av
Comstock
Ralston
Sunny Pl
Desert La
S Martin L King Dr
N Martin L King Dr
Las Vegas Blvd S (The Strip)
N Las Vegas Blvd
Central Pkwy
S Grand
Discovery Dr
S Commerce St
S Main St
S 1st St
S Casino Center Blvd
Fremont St
E Charleston Blvd
W Bonanza Rd
Veterans Memorial Dr
N Main St
Mt. Vermont Cir
E Washington Av
N Maryland Pkwy
Fantasy La
N Bruce St
N 18th St

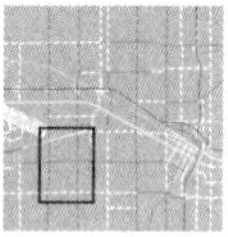

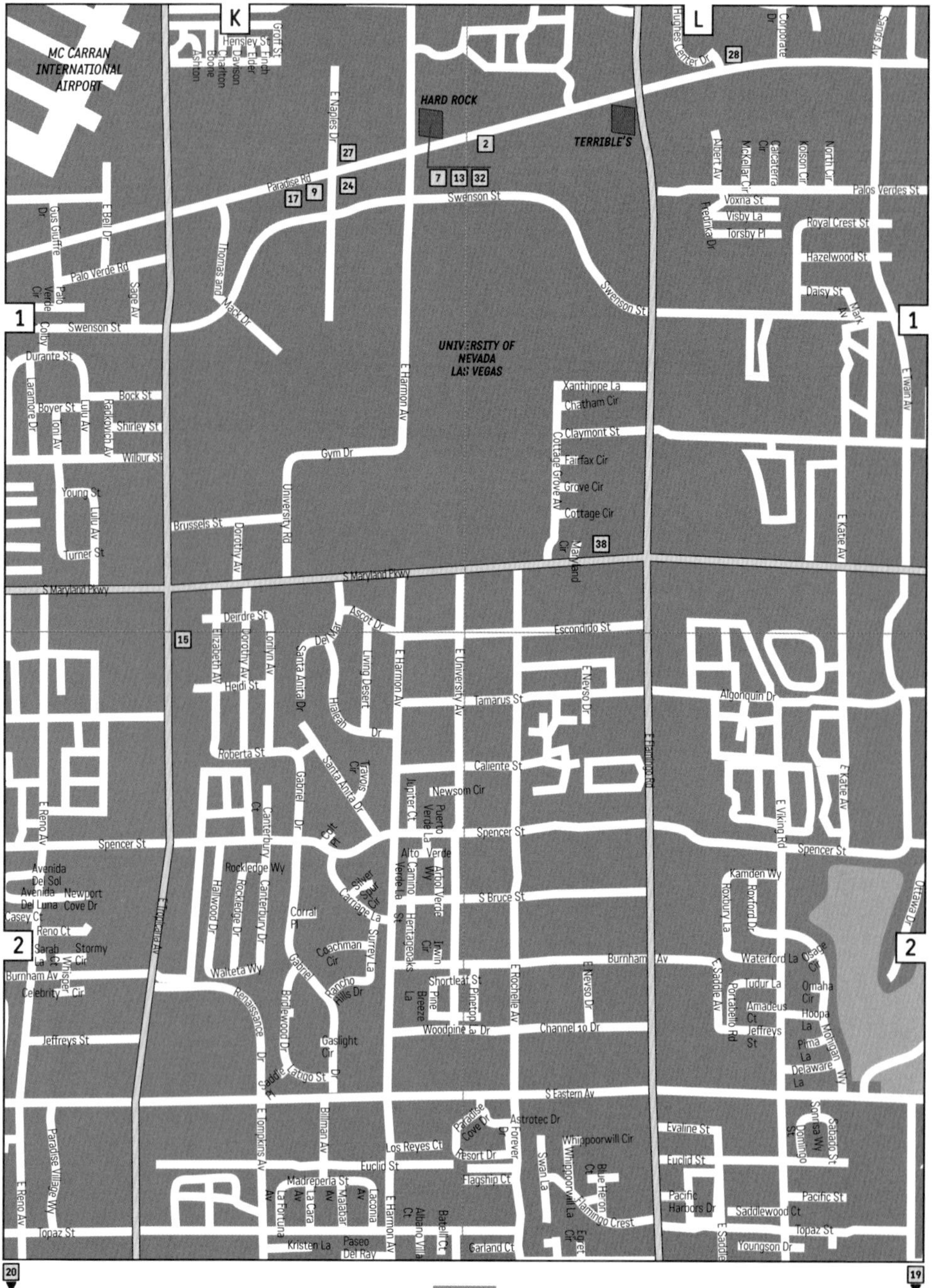

K L

1 1

2 2

MC CARRAN INTERNATIONAL AIRPORT

HARD ROCK

TERRIBLE'S

UNIVERSITY OF NEVADA LAS VEGAS

28 2 27 24 17 9 7 13 32 38 15

Hensley St Groff St Finch Elder Dawson Charlton Boone Ashton Hughes Center Dr Corporate Dr Sands Av

E Naples Dr Paradise Rd Swenson St Palos Verdes St Albert Av McKellar Cir Calcaterra Cir Kolson Cir North Cir Voxna St Visby La Torsby Pl Fredrika Dr Royal Crest St Hazelwood St Daisy St Mark Av

Gus Giuffre Dr E Bell Dr Palo Verde Rd Palo Verde Cir Sage Av Thomas and Mack Dr Swenson St

Colby Durante St Laramore Dr Boyer St Toni Av Lulu Av Radkovich Av Bock St Shirley St Wilbur St Young St Turner St E Harmon Av Gym Dr University Rd Brussels St Dorothy Av E Twain Av

Xanthippe La Chatham Cir Claymont St Cottage Grove Av Fairfax Cir Grove Cir Cottage Cir Maryland Cir E Katie Av

S Maryland Pkwy

Deirdre St Elizabeth Av Dorothy Av Lorilyn Av Heidi St Santa Anita Dr Del Mar Ascot Dr Living Desert Hialeah Dr E Harmon Av E University Av Escondido St Tamarus St E Nevso Dr Algonquin Dr

Roberta St Gabriel Dr Santa Anita Dr Travois Cir Jupiter Ct Caliente St Newsom Cir E Flamingo Rd E Viking Rd E Katie Av

E Reno Av Spencer St Canterbury Ct Colt Pl Puerto Verde La Spencer St Spencer St

Avenida Del Sol Avenida Del Luna Newport Cove Dr Casey Ct Reno Ct Sarah La Stormy Ct Whisper Cir Burnham Av Celebrity Cir Rockledge Wy Hallwood Dr Rockledge Dr Canterbury Dr Silver Spur Cir Carriage La Alto Camino Verde La Verde Arbol Wy Arbol Verde St S Bruce St Kamden Wy Roxbury La Roxford Dr Ottawa Dr

E Tropicana Av Corral Pl Coachman Cir Surrey La Heritage Oaks La Irwin Cir Burnham Av Waterford La Osage Cir

Walteta Wy Renaissance Dr Bridlewood Dr Gabriel Rancho Hills Dr Shortleaf St Pine Breeze Pinetop E Rochelle Av E Nevso Dr E Sadde Av Portabello Rd Tudur La Amadeus Ct Omaha Cir Hoopa La

Jeffreys St Gaslight Cir Woodpine La Dr Channel 10 Dr Jeffreys St Pima La Mohigan Wy Delaware La

Saddle Latigo St Dr S Eastern Av

Paradise Village Wy E Tompkins Av Billman Av Paradise Cove Dr Astrotec Dr Forever Whippoorwill Cir Evaline St Sonrisa Wy Sabado St Domingo St

Los Reyes Ct Resort Dr Euclid St Euclid St

E Reno Av Madreperla St La Fortuna Av La Cara Av Malabar Av Laconia Av E Harmon Av Albano Villa Ct Batelli Ct Flagship Ct Swan La Whippoorwill La Blue Heron Ct Flamingo Crest Egret Cir Pacific Harbors Dr Saddlewood Ct Pacific St

Topaz St Kristen La Paseo Del Rey Garland Ct Youngson Dr Topaz St E Sadde

20 19

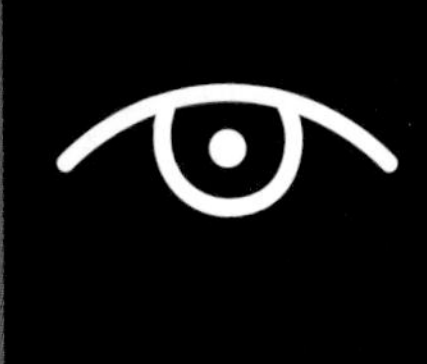

EXPLORE 5

Jesus wasn't born in Las Vegas, the old joke goes, because they couldn't find three wise men and a virgin. Like no other city in the world, this place is firmly rooted in the lower chakras, knocking out all who visit with the classic one-two punch of venial sin and mortal anti-intellectualism. It's easy to mock Vegas as simply being "fake," but that doesn't do justice to a place that should be awarding its most astute visitors with PhDs in kitsch. That's because Las Vegas is a fake that understands it is fake. Full appreciation of this city's truly sumptuous plasticity requires a refined sense of post-modernist irony—or the same suspension of disbelief that's necessary to trust you have a decent chance of becoming a millionaire with a single magic pull. Nobody—not even most UNLV students, it seems—comes here for highbrow pursuits. The local science museum? Fugetaboutit. In Las Vegas, "art" is more likely to be the name of your limousine driver.

The Best of Las Vegas...

Top Las Vegas Experiences
Forum Shops at Caesars Festival Fountains
The Fountains at Bellagio
Fremont Street Experience
Mirage Volcano
Sirens of TI Show
Stratosphere Tower

Top Museums & Galleries
Casino Legends Hall of Fame Museum
Elvis-A-Rama Museum
Guggenheim Hermitage Museum
Imperial Palace Auto Collection
Liberace Museum

Top Offbeat Sights
The Gun Store
The Little Church of the West
Gondola Rides at the Venetian
Welcome to Fabulous Las Vegas Sign

Top Parks & Gardens
Bellagio Botanical Conservatory
Flamingo Las Vegas Wildlife Habitat
Lion Habitat
Siegfried & Roy's Secret Garden & Dolphin Habitat

Top Places To Take Kids
Adventuredome Theme Park
GameWorks
Las Vegas Cyber Speedway
Merlin the Wizard Show
Shark Reef
White Tiger Habitat

Top Thrills
Flyaway Indoor Skydiving
Manhattan Express Rollercoaster
Mario Andretti Racing School
Speed—The Ride
Stratosphere Tower Rides
Wet 'n' Wild

Las Vegas Superlatives!

The largest city formed in the 20th century
Home to the 10 largest hotels in the world
Has the highest percentage of high school dropouts – 10.8%
Contains the world's largest pawn shop – Super Pawn
Performed the world's first execution by lethal gas – 1924

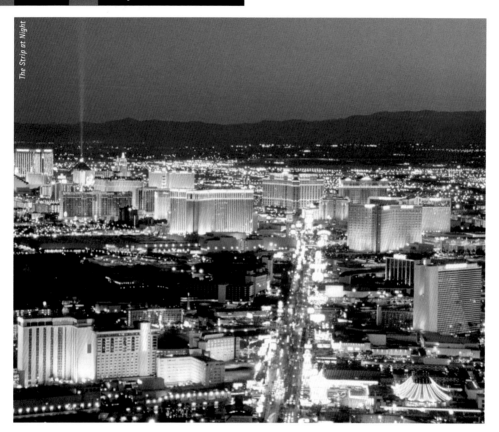

The Strip at Night

The Best Tours

Desert Fox Tours | 6265 Industrial Rd (at Post), Southwest, T 702.361.0676 The desert that surrounds Vegas is some of the most beguiling terrain anywhere. Yet most visitors never see it. You can simply drive your rental into the wilderness, or you can get off-road and onto obstacle-filled trails with one of Desert Fox's experienced guides driving a powerful, all-terrain Hummer. Tours last 3 to 6 hours.

Papillon Grand Canyon Helicopters | McCarran International Airport Executive Air Terminal, East Side, T 702.736.7243 or 800.528.2418 Several helicopter companies take visitors over the Strip, or to the Grand Canyon and beyond. Papillon, one of the largest, has an excellent Strip at Night tour and another that touches down for a champagne picnic on the floor of the Grand Canyon.

Scenic Airlines | North Las Vegas Airport, 2705 Airport Dr (at N Rancho), North Las Vegas, T 702.638.3275 or 800.634.6801 Scenic offers full-day, half-day and overnight tours to the Grand Canyon, Bryce Canyon, Monument Valley and Yosemite National Park. The Highlights Tour takes in Las Vegas, Lake Mead, Hoover Dam and the Colorado River, and the Grand Canyon. The company flies high-winged De Havilland Twin Otter airplanes that have been specially designed with large oversized windows for unobstructed views.

Adventuredome Theme Park

Circus Circus, 2880 Las Vegas Blvd S (at Circus Circus), Strip

T 702.734.0410 MAP G1 1

You could easily be forgiven for not noticing that "America's largest indoor theme park" (is there another one?) is hiding just behind the Strip. From the outside, the pink pleasure dome looks something like a Barnum & Bailey tent. Inside is a wacky environment built with fake stone cliffs, tunnels, caves and grottos, and almost two dozen rides and attractions. Top billing is given to the Canyon Blaster, a double-loop, double-corkscrew roller coaster, but it could just as well go to Chaos, an intense whirly ride, or the Inverter, whose name doesn't leave a lot to the imagination. There's also a cool virtual fun house, and a decent water-flume ride that will soak you, as well as bumper cars, a Ferris wheel, midway games, laser tag and IMAX Motion Rides. Admission is free, pay only for your rides.

AJ Hackett Bungy

Circus Circus, 2880 Las Vegas Blvd S (at Circus Circus), Strip

T 702.385.4321 MAP G1 2

After losing all your money and drinking yourself sick, what fun is left in this town? Pretend to end it all by taking a flying leap from a 200-foot (64-meter) tower into a sparkling pool. Take an elevator to the top, jump 18-stories, and get a T-shirt and certificate to prove you did it.

Bellagio Botanical Conservatory

Bellagio, 3600 Las Vegas Blvd S (at Flamingo), Strip

T 702.693.7444 MAP E2 4

The lobby of the Bellagio is home to the Botanical Conservatory, a gorgeous three-story, glass-domed garden filled with thousands of flowers and plants. The stunning floribundance changes seasonally and has included blazing fall colors of oranges and reds, Independence Day flower arrangements that appear to explode like fireworks against a solid backdrop, and Christmas decorations by pre-con Martha Stewart. This is no small feat: The hotel claims that it takes a team of 115 horticulturalists and about $8 million annually to maintain the conservatory. It's also proof that life can actually thrive in stunted casino air.

Bellagio Gallery of Fine Art

Bellagio, 3600 Las Vegas Blvd S (at Flamingo), Strip

T 702.693.7722 MAP E2 5

When MGM Grand Inc. acquired the Bellagio as part of its 2000 takeover of Mirage Resorts Inc., it didn't include

Bellagio Botanical Conservatory

this museum's celebrated collection of impressionist, post-Impressionist and modernist masters. Since that time, the Gallery has become an exhibition space for small temporary shows, like art from The Phillips Collection of Washington, D.C. (Degas, Cézanne, Picasso, Matisse, Monet and van Gogh), the Collection of Steve Martin (David Hockney, Edward Hopper, Roy Lichtenstein, Picasso), and an exhibit dedicated to kinetic sculpture by Alexander Calder. Sure, the entry fee is higher than New York's Metropolitan Museum of Art, but it includes an audio tour of the gallery, and we think it's worth it if they've got a show you want to see.

Casino Legends Hall of Fame Museum

Tropicana, 3801 Las Vegas Blvd S (at Tropicana), Strip

T 702.739.2222 MAP D2 6

With over 15,000 items of memorabilia from 738 casinos (most no longer existing), the Trop's gambling museum is crammed with thousands of "exhibitions" commemorating the city's larger-than-life personalities. You want chips? They're here, including one worth a quarter of a million smackers. You want swizzle sticks, gaming licenses, hotel china, Mike Tyson's boxing gloves, Vegas-themed movie clips, daredevil Robbie

The Fall of Atlantis at the Forum Shops

Knievel's jumpsuit, jai alai equipment, a bottle of Barbra Streisand Wine, drag queen dresses, Leroy Neiman paintings, a municipal tribute to flamboyant casino mogul Bob Stupak ("What he said will happen, did happen, and it happened in a city that was built on the odds"), and Marilyn Monroe and Joe DiMaggio's marriage license, not to mention comedian Buddy Hackett's 1963 performance contract, according to which Mr. Hackett was to be "provided oral gratification both before and after 'the show' by a showgirl of his choice"? Believe us, they're here, along with Pearl Bailey's dentures.

The Circus

Circus Circus, 2880 Las Vegas Blvd S (at Circus Circus), Strip

T 702.734.0410 MAP G1 7

Opened in 1968, Circus² was the second themed resort (after Caesars Palace) by the high-spirited entrepreneur Jay Sarno. It was also the first "family friendly" casino on the Strip. Lucky the Clown, the resort's neon mascot, has long been one of the brightest cultural images on Las Vegas Boulevard. Inside, above the main casino and under the fuchsia big-top, Russian aerialists and Chinese acrobats perform throughout the day. There are games of skill and chance on the Midway Mezzanine, and **The Adventuredome**, America's largest indoor theme park, is just out back.

Eiffel Tower Experience

Paris Las Vegas, 3655 Las Vegas Blvd S (at Harmon), Strip

T 702.946.7000 MAP E2 8

We're hard pressed to say which is cornier: ascending to the top of Vegas's 50-story replica of the Eiffel Tower, or sitting back for a gondola ride on the Grand Canal down the street. Both should be approached with the same sense of irony, and both are best experienced with a lover in tow. Romantic? Not really, but you can play along and *faux* it just like you're supposed to. While the Eiffel Tower is less than half the height of the **Stratosphere Tower** at the north end of the Strip, the lower vantage and more central location makes this small, mesh-covered observation deck a great place to view the city. Plus, this is the best spot to watch the Bellagio's prancing waters show just across the street. The vista is terrific both day and night, so why not double your pleasure and arrive at sunset when the city shimmers with color. Is this "experience" worth $20 for two? Probably not. But it's far more memorable than a losing hand of Blackjack. Cheapskates can get a free eagle-eye look at the Strip from the **VooDoo Lounge** atop the Rio, or the **Polo Lounge** atop Polo Towers.

Elvis-A-Rama Museum

3401 Industrial Rd (at Fashion Show), West Side

T 702.309.7200 MAP F2 9

Did you know that when Elvis Presley offered his old friend Dave Hebler a Cadillac as a gift and Hebler refused because Elvis had already given him a Cadillac, Elvis angrily pulled a gun on Hebler? And did you know that, on seeing the gun, "Hebler gladly accepted the car and said that he would enjoy owning it to drive around Memphis"? For the dry telling of that tale alone, we would adore this place, but it's such a professionally-run and well-appointed Elvis emporium that we would probably dig it anyway. And while a genuine interest in the King is necessary to fully enjoy it (there's only one black-velvet painting), anyone with a fulsome sense of irony will cotton to it enough to make the trip here worthwhile. The museum is full of goodies like Elvis' Glastron Bayflite speedboat, his American Express card (along with his 1969 application listing his annual

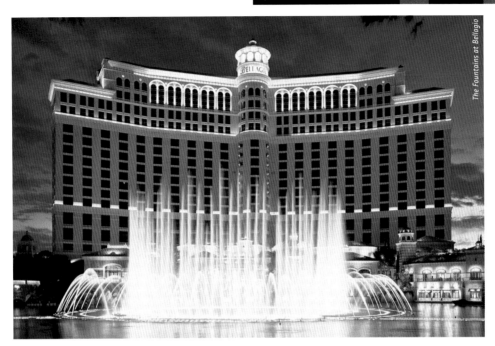

The Fountains at Bellagio

income at $3 million), letters to girlfriends ("the things we did and the desire we had for each other's body"), letters from his manager Colonel Parker (with a letterhead depicting a covered wagon and the words "We Cover The Nation"), a "Love Me Tender" briefcase, a "Don't Be Cruel" beach hat, ad nauseum. There are even regular small-scale shows put on by various Elvis impersonators, including the superb Sonny Boline and the teenage Justin Shandor (call for showtimes). Great giftshop too. If you're staying on the Strip, just tell your concierge that you've got a "Burning Love" and he'll ring the free shuttle for you. Make sure you specify that your "Burning Love" is for Elvis, though, or else you may receive a hotel room visit from the voluptuous Bellski twins, Stacey and Debbie, which will set you back—at least—five hundred clams.

Flamingo Las Vegas Wildlife Habitat

Flamingo, 3555 Las Vegas Blvd S (at Flamingo), Strip

T 702.733.3111 **MAP E2 10**

The Flamingo is not one of the Strip's swankiest hotels, but it's worth taking some time to explore the resort's extensive grounds that include rambling emerald gardens with tropical foliage, three-story waterfalls, Koi-stocked lagoons, African penguins and the hotel's trademark Chilean flamingos. The Habitat dates from the 1990's, when the last remnants of Bugsy's original hotel were demolished in favor of new towers. But the grounds still have the mood of old Vegas, complete with zigzagging water slides and kitschy flamingo fountains.

Flyaway Indoor Skydiving

200 Convention Center Dr (at Paradise), East Side

T 702.731.4768 **MAP G1 11**

This skydiving simulator is our favorite Vegas "sport." After a 20-minute training class, 15 minutes of equipment preparation and signing a two-page liability waiver, you get a 3-minute flight session in a padded wind tunnel that's supposedly similar to one the US Army uses for training. A DC-3 propeller in the floor creates a deafening roar and hurricane-force winds. Lie down on the mesh and the wind lifts you into the air. Mastering flying actually takes a lot of body control. And you need to be in fairly decent shape. But no worries about your parachute not opening. Flight suits, goggles and other gear are provided. They say that this is one of only a handful of skydiving simulators in the world, and we believe them because we've never seen anything like it. You've got to wear

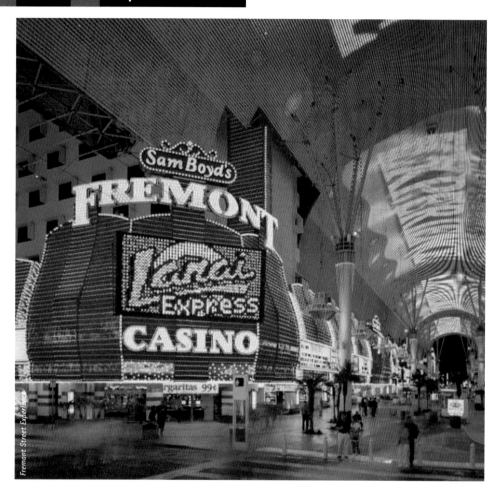

Fremont Street Experience

socks and soft-soled shoes and big people need not apply: you must weigh no more than 230 pounds to fly. Flyaway is located just off the Strip, a half-block east of the Stardust Hotel. Sessions cost about $50.

Forum Shops Festival Fountains

Caesars Forum Shops, 3570 Las Vegas Blvd S (at Flamingo), Strip

T 702.893.4800 — **MAP E2 12**

Newly expanded, the Forum Shops continue to be one of the city's highlights. At the "Talking" Roman Gods Show, animatronic statues narrate some kind of unintelligible "story" to the accompaniment of fire, lasers and booming sound. As asinine as it is enjoyable, this is a great 7-minute performance that's worth making a special trip for. At the other end of the mall, situated, appropriately enough, near the Cheesecake Factory, is the Fall of Atlantis Fountain Show, in which fire rains down from parted "skies" as the Children of Atlas fight for control of the Lost City. This is a spectacular production that has matured into one of the best-attended free sights in Vegas—which means it's always mobbed, though it hardly matters because there's not a bad sightline in the house. The show doubles as an advertisement for the adjacent Race for Atlantis IMAX 3-D ride that takes "mo-sim" to the next level and is one of the best of its kind in Vegas. See Shop for complete store information.

The Fountains at Bellagio

Bellagio, 3600 Las Vegas Blvd S (at Flamingo), Strip

T 702.693.7444 MAP E2 13

Waltzing waters were a trademark of local legend Liberace, who placed specially-built fountains on stage during his shows. The Bellagio has multiplied the theme a hundred-fold to create this stellar water attraction in front of the resort, directly on the Strip. To put it succinctly, more than a thousand computerized geysers shoot crisply choreographed spouts of water high into the air in time to synchronized stage lighting and popular music by the likes of Luciano Pavarotti, Frank Sinatra, and Gene Kelly. But the water doesn't just squirt straight up; it arcs, sways, swirls, and high-kicks like so many Vegas showgirls. The various 5- to 10-minute routines are anything but routine, and well worth making a special effort to see. Because the liquid chorus line runs along a block-long tree-lined promenade, there's plenty of room to watch. And if the wind is blowing, you'll even catch some spray (however, really high winds and inclement weather usually cause the show to be cancelled). Aside from standing on the sidewalk out front, there are several good vantage points from which to catch the show: Paris' **Eiffel Tower**, across the street, offers a particularly good view of the action as do the waterfront tables in most of the Bellagio's restaurants. Our favorite view is from the outdoor terrace of the Bellagio's **Fontana Bar**. You don't even have to buy anything, just confidently walk straight out to the patio. Shows run every 15-30 minutes throughout the day.

Fremont Street Experience

Fremont St (at Main), Downtown

T 702.678.5777 MAP I2 14

As the fortunes of the Strip ascended, those of Fremont Street fell into decline. In order to stay relevant and counter the wattage of the Strip, 11 Downtown hotels banded together in 1995 (along with the City of Las Vegas and the Las Vegas Convention and Visitors Authority) to create the Fremont Street Experience, in which four central blocks were pedestrianized and covered with a high-tech LED canopy. Each hour from dusk to midnight the street transforms into a free 7- to 9-minute light and sound show featuring concert-quality audio and a colorful computerized ballet of images created with 12.5 million synchronized lights. It's not the most amazing thing you'll ever see, but it's cool, free and worth making even a couple of trips for. With over a dozen different shows, it's unlikely you'll see the same one twice. The best place to stand is right in the middle, in front of the Horseshoe. Better yet, catch the multi-media spectacular from the small second-floor balcony of Lucky's Lookout bar at Fitzgerald's (take the escalator to the second level about 15 minutes early to beat the crowds). The "experience" includes a handful of retail shops, souvenir stands, street musicians, casino hawkers and a few local drunks singing in the middle of the street. And you can still find remnants of classic Vegas, including two of the city's most enduring icons: Vegas Vickie, the neon cowgirl that's perched above the Girls of Glitter Gulch strip club, and Vegas Vic, the ancient neon cowboy who used to wave to passing punters. Erected in 1950 and recently refurbished, Vic is once again the most colorful character in the neighborhood, though his deep voice, which once regularly intoned "Howdy Pardner!" can now only be heard occasionally.

GameWorks

Showcase Mall, 3785 Las Vegas Blvd S (at Tropicana Ave), Strip

T 702.432.4263 MAP D2 15

Sharing a mall with **M&Ms World**, next to the MGM Grand and across the street from New York-New York, GameWorks is the best games room outside a resort hotel. It's also probably the largest video arcade you've ever seen, bolstered by everything from old-time pinball machines to virtual-reality bobsleds which pit several racers against one another on the same icy course. There's a four-story rock-climbing wall too. The playing floor is continually updated with the latest games and, although this place is mostly mobbed with hormonal teenagers smelling like Clearasil, they've got a fully-stocked bar and lots of attractive drink specials.

Gondola Rides on the Grand Canal

Venetian Grand Canal Shoppes, 3355 Las Vegas Blvd S (at Sands), Strip

T 702.414.4500 MAP F2 16

The Venetian's attention to detail is so obsessive you'll think you're in the real thing; unless, of course, you've been to the real thing, in which case you'll just think this is kitsch of the highest order. Upon entering the resort, visitors are bowled over by the awesome Tiepolo-like frescoes on the ceilings of the entrance hall. But, its upstairs where the real fun awaits, in the guise of the **Grand Canal Shoppes** which are laid-out around a fake Grand Canal with real gondola rides complete with singing gondoliers. The ten-minute, half-mile (0.8 km) cruise up the center of the mall, under the gaze of the shopping hordes, is as ridiculous and kitschy as can

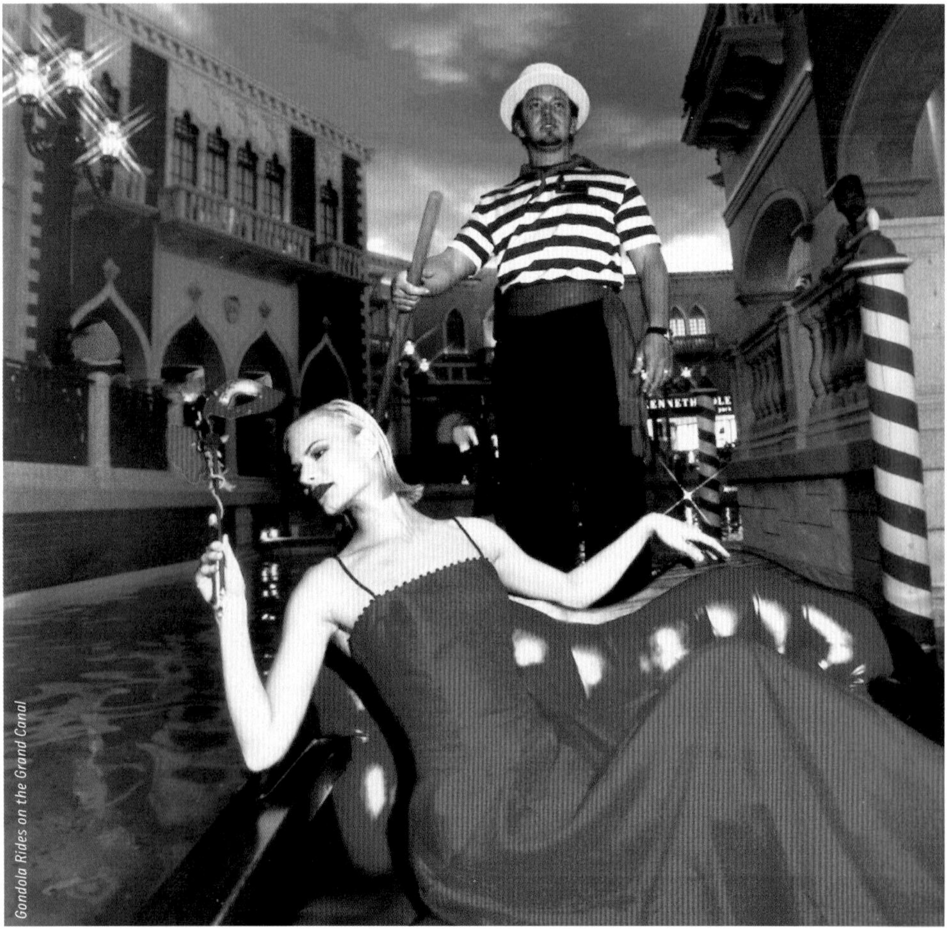

Gondola Rides on the Grand Canal

be. And it's not exactly a cheap thrill either. But for anyone with a refined sense of poor taste, this is a Vegas must-do, which is why they sell out every day. In fact, demand is so strong that they added gondola rides in the canal in front of the resort too. Each gondola seats four, so that couples are paired up with another party. Reservations are required and are only accepted on the day you ride. Get there early if you want to get on. If spectating is more your speed, then simply arrive any day at either 930am or 4pm to witness the Gondolier Parade, which floats the length of the Grand Canal—from the food court to St. Mark's Square.

Guggenheim Hermitage Museum

The Venetian, 3355 Las Vegas Blvd S (at Spring Mountain), Strip

T 702.414.2440 MAP F2 17

For visitors who feel guilty about gambling away their inheritance, getting drunk in strip clubs and waking up in the gutter, there's this novel joint venture between the American Solomon R. Guggenheim Foundation and the illustrious State Hermitage Museum of St. Petersburg, Russia. Hanging in this Rem Koolhaas-designed gallery, by way of powerful magnets, are several dozen works from one or both of the two museums or perhaps from some other museum altogether; exhibitions here change every six months. Recent exhibitions have included

"Masterpieces and Master Collectors" (Picasso, Renoir, Cézanne), "The Pursuit of Pleasure" (Velázquez, Kandinsky, Picasso), and American Pop Icons (Rauschenberg, Lichtenstein, Warhol).

The Gun Store

2900 E Tropicana Ave (at McLeod), East Side

T 702.454.1110 **MAP K2 18**

Be redneck chic at this quirky, one-of-a-kind Vegas spot where you can fire off a few rounds from machine guns that are illegal in most other states. Behind the boxy white facade is an indoor range where visitors without felonies can test not only a handgun or rifle, but Thomson sub machine guns, M16s, AK-47s and fully automatic Uzis too. A staff member will give you a brief safety talk, before handing over ear and eye protection and the gun of your choice. Fifty rounds of ammo costs about $30. But because Uzis are capable of firing 600 rounds per minute, this kind of fun can get expensive. Your bullet-ridden target is your souvenir. The Gun Store is situated about 3.5 miles (5.6 km) from the Strip. Visit their website (www.thegunstorelasvegas.com) for a discount coupon.

Imperial Palace Auto Collection

Imperial Palace, 3535 Las Vegas Blvd S (at Sands), Strip

T 702.794.3174 **MAP E2 19**

The best—no, only reason to visit this blue-roofed pagoda hotel is to see the spectacular Auto Collection, an enormous museum with over 200 antique and special-interest automobiles. The location—on the fifth floor of a parking garage—is unsavory, and the owner of the casino and the museum, one Ralph Engelstad, is more unsavory still, having been fined $1.5 million for openly displaying Nazi memorabilia and throwing two parties in honor of Hitler's birthday (complete with a swastika cake, German marching music and bartenders wearing T-shirts emblazoned with "Adolph Hitler European Tour 1939-45"). Yet the Auto Collection is one of the most rewarding museums in Vegas. Car freak or not, you'll find a plethora of rare and fascinating "rides" here. For Elvis enthusiasts, there's his 1976 Cadillac Eldorado. Fans of the Velvet Underground song "Sweet Jane" will finally learn what a Stutz Bearcat looks like (in the form of a '72 model once owned by Sammy Davis, Jr.). And even color-blind visitors will start to see yellow once they get a peep at the intensity of the hue on the '49 Egset Convertible, with matching surfboard. Of the two hundred cars on show (from a rotating collection of 750), all are for sale, complete with classic auto insurance, of course. A Ferrari 250 GTO was snapped up for $5.5 million and a Type 41 Bugatti Royale for a mere $11 million. Each is elegantly displayed and well-annotated, too. But wait, there's more! Alongside the cars are a number of other extremely eccentric displays: glowing Wurlitzer jukeboxes, Princess Diana dolls, chess sets with Apache chessmen, knives made from blown glass, an inexplicable Edwardian mannequin scene (a dapper couple picnicking amidst a mountain of pennies) and a Harley-Davidson doll called Bobby The Little Biker Baby ("His adventures may be confined to the nursery for now, but he dreams of hitting the open road"). You can often score free admission passes from the hotel's front desk or casino's cashier just by asking.

King Tut's Tomb & Museum

Luxor, 3900 Las Vegas Blvd S (at Tropicana), Strip

T 702.262.4555 **MAP D2 20**

According to ancient Egyptians, the human heart was the seat of intelligence. And when embalming a Pharaoh's corpse, the royal morticians sucked the brain out through the nose, chunk by chunk. That's no big deal, of course—a similar, very pleasurable service can be purchased today at Nevada's best-known specialty brothels. But what are we to make of a historical museum—actually, a modest-sized display attached to the inevitable gift shop—which consists entirely of reproductions of historical artifacts? The attraction purports to be an exact replication of King Tut's burial chamber as discovered by Egyptologist Howard Carter in 1922, and the detail is impressive. And sure, all these jewelry boxes, alabaster lamps, gold-plated sarcophagi, Styx-crossing wooden boats and shabti (statuettes made from calerite and limestone) all look authentic, and the glowing spotlights cutting through the dim, hushed surroundings lend them an indubitably dramatic vibe. Still, not even the grave robbers who broke into all the Pharaoh's tombs except for Tut's (which is why it remained so full of "wonderful things," as Carter put it on first beholding the treasure trove) would have been impressed by the stash here. And when you factor in the unpleasantly dizzying setting (the Luxor casino's cavernous—excuse us, pyramidal—interior), plus the sometimes inadvertently hilarious self-guided audio tour, and the high admission price, you might want to flee to the other side of the Nile—or other side of the Strip. Before you do, though, be advised that the history lesson on offer here is probably more academically serious than anything else in Vegas. So if academic seriousness has any place in your program, Tut's Tomb is worth every one of the twenty minutes it'll take to navigate through it. Just don't confuse your brain for your heart the way the ancient Egyptians did.

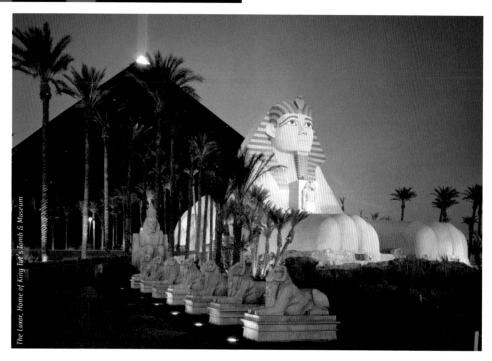

The Luxor, Home of King Tut's Tomb & Museum

Laser Quest

7361 W Lake Mead Blvd (at Tenaya), West Side

T 702.243.8881 | Closed MON MAP B1 21

Sure, there's something absurd about running around a black-lighted maze trying to zap your friends, but once you've done it (which, incidentally, is exactly the number of times you should do it) it's hard to knock this self-indulgent martial sport. Players don vests with laser-sensing targets, then hunt down enemies with a laser-shooting rifle. The war room is smartly designed with plenty of twists and turns plus some reflective surfaces which allow you to "shoot" around corners. Games last 20 minutes and players are ranked at the end by their number of "kills." Laser Quest is located off Highway 95, about 12 miles from the Strip.

Las Vegas Cyber Speedway

Sahara, 2535 Las Vegas Blvd S (at Sahara), Strip

T 702.734.7223 MAP G1 22

The Cyber Speedway is an enormously fun game in which you pilot mini race cars around a virtual track and hope to beat your friends to the checkered flag. Mounted on sophisticated hydraulic bases, the cars reach "speeds" up to 220 mph (352 kph). Wrap-around screens, intricate control panels, wind-in-your-hair effects and an excellent sound system round out this great experience.

Las Vegas Mini Grand Prix

1401 N Rainbow Blvd (at Ives), West Side

T 702.259.7000 MAP B1 23

There are several driving options here, including kiddie-carts and go-carts, but Las Vegas Mini Grand Prix earns Avant ink for its small-size Gran PriCars and Super Stock Cars, both of which you'll need a real driver's license to operate. Side attractions including a burlap-sack slide and a dragon-themed roller coaster.

Liberace Museum

1775 E Tropicana Ave (at Maryland), East Side

T 702.798.5595 MAP K2 24

Let's get this clear right from the start: the Liberace Museum is a genuine Vegas must-see. Upon visiting this amusing and unexpectedly inspiring tribute to "Mr. Showmanship" you'll

find yourself not laughing at the late Vegas performer, but with him—and learning a lesson to boot. The full-frontal assault of glitz is what makes this one of the hottest tourist spots in town. Liberace's countless possessions—his "happy-happies," as he called them—are so excessive and lavish they surpass self-parody. Dig them pianos: A sparkling rhinestone-bejeweled Baldwin, antiques formerly owned by Chopin and Gershwin, a miniature model made entirely from toothpicks! Dig them costumes: A red-white-and-blue hotpants outfit, the infamous "Lasagna" jumpsuit that "Lee" joked could be worn while cooking "because it doesn't show any stains!" And dig them cars: A rhinestone-encrusted Rolls, a red-white-and-blue Rolls convertible, even a mirrored Rolls! Yet, for all the gaudiness and mawkishness, the awful taste and materialistic narcissism, Liberace, who died in 1987, had heart, and by all accounts he never failed to give freely of this heart to fans, friends, family and strangers alike through acts of charity large and small. Although he was never publicly gay, Liberace was best known for startling middle-American audiences by contradicting every cliché about masculinity. Strangely, although he paved the way for the pansexuality of David Bowie, Elton John and many others, there is not a single reference to his greatest contribution here. The museum is located 2.5 miles east of the Strip.

Lion Habitat

MGM Grand, 3799 Las Vegas Blvd S (at Tropicana), Strip

T 702.891.1111 MAP D2 25

If more proof were needed that Vegas is truly a zoo, this indoor environment offers its main attractions—descendants of MGM's first marquee lion, Metro—protected from the hordes behind a heavy glass enclosure. Press your nose against it and watch the big cats saunter about, bat giant toys around, lick themselves and (mostly) sleep. Of course, the lion cubs are the cutest beasts here and, if you've got a Jackson you can get a photo of yourself cuddling one for a mere $20 (most days from 11am-2pm). Because admission is free, crowds can be brutal. And, of course, there's a gift shop nearby selling souvenirs, logowear and cuddly lion plush toys.

The Little Church of the West

4617 Las Vegas Blvd S (at Russell), Strip

T 702.739.7971 MAP C2 26

Opened in 1942, the city's first wedding chapel has been the site of numerous celebrity nuptuals and remains one of the most popular places to get hitched. It's also one of the few "historic" structures in the city. It hasn't always been located here, though; until 1996 the "church" was situated in front of the Hacienda Casino, which has since been blown up. Because blood tests are not required, there is no waiting period, and it represents the epitome of ironic kitsch—getting hitched in Vegas is as popular as getting divorced once was. Why not do it yourself? Or just show up and offer to be a witness.

Madame Tussaud's Wax Museum: The Celebrity Encounter

The Venetian, 3355 Las Vegas Blvd S (at Sands), Strip

T 702.367.1847 MAP F2 27

The original Madame T was a French aristocrat who was coerced during the Revolution into making death masks of her fellow nobles. Of course, celebrity is the new aristocracy, so Tussaud's spiritual heirs now do their thing with stars rather than royalty; making some 150 measurements of each, then spending six months shaping the wax, hand-painting the eyes and suggesting the veins with delicate red silk thread. Nevertheless, despite all this tradition and technique and expense—not to mention an enormous "interactive" space (which means that you're allowed to touch the dummies)—isn't some $15 a bit too rich of an admission price? We think so, unless you're too drunk or drugged to notice... which we assume is exactly what Madame T is counting on.

Manhattan Express Rollercoaster

New York-New York, 3790 Las Vegas Blvd S (at Tropicana), Strip

T 702.740.6969 MAP D2 28

Manhattan Express is a great rollercoaster. It's fast, filled with lots of loops and dives, and offers great views over both phony Manhattan and genuine Las Vegas. Lines can be long for this three-minute wild taxi ride, but at least it's safer than the real thing. Inside the hotel you'll find Coney Island Emporium, a massive room full of virtual-reality attractions and plenty of old-fashioned carnival games that is considered by lots of Las Vegans to be the best arcade in town.

Mario Andretti Racing School

6915 Speedway Blvd (at I-15), East Side

T 702.651.6300 or 877.227.8101 | www.driving101.com MAP J2 29

Andretti's specially-designed, two-seat, Champ Cars reach speeds up to 180 mph, which, by the way, we did on our last drive from Vegas to LA. Still, their basic ride, a simple 4.5-mile course, looks like fun. After completing a written exam, you can get behind the wheel for a longer session. None of this excitement comes cheap ($150-$800) and reservations are required.

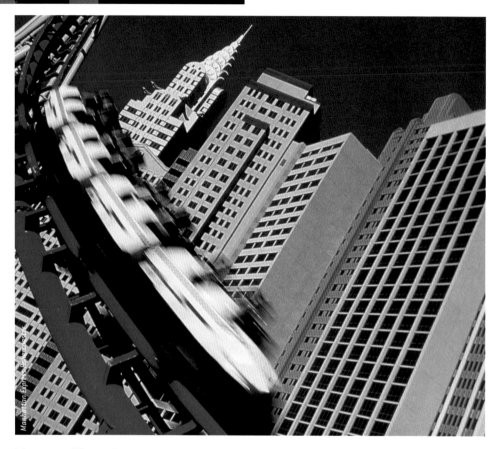

Manhattan Express Rollercoaster

Merlin the Wizard Show

Excalibur, 3850 Las Vegas Blvd S (at Tropicana), Strip

T 702.597.7700 MAP D2 30

The Excalibur is a whimsical riot of candy-colored turrets and towers, complete with a moat and drawbridge of sorts. You wouldn't make a special trip just to see the show that happens out front, in which Merlin the wizard shoos away a fire-breathing dragon, but if you happen to be walking by this cartoonish resort...well, it's worth pausing by the mist-filled moat to spy the campy action. In other words, this show is just your average animatronic dragon battle, though the beast's loud snorting beneath the drawbridge is cool, as are the breathless gasps from the oodles of children who gather to watch the show. Inside the "land of Sir Lose-A-Lot," you'll find Merlin's Magic Motion Machines simulator rides and the **Fantasy Faire Arcade** of carnival games and fairground attractions, plus people in knights' and witches' costumes and some Renaissance-type who tries to guess your weight.

Mirage Volcano

The Mirage, 3400 Las Vegas Blvd S (at Spring Mountain), Strip

T 702.791.7111 MAP F2 31

The first tourist attraction to be put in a hotel's front yard, the Mirage Volcano remains one of the city's best-loved sights. Beginning each night at sundown, the volcano "erupts" with brilliant bursts of fire, flashing lights and churning water which explodes with another ring of fire. The best place to watch the show is on the Strip directly in front of the Volcano. You can also watch from the safety of another city: beneath the Venetian's Campanile Tower, directly across the street. While the volcano is

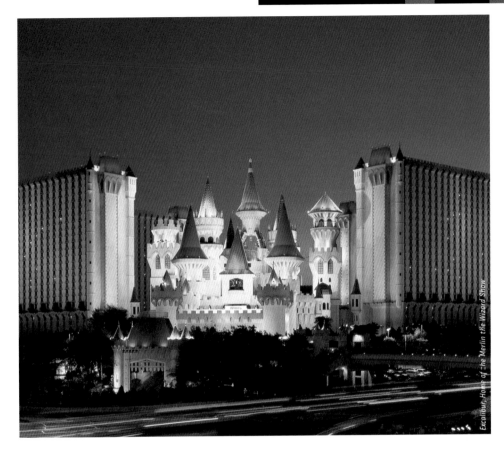

Excalibur, Home of the Merlin the Wizard Show

not worth planning your visit around, it's certainly worth a drive-by, or a stroll to the sidewalk. Crowds can be heavy, but you only need to wait fifteen minutes for a better view during the next show. There's lots of entertainment inside the resort as well, including a beautiful plant-filled atrium "rainforest" in the lobby and a spectacular 20,000-gallon coral reef aquarium behind the front desk. There are indoor tiger and dolphin habitats too.

Shark Reef

Mandalay Bay, 3950 Las Vegas Blvd S (at Mandalay Bay), Strip

T 702.632.7777 MAP C2 32

What the hell is an enormous saltwater reef doing in the middle of the desert? Even if this amazing aquarium were next to the sea it would be one of the best of its kind in the world. That's because, instead of simply offering a home to colorful cute and cuddlies, this tank is filled with some of the scariest predators of the deep. Sure, there are dozens of kinds of sharks, but that's just the beginning. Thousands of other animals include venomous fish, golden crocodiles, green sea turtles, slithery water monitors, moray eels and hundreds of iridescent jellyfish (in an oval tank bathed in black light). The main tanks are built with transparent tunnels through which visitors walk completely surrounded by water. And this being Vegas, the tanks are decorated with kitschy "treasures" that include a sunken galleon and the ruins of an Asianesque temple. In addition to the main event, there are lots of ancillary aquaria, plus a "touch tank" where you can pet crabs and sting rays and a baby zebra shark, if you dare. A large staff of naturalists are on hand to answer questions, and admission includes a self-guided audio tour to help convince you that this place is educational too.

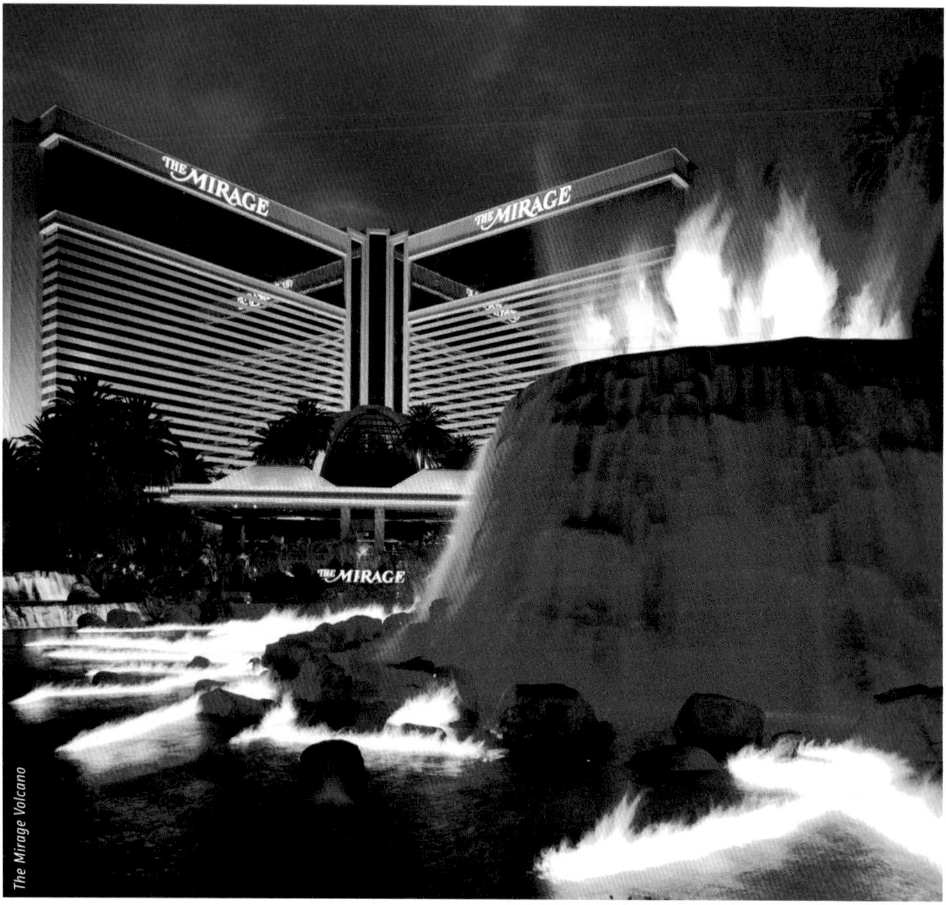

The Mirage Volcano

Siegfried & Roy's Secret Garden & Dolphin Habitat

The Mirage, 3400 Las Vegas Blvd S (at Spring Mountain), Strip

T 702.791.7111 MAP F2 33

The Secret Garden is a great name for what is essentially a mini zoo where the magicians house some of their animals. There are actually a half-dozen habitats here for these rarest performers, including white tigers, white lions, a black panther, a snow leopard, gray elephants and almost two dozen other exotics. Although these jungle creatures appear to live better than most humans we know, animal liberationists may still want to avoid this place. Everyone else, however, should probably go, because the animals really are amazing and this is the closest you'll probably ever get to them. And when you go, be sure to show up when Dolphin Habitat is open too (hours are sporadic) so you can play catch with a family of Atlantic bottlenose dolphins (ask the handlers), watch them swim from below water level, and see a cool video of dolphins giving birth.

Sirens of TI Show

Treasure Island, 3300 Las Vegas Blvd S (at Spring Mountain), Strip

T 702.894.7111 MAP F2 34

It's a toss up whether the best free show on the Strip is the Bellagio Fountains or this over-the-top outdoor spectacular, in which busty female "sirens" and renegade male "pirates" sing, dance and swordplay on very real looking, multi-masted frigates that float on the lagoon in front of the hotel. The 10-minute pyrotechnic stunt show is such silly fun to watch, as the drama-student actors take their flying leaps into the water so seriously. And the actual sinking of one of the ships at the end is amazing. But because this is also one of the most popular attractions in the city, it's usually impossibly crowded, with some spectators jamming the front of the hotel a full hour before show time. The best viewing is from the very center of resort's wooden boardwalk entrance. If you really have no life, then by all means arrive as early as you can. Better yet, exit the hotel's front entrance about fifteen minutes before showtime and resign yourself to an only-slightly-obstructed perch close to the front door. Weather permitting, performances usually run every 90 minutes beginning at 6pm.

Speed—The Ride

Sahara, 2535 Las Vegas Blvd S (at Sahara Ave), Strip

T 702.734.7223 **MAP G1 35**

Short and fast, Speed is widely considered to be the best rollercoaster in town. It's certainly one of the scariest. Powered by magnetic propulsion, riders are shot out of the gate like a rocket, accelerating from 0 to 70 mph (112 kph) in four seconds. The entire ride—around a curve, down a misty underground tunnel, through the resort's marquee to the top of a tower—takes just 20 seconds. Then it does it again, in reverse. Be sure to sit in front and, oh yeah, go to the bathroom first.

Star Trek: The Experience

Las Vegas Hilton, 3000 Paradise Rd (at Sahara), East Side

T 702.732.5111 **MAP G1 36**

Part simulator ride, part live-action show, it's hard to classify this future-schlock "experience" because it truly goes where no man has gone before. Upon assuming the identity of a Star Trek crew member, visitors are treated to an audio-visual "history of the future" before being "beamed aboard" a very cool replica of the bridge on the USS Enterprise, complete with live crew, some of whom really seem to believe that they're Starfleet officers from the year 3271. Then comes a four-minute "ride" through space which deposits you on the Deep Space Nine space station promenade where you'll find a bar and restaurant (bad food, great cutlery), an enormous gift shop, and a space-themed casino in which dealers wear sci-fi outfits and HD-TVs are positioned to look like windows into space. Die hards should also visit **Borg Invasion 4D**, a special effects laden film in which the fourth dimension is touch. For trekkies, the 22-minute Experience is a must-see. Some even cry. But if you've never heard of Lieutenant Geordi LaForge then you're better off simply visiting the bar and casino.

Sirens of TI Show

Stratosphere Tower

Stratosphere, 2000 Las Vegas Blvd S (at Charleston), Strip

T 702.380.7777 **MAP H1 37**

The Stratosphere is the Strip resort Las Vegans most love to hate. Wags joke that the best reason to visit the 113-story tower is because it's the only building in the city from which it can't be seen. No matter what you think of the architecture, the tallest free-standing lookout tower in America has become

a bona fide Las Vegas landmark, with indoor and outdoor observation decks and **Top of the World**, a very good revolving restaurant and lounge. On the very top are several thrill rides including the High Roller rollercoaster (where would it go if it derailed?), Insanity, which dangles and spins riders in mid-air out over the tower, XScream, a fast, floorless hurtle several feet over the edge of the tower, and the G-force-defying Big Shot, a mega-shot of compressed air that sends crazy drunks screaming to the very top of the mast in 2.5 seconds before free-falling weightless on a bungee cord back to the launching pad. Go at night for a great view, assuming you can keep your eyes open. Back on earth, in the Strat-O-Fair midway there's the Little Shot, a smaller version of the ride for kids and wimps. The tower itself was smartly designed with huge windows that angle outward, which increases the vertiginous perspective while allowing you to soak-in unobstructed 360-degree views of the entire Las Vegas Valley (and much of Southern Nevada). The top of the tower is a great place to get your bearings, put the entire Strip into perspective and see the ugly checkerboard of "leapfrog" development spreading out in all directions. Catch it at sunset and you'll be treated to an exquisite kaleidoscope of color, courtesy of the city's severe smog. The tower is open until late, weather permitting.

Welcome to Fabulous Las Vegas Sign

Las Vegas Blvd S (at Russell), Strip MAP C2 38

Erected at the southernmost end of the Strip in 1959, this Vegas icon is one of the city's few historical cultural landmarks. A beacon to motorists from Los Angeles, the luminous diamond shaped sign was created by local graphic designer Betty Willis with a two-tone flickering eight-point star and seven silver dollars. Situated on a happy median amid bruising traffic, the sign has become a powerful combination of mythology, symbolism and kitsch that inspires endless throngs of jaywalkers, their hazard lights blinking, to risk their lives for a photo-op.

Wet 'n' Wild

2601 Las Vegas Blvd S (at Sahara), Strip

T 702.765.9700 | CLOSED Oct-Mar MAP G1 39

It's pretty amazing that this giant waterpark is still here, considering that its on prime Stripfront land that must be worth tens of millions of dollars. But we're happy it is because, on scorching summer weekends, this is a great place to have some childish fun. There's a half-dozen or so gigantic slides, including one which drops you out of a bomb-shaped compartment, one that flushes you down an immense chute, one that spins you around a giant bowl, and one that's said to be the fastest and highest water slide in the world (keep your legs closed!). Monster wave simulators and a lazy river ride offer slower thrills. Admission is not cheap, and there are several extra charges, including inner tube rentals and lockers. Bring a towel, and a picnic if you'd like. And arrive early to beat the lines.

White Tiger Habitat

The Mirage, 3400 Las Vegas Blvd S (at Spring Mountain), Strip

T 702.791.7111 MAP F2 40

Not to be outdone by MGM's Lion Habitat, the Mirage offers its own glassed-in enclosure for Siegfried & Roy's trademark white tigers ("wis ice blue ice," the blond guy ominously narrates in his Germanic accent on an overhead video). Usually they just lie around doing nothing. But the tigers are awesome and majestic, and, unlike their owners, these cats have naturally colored hair. Anyway, it costs nothing to take a peek.

Map	Area	Sight	Address	Phone
		Top Las Vegas Experiences		
E2 [12]	Strip	Forum Shops Festival Fountains	Caesars Forum Shops	702.893.4800
E2 [13]	Strip	The Fountains at Bellagio	Bellagio	702.693.7444
F2 [31]	Strip	Mirage Volcano	The Mirage	702.791.7111
F2 [34]	Strip	Sirens of TI Show	Treasure Island	702.894.7111
H1 [37]	Strip	Stratosphere Tower	Stratosphere	702.380.7777
I2 [14]	Downtown	Fremont Street Experience	Fremont St	702.678.5777
		Museums and Galleries		
E2 [5]	Strip	Bellagio Gallery of Fine Art	Bellagio	702.693.7722
D2 [6]	Strip	Casino Legends Hall of Fame Museum	Tropicana	702.739.2222
F2 [17]	Strip	Guggenheim Hermitage Museum	The Venetian	702.414.2440
E2 [19]	Strip	Imperial Palace Auto Collection	Imperial Palace	702.794.3174
D2 [20]	Strip	King Tut's Tomb & Museum	Luxor	702.262.4555
K2 [24]	East Side	Liberace Museum	1775 E Tropicana Ave	702.798.5595
F2 [9]	West Side	Elvis-A-Rama Museum	3401 Industrial Rd	702.309.7200
		Thrills		
G1 [2]	Strip	AJ Hackett Bungy	Circus Circus	702.385.4321
F2 [16]	Strip	Gondola Rides	Venetian Grand Canal Shoppes	702.414.4500
K2 [18]	East Side	The Gun Store	2900 E Tropicana Ave	702.454.1110
D2 [28]	Strip	Manhattan Express Rollercoaster	New York-New York	702.740.6969
G1 [35]	Strip	Speed—The Ride	Sahara	702.734.7223
G1 [39]	Strip	Wet 'n' Wild	2601 Las Vegas Blvd S	702.765.9700
G1 [11]	East Side	Flyaway Indoor Skydiving	200 Convention Center Dr	702.731.4768
J2 [29]	East Side	Mario Andretti Racing School	6915 Speedway Blvd	702.651.6300
B1 [23]	West Side	Las Vegas Mini Grand Prix	1401 N Rainbow Blvd	702.259.7000
B1 [21]	West Side	Laser Quest	7361 W Lake Mead Blvd	702.243.8881
		Churches & Monuments		
E2 [8]	Strip	Eiffel Tower Experience	Paris Las Vegas	702.946.7000
C2 [26]	Strip	The Little Church of the West	4617 Las Vegas Blvd S	702.739.7971
C2 [38]	Strip	Welcome to Fabulous Las Vegas Sign	The Strip at Russel Rd	none

Map	Area	Sight	Address	Phone
		Parks & Gardens		
E2 [4]	Strip	Bellagio Botanical Conservatory	Bellagio	702.693.7444
E2 [10]	Strip	Flamingo Las Vegas Wildlife Habitat	Flamingo	702.733.3111
D2 [25]	Strip	Lion Habitat	MGM Grand	702.891.1111
F2 [33]	Strip	Siegfried & Roy's Secret Garden and Dolphin Habitat	The Mirage	702.791.7111
		Places to Take Kids		
G1 [1]	Strip	Adventuredome Theme Park	Circus Circus	702.734.0410
G1 [7]	Strip	The Circus	Circus Circus	702.734.0410
D2 [15]	Strip	GameWorks	3785 Las Vegas Blvd South	702.432.4263
G1 [22]	Strip	Las Vegas Cyber Speedway	Sahara	702.734.7223
F2 [27]	Strip	Madame Tussaud's Wax Museum: The Celebrity Encounter	The Venetian	702.367.1847
D2 [30]	Strip	Merlin the Wizard Show	Excalibur	702.597.7700
C2 [32]	Strip	Shark Reef	Mandalay Bay	702.632.7777
F2 [40]	Strip	White Tiger Habitat	The Mirage	702.791.7111
G1 [36]	East Side	Star Trek: The Experience	Las Vegas Hilton	702.732.5111
		Tours		
	East Side	Papillon Grand Canyon Helicopters	McCarran Airport	702.736.7243
	North Las Vegas	Scenic Airlines	North Las Vegas Airport	702.638.3275
	Southwest	Desert Fox Tours	6265 Industrial Rd	702.361.0676

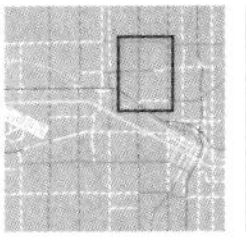

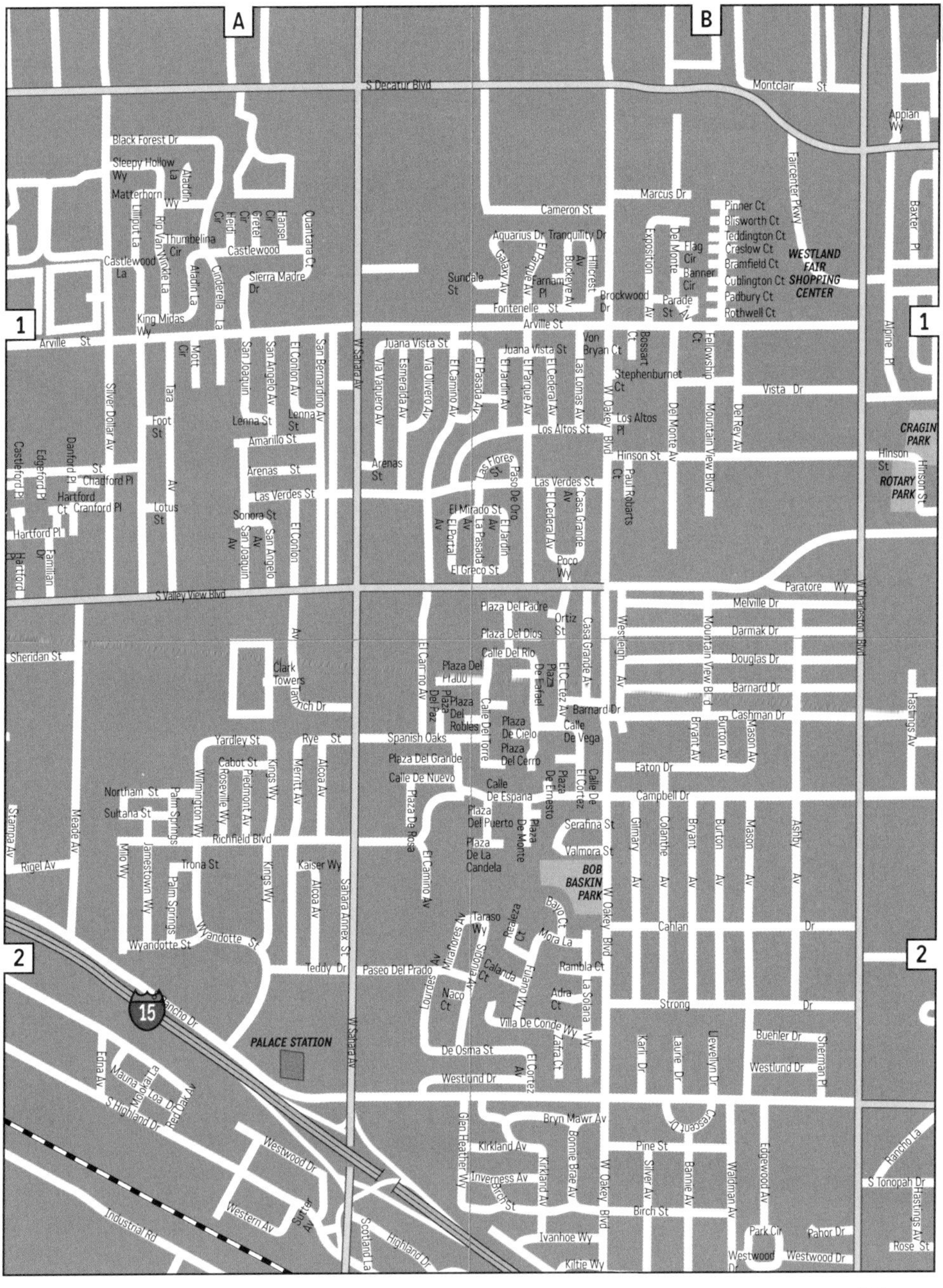

A
B
1
2
21
23

S Decatur Blvd
Montclair St
Appian Wy
Black Forest Dr
Sleepy Hollow Wy
Aladdin La
Matterhorn Wy
Lilliput La
Rip Van Winkle La
Thumbelina Cir
Heidi Cir
Gretel Cir
Hansel Cir
Quantana Ct
Castlewood
Castlewood La
Aladin La
Cinderella La
Sierra Madre Dr
King Midas Wy
Arville St
Mott Cir
San Joaquin
San Angelo Av
El Conlon Av
San Bernardino Av
W Sahara Av
Silver Dollar Av
Tara
Foot St
Lenna St
Lenna St
Amarillo St
Arenas St
Las Verdes St
Sonora St
San Joaquin Av
San Angelo Av
El Conlon
Lotus St
Av
Castleford Pl
Edgeford Pl
Danford Pl
Chadford Pl
St
Hartford Ct
Cranford Pl
Hartford Pl
Familian Dr
Hartford
S Valley View Blvd
Marcus Dr
Cameron St
Faircenter Pkwy
Baxter Pl
Pinner Ct
Blisworth Ct
Teddington Ct
Creslow Ct
Bramfield Ct
Cublington Ct
Padbury Ct
Rothwell Ct
WESTLAND FAIR SHOPPING CENTER
Aquarius Dr
Tranquility Dr
Galaxy Av
El Parque Av
Buckeye Av
Farnam Pl
Hillcrest
Exposition Av
Del Monte
Flag Cir
Banner Cir
Parade St
Brockwood Dr
Sundale St
Fontenelle St
Arville St
Juana Vista St
Juana Vista St
Via Vaquero Av
Esmeralda Av
Via Olivero Av
El Camino Av
El Pasada Av
El Jardin Av
El Parque Av
El Cederal Av
Las Lomas Av
Von Bryan Ct
Bossart Ct
Fellowship Ct
Stephenburnet Ct
W Oakey Blvd
Alpine Pl
Vista Dr
Del Monte Av
Mountain View Blvd
Del Rey Av
Los Altos Pl
Los Altos St
Hinson St
Hinson St
CRAGIN PARK
ROTARY PARK
Hinson St
Arenas St
Las Flores St
Paso De Oro
Las Verdes St
El Cederal Av
Casa Grande
Paul Robarts
El Mirado St
El Portal Av
La Pasada Av
El Jardin Av
El Greco St
Poco Wy
Paratore Wy
W Charleston Blvd
Melville Dr
Darmak Dr
Douglas Dr
Barnard Dr
Cashman Dr
Plaza Del Padre
Ortiz St
Casa Grande Av
Wesleigh Av
Mountain View Blvd
Plaza Del Dios
Calle Del Rio
Plaza Del Prado
El Camino Av
Plaza De Rafael
El Cortez Av
Barnard Dr
Plaza Del Paz
Plaza Del Robles
Calle Del Torre
Plaza De Cielo
Calle De Vega
Plaza Del Cerro
Bryant Av
Burton Av
Mason Av
Hastings Av
Sheridan St
Clark Towers
Tamarich Dr
Yardley St
Rye St
Spanish Oaks
Plaza Del Grande
Cabot St
Roseville Wy
Piedmont Av
Kings Wy
Merritt Av
Alcoa Av
Calle De Nuevo
Calle De Espana
Plaza De Ernesto
Calle De El Cortez
Eaton Dr
Northam St
Sultana St
Wilmington Wy
Palm Springs
Campbell Dr
Plaza De Rosa
Plaza Del Puerto
Plaza De Monte
Serafina St
Gilmary Av
Colanthe Av
Bryant Av
Burton Av
Mason Av
Ashby Av
Stampa Av
Meade Av
Richfield Blvd
Plaza De La Candela
Valmora St
Rigel Av
Mio Wy
Jamestown Wy
Trona St
Palm Springs
Kings Wy
Kaiser Wy
Alcoa Av
Sahara Annex St
El Camino Av
BOB BASKIN PARK
Wyandotte St
Wyandotte St
Taraso Wy
Realeza Ct
Bayo Ct
Mora La
Cahlan Dr
Teddy Dr
Paseo Del Prado
Lourdes Av
Miraflores Av
Moapa Ct
Calanda Ct
Eduano Wy
Rambla Ct
Naco Ct
Adra Ct
La Solana Wy
Strong Dr
15
Rancho Dr
Villa De Conde Wy
PALACE STATION
De Osma St
Zafra Ct
Karli Dr
Laurie Dr
Lewellyn Dr
Buehler Dr
Sherman Pl
Westlund Dr
Edna Av
Mauna Loa Dr
Molokai La
Red Oak Av
S Highland Dr
Westlund Dr
El Cortez Av
Bryn Mawr Av
Crescent Dr
Glen Heather Wy
Kirkland Av
Bonnie Brae Av
Pine St
Edgewood Av
Rancho La
Westwood Dr
Inverness Av
Kirkland Av
Silver Av
Bannie Av
Waldman Av
S Tonopah Dr
Hastings Av
Birch St
Birch St
Western Av
Sutter Av
Industrial Rd
Scotland La
Highland Dr
Ivanhoe Wy
Park Cir
Pahor Dr
Rose St
Westwood Dr
Westwood Dr
Kiltie Wy

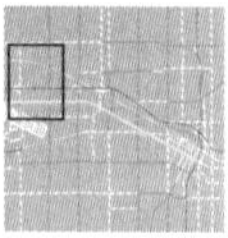

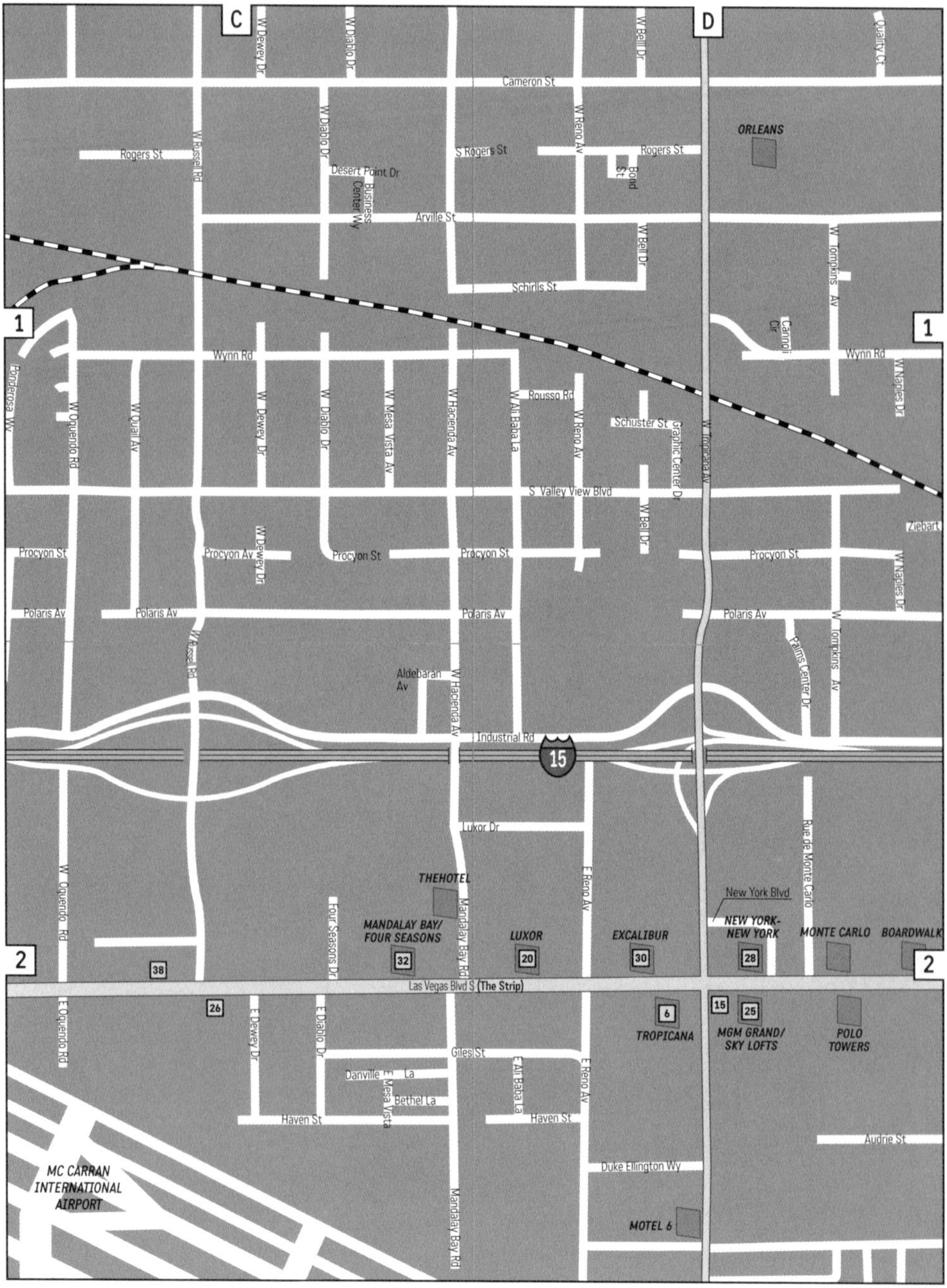

C
D
1
2
W Dewey Dr
W Diablo Dr
W Bell Dr
Quality Ct
Cameron St
ORLEANS
W Russel Rd
W Diablo Dr
W Reno Av
Rogers St
S Rogers St
Rogers St
Bond St
Desert Point Dr
Business Center Wy
Arville St
W Bell Dr
W Tompkins Av
Schirlls St
Cannoli Cir
Wynn Rd
Wynn Rd
Ponderosa Wy
W Oquendo Rd
W Quail Av
W Dewey Dr
W Diablo Dr
W Mesa Vista Av
W Hacienda Av
W Ali Baba La
Rousso Rd
W Reno Av
Schuster St
Graphic Center Dr
W Tropicana Av
W Naples Dr
S Valley View Blvd
W Bell Dr
Ziebart
Procyon St
Procyon Av
W Dewey Dr
Procyon St
Procyon St
Procyon St
W Naples Dr
Polaris Av
Polaris Av
Polaris Av
Polaris Av
W Russel Rd
Aldebaran Av
W Hacienda Av
Palms Center Dr
W Tompkins Av
Industrial Rd
15
Luxor Dr
THEHOTEL
W Oquendo Rd
Four Seasons Dr
Mandalay Bay Rd
E Reno Av
Rue de Monte Carlo
New York Blvd
MANDALAY BAY/ FOUR SEASONS
LUXOR
EXCALIBUR
NEW YORK-NEW YORK
MONTE CARLO
BOARDWALK
38
32
20
30
28
Las Vegas Blvd S (The Strip)
26
E Oquendo Rd
E Dewey Dr
E Diablo Dr
6
TROPICANA
15
25
MGM GRAND/ SKY LOFTS
POLO TOWERS
Giles St
Danville La
E Mesa Vista
Bethel La
E Ali Baba La
E Reno Av
Haven St
Haven St
Audrie St
Duke Ellington Wy
MC CARRAN INTERNATIONAL AIRPORT
Mandalay Bay Rd
MOTEL 6

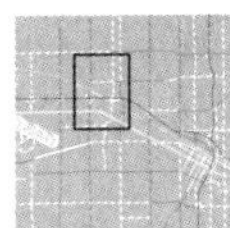

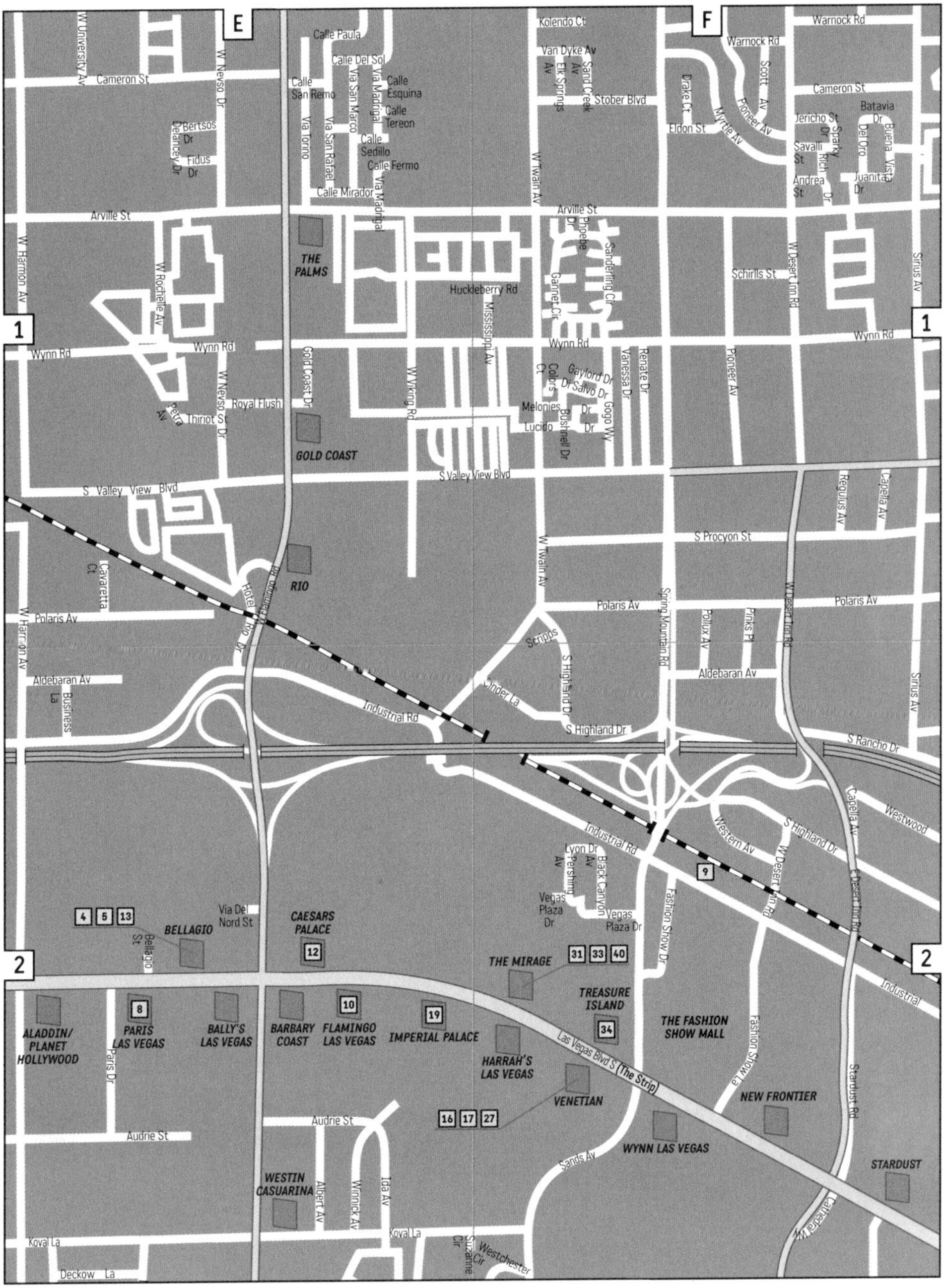

E
F
1
2

W University Av
Cameron St
W Nevso Dr
Bertsos Dr
Delancey Dr
Fidus Dr
Calle Paula
Calle Del Sol
Calle San Remo
Via San Marco
Via Madrigal
Calle Esquina
Calle Tereon
Via Torino
Via San Rafael
Calle Sedillo
Calle Fermo
Calle Mirador
Via Madrigal
Kolendo Ct
Van Dyke Av
Elk Springs Av
Sand Creek Av
Stober Blvd
W Twain Av
Warnock Rd
Drake Ct
Scott Av
Pioneer Av
Myrtle Av
Eldon St
Jericho St
Sparky Dr
Savalli St
Rich Dr
Andrea St
Batavia Dr
Del Oro
Buena Vista
Juanita Dr
Arville St
W Harmon Av
W Rochelle Av
THE PALMS
Arville St
Phoebe Dr
Sanderling Cir
Garnet Cir
Huckleberry Rd
Mississippi Av
Schirlls St
W Desert Inn Rd
Sirius Av
Wynn Rd
Wynn Rd
Wynn Rd
Wynn Rd
Gold Coast Dr
W Viking Rd
Colors Ct
Gaylord Dr
Di Salvo Dr
Vanessa Dr
Renate Dr
Pioneer Av
Melonies Dr
Lucido Dr
Bushnell Dr
Gogo Wy
Royal Hush
Petra Av
Thiriot St
GOLD COAST
S Valley View Blvd
S Valley View Blvd
Regulus Av
Capella Av
S Procyon St
Cavaretta Ct
RIO
Flamingo Rd
Hotel Rio Dr
W Twain Av
Polaris Av
Polaris Av
Polaris Av
W Harmon Av
Scripps
Spring Mountain Rd
Pollux Av
Pinks Pl
W Desert Inn Rd
Aldebaran Av
Aldebaran Av
Business La
S Highland Dr
Cinder La
Industrial Rd
S Highland Dr
S Rancho Dr
Sirius Av
Industrial Rd
Western Av
S Highland Dr
Capella Av
Westwood
Lyon Dr
Pershing Av
Black Canyon Av
W Desert Inn Rd
E Desert Inn Rd
9
Fashion Show Dr
Vegas Plaza Dr
Vegas Plaza Dr
4 5 13
BELLAGIO
Bellagio St
Via Del Nord St
CAESARS PALACE
12
THE MIRAGE
31 33 40
TREASURE ISLAND
34
THE FASHION SHOW MALL
Industrial
ALADDIN/ PLANET HOLLYWOOD
8
PARIS LAS VEGAS
BALLY'S LAS VEGAS
BARBARY COAST
10
FLAMINGO LAS VEGAS
19
IMPERIAL PALACE
HARRAH'S LAS VEGAS
Las Vegas Blvd S (The Strip)
VENETIAN
Fashion Show La
NEW FRONTIER
Stardust Rd
Paris Dr
Audrie St
Audrie St
16 17 27
Sands Av
WYNN LAS VEGAS
STARDUST
WESTIN CASUARINA
Albert Av
Winnick Av
Ida Av
Cathedral Wy
Koval La
Koval La
Suzanne Cir
Westchester Cir
Deckow La

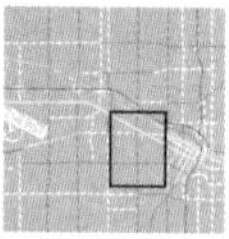

G
H
1
2
STARDUST
CIRCUS CIRCUS
RIVIERA
ALGIERS
STRATOSPHERE
SAHARA
LAS VEGAS HILTON
LAS VEGAS CONVENTION CENTER
LAS VEGAS COUNTRY CLUB
BAKER PARK
1
2
7
11
22
35
36
37
39
Circus Circus Dr
Kishner Dr
Convention Center Dr
Riviera Blvd
Las Vegas Blvd S (The Strip)
La South Bridge
Northbridge St
W Sahara Av
E Sahara Av
Highland Av
Western Av
Industrial Rd
Martin L. King Blvd
W Oakey Blvd
W Wyoming Ave
Westwood Dr
Shadow La
Jaylar Cir
Ellis Av
Ormsby St
Mercedes Cir
Richard Ct
Charmast La
Wall St
Tam Dr
W Boston Av
W St Louis Av
W Philadelphia Av
W Chicago Av
W New York Av
W Cincinnati Av
W Cleveland Av
W Baltimore Av
Fairfield Av
W Utah Av
W Imperial Av
W Colorado Av
S Commerce St
S Main St
E Utah Av
E Imperial Av
E Colorado Av
E California St
Casino Center Blvd
S 3rd St
S 4th St
Paradise Rd
Av of the Hiltons
Joe W Brown Dr
Santa Clara Dr
Santa Paula Dr
Santa Rita Dr
Santa Rosa Dr
Santa Ynez Dr
Van Patten Pl
San Pablo Dr
Weldon Pl
El Centro Pl
Rexford Dr
Rexford Pl
Houssels Av
Karen Ct
Lynnwood St
Van Patten St
Sherwood St
Kendale St
State St
Oakmont Pl
Oakmont Av
Oakmont Dr
Queens Dr
Queens Courtyard
Augusta Dr
Bel Air Cir
Bel Air
Broadmoor Av
Pinehurst Dr
Vegas Valley Dr
Tam O'Shanter
Karen Av
E St Louis Av
Bonita Av
Barbara Wy
Ellen Wy
E Oakey Blvd
Griffith Av
Bracken Av
Sweeney Av
5th Pl
S 6th St
S 7th St
Park Paseo
Alhambra Cir
Alhambra Dr
Santiago St
Cordova St
Canosa Av
S 8th St
8th Pl
S 9th St
S 10th St
Hasseth Av
Howard Av
Franklin Av
Wengert Av
Norman Av
Jessica Av
Francis Av
S 11th St
Almond Tree La
S Maryland Pkwy
San Pedro Av
Exley Av
Phillips Av
Art and Mary Thomas La
Canosa Av
St. Jude Cir
St. Joseph Cir
S 13th St
S 14th St
Maroney St
Pardee Pl
S 15th St
Chapman Dr
Hartke Pl
Cochran St
S 16th St
Becke Cir
Concordia Pl
Maria Elena Av
Hillside Pl
Curtis Dr
S 17th St
Spencer St
Pauline Wy
Kassabian Av
Lamplighter La
Moore St
S Bruce St
Casa Vegas St
Corona Av
Topanga St
Hermosa St
Laguna Av
Malibu St
La Canada St
Serenada Av
El Cajon St
Silver Mesa Wy
Raindance Wy
Golden Arrow Dr
Palora Av
Capistrano Av
Palma Vista Av
Izabella Av
La Jolla Av
Coronado Av
El Segundo Av
Iglesia St
Meteoro St
Del Mar Av
Playa Del Rey St
Talbot St
Talbot Cir
Sundown Dr
Seneca Dr
Medicine Man Wy
Caballero Wy
Berman St
Palma Vista Cir
La Vante Av
La Brisa Av
Balboa Av
Del Mar Pl
Del Mar Ct
El Toreador St

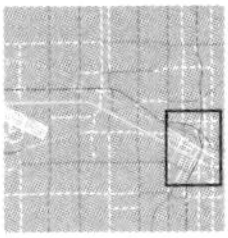

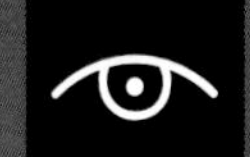

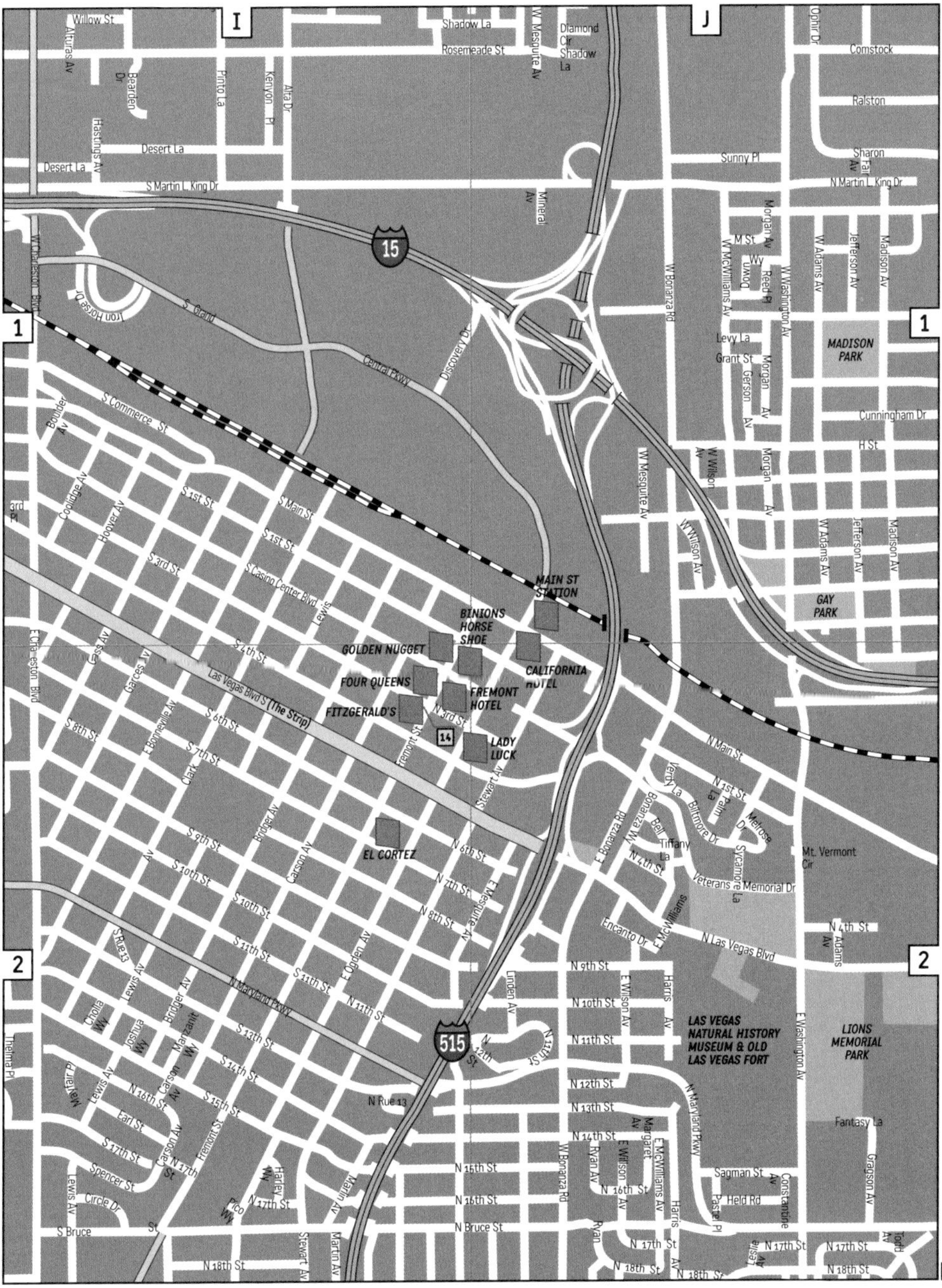

I
J
1
2
Willow St
Alturas Av
Bearden Dr
Pinto La
Kenyon Pl
Alta Dr
Shadow La
Rosemeade St
W Mesquite Av
Diamond Cir
Shadow La
Ophir Dr
Comstock
Ralston
Sharon
Fair Av
Hastings Av
Desert La
Desert La
S Martin L King Dr
Sunny Pl
N Martin L King Dr
Mineral Av
15
W Charleston Blvd
Iron Horse Dr
S Grand
Central Pkwy
Discovery Dr
M St
Morgan Av
Down Wy
W McWilliams Av
Reed Pl
W Washington Av
W Adams Av
Jefferson Av
Madison Av
W Bonanza Rd
Levy La
Grant St
Gerson Av
Morgan Av
MADISON PARK
Cunningham Dr
H St
W Wilson Av
W Mesquite Av
Morgan Av
W Wilson Av
W Adams Av
Jefferson Av
Madison Av
Boulder Av
S Commerce St
3rd Pl
Coolidge Av
Hoover Av
S 1st St
S Main St
S 1st St
S 3rd St
S Casino Center Blvd
Lewis
MAIN ST STATION
BINIONS HORSE SHOE
GAY PARK
GOLDEN NUGGET
E Charleston Blvd
Cass Av
Garces Av
S 4th St
CALIFORNIA HOTEL
FOUR QUEENS
FREMONT HOTEL
Las Vegas Blvd S (The Strip)
FITZGERALD'S
N 3rd St
S 8th St
E Bonneville Av
S 6th St
Fremont St
14
LADY LUCK
S 7th St
Clark
N Main St
Stewart Av
Veredy La
N 1st St
Palm Dr
Bonanza Wy
Biltmore Dr
Melrose
Bridger Av
Bell
E Bonanza Rd
Tiffany La
Sycamore La
Mt. Vermont Cir
S 9th St
EL CORTEZ
N 6th St
N 4th St
Veterans Memorial Dr
S 10th St
Carson Av
N 7th St
E Mesquite Av
S 10th St
N 8th St
E McWilliams
Encanto Dr
N 4th St
Adams Av
S Rue 13
Lewis Av
S 11th St
S 11th St
E Ogden Av
N Las Vegas Blvd
N 9th St
N Maryland Pkwy
N 10th St
E Wilson Av
Linden Av
Harris Av
Cholla Wy
Joshua Wy
Bridger Av
Manzanita Wy
S 13th St
N 11th St
515
N 12th St
N 11th St
N 11th St
LAS VEGAS NATURAL HISTORY MUSEUM & OLD LAS VEGAS FORT
E Washington Av
LIONS MEMORIAL PARK
Thelma Pl
Mayfair Pl
Lewis Av
N 16th St
Carson Av
S 14th St
S 15th St
N 12th St
N Maryland Pkwy
N Rue 13
Earl St
N 13th St
Fantasy La
S 17th St
Carson Av
N 17th St
Fremont St
N 14th St
Margaret Av
E McWilliams Av
Spencer St
N 15th St
Ryan Av
E Wilson Av
Sagman St
Gragson Av
Lewis Av
Circle Dr
Harley Wy
N 17th St
Marlin Av
N 16th St
W Bonanza Rd
N 16th St
Harris Av
Pastel Pl
Held Rd
Constantine Av
Pico Wy
S Bruce St
N Bruce St
Ryan
N 17th St
Tesla Av
N 17th St
N 17th St
Todd Av
N 18th St
Stewart Av
Martin Av
N 18th St
N 18th St
N 18th St
29

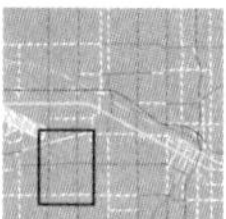

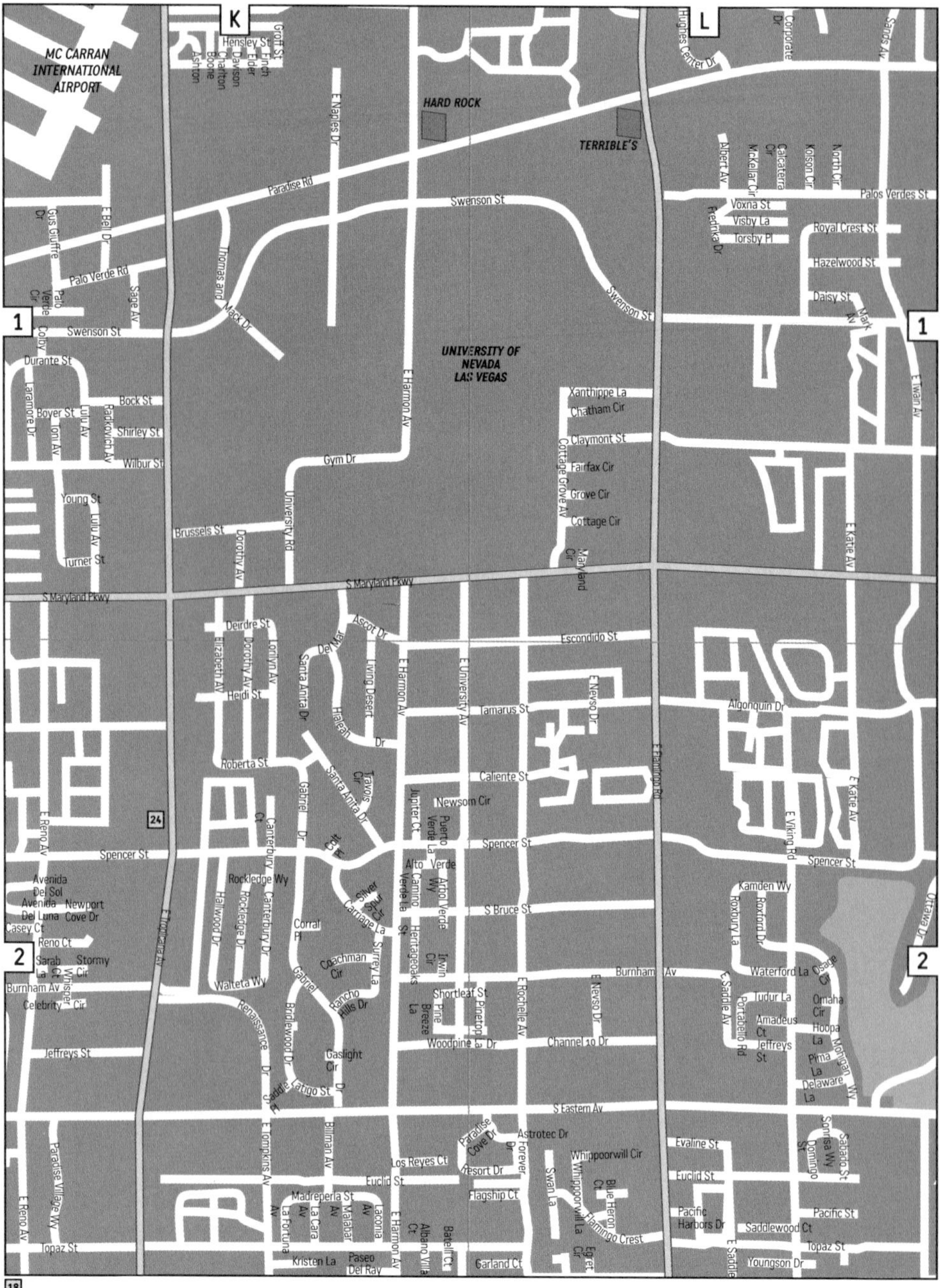

K
L
1
2
MC CARRAN INTERNATIONAL AIRPORT
HARD ROCK
TERRIBLE'S
UNIVERSITY OF NEVADA LAS VEGAS
Paradise Rd
Swenson St
S Maryland Pkwy
E Flamingo Rd
E Tropicana Av
E Harmon Av
University Rd
E Naples Dr
Gym Dr
Brussels St
Dorothy Av
Thomas and Mack Dr
Palo Verde Rd
Gus Giuffre Dr
E Bell Dr
Sage Av
Palo Verde Cir
Colby
Durante St
Laramore Dr
Boyer St
Toni Av
Lulu Av
Radkovich Av
Bock St
Shirley St
Wilbur St
Young St
Turner St
Hensley St
Groff St
Finch
Elder
Davison
Charlton
Boone
Ashton
Hughes Center Dr
Corporate Dr
Sandhill Rd
Albert Av
McKellar Cir
Calcaterra Cir
Kolson Cir
North Cir
Palos Verdes St
Voxna St
Visby La
Torsby Pl
Fredrika Dr
Royal Crest St
Hazelwood St
Daisy St
Mark Av
E Twain Av
E Katie Av
Xanthippe La
Chatham Cir
Claymont St
Fairfax Cir
Grove Cir
Cottage Cir
Cottage Grove Av
Maryland Cir
Escondido St
Deirdre St
Elizabeth Av
Dorothy Av
Ionlyn Av
Ascot Dr
Del Mar
Santa Anita Dr
Living Desert
Heidi St
Hialeah Dr
E University Av
Tamarus St
E Nevso Dr
Algonquin Dr
Roberta St
Travois Cir
Caliente St
Newsom Cir
Jupiter Ct
Puerto Verde La
Gabriel Dr
Canterbury Ct
Colt Pl
Spencer St
Alto Verde
Camino Verde La
Arbol Verde Wy
E Viking Rd
E Reno Av
Avenida Del Sol
Avenida Del Luna
Newport Cove Dr
Casey Ct
Reno Ct
Sarah La
Stormy Cir
Whisper Ct
Burnham Av
Celebrity Cir
Rockledge Wy
Hallwood Dr
Rockledge Dr
Canterbury Dr
Corral Pl
Silver Spur Cir
Carriage La
Surrey La
S Bruce St
Heritageoaks La
Irwin Cir
Kamden Wy
Roxbury La
Roxford Dr
Ottawa Dr
Waterford La
Osage Cir
Coachman Cir
Walteta Wy
Rancho Hills Dr
Shortleaf St
Pine Breeze La
Pinetop La
E Rochelle Av
E Nevso Dr
E Saddle Av
Portabello Rd
Tudur La
Amadeus Ct
Jeffreys St
Omaha Cir
Hoopa La
Pima La
Mohigan Wy
Delaware La
Renaissance Dr
Bridlewood Dr
Gaslight Cir
Woodpine Dr
Channel 10 Dr
Saddle Latigo St
S Eastern Av
Paradise Village Wy
E Tompkins Av
Billman Av
Paradise Cove Dr
Astrotec Dr
Forever Dr
Whippoorwill Cir
Evaline St
Sonrisa Wy
Domingo St
Sabado St
Los Reyes Ct
Resort Dr
Swan La
Euclid St
Flagship Ct
Blue Heron Ct
Whippoorwill La
Madreperla St
La Fortuna Av
La Cara Av
Malabar Av
Laconia Av
Albano Villa Ct
Batelli Ct
Flamingo Crest
Pacific Harbors Dr
Pacific St
Saddlewood Ct
Topaz St
Kristen La
Paseo Del Rey
Garland Ct
Egret Cir
Youngson Dr
24
18

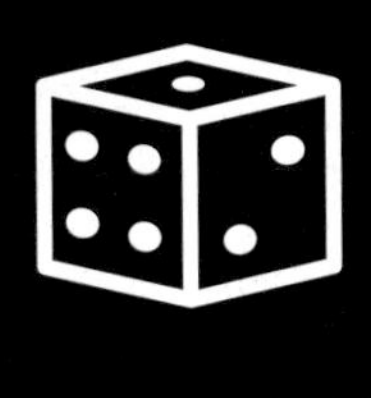

GAME 6

Did you know that gambling is legal in Las Vegas? No really, it's true! Although in Vegas it hasn't been called gambling since the mob lost control. Today, it's *gaming*—a euphemism that's less offensive to the enormous publicly-held corporations that operate the city's largest casinos. To its detractors, legalized gambling is nothing more than a tax on people who are bad at math, because, in the long run, there is no way you can win. The odds are literally stacked against you. Sure, you can have a great run, or hit a massive jackpot. But, statistically, the longer you play the more you'll lose. Period. So no matter what you play, it's best to play slowly. Don't expose your bankroll to the house-edge for 100 hands an hour playing alone against the dealer if you can have just as much (or more) fun playing just 45 hands an hour at a full table. Likewise, as long as you enjoy it just the same, it's better to opt for 200 spins an hour hand-feeding coins into a slot machine and pulling its arm, rather than 250 spins an hour hitting the Spin button like a lab rat.

Comps & Players Clubs | Comps are any kind of "complimentary" gifts that casinos give to loyal players, and are directly related to the amount of time you spend gambling and/or the rate at which you win. Comps range from free meals, which almost anyone can score, to transport on private jets for "whales," the casino's highest-rolling customers. The most common comps are rooms, food and beverages, the trio of which are collectively referred to as RFB when they're offered as a package to better customers.

To receive comps you must allow the casino to "rate" your play, that is, keep tabs on how much money you put in their machines and lay out on their tables. You do this by joining their players' club, receiving a plastic frequent-gamblers card, and then presenting it to the pit boss (a.k.a. the compcierge) or inserting it into your machine each time you play. It costs nothing and often you'll even get something just for signing up. Plus, being a club member almost certainly guarantees you will receive offers in the mail for room discounts, free shows and other incentives for future visits.

Each casino has a different comps policy. Coffee shop lunches at most places are usually an easy score. At the Bellagio it's buffets for the $25-a-hand bettor and nothing for the rest of us. At "locals" casinos and Downtown, the same play gets you the casino rate for a room (if you're already staying there, they'll take it off your credit card). What it takes to get comped isn't a mystery. Casinos are happy to tell you what you need to do, and some, like Stations Casinos, even let you view your "points" on their website. When you sit down at a table, don't be shy to ask the pit boss "How long do I have to play to get comped at the buffet?" In fact, you almost always have to ask for comps as they rarely come looking for you.

If you immediately hit a $1000 jackpot, expect to be treated very nicely; the casino will want to keep you playing so they can win their money back. Even if you're a lowly cheapskate, as long as you're gambling, most casinos are happy to cloud your judgment with free drinks. And the next time you're ordering don't forget to ask for a free cigar too. Many Strip hotels are now keeping these stinky stogies on hand for just such an occasion.

Gambling Lessons | In order to hook new addicts and get more business, many casinos offer fun, free gambling lessons to newbies. Choose your poison and there's an expert to learn you the rules, language, etiquette and the finer points of play. Once you're on a table, don't be shy about asking your dealer for advice. Helping you spend your money is what they're paid to do. And remember, when you hit the jackpot, collect your dough from the cashier and request a security escort to the hotel safe. Our favorite classes are Bally's Gaming University (tel. 702.739.4111), Caesars Palace (tel. 702.731.7110) and MGM Grand (tel. 702.891.5110). Phone for games and times.

Betting With Your Head | If you have an addictive personality, there is only one bit of (rarely heeded) advice we know of to keep you from blowing your entire savings in one go: Divide your gambling money into daily portions. When each day's portion is gone, simply stop playing until the next day. Then there was the visitor who lost all her money at the tables on her very first day in Vegas. But because she still had several vacation days left, she stood around and bet mentally. But in a few hours she lost her mind as well (hee hee).

Minimums & Maximums | Each gaming table sets a limit on the minimum and maximum allowable bet. It's posted on a little sign beside the dealer. Most players wager close to the minimum. In Blackjack, if you play two hands simultaneously, you are usually required to bet twice the minimum on each hand. In Roulette, the minimum refers to the sum total of all your bets during a single spin of the wheel.

AVANT-GUIDE COMP GUIDE

After several hours play

$ Per Hand	Comp
$5–$10	Coffee shop breakfast or lunch
$10–$25	Coffee shop, buffet, casino rate on room
$25–$100	Shows, club passes, gourmet restaurants
$100–$250	Room, food, beverage (RFB)
$250–$1000	RFB, suite, limo, golf, airfare
$1000+	Private plane, slave girls peeling grapes

LAWS & TAXES | According to Nevada law, players must be at least 21 years of age to gamble. People under 21 are not even allowed in casinos and, more importantly, if they hit the jackpot won't be able to keep their winnings. Casino winnings are taxable, and Uncle Sugar requires residents to report them as income. Losses too are deductible, but limited to the amount of winnings declared. The IRS considers "comps" to be earnings too, though few players seem to report them. Before paying you big, the casino will require two forms of identification. Non-resident aliens are subject to a 30-percent withholding tax, deducted from their winnings. Ouch.

AVANT-GUIDE CASINO TEN COMMANDMENTS

1. Thou shalt not touch your bet after you have placed it.
2. Thou shalt not wish ill on thy neighbor.
3. Thou shalt not handle dice with both hands.
4. Thou shalt not sit in thy neighbor's lucky seat.
5. Thou shalt not use thy Kino caller's name in vain.
6. Thou shalt not holler false "Bingo."
7. Thou shalt not slobber on dice while kissing them.
8. Thou shalt not split 10s.
9. Thou shalt not covet thy neighbor's machine.
10. Thou shalt not lie about thy losings.

WHERE TO PLAY

THE STRIP | Why lose your money in a shabby "grind joint" when you can blow the kids' college fund in the splendor of a billion-dollar resort? The Strip, of course, is where most visitors tend to play, and each of the giant mega-resorts competes fiercely with one another for the hearts and wallets of the gambling, er, gaming public. If truth be told, most of these top resorts have almost identical casinos. That's why most players choose where to gamble based on a casino's non-gaming attributes: like location, restaurants, nightlife or proximity to bed.

Especially in fancier places, table minimums will quickly jump when the joint is jumping, which means it's difficult to find a $5 Blackjack game most nights and weekends. And when a big convention is in town, minimums can be as high as $25 a hand at upmarket casinos like the Bellagio and the Mirage.

For all-around fun, our three favorite Strip casinos are Wynn, Mandalay Bay and the Venetian, all of which are hip spots with great casinos and plenty of diversions. Paris, Caesars, the Mirage, and the Bellagio are also good choices for comprehensive casino action. The London Club, a private gaming salon with its own restaurant and 24-hour butler service, is a good place to play $10,000-a-hand Blackjack without worrying you'll be spotted by your ex-wife's alimony lawyer. The least-loved of the major strip casinos are New York-New York because of dense crowds, Treasure Island and Circus Circus because of their popularity with kids, Stratosphere because many people think the tower is an eyesore, and MGM Grand because of its daunting size: When the hotel opened, it took two days and $3.5 million just to fill the machines.

DOWNTOWN | Downtown casinos tend to be less expensive and more "old Vegas," because, well... they *are* old Vegas. This part of the city has been caught in a proverbial vice, having lost the big betters to the Strip, and locals to more distant casinos. What's left is a handful of hotels that try to make themselves appealing to visitors by offering some of the best odds, cheapest games and least expensive extras in Vegas. Downtown casinos are usually no-nonsense game rooms that are full of the ghosts of gangsters past; home to single-deck Blackjack (Binion's), penny Video Poker (Gold Spike), and 99-cent shrimp cocktails (Golden Gate). And the nightly **FREMONT STREET EXPERIENCE** sound and light show even gives some of the larger Strip resorts a run for their money.

LOCALS CASINOS | With a few notable exceptions (Hard Rock, The Palms, Rio), casinos that are not located Downtown or on the Strip are broadly categorized as "Locals" because that's largely the hip-resistant audience they cater to with better odds, bigger comps and cheaper prices all around. Another truism is that minimums are lowered and odds are increased in direct relation to a given casino's shabbiness and distance from the Strip. With more than a half-dozen properties, Stations Casinos is the largest chain of Locals, and includes Palace Station, Boulder Station, Sunset Station, Santa Fe Station, Wild Wild West, and the Fiesta. The company continues to build more casinos and owns small chunks of many others, including the Palms. The greatest concentration of locals casinos is along Boulder Highway, which runs southeast from Downtown to Henderson. Here you'll find several Station Casinos as well as Sam's Town and many others.

The Games

BINGO

As long as tongue is firmly in cheek, Bingo can be a lot of fun. In addition to being a terrific place to pick-up elderly widows, this venerable pastime offers a window into Americana that's as real as bowling and trailer parks. And, according to a study by the University of Southampton, playing Bingo helps people "minimize memory loss, preserve visual acuity and bolster hand-eye coordination." Whoa. **Avant-Guide Fun Fact**: Bingo dates back to a 16th century Italian lottery and was popularized in America in the early 1930s by toy maker Ed Lowe who called it "Beano." He sold the game to Milton Bradley in 1973 for $26 million.

How | Players purchase cards with 25 arbitrarily numbered boxes on each. As the caller randomly picks each of 75 possible numbers, players mark off their cards. The winners are the first to mark a full row of boxes—either horizontally, vertically or diagonally.

Where | Harrah's began as a chain of Bingo parlors in California in the 1930s. It was such a success that, when the first Harrah's casino opened in Reno in 1946 it was called "The House That Bingo Built." In Las Vegas, Bingo is the preserve of "locals" hotels, all of which are located off-Strip. Arizona Charlie's, 740 S Decatur Blvd (at Charleston—West Side; tel. 702.258.5111), has the only 24-hour Bingo room in the city. It's such rollicking action that most of the old ladies who play here only get up from their seats to keep their support hose from completely cutting off their circulation. Gold Coast, 4000 W Flamingo Rd (at Valley View—West Side; tel. 702.367.7111), is Las Vegans' favorite place for Bingo. It's also full with chimneyfish (read: hard-drinking chain smokers) and is so smoky you can get the sensation of inhaling an entire pack of cigarettes without the pesky inconvenience of actually having to light one up.

BLACKJACK

Blackjack is easily the most popular game in the Green Felt Jungle. It's also one of the easiest to learn, though few people actually follow the conventions, preferring to follow their "feelings."

How | The basic premise, of course, is to beat the dealer by coming closest to 21 without going over. Unless you're counting cards, you should always abide by the following principles:

Black Jack at New York-New York

- Stand on 12 to 16 against the dealer's 2 to 6, but hit on 12 to 16 against the dealer's 7, 8, 9, 10 and ace.
- Stand on 17 to 21, but always hit soft 17. Hard 17 is called a "Mother-in-Law Hand" because it's a bad hand and you'd like to hit her, but you can't.
- Always split aces and 8s, but never split 4s and 10s.
- Double down on 10s and 11s against the dealer's 2s to 9s.
- Insurance is for suckers.

Where | If you're serious about winning you'd be wise to leave the Strip, where games are dealt from multi-deck shoes, and head Downtown or to a far-flung Locals place for a hand-held single-deck game in which your odds improve dramatically. There are some hotels on and near the Strip advertising "single-deck 21"—most notably Rio—but once inside you'll find only one or two of these tables and usually at higher limits, often $25 minimum. Slots-a-Fun, 2890 Las Vegas Blvd S (at Desert Inn—Strip; tel. 702.734.0410), or "Slots-a-

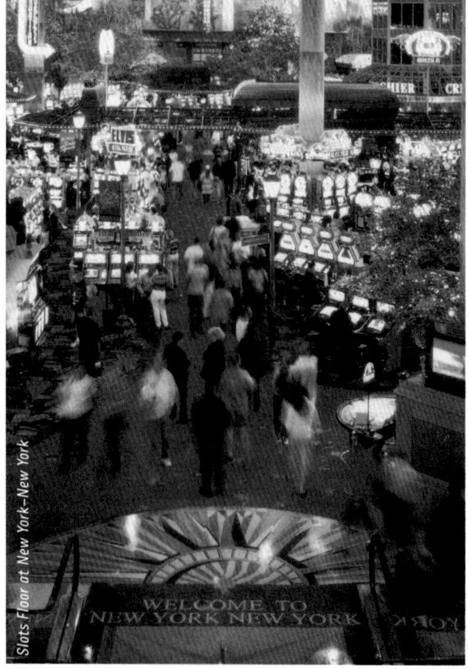

Slots Floor at New York–New York

Dumb" as it's affectionately known, is a downscale place with single-deck games and terrific rules that reduce the house edge to a razor-thin margin. If fun is more important than winning then almost any casino will do, though some, like the Hard Rock Hotel, are particularly high-energy places that up the joy-ante. Speaking of the Hard Rock, they're one of several casinos (along with the Tropicana and The Palms) offering swim-up Blackjack out by the pool. Unfortunately, you've got to be a guest of the hotel to play in their pool area.

CRAPS

When baby needs a new pair of shoes, Craps is the game to play. Fans will tell you that Craps has the best odds of any table game in the casino, and they're right, just as long as you play it by the book.

HOW | Craps is a bit complicated and requires instruction and practice. Although we don't attempt to teach you to play in these pages, we will once again refer you to the free gambling lessons that are offered at most major casinos and give you some tips to maximize your winnings:

- Play the line and the Come, and either Pass or Don't Pass. These two areas offer the best possible odds with house advantages of just 1.414% and 1.402%.
- When betting the Pass line, always take full odds in back of your pass line bet. Some casinos advertise double odds (or higher). Always take advantage of this option.
- Six and Eight pay 7-6. True odds are 6-5 so the house only has a 1.51% edge.
- Never bet Eleven. It pays 14-1, but true odds are 17-1, giving the house a 16.66% advantage.
- Increase bets on wins. Don't double up on losses.

WHERE | The best Craps rooms are either the ones that are the most fun to play in, or the ones that give you the best odds. Unfortunately, these two places are usually mutually exclusive. To shoot with well-dressed players in beautiful surroundings, head straight for Bellagio, the Mirage, Mandalay Bay, the Venetian, Wynn Las Vegas or any other top-of-the-line Strip resort. Downtown's Binion's is also known far and wide for its lively and raucous Craps action, as is the Golden Nugget nearby. For the other kind of play, the Sahara almost always has $1 dollar Craps with 5x odds, and the Stratosphere sometimes offers 100x odds. Casinos often include Craps in various promotions, so you should keep an eye out for advertisements touting odds specials.

KENO

Keno came to America by way of China, where it was invented more than two centuries ago. Now played nonstop in Vegas, this "Chinese lottery" is very similar to America's weekly state-run lotteries, offering jackpots that can reach into the millions.

HOW | Using a Keno ticket imprinted with the numbers 1 through 80, mark your favorite numbers, determine how much money you want to lose and how many games you're playing, then give your ticket to a runner. You can usually play anywhere from one to 15 spots. Rules and payouts vary with each casino, but they are always posted in the Keno lounge, on dining tables and on the back of each ticket. Frankly, it's all a bit complicated for the first-timer, but the runner can help you fill out the ticket properly.

WHERE | Keno is most fun when played in restaurants, where runners walk in for every game calling "Keno?" Play ten games for $1 per game, then enjoy your meal with an eye on the Keno

board and, with any luck, you'll be rich by the time dessert arrives. Serious players—and there are serious players—will want to spend some time in a casino Keno Parlor. The top-rated Keno lounges on the Strip are at MGM Grand, Luxor and Excalibur, while Gold Coast and the Golden Nugget win off-Strip honors. **Avant-Guide Table Tip**: If you don't want to gamble with the casino, try playing "Freeno"—or theoretical Keno—with your friends at the dining table: everyone chooses their own six numbers and the ones with the fewest hits at the end pay for the meal.

MINI-BACCARAT

Baccarat has a sophisticated air about it, bolstered by the fact that it's often played in roped off areas with tuxedo-wearing dealers. Needless to say, such refinement is rare in Vegas. Far more common is Mini-Baccarat, which is almost identical to its elite cousin, except that it's played in the regular casino area, the players might be wearing Bermuda shorts, and the casino's personnel are the only ones handling the cards.

HOW | The game is mind-numbingly simple. Dealt from an eight-deck shoe, Mini-Baccarat is not much different than betting on a coin toss, with players choosing which of two sets of cards will create a higher hand. Because it's basically an even-money game, the house takes 5% (or more) commission from every hand.

WHERE | Anyplace where there's fools and money.

POKER

Poker players, so we're told, are a quirky lot marked by a geeky above-average intelligence. One indication of their smarts is simply the fact that they play Poker at all, instead of games where losses usually mount much faster—like Blackjack, Craps and Roulette.

HOW | Poker is easy to play but difficult to master, so if you don't know the basics Vegas is not the place to learn. On the other hand, low-limit games offer some of the cheapest thrills around, so that you can consistently lose and still make a benjamin last several hours. Not bad, especially when drinks are free. Many off-Strip casinos will also comp players with food after several hours of play. Texas Hold'em and 7-Card Stud are the two most popular games. These are straightforward conservative games, with no deuces wild, no one-eyed jacks or suicide kings or anything. To join a game, find

The Venetian's Hallway to the Casino

a Poker room, belly up to the desk and ask the manager what games they're playing. Don't be shy about asking him to clarify the rules for you before you sit down, including table limits. If there's no space, the manager will put your name on a waiting list. Downtown and Locals casinos offer the cheapest games, often $1/$3, which means a minimum of $1 and maximum of $3 per bet. You usually need at least 20-times the maximum bet to "buy-in" your first load of chips; $100 usually gets you into a game on the Strip. **Avant-Guide Table Tip**: Always be vigilant. As the saying goes, if you don't know who the sucker at the table is, it's probably you.

WHERE | The wild success of TV Poker programs and the World Series of Poker has made this game a growth industry in Vegas. Many casinos have decided to get into the Poker business, and others have increased the number of tables dramatically. The Mirage, Bellagio and Wynn Las Vegas operate the dominant high-roller games on the Strip. But lots of other Strip resorts offer Poker too, including the Golden Nugget, Mandalay Bay, Luxor, Excalibur, Monte Carlo, Flamingo, Riviera, Stardust, Circus Circus and the Stratosphere. Off-Strip "locals"

Palms Girls at the Slots

casinos are the places to go to take Social Security money from grandmothers and grandfathers. The Orleans, 4500 W Tropicana Ave (at Decatur—West Side; tel. 702.365.7111), has one of the largest Poker rooms of any "locals" casino. It's our top pick for good action with moderately astute players. Drinks are always free-flowing and you can usually get a $5 food discount just for asking. Binion's, birthplace of the World Series of Poker, is a popular place to play year-round. For many gamblers, playing at Binion's is akin to taking to the court at Madison Square Garden, and you'd better be that good if you want to play here.

ROULETTE

With few exceptions, we avoid Roulette in Vegas because the odds are far worse here than they are in Europe. That's because American wheels have two zero positions (marked 0 and 00), as opposed to the ones in Europe which only have one. That difference nearly doubles the house edge from 2.7% to 5.26%. There are also fewer betting options in Vegas (no "neighbors" bets, for example) which, for us, make these wheels far less fun to play.

How | Table and chip minimums are clearly marked. The table minimum refers to the sum total of all your bets. It's also the minimum required for an "outside" bet, like Black or Red, for example. The chip minimum tells you the smallest amount you can bet on a single number. Exchange your cash or casino chips at the table for "wheel chips," which come in several different colors so the dealers can distinguish each players' bets. You must also inform the dealer of the denomination you want your chips to be. If you give the dealer $50 and want to bet dollars, he'll give you back 50 wheel chips worth $1 each. At the same time, a fellow player might be betting with chips worth $25 apiece. **Avant-Guide Table Tip**: The double-zero game has one bet that you should always avoid: the five-number bet on 0, 00, 1, 2, 3. It has a whopping casino edge of 7.89%.

Where | If you have to take a test spin, find a casino with a Euro wheel. On the Strip that means the Monte Carlo, though Caesars, MGM Grand and some others sometimes have one or two single-0 wheels spinning too, but usually with high table minimums.

SLOTS

The allure of the "idiot pull" is the promise of instant wealth in return for a meager investment, an enticing concept that has always been embraced chiefly by the lower and middle classes. Originally placed in casinos to amuse women while their men gambled at the tables, slots have "evolved" to become the casinos' leading source of income, accounting for more than 60% of revenues.

HOW | "One-armed banditry" makes money because of its built-in house advantage, called the vigorish, or "vig" for short. For every dollar dropped in, a machine will return somewhere between 90% and 99%—over the long run, that is. But these numbers are misleading because they refer to the total amount a player puts into the machine, not the total amount he or she originally brings to it. In other words, a slot jockey who comes to a machine with $100 and bets $1 per pull sometimes wins and sometimes loses. But because the player keeps reinvesting winnings, the total amount of play might be closer to $500 after a given time. If the machine retains just 5% of that amount, that's equivalent to $25, or 25-percent of the player's original drop. Capiche? Furthermore, many casinos brashly promote "loose" slots that return "up to 99.9%". But this can mean just a single machine hidden somewhere on the floor that will make such a payout in total over a number of weeks, or months. It's simply impossible to know. Anyway, no matter how "loose" a machine is, you're still likely to lose your money, just not as fast as on some other machines. Today's one-armed bandits are controlled by microprocessors known as Random Number Generators (RNG) that continuously generate strings of numbers associated with the various wheel combinations. When the slot machine's arm is pulled, or its "spin" button is pressed, the RNG pauses at that exact moment and "tells" the wheels where to stop. In this way, casinos can precisely program and control each machine's payout ratio. Top players always follow the following:

* Always bet the maximum number of coins allowed. That's the only way your overall odds increase (as stated on the payout schedule) and the only way you can claim the jackpot should all the wheels align in your favor. If you're looking to bet $1 per pull, you're better off playing maximum coins in a quarter machine than you are dropping a single dollar in a dollar machine.
* Non-progressive machines are "looser" (i.e. they pay out more often) than progressive machines. If you can relinquish your dreams of becoming an instant millionaire, your chances are better of winning something, simply because the payout will be smaller.
* When you find a good machine, hang on to it. We can't tell you how many times we've stepped away from our "workstation" for two seconds to go to the bathroom only to return and find a "lurker" putting coins in *our* machine.

WHERE | Everyone's got slots, but Bally's is home to the Champagne Slots Lounge which has a variety of high-denomination machines, some as much as $500 a pull. At the other end of the food chain is Arizona Charlie's, 740 S Decatur Blvd (at Charleston—West Side; tel. 702.258.5111) and Sunset Station, 1301 W Sunset Rd (at I-95—Henderson; tel. 702.547.7777), both of which offer Player's Wrist Pads which can be attached to most machines and save you all the pesky trouble of having to bear the weight of your own arm.

SPORTS & RACE BOOKS

In short, sports and race books bring together three great American pastimes: watching sports, betting and getting drunk. You can think of a Book as a very good sports bar in which you can watch multiple games on jumbo screens, place wagers on your favorite teams and get all your drinks free. Of course, it's not this good everywhere, but there are plenty of excellent places to play in Vegas.

HOW | Most sports books have large LED boards listing that day's athletic events along with the odds being offered. Future match-ups for which bets are being taken are usually posted as well. Aside from special events, like the Super Bowl, NCAA Basketball Tournament and playoffs in different sports, Books are most crowded on Saturday and Sunday afternoons during football season. And, unless a big game is just about to begin, bet-takers are usually happy to help you figure out how things work. Vegas Books operate on a pay-as-you-go basis, meaning you have to come up with all the cash in advance rather than settling-up on Thursday. To make a straight bet, you wager $11 to win $10. If you win, you get $21 back. A minus sign on the board denotes the favorite and a plus sign denotes the underdog. To win, your team must cover the point spread which follows the plus/minus sign. The minimum bets are usually $5 to $10.

WHERE | Sports books are a growing phenomenon in Vegas. The largest are at Circus Circus, Las Vegas Hilton, Stardust and Caesars Palace, a high-energy spot that takes some of the

Video Poker at The Palms

highest wagers in the city. All have lots of seats, big screens and numerous betting options. The Mirage and Imperial Palace are also good bets for people who want to roll out of bed and hang out in the sports book all day. Even if you're not really playing, you can always buy a cheap ticket to get free drinks.

VIDEO POKER

Pros like to say that Video Poker is one of the few casino games in which educated players can actually have the odds on their side. That's why this game has such a hardcore local following in Vegas. Luckily for casinos, however, most players are "videots."

HOW | The main thing you need to know is that not all machines pay out according to the same schedule. Not surprisingly, the vast majority of Video Poker machines contain a built-in house edge, but not all. If played mathematically, the house edge can be reversed on some full-pay "Double Bonus" machines, kicking back a return slightly over 100 percent for computer-perfect play. This, in some people's minds, raises Video Poker to a game of skill. Before you get too excited, note that computer-perfect play is hard to do, especially since every deal comes from a freshly shuffled 52-card deck. You can locate the high-paying equipment because state law requires the pay schedule to be posted on the front of each machine. Here's how to look like a pro:

- You must play the maximum number of coins (usually 5) to get the best odds.
- Never hold a "kicker" (unpaired or unsuited high card).
- Never draw to an inside straight (for example, hoping for a 5 when you're holding 4, 6, 7, 8).
- Always go for the royal flush if you hold the other four cards, even if that means sacrificing a flush.

WHERE | Full-pay Double Bonus machines can be found in most of the bigger Locals casinos, including Arizona Charlie's, Fiesta and the Orleans. If you don't know what they look like, then ask. None of the major Strip resorts have them.

KNOW 7

Las Vegas exists solely because of its proximity to Los Angeles. In a saner world, there wouldn't be a city here (it's in the middle of the desert, for God's sake!), which makes it doubly hard to believe that just a century ago Las Vegas was little more than a dusty railroad hamlet at the corner of Main and Fremont streets. The history of Las Vegas is short. But, as they say around here, brevity is the soul of cocktail waitress uniforms. Although the New York skyline, the Eiffel Tower and Venetian canals reside in the same ZIP code, Las Vegas is a "city" in name only. Really it's a giant company town; home to two million people who cater to over 36 million visitors a year. Locals' Las Vegas is a white trash Mecca filled with endless strip malls and anonymous chain stores built to service ever-growing pre-fab stucco tract communities of retirees, dropouts, run-aways and God-knows-who. The state ranks dead last in the nation in sending its high school grads to college, and the town is chock-full of losers who arrived by Greyhound then found trailers in which to spend their remaining days. By the way, if you ever meet a genuine local, don't ask any stupid questions like "Which hotel do you live in?" or "Have you hit the big one yet?" And remember, the "a" in the middle of Nevada is pronounced like "Gap," and not "Prada."

KNOW YOUR NEIGHBORHOODS

See inside front cover for neighborhoods map

THE STRIP | The Strip, a.k.a. Las Vegas Boulevard South, is approximately four miles (6.2 km) from Mandalay Bay (Russell Rd) to the Stratosphere (Main St). Dominated by some of the world's most extravagantly garish architecture, the street's entire length is fronted on both sides by the world's biggest mega-resorts, interspersed with tacky souvenir shops, retro diners and some enormously valuable vacant lots that are simply biding their time before they too become part of the architectural hysteria. First and foremost, the Strip is a study in excess. Its overwhelming neon signage has itself been overwhelmed by the audacious architecture of the monoliths they front; a Disneyesque world of themed lands that take you around the globe—from New York and Paris to Venice and Arabia—in just a matter of blocks. The Strip is all about The Spectacle, as each casino endeavors to outdo its neighbors for the attentions of would-be gamblers. The result is the most wonderfully awesome and wacky display anywhere. Millions of visitors from all over the world come to gawk as waters prance, a volcano spews and sirens dance; all part of the gaudy freak sideshow that fronts the world's largest adult playground.

DOWNTOWN | In 1925 Fremont Street became the first paved street in Las Vegas. It's still the heart of Downtown, and although it now has the flavor of a shopping mall, the neighborhood still retains its rat-pack appeal. Situated about three miles north of the Strip, Downtown is where Vegas began—before reality became virtual and hype replaced history. This is the original Glitter Gulch; low-ceiling casinos full with one-armed-banditry, smoky poker rooms, penny slots, nickel roulette and margaritas for a buck. Downtown Las Vegas has stood the test of time and then some. But as the fortunes of the Strip ascended, so Fremont Street fell into decline. In order to stay relevant and counter the wattage of the Strip, eleven Downtown hotels banded together in 1995 (along with the City of Las Vegas and the Las Vegas Convention and Visitors Authority) to create the covered mall that is the **FREMONT STREET EXPERIENCE**. If you long for the bad old days of pickpockets, prostitutes, porno parlors and psychodramatic panhandlers, simply continue east on Fremont Street, past El Cortez hotel and you'll be treated to the world's most beautiful stretch of seedy motels and their attendant vintage signs. Even as Las Vegas builds toward the heavens, this section of town keeps close to the ground. But watch your ass.

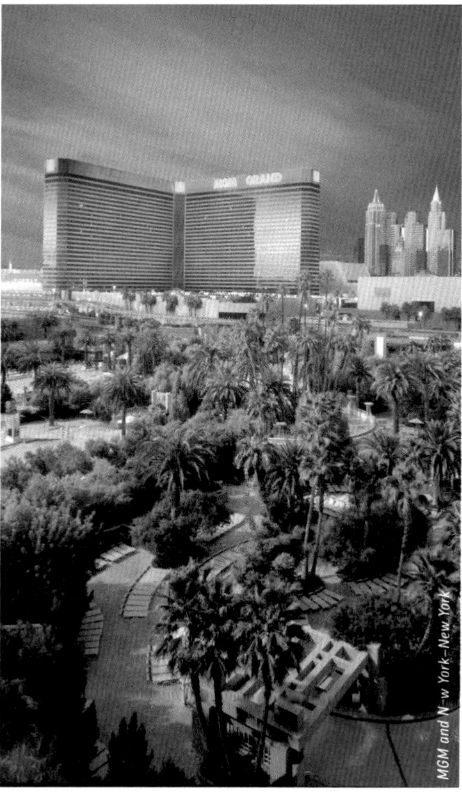

MGM and N-w York–New York

BOULDER HIGHWAY | Also known as the Boulder Strip, this long stretch of road runs southeast from Downtown all the way to **Henderson**, a work-a-day extension of the suburban city. The Boulder Strip is home to many of the city's largest "locals" hotels, including Boulder Station and Sam's Town. Henderson is home to a big shopping mall and several good restaurants which, aside from cultural slumming, is probably the only reason you'll visit.

SUMMERLIN | Situated to the far west of the Strip, Summerlin is the "Beverly Hills" of Las Vegas. Much of this area is a "master-planned" community, a town-sized swath of privately-owned land that was developed as a stand-alone suburb, complete with commercial districts and housing in several price brackets. This is the American Dream, sterilized. There's not much here for visitors, but it makes an interesting cultural study.

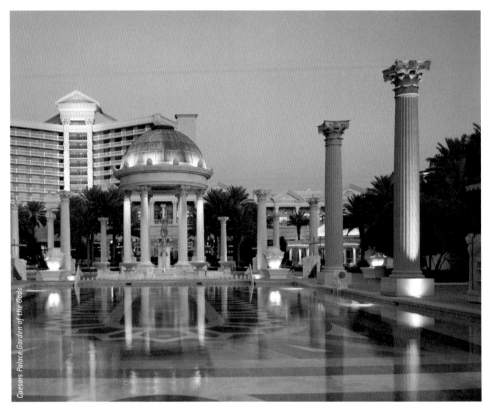

Caesars Palace Garden of the Gods

LEAVING THE AIRPORT

Your transport options between McCarran International Airport (tel. 702.261.5211) and the city are as follows:

TAXI | The fastest and easiest way to your hotel is by taxi. Cabs line up in front of each terminal. If two or more are traveling together in a cab, so much the better—in Vegas, there are no extra charges for additional passengers (up to a limit of 4 in most cabs) or for baggage placed in the trunk. The average fare is about $15 to the Strip and $18 to Downtown, including a small airport surcharge. Fifteen percent tip is customary. The trip takes about 10 to 20 minutes.

SHUTTLE VAN | Vans line up outside of the baggage claim area. There are several competing companies, all offering the same door-to-door service for about $7 per person to the Strip and $8 per person to a destination Downtown. Trips to off-Strip hotels cost $10-$18, depending on how far they are. When you're ready to head back to the airport, ask your hotel to book a shuttle or reserve with **Bell Trans** (tel. 702.739-7990 or 800.274-7433), **CLS Transportation** (tel. 702.740-4050), or **Star Transit** (tel. 702.646-4661).

SHUTTLE LIMOUSINE | **Las Vegas Limousine** (tel. 702.739.8414) is essentially a group shuttle service that happens to be by limo rather than passenger van. Several other limo-share companies also line up outside the airport's Door 14.

LIMOUSINE | Arrive in the style to which you're accustomed by calling **Ambassador Limousine** (tel. 702.362.6200 or 888.519.5466) or **Executive Coach & Carriage** (tel. 702.367.7774 or 866.367.7774). Both offer meet-and-greet service for about $75. Super-Stretch limos are about $95.

LOCAL TRANSPORT

CAR | Las Vegas is an autopia. Unless you're not planning to move around much, we highly recommend that you have wheels. Rentals are cheap, parking is easy and you'll save a mint on taxi fares. Free valet parking is offered at most hotels: Just tip $1 when you retrieve your car. If valet parking is "full," be bold and they'll likely find a space for you. Cash will also get you a spot no matter what the sign says.

MONORAIL | The **Las Vegas Monorail** travels from Sahara Avenue to the MGM Grand. Operated by computer, the driverless "transportainment" system follows a four-mile route just east of the Strip and takes 15 minutes to visit all of the stations: Sahara, Las Vegas Hilton, Las Vegas Convention Center, Harrah's-Imperial Palace, Flamingo-Caesars Palace, Bally's-Paris and MGM Grand. Extensions of the line are planned for Downtown, McCarran Airport and the corridor just west of the Strip.

TAXI | Even if you have your own wheels you'll find it useful to take a cab every once in a while (read: when drunk). Taxis line up outside every major hotel. And when they're not already waiting, you can easily phone for one (or ask your bartender to call for you). There are lots of cab companies, including **Checker**, **Star** and **Yellow**, all of which are contacted on tel. 702.873.2000.

LIMOUSINE | There are probably more limos per capita in Vegas than anywhere else on the planet. Prices vary from the basic stretch at about $45 an hour to flamboyant super-stretch cars that cost about twice as much. Reputable companies include **Ambassador Limousine** (tel. 702.362.6200 or 888.519.5466) and **Executive Coach & Carriage** (tel. 702.367.7774 or 866.367.7774).

Mc Carran International Airport

CASINO TRAM | Three casino-financed and operated monorails run between several of the largest hotels on the Strip. All should be thought of as entertainment first and transportation second, because in all cases it's usually quicker to walk. The **Bellagio-Monte Carlo** tram runs 24 hours a day with departures every two minutes or so. The swanky waiting areas at both termini are indoors and air-conditioned. The **Mandalay Bay-Luxor-Excalibur** monorail also operates nonstop with trains departing every 3-7 minutes. There are two tracks: One serves all the stations along the route, while the other provides express service between the two end stations. The **Mirage-Treasure Island** tram operates every 15 minutes or less, between 9am and 1am. The journey is just four minutes long and most able-bodied people prefer to walk.

STRIP TROLLEY | **Las Vegas Strip Trolley** (tel. 702.382.1404) operates cute-looking trolley buses that ply the Strip from Mandalay Bay to the Stratosphere, stopping in front of almost every major hotel in-between. Trolleys run about every 15 minutes, daily from 9.30am to 2am.

7 | KNOW

HISTORY IN A HURRY

1000 Native American Anasazi and Paiutes live in the area.

1829 Spanish traders en route to Los Angeles discover a desert spring and name it Las Vegas (The Meadows).

1844 Explorer John Fremont writes about the Las Vegas Valley.

1855 Mormon missionaries build an adobe fort in Las Vegas in a failed attempt to convert native Paiute Indians.

1860 Wells Fargo opens state's first bank in Virginia City.

1864 Nevada becomes the 36th US state.

1885 State Land Act offers parcels at $1.25 per acre.

1892 US Postal Service opens Las Vegas office.

1895 Slot machine invented in San Francisco.

1905 Railway through Vegas linking Southern California with Salt Lake City completed; Railroad company sells 1200 lots of land at auction; Town of Las Vegas established on May 15th.

1907 Town's first electric light installed on Fremont Street.

1909 Las Vegas becomes county seat for the newly established Clark County.

1911 City of Las Vegas incorporates; Population 800.

1917 Fire department buys its first truck.

1925 Fremont Street becomes first paved street in Vegas.

1926 Western Airlines makes first commercial flight into Vegas.

1930 Las Vegas population 5165.

1931 Hoover Dam construction begins, bringing thousands of workers to the area; Gambling legalized in Nevada, six gaming licenses issued; Governor signs quickie 6-week divorce law.

1933 Prohibition repealed.

1935 Hoover Dam dedicated by President Franklin Roosevelt.

1940 Las Vegas population 8422.

1941 El Rancho resort is first to open on the Strip; El Cortez Hotel opens downtown; World War II brings defense industry to the Valley.

1942 Last Frontier Hotel opens.

1946 Bugsy Siegel opens 105-room Flamingo Hotel on New Year's Eve.

1950 Desert Inn opens on the Strip with Vegas' first golf course; Las Vegas population 24,624.

1951 Nuclear bomb testing begins on range just 65 miles from Vegas.

1953 KLAS, the city's first commercial TV station starts broadcasting.

1954 The Showboat hotel opens and originates the all-you-can-eat buffet.

1955 Gaming Control Board created by Nevada Legislature.

1956 Elvis makes his first Vegas appearance at the New Frontier Hotel on April 23rd.

1957 "Minsky Goes to Paris" at The Dunes hotel is the first production to feature topless showgirls; Nevada Southern University (now UNLV) opens.

1959 Las Vegas Convention Center opens; Dawn Wells, who would play Maryann on Gilligan's Island, becomes Miss Nevada.

1960 Las Vegas population 64,405.

1963 Major casinos close for the only time in history from 7am to midnight on November 25th to mourn the assassination of President Kennedy; McCarran International Airport opens.

1964 Elvis and Ann Margaret star in Presley's 15th film, "Viva Las Vegas."

1966 Howard Hughes buys six Vegas hotels, moves into the penthouse of the Desert Inn and doesn't emerge for the next four years; Caesars Palace opens.

1967 Elvis Presley and Priscilla Anne Beaulieu wed at the Aladdin; Nevada law allows public corporations to obtain gambling licenses.

1968 Someone figures out that the anagram for "slot machines" is "cash lost in 'em."

1969 International Hotel (now the Las Vegas Hilton) opens with Barbra Streisand headlining in the showroom; Elvis makes his comeback with a sold-out 57-show engagement.

1970 Culinary & Bartenders strike cripples major hotels for four days in March; Las Vegas population 125,787.

1975 State gambling revenues top $1 billion.

1976 Elvis appears at the Hilton for a two-week engagement that would be his final Las Vegas appearance.

1977 Clark County gambling revenues top $1 billion per year.

1980 Fire devastates the MGM Hotel, killing 84 people and injuring over 700 more; Las Vegas population 164,674.

1981 Siegfried and Roy open at the Frontier.

1985 First National Finals Rodeo held in Las Vegas.

1989 Mirage opens with an erupting volcano and 3039 rooms.

1990 Excalibur opens as the world's largest resort hotel with 4032 rooms; UNLV wins first NCAA basketball title; Las Vegas population 258,295.

1992 First Las Vegas Bowl held at Silver Bowl.

1993 Flamingo Hilton announces plans to raze Bugsy's suite and office; Dunes Hotel sold to Steve Wynn's Mirage Inc.; Nevada casino winnings top $6 billion; ITT Sheraton Corp. buys Desert Inn Hotel from Kirk Kerkorian's Tracinda Corp.; Luxor, Treasure Island hotels open; MGM Grand opens with 5,005 rooms to become the largest resort hotel in the world.

1994 Fremont Street Experience begins construction; Four "skywalks" are built over the Las Vegas Strip.

1995 Hard Rock Hotel opens; Monorail begins running between MGM Grand and Bally's; ITT Corp. buys Caesars World Inc. for $1.7 billion, including Caesars Palace on the Las Vegas Strip; Construction begins on Steve Wynn's $1.7 billion Bellagio; $70 million Fremont Street Experience opens; Statewide gross gaming revenue tops $7.3 billion; Las Vegas population 368,360

1996 Wayne Newton celebrates 25,000th Las Vegas performance; Siegfried and Roy celebrate 15,000th Las Vegas performance; Stratosphere Tower opens; Hilton Hotels Corp. purchases Bally's Entertainment Corp. for $3 billion; Monte Carlo opens; Las Vegas Motor Speedway opens; Clark County population hits 1.1 million.

1997 New York-New York opens.

1998 Starwood Hotels & Resorts buys ITT Corp. for $14.6 billion, acquiring Caesars Palace and the Desert Inn; Bellagio, billed as the most expensive hotel in the world ($1.7 billion) opens; A 66-year-old Las Vegas resident hits a $27.58 million Megabucks jackpot at Palace Station; Nevada's annual gross gaming revenue hits $8.1 billion; Annual number of visitors to Las Vegas totals 30.6 million.

1999 Mandalay Bay, Four Seasons, Paris Las Vegas, and the Venetian hotels open; Harrah's Entertainment Inc. purchases the Rio Hotel for $888 million; MGM Grand Inc. buys Primadonna Resorts Inc., taking full ownership of New York-New York.

2000 Park Place Entertainment buys Caesars World Inc. for $3 billion; Kirk Kerkorian's MGM Grand Inc. buys Steve Wynn's Mirage Resorts Inc., creating the largest corporate buyout in gaming history; Aladdin hotel opens; Las Vegas population approx. 460,000; Clark County population approx. 1.4 million.

2001 $150 million expansion nearly doubles exhibit space of the Vegas Convention Center; Vegas takes a huge financial hit following terrorist attacks on the World Trade Center and the Pentagon.

2005 Wynn Las Vegas opens on the former Desert Inn property; Vegas celebrates its 100th birthday; Vegas population tops 2 million.

2006 Cirque du Soleil's fifth Vegas show opens at the Mirage, showcasing the music of the Beatles.

7 | KNOW

Las Vegas Lingo

Boat People | Gamblers who arrive on tour buses
Buy In | The initial exchange of cash for casino chips, usually in Poker
Cage | The main cashier for redeeming chips for cash
Carousel | Group of slot machines usually connected to a progressive jackpot
Carpet Joint | Casino catering to high rollers
Change Color | Trade chips for ones of a higher or lower denomination
Coffeehouser | *see* Kibitzer
Comp | Free or complimentary items given to players
Compcierge | The pit boss who's responsible for rating play and giving comps.
Copper Mine | A group of penny slot machines
Drop | The sum of all chips, cash and markers taken in at a gaming table
Drop Box | The locked box on gambling tables in which dealers deposit paper money
European Wheel | A Roulette wheel with no 'oo' position
Eyes in the Sky | Video surveillance cameras
Flotsam and Rejectsam | The refuse and excess left on your plate at a buffet
Freeno | Theoretical Keno, played without money
Grind | A low roller; *also*, Sucker or Tinhorn
Grind Joint | A casino with low table minimums and small-denomination slot machines
Handicap | A race in which the horses carry different weights in their saddles
House Advantage | The casino's advantage, expressed as a percentage
In Action | To have a wager on an event, usually sports-related
In Red | The color in which "comped" players' names are usually written in restaurants' reservation books
Iron Duke | An unbeatable card hand
Junket | An organized gambling tour offering low travel rates
Kibitzer | A mouthy onlooker at a card game (Yiddish for talker)
King George | A big tipper
Law Suit | When a Craps shooter misfires and hits another player with the dice
Lick Me | In Blackjack, another way to say "hit me"
Loose | Slots with frequent payouts
Marker | Credit extended by a casino to a player
Para-Mutual | Races in which the odds change based on how other players bet
Pit | The employee area behind gaming tables
Pit Bull | The chief who oversees numerous table dealers; *also* Pit Boss
Progressive Jackpot | A payout that increases with each coin played
Rated Player | Player whose gambling habits are assessed by the casino
River Card | The final community card in Texas Hold'em
Rock | Poker professional who only plays the very best cards (and otherwise just sits)
RFB Comp | Free room, food and beverage for bigger players
Shill | Casino employee who plays with house money at empty tables to encourage business
Shoe | Container for decks of cards, especially on Blackjack tables
Stiff | A winning player who doesn't tip the dealer
Toke | Tip or gratuity given to dealers
Turkey | A player who is unpleasant to the dealer and other players
Whales | The highest of the high-rollers; also Premium Players

INDEXES

BOOK INDEX

=#=

10 Things to Buy 76
3950 38
55 Degrees Wine + Design 77
808 38
99¢ shrimp cocktail 54

=A=

Adult Superstore 77
Adventuredome Theme Park 14, 129
Agassi, Andre 111
Agent Provocateur 77
AGLN 11
Ah Sin 38
airplane tours 128
airport transportation 164
AJ Hackett Bungy 129
Aladdin/Planet Hollywood Hotel 12
Albion Book Company 77
Alcott, Louisa May 20
Alex restaurant 38
Algiers Hotel 12
Alizé 39
Altreche, Suzanne 44
André's 39
Andretti Racing School 137
Antique Mall 78
Antiques at the Market 78
area codes 37
areas 163
Arizona Charlie's East 12
Art of Shaving, The 78
Attic, The 78
Aureole 39
Auto Collection 135
automobile racing school 137
Avant-Guide Lifestyle Network 11

=B=

Backstreet Saloon & Dancehall 105
Baja Fresh Mexican Grill 39
Bally's Hotel 12
Bally's Sterling Brunch 57
Bangkok Orchid 40
Barbary Coast 12
Bare Essentials 78
Barish, Chris 106
Barnes & Noble 79
bars 101
bars & clubs A—Z 105
Bass Pro Shops 79
Bathhouse, The 74
Beach, The 105
Beano 155
Bellagio Botanical Conservatory 129
Bellagio Buffet 40
Bellagio Fountains 133
Bellagio Gallery of Fine Art 129
Bellagio Hotel 13
Berlin Wall, the 20
best bars to... 103
best hotels to... 11
best sights in Las Vegas 127
betting with your head 153
Big Al's Oyster Bar 40
Big B's CDs & Records 79
Big Mama's Rib Shack 40
Big Shot ride 142
Bingo parlors 155
Binion's Coffee Shop 40
Binion's Ranch Steakhouse 41
Blackjack 155
Blarney Castle 16
Blau, Elizabeth 55
Blockbuster Video 79
Bloomingdale's Home 71
Blue Agave Oyster & Chilé Bar 41
BOA Steakhouse 41
Body English 105
Bonanza Gift Shop 79
Boogie Knights 106
Borders Books, Music & Cafe 79
Borg Invasion 4D 141
Boston Grill & Bar 105
Botanical Conservatory 129
Bouchon 41
Boulder Highway 163
Boulder Station 13
Boulder Strip 163
Boulevard Mall 71
Bowie, David 137
Brennan, Brad 37
British Foods, Inc. 79
Broadacres Swap Meet 74
Buffalo Exchange 79
Buffalo, The 105
Buffet, The 41
buffets 37
bungy jumping 129
Burdsall, Brad 44
Burger Bar 41

=C=

Ca' d'Oro 79
cabs 165
Café Bellagio 42
Café Lago 42
Canaletto 42
Canyon Ranch SpaClub 74
Capriotti's Sandwich Shop 42
car museum 135
Caramel 106
Carnival Court 106
Carnival World Buffet 42
Carolina Herrera 80
Carter, Howard 135
Casey's Cameras 80
Casino Legends Hall of Fame Museum 129
casino slang 168
Casino Ten Commandments 154
Casuarina Hotel & Spa 26
celebrity restaurateurs 37
Cellar Lounge 106
Center Bar, The 106
Chanel 80
Charlie Palmer Steak 43
Cheesecake Factory, The 43
Cheetah's Topless Lounge 104
Chi, Tony 24
Chihuly, Dale 13
Chinois 43
Christina, Christina 111
Circuit City 80
Circus Circus 14
Circus, The 130
Cirque du Soliel 13
city telephone code 37
Club Paradise 104
Club Rio 106
clubs 101
Coachman's Inn 44
Coffee Pub 44
Colicchio, Tom 37, 44, 58
Commander's Palace 44
comp guide 153
comps 153
coral reef aquarium 139
country code 37
Craftsteak 44
Craps 156
Cravings 44
Crazy Horse Too 104
Crown & Anchor 106
Cuba Libre 80
Cue Club 106
custard 49
Cyber Speedway 136

=D=

Davante 80
day spas 74
Dead Poet Books 80
Dealers Room Casino Clothiers 81
dealer's uniforms 76
Delmonico 44
Desert Fox Tours 128
Desert Passage 71
dice clocks 76
Dion, Celine 111
directions 163
Dolphin Habitat 140
Don Pablo Cigar Co. 81
Double Down Saloon 106
Dougall Design Associates 25
Downtown 163
Drai, Victor 107

Drai's 107
Ducasse, Alain 37, 38, 50
Dylan's Dance Hall & Saloon 107

=E=

Eagle, The 107
eating 35
Eddie Rodriguez 81
Egg & I, The 44
Eiffel Tower Experience 130
Eiffel Tower restaurant 45
El Cortez 15
El Rancho 166
Electra, Carmen 111
Elemis Spa 74
Ellis Island Lounge 107
Elvis Glasses 76
Elvis 166
Elvis-A-Rama Museum 130
Elvis-A-Rama Museum Shop 81
Emeril's New Orleans Fish House 45
Engelstad, Ralph 135
English, Todd 37, 51
Ethel M. Chocolates 83
Excalibur hotel 15
Excalibur Wizard Show 138
exploring 125

=F=

Fall of Atlantis Fountain Show 132
Fantastic Indoor Swap Meet 74
Fantasy Faire Arcade 138
FAO Schwarz 81
Fashion Outlets Las Vegas 71
Fashion Show Mall 71
Festival Fountains 132
Fitzgerald's 15
Fix 46
Flamingo Las Vegas 16
Flamingo Las Vegas Wildlife Habitat 16, 131
Flay, Bobby 50
Fleur de Lys 46
flightseeing tours 128
Flyaway Indoor Skydiving 131
Fontana Bar 108
Forum Shops Festival Fountains 132
Forum Shops, The 71
Foundation Room 108
Fountains at Bellagio 133
Four Queens 17
Four Seasons Las Vegas 16
Frederick's of Hollywood 81
Free Zone 108
Fremont Hotel & Casino 17
Fremont Street Experience 133
Fremont Street 163
Fremont, John 166
frozen custard 49
Fry's Electronics 81

=G=

Galleria at Sunset 72
Gallery of Fine Art 129
Gamblers Book Club 82
Gamblers General Store 82
gambling lessons 153
gambling 151
GameWorks 133
gaming laws 154
gaming 151
Garden Court Buffet 37
Garden of the Gods 14
Garduños 46
Ghostbar 108
Gilley's Dancehall Saloon 108
Gipsy 108
Girls of Glitter Gulch 133
Glitter Gulch 163
Golden Nugget 17
Gondola Rides 133
Gondolier Parade 134
Gordon Biersch Brewery 108
Gramercy Tavern 44
Grand Canal Shoppes 72
Grand Canal 133
Grand Lux Café 47
Guggenheim Hermitage Museum 134
Gun Store, The 135
Guy Savoy 47
Gypsy Caravan Antique Mall 82

=H=

Hand Of Faith nugget 17
Hard Rock Hotel 18
Harrah's 18
Harrie's Bagelmania 47
Hebler, Dave 130
Helicopter tours 128
Henderson 163
Herbst brothers 25
High Roller rollercoaster 142
Hilton hotel 18
history in a hurry 166
Holiday Inn Boardwalk's Surf Buffet 37
Hookah Lounge 110
hotel upgrades 11
hotels A—Z 12
hotels 9
House of Blues 108
Hughes, Howard 166
Hush Puppy 47

=I=

Ice Accessories 82
Ice Las Vegas 108
Il Fornaio 42
Il Prato 82
IMAX 3-D ride 132
IMAX Motion Rides 129
Imperial Palace 18
Imperial Palace Auto Collection 135
indoor skydiving 131
In-N-Out Burger 48
Insanity ride 142
International Marketplace 82
Isla Mexican Kitchen & Tequila Bar 48
Ivan Kane's Forty Deuce 109

=J=

Jacqueline Jarrot 82
Jarr, Cook E 106
John, Elton 137
Johns, Jasper 25
Johnson, Brad 115
Joint, The 18, 109
Josselin, Jean-Marie 37
Judd, Donald 25
Judith Leiber Boutique 83
Juicy Couture 83

=K=

Keller, Hubert 41, 46
Keller, Thomas 37, 41
Keno 156
King Tut's Tomb & Museum 135
Kipling, Rudyard 20
Koolhaas, Rem 134

=L=

La Brea Bakery 40
LaForge, Lieutenant Geordi 141
Lagasse, Emeril 37, 44, 45
Las Vegas Cyber Speedway 136
Las Vegas Hilton 18
Las Vegas Limousine 164
Las Vegas lingo 168
Las Vegas Mini Grand Prix 136
Las Vegas Monorail 165
Las Vegas Outlet Center 72
Las Vegas Premium Outlets 72
Las Vegas sign 142
Las Vegas Strip Trolley 165
Las Vegas superlatives! 127
Las Vegas T-shirts 76
Las Vegas Wildlife Habitat 131
Laser Quest 136
laws 154
Le Boulevard mall 72
Le Café Île St. Louis 48
Le Village Buffet 49
Lee's Discount Liquor 83
Lenin's head 112
Leonard's Wide Shoes 83
Lessons, gambling 153
Liberace Museum Gift Shop 83

BOOK INDEX

Liberace Museum 136
Liberace Refrigerator Magnets 76
Light 109
limousines 164, 165
lingo 168
Lion Habitat 21, 137
Little Buddha Café 49
Little Church of the West 137
local transport 165
locals casinos 154
London Club, The 154
Lord & Taylor 71
Lotus 115
Louis XV restaurant 50
Lowe, Ed 155
Luv-It Frozen Custard 49
Luxor 19

=M=

M&Ms World 83
Maccioni family 52
Macy's 71
Madame Tussaud's Wax Museum 137
Main Street Station 19
malls 71
Maloof family 23
Mandalay Bay 20
Mandalay Place 73
Mandara Spa 75
Manhattan Express Rollercoaster 137
Mansions, The 21
Mario Andretti Racing School 137
markets 74
marriages 137
Masa 52
Masquerade Show in the Sky 23
Matsuhisa, Nobu 37, 51
Mayflower Cuisinier 49
Mazzon, Maurizio 37
McCarran International Airport 164
McWhorter, Dargin 40
Medieval Village 15
Memphis Championship Barbecue 49
Merlin the Wizard Show 138
Merlin's Mystic Shop 84
Mesa Grill 50
Metro Pizza 50
MGM Grand Spa 75
MGM Grand hotel 21
Midway Mezzanine 14
Mini Grand Prix 136
Mini-Baccarat 157
minimums & maximums 153
Mirage Volcano 138
Mirage, The 21
Mix 50, 109
Mon Ami Gabi 50
monorail 165
Monte Carlo hotel 21
Monte Carlo Pub & Brewery 109
Montesano's Italian Deli 51
Moorea Beach Ultra Lounge 109
Morgan, Cheleen 78
Morton, Michael 51
Morton, Peter 51
Morton's of Chicago 51
Motel 6 22
Motion Machines simulator rides 138
Mr. Bill's Pipe & Tobacco 84
Mr. Lucky's 24/7 51
Mr. O'Lucky 15
Murphy, Brittany 111
Musette 84
museums 125

=N=

N9ne 51
Nanette Lepore 84
NASCAR Cafe 24
National Finals Rodeo 107
Native Americans 166
neighborhoods 163
Neiman Marcus 84
Neonopolis 73
New York-New York 22
Newton, Wayne 24
Nicolas & Osvaldo Antiques 84
Nieman Marcus 71
nightlife 101
Nobu 51
Nordstrom 71
nuclear bomb testing 166

=O=

Oculus 85
Olives 51
Olympic Gardens Cabaret 104
O'Neal, Shaquille 111
OPM 110
Opportunity Village 85
Orleans, The 22
Osteria del Circo 52
outlet shopping 72

=P=

Paiute Tribal Smoke Shop 85
Palmer, Charlie 37, 39, 43
Palms, The 23
Papillon Grand Canyon Helicopters 128
Paradise Electro Stimulations 85
Paris Las Vegas 23
Paris Spa by Mandara 75
Paymon's Hookah Lounge 110
Peppermill's Fireside Lounge 110
PF Chang's China Bistro 52
Picasso 52
Piero Selvaggio Valentino 52
Pink E's Lounge 110
Pink Taco 53
Pinot Brasserie 53
Planet Hollywood Hotel 12
Players Clubs 153
Plaza Athenee 50
Poker 157
Polo Lounge 111
Postrio 53
Presley, Elvis 167
Prime 53
prostitution 104
Prudhomme, Paul 44
PS Italian Grill 53
Puck, Wolfgang 37, 43, 53, 56
Pure 111
Pussycat Dolls Lounge 111

=R=

Ra 111
Rabin, David 115
Race Books 159
Race for Atlantis 132
racing school 137
Rain 112
Rainbow Feather Company 85
Raushenberg, Robert 25
Ray's Beaver Bag 86
Reading Room, The 86
Record City 86
Red Rooster Antique Mall 86
Red Square 112
Regan, Will 115
Reichl, Ruth 53
reservations, hotel 11
reservations, restaurant 37
restaurant reservations 37
restaurants 35
restaurants A—Z 38
restaurateurs, celebrity 37
Richardson Sadeki 74
Rio 23
Ripa di Monti 86
Risqué 112
Roasted Bean 54
Roberto Cavalli 86
Rochat, André 37, 39
rollercoasters 137, 141, 142
Roman Gods Show 132
Romano's Macaroni Grill 54
Roosevelt, Teddy 20
Roulette 158
Round Table Buffet 15
Rumjungle 113

=S=

Sacramento Kings 23
Sahara 24
Saks Fifth Avenue 71, 86

San Francisco Shrimp Bar 54
Sand Dollar Blues Lounge 113
Sasson, Andrew 106
Savers Thrift Shop 86
Savoy, Guy 37, 47
Scenic Airlines 128
Scoop NYC 87
Secret Garden 140
Serges Showgirl Wigs 87
Serra, Richard 25
Serrano 37
Serrano, Julian 37, 52
sex scenes 104
Shadow 114
Shalimar 55
Shanghai Lilly 55
Shark Reef 139
Sheplers Western Store 87
Shibuya 55
shopping 69
shopping malls 71
shops A—Z 77
Showcase Slots & Antiquities 87
shrimp cocktail 54
shuttle services 164
shuttle vans 164
Siegel, Benjamin "Bugsy" 16, 166
Siegfried and Roy 167
Siegfried & Roy Boutique 87
Siegfried & Roy calendar 76
Siegfried & Roy's Secret Garden 140
sights 125
sights A—Z 129
Simon Kitchen & Bar 55
Simon, Kerry 37, 55
Sirens of TI Show 140
skydiving 131
SkyLofts at MGM 24
slang 168
sleeping 9
Slightly Sinful 87
slot clubs 153
Slots 159
Sourdough Cafe 56
Spago 56
spas 74
Speed—The Ride 141
Splichal, Joachim 37, 53
Sports Books 159
Star Trek: The Experience 141
Stardust 24
statehood 166
Station Resorts 13
Steak House, The 15, 57
Steakhouse at Camelot 15
Stefani, Gwen 111
Sterling Brunch 57
Stevenson, Robert Louis 25
Stewart, Martha 129
stores 69
Stratosphere hotel 24
Stratosphere restaurant 57
Stratosphere Tower 141
Stratta 37
Stratta, Alessandro 37, 38
Strings by Judith 87
Strip, The 163
strip clubs 104
Strip trolley 165
Studio 54 114
Summerlin 163
Sunset Room 115
Sunset Station 24
Superpawn 87
Surf Buffet 37
Sushi Roku 57
swap meets 74

=T=

Tabu 114
Talking Roman Gods Show 132
Talulah G 87
taxes 154
taxis 164, 165
Teatro 114
telephone area code 37
Ten Commandments 154
Terrazza 57
Terrible's 25
THEhotel 25
things to buy 76
Thriller Clothing Company 88
TI hotel 25
TI show 140
Tiffany & Co. 88
Tihany, Adam 39, 41, 52, 114
Toe Rings and Foot Things 88
Tommy Rocker's 114
Tony Chi & Associates 55
Top of the World 57
tours 128
Tower Records 88
trams 165
transport 165
Treasure Island Show 140
Treasure Island 25
Triple 7 Brewpub 114
T-shirts 76

=U=

ultralounges 102
Unica Home 88
upgrades, hotel 11

=V=

V Bar 115
Valentino 52
Valentino, Piero Selvaggio 37, 52
Vegas Vic 133
Vegas Vickie 133
Venetian, The 26
Venetian Grand Canal 133
Verandah, The 57
Via Bellagio 74
Video Poker 160
Village Meat & Wine 88
Village Seafood Buffet 57
Viper Room 111
Virgin Megastore 88
Viva Mercado's 58
Vivid 115
Volcano at the Mirage 138
Vongerichten, Jean-Georges 37, 53
VooDoo Lounge 116
Vosges Haut Chocolat 88

=W=

Warhol, Andy 25
waterpark 142
Wax Museum 137
wedding chapel 137
Welcome to Fabulous Las Vegas Sign 142
Wells, Dawn 166
Westin Casuarina Hotel & Spa 26
Wet 'n' Wild 142
where to gamble 154
White Tiger Habitat 142
'Wichcraft 58
Wild Oats Community Market 88
Wildlife Habitat 131
Willis, Betty 142
Wine Cellar & Tasting Room 88
Wynn Las Vegas 26
Wynn Las Vegas Shops 74
Wynn, Steve 26

=X=

XScream 142

=Z=

Z'Tejas Grill 58

MAP INDEX

=#=

3rd Pl I1
5th Pl H1
8th Pl H2

=A=

Adams Av J2
Adra Ct B2
Aladdin La A1
Albert Av E2
Albert Av L1
Alcoa Av A2
Aldebaran Av C2, E2, F2
Algonquin Dr L2
Alhambra Cir H2
Alhambra Dr H2
Almond Tree La H2
Alpine Pl B1
Alta Dr I1
Alto Verde Dr K2
Alturas Av I1
Amadeus Ct L2
Amarillo St A1
Andrea St F1
Appian Wy B1
Aquarius Dr B1
Arbol Verde Wy K2
Arenas St A1
Art and Mary Thomas La H2
Arville St A1, B1, C1, D1, E1, F1
Ascot Dr K1
Ashby Av B1, B2
Ashton St K1
Astrotec Dr L2
Audrie St D2, E2
Augusta Dr G2
Av of the Hiltons G1
Avenida Del Luna K2
Avenida Del Sol K2

=B=

Balboa Av G2
Banner Cir B1
Bannie Av B2
Barbara Wy H1
Barnard Dr B2
Batavia Dr F1
Batelli Ct K2
Baxter Pl B1
Bayo Ct B2
Bearden Dr I1
Becke Cir H2
Bel Air Cir G2
Bel Air Dr G1, G2
Bell Dr J2
Bellagio St E2
Berman St G2
Bertsos Dr E1
Bethel La C2
Billman Av K2
Biltmore Dr J2
Birch St A2, B2
Black Canyon Av F2
Black Forest Dr A1
Blisworth Ct B1
Blue Heron Ct L2
Bock St K1
Bonanza Wy J2
Bond St D1
Bonita Av H1, H2
Bonnie Brae Av B2
Boone St K1
Bossart Ct B1
Boulder Av I1
Boyer St K1
Bracken Av H1, H2
Bramfield Ct B1
Bridger Av I1, I2
Bridlewood Dr K2
Broadmoor Av G2
Brockwood Dr B1
Brussels St K1
Bryant Av B2
Bryn Mawr Av B2
Buckeye Av B1
Buehler Dr B2
Buena Vista Dr F1
Burnham Av K2, L2
Burton Av B2
Bushnell Dr F1
Business Center Wy C1
Business La E2

=C=

Caballero Wy G2
Cabot St A2
Cahlan Dr B2
Calanda Ct B2
Calcaterra Cir L1
Caliente St K2, L2
Calle De El Cortez B2
Calle De Espana A2, B2
Calle De Nuevo A2
Calle De Vega B2
Calle Del Rio B2
Calle Del Sol E1
Calle Del Torre B2
Calle Esquina E1
Calle Fermo E1
Calle Mirador E1
Calle Paula E1
Calle San Remo E1
Calle Sedillo E1
Calle Tereon E1
Cameron St B1, C1, D1, E1, F1
Camino Verde La K2
Campbell Dr B2
Cannoli Cir D1
Canosa Av H1, H2
Canterbury Ct K2
Canterbury Dr K2
Capella Av F1, F2
Capistrano Av G2
Carriage La K2
Carson Av I1, I2
Casa Grande Av B1, B2
Casa Vegas St G2
Cashman Dr B2
Casino Center Blvd H1
Castleford Pl A1
Castlewood La A1
Cathedral Wy F2
Cavaretta Ct E1
Celebrity Cir K2
Chadford Pl A1
Channel 10 Dr L2
Chapman Dr H2
Charlton St K1
Charmast La H1
Chatham Cir L1
Cholla Wy I2
Cinder La F2
Cinderella La A1
Circle Dr I2
Circus Circus Dr G1
Clark Av I1, I2
Clark Towers Ct A2
Claymont St L1
Coachman Cir K2
Cochran St H2
Colanthe Av B2
Colby Av K1
Colors Ct F1
Colt Pl K2
Concordia Pl H2
Constantine Av J2
Convention Center Dr G1
Coolidge Av I1
Cordova St H2
Cornstock Dr J1
Corona Av G2
Coronado Av G2
Corporate Dr L1
Corral Pl K2
Cottage Cir L1
Cottage Grove Av L1
Cranford Pl A1
Crescent Dr B2
Creslow Ct B1
Cublington Ct B1
Cunningham Dr J1
Curtis Dr H2

=D=

Daisy St L1
Dalton Dr K1
Danford Pl A1
Danville La C2
Darmak Dr B1
Davison St K1
De Osma St A2, B2
Deckow La E2
Deirdre St K1
Del Mar Av G2
Del Mar Ct G2
Del Mar Pl G2
Del Mar St K1, K2
Del Monte Av B1
Del Oro Dr F1
Del Rey Av B1
Delancey Dr E1
Delaware La L2
Desert La I1
Desert Point Dr C1
Di Salvo Dr F1
Diamante Cir L2
Diamond Cir J1
Discovery Dr I1, J1
Domingo St L2
Dorothy Av K1, K2
Douglas Dr B2
Down Wy J1
Drake Ct F1
Duke Ellington Wy D2
Durante St K1

=E=

E Ali Baba La D2
E Bell Dr K1
E Bonanza Rd J2
E Bonneville Av I1, I2
E California St H1
E Charleston Blvd I1, I2
E Colorado Av H1
E Desert Inn Rd F2
E Dewey Dr C2
E Diablo Dr C2
E Flamingo Rd L1, L2
E Harmon Av K1, K2
E Imperial Av H1
E Katie Av L1, L2
E McWilliams Av J2
E Mesa Vista Av C2
E Mesquite Av I2, J2
E Naples Dr K1
E Nevso Dr L2
E Oakey Blvd H1, H2
E Ogden Av I2, J1, J2
E Oquendo Rd C2
E Reno Av D2
E Reno Av K1, K2
E Rochelle Av L1, L2
E Saddle Av L2
E Sahara Av G1, G2
E St Louis Av H1, H2
E Tompkins Av K2
E Tropicana Av K1, K2
E Twain Av L1, L2
E University Av K1, K2
E Utah Av H1
E Viking Rd L2
E Washington Av J2
E Wilson Av J2
Earl St I2
Eaton Dr B2
Edgeford Pl A1
Edgewood Av B2
Edna Av A2
El Cajon St G2
El Camino Av A1, A2
El Cederal Av B1
El Centro Pl H1
El Conlon Av A1
El Cortez Av B1, B2
El Greco St A1, B1
El Jardin Av B1
El Mirado St A1, B1
El Parque Av B1
El Pasada Av B1
El Portal Av A1
El Segundo Av G2
El Toreador St G2
Elder St K1
Eldon St F1
Elizabeth Av K1, K2
Elk Springs Av F1
Ellen Wy H1
Ellis Av H1
Encanto Dr J2
Escondido St K2, L1, L2
Esmeralda Av A1
Euclid St K2, L2
Evaline St L2
Exley Av H2
Exposition Av B1

=F=

Fair Av J1
Faircenter Pkwy B1
Fairfax Cir L1
Fairfield Av G1, H1
Familian Dr A1
Fantasy La J2
Farnam Pl B1
Fashion Show Dr F2
Fashion Show La F2
Fellowship Ct B1
Fidus Dr E1
Finch St K1
Flag Cir B1
Flagship Ct L2
Flamingo Crest Dr L2
Fontenelle St B1
Foot St A1
Forever Dr L2
Four Seasons Dr C2

Francis Av H2
Franklin Av H1, H2
Fredrika Dr L1
Fremont St I2
Fulano Wy B2

=G=

Gabriel Dr K2
Galaxy Av B1
Gannet Cir F1
Garces Av I1, I2
Garland Ct L2
Gaslight Cir K2
Gass Av I1, I2
Gaylord Dr F1
Gerson Av J1
Giles St C2, D2
Gilmary Av B2
Glen Heather Wy A2
Gogo Wy F1
Gold Coast Dr E1
Golden Arrow Dr G2
Gragson Av J2
Grant St J1
Graphic Center Dr D1
Gretel Cir A1
Griffith Av H1, H2
Groff St K1
Grove Cir L1
Gus Giuffre Dr K1
Gym Dr K1

=H=

H St J1
Hallwood Dr K2
Hansel Cir A1
Harley Wy I2
Harris Av J2
Hartford Pl A1
Hartke Pl H2
Hasseth Av H2
Hastings Av B2, I1
Haven St C2, D2
Hazelwood St L1
Heidi Cir A1
Heidi St K2
Held Rd J2
Hensley St K1
Heritageoaks St K2
Hermosa St G2
Hialeah Dr K2
Highland Av H1
Highland Dr A2
Hillcrest Av B1
Hillside Pl H2
Hinson St B1
Hoopa La L2
Hoover Av I1, I2
Hotel Rio Dr E1, E2
Houssels Av H1
Howard Av H2
Huckleberry Rd F1
Hughes Center Dr L1

=I=

Ida Av E2
Iglesia St G2
Industrial Rd A2, C2, D2, E2, F2, G1, H1
Inverness Av A2, B2
Iron Horse Dr I1
Irwin Cir K2
Ivanhoe Wy B2
Izabella Av G2

=J=

Jamestown Wy A2
Jaylar Cir H1
Jefferson Av J1, J2
Jeffreys St K2, L2
Jericho St F1
Jessica Av H2
Joe W Brown Dr G1
Joshua Wy I2
Juana Vista St A1, B1
Juanita Dr F1
Jupiter Ct K2

=K=

Kaiser Wy A2
Kamden Wy L2
Karen Av G1, G2
Karen Ct G1
Karli Dr B2
Kassabian Av H2
Kendale St G1
Kenyon Pl I1
Kiltie Wy B2
King Midas Wy A1
Kings Wy A2
Kirkland Av A2, B2
Kishner Dr G1
Kolendo Ct F1
Kolson Cir L1
Koval La E2, F2
Kristen La K2

=L=

La Brisa Av G2
La Canada St G2
La Cara Av K2
La Fortuna Av K2
La Jolia Av G2
La Pasada Av B1
La Solana Wy B2
La Vante Av G2
Laconia Av K2
Laguna Av G2
Lamplighter La H2
Laramore Dr K1
Las Flores St B1
Las Lomas Av B1
Las Vegas Blvd S (the Strip) C2, D2, E2, F2, G1, H1, I1, I2, J2
Las Verdes St A1, B1
Latigo St K2
Laurie Dr B2
Lenna St A1
Leslie Av J2
Levy La J1
Lewis Av I1, I2
Lilliput La A1
Linden Av J2
Living Desert Dr K1, K2
Llewellyn Dr B2
Loch Lomond Wy B2
Lorilyn Av K1, K2
Los Altos Pl B1
Los Altos St A1, B1
Los Reyes Ct K2
Lotus St A1
Lourdes Av A2
Lucido Dr F1
Lulu Av K1
Luxor Dr C2, D2
Lynnwood St G1
Lyon Dr F2

=M=

M St J1
Madison Av J1, J2
Madreperla St K2
Malabar Av K2
Malibu St G2
Mandalay Bay Rd C2
Manzanit Wy I2
Marcus Dr B1
Margaret Av J2
Maria Elena Av H2
Mark Av L1
Marlin Av I2
Maroney Av H2
Martin L. King Blvd H1
Maryland Cir L1
Mason Av B2
Matterhorn Wy A1
Mauna Loa Dr A2
Mayfair Pl I2
McKellar Cir L1
Meade Av A1, A2
Medicine Man Wy G2
Melonies Dr F1
Melrose Dr J2
Melville Dr B1
Mercedes Cir H1
Merritt Av A2
Meteoro St G2
Metropolitan St B1
Milo Wy A2
Mineral Av J1
Miraflores Av A2
Mississippi Av F1
Mohigan Wy L2
Molokai La A2
Montclair St B1
Moore St H2
Mora La B2
Morgan Av J1
Mott Cir A1
Mount Vernon Cir J2
Mountain View Blvd B1, B2
Myrtle Av F1

=N=

N 10th St I2, J2
N 11th St I2, J2
N 12th St J2
N 13th St I2, J2
N 14th St I2, J2
N 15th St I2, J2
N 16th St I2, J2
N 17th St I2, J2
N 18th St I2, J2
N 1st St J2
N 3rd St I2, J2
N 4th St I2, J2
N 6th St I2, J2
N 7th St I2, J2
N 8th St I2, J2
N 9th St I2, J2
N Bruce St I2, J2
N Las Vegas Blvd J2
N Main St J1, J2
N Martin L King Dr J1
N Maryland Pkwy I2, J2
N Rue 13 I2
Naco Ct A2
New York Blvd D2
Newport Cove Dr K2
Newsom Cir K2
Norman Av H2
North Cir L1
Northam St A2
Northbridge St G1

=O=

Oakmont Av G1
Oakmont Dr G1
Oakmont Pl G1
Omaha Cir L2
Ophir Dr J1
Ormsby St H1
Ortiz St B1
Osage Cir L2

=P=

Pacific Harbors Dr L2
Pacific St L2
Padbury Ct B1
Pahor Dr B2
Palm La J2
Palm Springs Wy A2
Palma Vista Av G2
Palma Vista Cir G2
Palms Center Dr D1, D2
Palo Verde Cir K1
Palo Verde Rd K1
Palora Av G2
Palos Verdes St L1
Parade St B1
Paradise Cove Dr K2, L2
Paradise Rd G1, H1, K1, L1
Paradise Village Wy K2
Paratore Wy B1
Pardee Pl H2
Paris Dr E2
Park Cir B2
Park Paseo H1, H2
Paseo Del Prado A2
Paseo Del Ray K2
Paso De Oro Av B1
Pastel Pl J2
Paul Robarts Ct B1
Pauline Wy H2
Pershing Av F2
Petra Av E1
Phillips Av H2
Phoebe Dr F1
Pico Wy I2
Piedmont Av A2
Pima La L2
Pine Breeze La K2
Pine St B2
Pinehurst Dr G2
Pinetop La L2
Pinks Pl F1, F2
Pinner Ct B1
Pinto La I1
Pioneer Av F1
Playa Del Rey St G2
Plaza De Cielo B2
Plaza De Ernesto B2
Plaza De La Candela B2
Plaza De Monte B2
Plaza De Rafael B2
Plaza De Rosa A2
Plaza Del Cerro B2
Plaza Del Dios B1
Plaza Del Grande A2
Plaza Del Padre B1
Plaza Del Paz A2
Plaza Del Prado A2, B2
Plaza Del Puerto B2
Plaza Del Robles A2, B2
Poco Wy B1
Polaris Av C1, D1, E1, F1

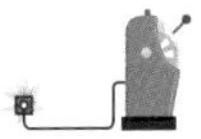

MAP INDEX

Pollux Av F1, F2
Ponderosa Wy C1
Portabello Rd L2
Procyon St C1, D1, F1
Puerto Verde La K2

=Q=

Quality Ct D1
Quantana Ct A1
Queens Courtyard Dr G1, G2

=R=

Radkovich Av K1
Raindance Wy G2
Ralston Dr J1
Rambla Ct B2
Rancho Hills Dr K2
Rancho La B2
Realeza Ct B2
Red Oak Av A2
Reed Pl J1
Regulus Av F1
Renaissance Dr K2
Renate Dr F1
Reno Ct K2
Resort Dr K2, L2
Rexford Dr H1
Rexford Pl H1
Rich Dr F1
Richard Ct H1
Richfield Blvd A2
Rigel Av A2
Rip Van Winkle La A1
Riviera Blvd G1
Roberta St K2
Rockledge Dr K2
Rockledge Wy K2
Rogers St C1, D1
Rose St B2
Rosemeade St I1, J1
Roseville Wy A2
Rothwell Ct B1
Roxbury La L2
Roxford Dr L2
Royal Crest St L1
Royal Flush Wy E1
Rue de Monte Carlo D2
Ryan Av J2
Rye St A2

=S=

S 10th St H2, I2
S 11th St I2
S 13th St H2, I2
S 14th St H2, I2
S 15th St H2, I2
S 16th St H2, I2
S 17th St H2, I2
S 1st St I1, J2
S 3rd St H1, I1, I2
S 4th St H1, I1, I2
S 6th St G1, H1, I1, I2
S 7th St H1, H2, I2
S 8th St H2, I2
S 9th St H2, I2
S Bruce St G2, H2, I2, K2, L2
S Casino Center Blvd I1, I2
S Commerce St H1, I1
S Eastern Av K2, L2
S Grand Central Pkwy I1, J1
S Highland Dr A2, F1, F2
S Main St H1
S Main St I1, J1
S Martin L King Dr I1, J1
S Maryland Pkwy G2, H2, K1, L1
S Rancho Dr A2, B2, F1, F2
S Rogers St C1, D1
S Rue 13 I2
S Tonopah Dr B2
S Valley View Blvd A1, B1, C1, D1, E1, F1
Sabado St L2
Saddle Pl K2
Saddlewood Ct L2
Sage Av K1
Sagman St J2
Sahara Annex St A2
San Angelo Av A1
San Bernardino Av A1
San Joaquin Av A1
San Pablo Dr G1, H1
San Pedro Av H2
San Pedro St H2
Sand Creek Av F1
Sanderling Cir F1
Sands Av F2, L1
Santa Anita Dr K2
Santa Clara Dr G1, H1
Santa Paula Dr G1, H1
Santa Rita Dr G1, H1
Santa Rosa Dr G1, H1
Santa Ynez Dr H1
Santiago St H2
Sarab La K2
Savalli St F1
Schirlls St C1, D1, F1
Schuster St D1
Scotland La A2
Scott Av F1
Scripps Dr F1
Seneca Dr G2
Serafina St B2
Serenada Av G2
Shadow La H1, I1, J1
Sharon Rd J1
Sheridan St A2
Sherman Pl B2
Sherwood St G1
Shirley St K1
Shortleaf St K2, L2
Sidonia Av A2, B2
Sierra Madre Dr A1
Silver Av B2
Silver Dollar Av A1
Silver Mesa Wy G2
Silver Spur Cir K2
Sirius Av F1, F2
Sleepy Hollow Wy A1
Sonora St A1
Sonrisa Wy L2
South Bridge La G1
Spanish Oaks Dr A2, B2
Sparky Dr F1
Spencer St H2, I2, K2, L2
Spring Mountain Rd F1, F2
St Joseph Cir H2
St Jude Cir H2
Stampa Av A2
Stardust Rd F2
State St G2
Stephenburnet Ct B1
Stewart Av I2, J2
Stober Blvd F1
Stormy Cir K2
Strip (Las Vegas Blvd S) C2, D2, E2, F2, G1, H1, I1, I2, J2
Strong Dr B2
Sultana St A2
Sundale St B1
Sundown Dr G2
Sunny Pl J1
Surrey La K2
Sutter Av A2
Suzanne Cir E2
Swan La L2
Sweeney Av H1, H2
Swenson St K1, L1
Sycamore La J2

=T=

Talbot Cir G2
Talbot St G2
Tam Dr G1, H1
Tam O'Shanter G1, G2
Tamarus St K2, L2
Tamrich Dr A2
Tara Av A1
Teddington Ct B1
Teddy Dr A2
Thelma Pl I2
Thiriot St E1
Thomas and Mack Dr K1
Thumbelina Cir A1
Tiffany La J2
Tiraso Wy B2
Todd Av J2
Toni Av K1
Topanga St G2
Topaz St K2, L2
Torsby Pl L1
Tranquility Dr B1
Travois Cir K2
Trona St A2
Trotter Cir B2
Tudur La L2
Turner St K1

=U=

University Rd K1

=V=

Valmora St B2
Van Dyke Av F1
Van Patten Pl G1, H1
Van Patten St G1
Vanessa Dr F1
Vegas Plaza Dr F2
Vegas Valley Dr G1, G2
Verdy La J2
Veterans Memorial Dr J2
Via Del Nord St E2
Via Madrigal E1
Via Olivero Av A1
Via San Marco E1
Via San Rafael E1
Via Torino E1
Via Vaquero Av A1
Villa De Conde Wy B2
Visby La L1
Vista Dr B1
Von Bryan Ct B1
Voxna St L1

=W=

W Adams Av J1
W Ali Baba La D1, D2
W Baltimore Av H1
W Bell Dr D1
W Bonanza Rd J1, J2
W Boston Av H1
W Charleston Blvd B1, B2, I1
W Chicago Av H1
W Cincinnati Av H1
W Cleveland Av H1
W Colorado Av H1
W Desert Inn Rd F1, F2
W Dewey Dr C1
W Diablo Dr C1
W Flamingo Rd E1, E2
W Hacienda Av C1, C2
W Harmon Av E1, E2
W Imperial Av H1
W McWilliams Av J1
W Mesa Vista Av C1
W Mesquite Av J1
W Naples Dr D1
W Nevso Dr E1
W New York Av H1
W Oakey Blvd B1, B2, H1
W Oquendo Rd C1, C2
W Philadelphia Av H1
W Quail Av C1
W Reno Av D1
W Rochelle Av E1
W Russell Rd C1, C2
W Sahara Av A1, A2, G1
W St Louis Av H1
W Tompkins Av D1, D2
W Tropicana Av D1, D2
W Twain Av E2, F1, F2
W University Av E1
W Utah Av H1
W Viking Rd E1
W Washington Av J1, J2
W Wilson Av J1
W Wyoming Av H1
Waldman Av B2
Wall St H1
Walteta Wy K2
Warnock Rd F1
Waterford La L2
Weldon Pl H1
Wengert Av H2
Westchester Cir F2
Western Av A2, F2, H1
Westland Dr A2, B2
Westleigh Av B1, B2
Westlund Dr B2
Westwood Dr A2, B2, F2, H1
Whippoorwill Cir L2
Whippoorwill La L2
Whisper Ct K2
Wilbur St K1
Willow St I1
Wilmington Wy A2
Winnick Av E2
Woodpine Dr K2, L2
Wyandotte St A2
Wynn Rd C1, D1, E1, F1

=X=

Xanthippe La L1

=Y=

Yardley St A2
Young St K1
Youngson Dr L2

=Z=

Zafra Ct B2
Ziebart Pl D1